Neighbourhood and Society

A London Suburb in the Seventeenth Century

*Cambridge Studies in Population, Economy and
Society in Past Time* 5

Series Editors:

PETER LASLETT, ROGER SCHOFIELD and E. A. WRIGLEY

ESRC Cambridge Group for the History of Population and Social Structure

and DANIEL SCOTT SMITH

University of Illinois at Chicago

Recent work in social, economic and demographic history has revealed much that
was previously obscure about societal stability and change in the past. It has also
suggested that crossing the conventional boundaries between these branches of
history can be very rewarding.

This series will exemplify the value of interdisciplinary work of this kind, and
will include books on topics such as family, kinship and neighbourhood; welfare
provision and social control; work and leisure; migration; urban growth; and legal
structures and procedures, as well as more familiar matters. It will demonstrate that,
for example, anthropology and economics have become as close intellectual
neighbours to history as have political philosophy or biography.

Neighbourhood and Society

A London Suburb in the Seventeenth Century

JEREMY BOULTON

New Hall, Cambridge

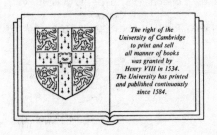

The right of the
University of Cambridge
to print and sell
all manner of books
was granted by
Henry VIII in 1534.
The University has printed
and published continuously
since 1584.

CAMBRIDGE UNIVERSITY PRESS

Cambridge

London   New York   New Rochelle
Melbourne   Sydney

Published by the Press Syndicate of the University of Cambridge
The Pitt Building, Trumpington Street, Cambridge CB2 1RP
32 East 57th Street, New York, NY 10022, USA
10 Stamford Road, Oakleigh, Melbourne 3166, Australia

First published 1987

Printed in Great Britain by the University Press, Cambridge

British Library cataloguing in publication data

Boulton, Jeremy
Neighbourhood and society: a London suburb
in the seventeenth century. – (Cambridge studies in population, economy and
society in past time; 5)
1. Borough (London, England) – Social conditions
2. London (England) – Social conditions
I. Title
942.1′64   HN398.B6/

Library of Congress cataloguing in publication data

Boulton, Jeremy.
Neighbourhood and society.
(Cambridge studies in population, economy, and society in past time; 5)
Based on the author's thesis (doctoral–Cambridge University, 1983)
Bibliography.
Includes index.
1. London (England) – Social conditions.
2. Southwark (London, England) – Social conditions.
3. London (England) – Economic conditions. 4. Southwark
(London, England) – Economic conditions. 5. Neighborhood
– England – London – History – 17th century. I. Title.
II. Series.
HN398.L7B68   1987   306′.09421   86-1010

ISBN 0 521 26669 6

7-13-90.

For Jackie and Kirsty

Contents

Figures

Tables

xi

Preface

This book is an analysis of the society of a parish in seventeenth-century London. In spirit and approach the work owes much to the sociological, anthropological and historical techniques used so effectively by Keith Wrightson and David Levine in their pioneering study of the Essex village of Terling. By using and adapting their approach to a district of seventeenth-century London I hope I have been able to make a significant contribution to the social and economic history of London and to shed some light on the similarities and differences between rural and metropolitan society in early modern England.

Since I started my historical research in 1978 I have built up numerous intellectual debts. Like all academics I have drawn inspiration, strength and references from my colleagues working in the same general area.

Firstly I owe a great debt to Keith Wrightson whose social history seminars in St Andrews kindled my interest in British social history. In particular, too, I am conscious of a great debt to the supervisor of my Ph.D research, Brian Outhwaite, whose perceptive comments on innumerable drafts and timely words of encouragement when my energies flagged were all very much appreciated. I owe much too, to the kind and constructive criticisms made by Paul Slack and Valerie Pearl who examined my Ph.D thesis in 1983. Subsequently Roger Schofield has been a tolerant and perceptive editor and has done much to help in the metamorphosis of caterpillar thesis to butterfly book.

In addition to the above I have benefited from discussions with Richard Wall, Peter Laslett, Ruth Gladden, Beatrice Shearer, Tim Harris and from many other individuals encountered in seminars held at Cambridge and elsewhere.

I should also like to thank Professor J. S. Cockburn for allowing me to make xerox copies of the typescript of a forthcoming book and the Corporation of the Wardens of St Saviour's for giving permission for microfilm copies of some of the records of the Corporation to be made.

The staffs of the following record offices were particularly helpful: the Public Record Office, Chancery Lane; the Corporation of London Record Office; the Guildhall Library; the British Library; the Surrey Record Office; the John Harvard Library; the Minet Library. In particular I would like to thank the staff of the Greater London Record Office for their efficiency and help and the staff of St Olave's Grammar School, Orpington, for their hospitality. I am also indebted to Mr J. W. Pinder, Churchwarden of St George the Martyr, Southwark, for his work on the parish register of that church.

Much of the initial research for this book was supported by an SSRC (now ESRC) grant whose help I gratefully acknowledge. A preliminary version of this book was awarded a Ph.D by the University of Cambridge in 1983. Subsequent revisions and the collection of new material have been funded by a generous personal research grant from the Board of the British Academy whom I would also like to take this opportunity of thanking.

The book was written while I held a Junior Research Fellowship at New Hall, Cambridge. I would like to thank the President and Fellows of New Hall for their friendship and support during this period.

I am also grateful to the staff of Cambridge University Press for their help with the text.

Last of all I should like to thank my parents for their encouragement and most of all my wife, Jackie, who kept me going.

Abbreviations

P.R.O.	Public Record Office, Chancery Lane
P.C.C.	Prerogative Court of Canterbury, Will Registers
G.L.R.O.	Greater London Record Office, Clerkenwell
C.L.R.O.	Corporation of London Record Office
C.S.P.D.	Calendar of State Papers, Domestic series
Rep.	Repertories, Proceedings of the Court of Aldermen

For the purposes of clarification where contemporary sources are quoted the spelling has been modernised.

1

Introduction

1.1 London in the seventeenth century: an agent of social change?

During the sixteenth and seventeenth centuries London became the largest
city in Europe. In terms of size the capital moved progressively up the
European urban hierarchy from a position of perhaps seventh or eighth
biggest in 1550 to third in 1600 (exceeded by Paris and Naples) and second
in 1650 (behind Paris). By 1700 London was, and throughout the eighteenth
century remained, the largest European city. The capital's growth in the
seventeenth century was mainly responsible for the doubling of that
proportion of England's population living in urban settlements of 10,000
or more at a time when the rest of Europe experienced stagnation in this
respect. After 1700 London's share of, and contribution to, the unique
urbanisation experienced by England between 1600 and 1800 declined. In
eighteenth-century England the proportion of the nation's population living
in towns of 10,000 or more again nearly doubled, reaching 24% by 1800.
London's share of this population, however, declined from 86% in 1700
to 66% in 1750 and only 46% by the end of the century. In the context
of European urbanisation the growth of England's capital city was most
striking in the seventeenth century.[1]

The importance of London's rapid population growth and its effects on
the economy of sixteenth- and seventeenth-century England are now well
established. London's increasing demand for agricultural products was a
significant factor in the development of an integrated national market, an
agent promoting regional agricultural specialisation and commercial farming

[1] This brief summary of European urban growth is based largely on E. A. Wrigley, 'Urban growth
and agricultural change: England and the Continent in the early modern period', *Journal of
Interdisciplinary History* 15 (1985), 683–728. A convenient table of European cities ranked by size
is in J. de Vries, *European Urbanization 1500–1800*, London, 1984, pp. 269–87. See, also,
E. A. Wrigley, 'A simple model of London's importance in changing English society and economy
1650–1750', *Past and Present* 37 (1967), 44.

1

for the metropolitan markets. By stimulating agricultural efficiency in this way food prices were reduced and labour released for non-agricultural pursuits. London's growth further helped to free industry from constraints on expansion by accelerating the substitution of mineral fuel (coal) for natural fuel (wood). To supply the capital the nation's transport network was improved and unit costs thereby reduced.[2] Moreover the capital's insatiable demand for people to fuel and maintain its growth acted, notably in the period 1650 to 1750, as an important regulator and brake on national population growth. Indeed in the second half of the seventeenth century London's demographic impact turned a small *surplus* of births in the rest of England into an overall national *deficit* causing a fall in the national population. In this way London's growth is thought to have contributed to the rise in real wages in the late seventeenth century by reducing population pressure on a (growing) food supply.[3] The nature of the society produced by metropolitan expansion and its relationship to the wider society of seventeenth-century England is less easy to summarise.

The historical importance of London society and its possible influence on that of the rest of England rests both on the capital's unique size and growth and on the large proportion of the nation's population which experienced life in the metropolis. Recent research now enables us to place London's growth reasonably accurately within the context of national population movements (see Table 1.1). London grew most rapidly in the last half of the sixteenth century. At this time her rate of growth was more than three times that of the national population. Thereafter, until the last half of the eighteenth century, the capital's growth rate *slowed* progressively, from 1.4% per annum in the first half of the seventeenth century to 0.73% in the second half and 0.32% in the first fifty years of the eighteenth century. In the eighteenth century London's population growth rate was similar to, or *exceeded* by, that of the national population. Before about 1670 the capital was the fastest growing, as well as the biggest, urban centre in England. After that date however, London's rate of growth was equalled and then outstripped by the burgeoning new manufacturing towns in the North and the Midlands and by some provincial ports.[4] The number of persons inhabiting urban centres of more than 10,000 (other than London) grew

---

[2] See, for example, F. J. Fisher, 'The development of the London food market, 1540–1640', in E. M. Carus-Wilson (ed.), *Essays in Economic History*, London, 1954, 134–51; F. J. Fisher, 'London as an engine of economic growth', in P. Clark (ed.), *The Early Modern Town*, London, 1976, pp. 205–15; Wrigley 1967: 44–70; A. Everitt, 'The marketing of agricultural produce', in J. Thirsk (ed.), *The Agrarian History of England and Wales*, IV: *1500–1640*, Cambridge, 1967, pp. 507–16.

[3] See, M. J. Daunton, 'Towns and economic growth in eighteenth-century England', in P. Abrams and E. A. Wrigley (eds.), *Towns in Societies: Essays in Economic History and Historical Sociology*, Cambridge, 1979 edn, pp. 255–6; E. A. Wrigley and R. S. Schofield, *The Population History of England 1541–1871*, London, 1981, pp. 166–70; Wrigley 1967: 44–50.

[4] For the different patterns of urban growth in early modern England see Wrigley 1985: 689–93.

Table 1.1. *Population growth in London, towns of 10,000+ and England 1550–1800*

| | Population of | | Per cent English population living in | | Compound annual percentage growth rates | | |
	London	England	London	Towns of 10,000+ excluding London	England	London	Towns of 10,000+
1550	70,000	3,011,000	2.3	—	—	—	—
1600	200,000	4,110,000	4.9	1.1	0.62	2.12	—
1650	400,000	5,229,000	7.7	—	0.48	1.40	—
1700	575,000	5,058,000	11.4	1.9	−0.07	0.73	—
1750	675,000	5,772,000	11.7	6.0	0.26	0.32	2.40
1800	959,000	8,665,000	11.1	13.0	0.82	0.71	2.38

Sources: Finlay 1981: 51; Wrigley and Schofield 1981: 531–4; Wrigley 1985: 686–708.

more than *seven times* faster in the first half of the eighteenth century and three times faster in the second half than the capital's population. The capital's share of England's population grew in like fashion. From a modest 2.3% in 1550 to 4.9% in 1600 and reaching 11.4%, more than one person in nine, by 1700. This share increased only slightly by 1750 and declined to 11.1% by 1800.

Direct experience of London life, however, was undoubtedly more widespread than the latter figures suggest. Since many more people died in the capital than were born there most of London's growth was sustained by immigration – particularly the immigration of young adults. Using this premise it has been calculated that in the period 1650 to 1750 one in six of the survivors of all those born in England would have had to become Londoners at some point in their lives if the capital's growth was to be maintained. A similar calculation for the period 1550 to 1650 finds that one in eight of the survivors of the nation's births would have been destined to have direct experience of life in the capital.[5]

If there were proportionately more Englishmen and women experiencing London life in the later seventeenth and early eighteenth centuries than in the earlier period it also seems likely that the metropolitan experience became, increasingly, restricted to those living in regions adjacent to the capital. London society may have had a more truly *national* impact in the period before 1650. Evidence of the distances travelled to London by

[5] Wrigley 1967: 48–50; R. Finlay, *Population and Metropolis: The Demography of London 1580–1650*, Cambridge, 1981, p. 9.

immigrants suggests that the proportion of long distance migrants coming to the capital fell significantly after the middle of the seventeenth century. In fact all over England in this period urban catchment areas shrank both as population pressure on resources lessened, thus cutting back long distance 'subsistence' migration, and as the alternative centres of attraction for migrants arose in the north Midlands and the northern counties of England.[6] Thus, for example, between 1551 and 1553, 26.0% of London freemen originated from the Home Counties and the south Midlands; in 1690, 43.2% did so. Freemen from the north-eastern and north-western counties comprised 36.9% of all freemen in the mid-sixteenth century but only 11.1% in 1690.[7]

A study of seventeenth-century London society therefore could be justified solely on the grounds of the large proportion of the nation's population which participated in and experienced its formal and informal social institutions. London's unique size, however, is also thought to have resulted in a particular *type* of society, the experience of which, by itself, is thought to have acted as an important agent of social change in early modern England.

In his classic and influential article, written in 1967, Wrigley advanced the idea that London life was *qualitatively* as well as *quantitatively* different from that of the rest of England. The experience of London life was a force promoting the modernisation of English society, 'a powerful solvent of the customs, prejudices and modes of action of traditional rural England'.[8] Following sociological theory Wrigley suggested that London society, where a higher proportion of daily contacts were casual and associated with a particular transaction rather than with custom and tradition, promoted 'rational' rather than 'traditional' patterns of behaviour. Thus the crowded city, a centre for conspicuous consumption, increased the possibility of social emulation in dress and life-style; tangible reasons for taking the higher wages of the late seventeenth century in the form of increased income rather than in increased leisure which was, apparently, the customary practice.[9]

---

[6] See, Finlay 1981: 64–6; S. R. Smith, 'The social and geographical origins of the London apprentices, 1630–60', *Guildhall Miscellany* 4, 4 (1973), 195–207; J. Wareing, 'Changes in the geographical distribution of the recruitment of apprentices to the London Companies, 1486–1750', *Journal of Historical Geography* 6, 3 (1980), 241–9; P. Clark, 'The migrant in Kentish towns 1580–1640', in P. Clark and P. Slack (eds.), *Crisis and Order in English Towns 1500–1700*, London, 1972, 117–63; P. Clark, 'Migration in England during the late seventeenth and early eighteenth centuries', *Past and Present* 83 (1979), 57–90.

[7] Finlay 1981: 64–6.   [8] Wrigley 1967: 50.

[9] Wrigley 1967: 51. See also, F. J. Fisher, 'The development of London as a centre of conspicuous consumption', *Transactions of the Royal Historical Society*, 4th ser., 30 (1948), 37–50. For leisure preference or the 'backward sloping labour supply curve', see, D. Coleman, 'Labour in the English economy of the seventeenth century', *Economic History Review*, 2nd ser., 8 (1956), 280–95. The potency of this strand of Wrigley's argument is diluted by the fact that the higher wages of early

London society was said to have been different from that of rural England in other ways: population turnover was higher and the environment impersonal; literacy was higher, kin less likely to live near at hand and, in central areas at least, households were larger containing exceptional numbers of servants and lodgers.[10]

Despite its importance, however, metropolitan society has been relatively neglected by social historians. Wrigley himself was forced to qualify his own argument with the complaint that 'Too little is known of the sociological differences between life in London and life in provincial England to afford a clear perception of the impact of London's growth upon the country as a whole.'[11] More recently other authorities have echoed this reservation that despite its numerical size and the wide experience of London life, little is as yet known of *how* the capital's inhabitants actually lived.[12]

This book aims to shed more light on the society of which so many persons had direct experience in seventeenth-century England. Using a fresh methodological approach it seeks to reconstruct the social and economic institutions within which Londoners lived their lives and, hopefully, to provide a blueprint for and stimulus to, further similar studies of city society in pre-industrial England.

1.2 *Methodology: an intensive area study of a London parish*

In order to shed new light on seventeenth-century London society a small area of the capital has been studied intensively. Historians have already used this approach to make original and important contributions to the study of the societies of nineteenth- and twentieth-century cities.[13] In the absence of analogous source material similar reconstructions of districts of pre-industrial cities have as yet barely begun.[14] The methodology used in this study combines the intensive area study approach with that used in the community studies carried out recently by Wrightson and Levine, and Macfarlane on two pre-industrial Essex villages. These authors, by combining

eighteenth-century London seem to have been spent, initially at least, largely on gin, Daunton 1979: 255.

[10] Wrigley 1967: 50–4.   [11] Wrigley 1967: 50.

[12] P. Clark and P. Slack, 'Introduction', in P. Clark and P. Slack (eds.), *Crisis and Order in English Towns 1500–1700*, London, 1972, p. 35.

[13] See, for example, M. Anderson, *Family Structure in Nineteenth-Century Lancashire*, Cambridge, 1971, pp. 20 and *passim*; C. G. Pooley, 'Residential mobility in the Victorian city', *Transactions of the Institute of British Geographers*, n.s., 4, 2 (1979), 258–77; M. Young and P. Willmott, *Family and Kinship in East London*, London, 1957.

[14] For London see the first fruits of a study of Cheapside housing reported in D. Keene, 'A new study of London before the Great Fire', *Urban History Yearbook* (1984), 11–21. See also, P. Clark and Jennifer Clark, 'The social economy of the Canterbury suburbs: the evidence of the census of 1563', in A. Detsicas and N. Yates (eds.), *Studies in Modern Kentish History*, Maidstone, 1983, pp. 65–86.

information from as many historical sources as possible, were able to ask and answer new questions about the social and economic lives of ordinary villagers.[15] By using such techniques to study one area of London it was possible to penetrate deeper than ever before into the lives and behaviour of the more humble seventeenth-century Londoners.

Although parish histories have a long tradition in London, a detailed reconstruction of the lives of the inhabitants of any particular area has not yet been attempted.[16] Antiquarian works tend to reflect local pride and undisciplined curiosity rather than the current concern with social and economic themes.[17] The more recent studies of London parishes have tended to concentrate on one particular aspect of their history such as poor relief, occupational structure, housing, religious behaviour or demography.[18] The only detailed reconstruction of a London street that has been made so far predated the upsurge in interest in social and economic history and was based on a small and unrepresentative number of individuals.[19]

The Boroughside district of the parish of St Saviour's, Southwark, (see Fig. 1.1 below), was selected for intensive study because of the variety of the extant records of the Corporation of the Wardens of St Saviour's. The availability of these records, which are particularly extensive in the late sixteenth and early seventeenth centuries, partly determined the time period covered by this study. Methodological considerations also played some part.

Originally the study had been intended to extend over a long period of time in the pre-industrial era. However, the large population size and

---

[15] See, A. Macfarlane, *Reconstructing Historical Communities*, Cambridge, 1977; K. Wrightson and D. Levine, *Poverty and Piety in an English Village. Terling 1525–1700*, London, 1979. For a call for the adoption of an anthropological perspective of pre-industrial cities, see, P. Burke, 'Urban history and urban anthropology of early modern Europe', in D. Fraser and A. Sutcliffe (eds.), *The Pursuit of Urban History*, London, 1983, pp. 69–82.

[16] For a review of some recent parish studies see, D. A. Reeder, 'Keeping up with London's past', *Urban History Yearbook* (1977), 48–54.

[17] For Southwark see in particular the following works: W. Rendle and P. Norman, *The Inns of Old Southwark*, London, 1888; W. Rendle, *Old Southwark and Its People*, London, 1878; W. Taylor, *Annals of St Mary Overy; an Historical and Descriptive Account of St Saviour's Church and Parish*, London, 1833.

[18] See, R. W. Herlan, 'Poor relief in the London parish of Dunstan in the West during the English Revolution', *Guildhall Studies in London History* 3, 1 (1977), 13–36; R. W. Herlan, 'Poor relief in the London parish of Antholin's Budge Row, 1638–64', *Guildhall Studies in London History* 2, 4 (1977), 179–99; M. J. Power, 'Shadwell: the development of a London suburban community in the seventeenth century', *London Journal* 4 (1978), 29–46; D. A. Kirby, 'The radicals of St Stephen's, Coleman Street, London, 1624–42', *Guildhall Miscellany* 3, 2 (1970), 98–119; D. A. Williams, 'London puritanism: the parish of St Botolph Without Aldgate', *Guildhall Miscellany* 2, 1 (1960), 24–48; T. R. Forbes, 'Weaver and cordwainer: occupations in the parish of St Giles Without Cripplegate, London, in 1654–93 and 1729–43', *Guildhall Studies in London History* 4, 3 (1980), 119–32; T. R. Forbes, *Chronicle from Aldgate: Life and Death in Shakespeare's London*, London, 1971.

[19] T. F. Reddaway, 'Elizabethan London–Goldsmiths' Row in Cheapside, 1558–1645', *Guildhall Miscellany* 2, 5 (1963), 181–206.

high turnover of urban societies in the past greatly increase the number of individuals who are included in an intensive study. Moreover, when several sources are combined, as in the village reconstructions of Wrightson and Levine, and Macfarlane the burden of record linkage becomes very great indeed.[20] To meet this problem the study was restricted to a much shorter time period than had originally been envisaged, the period chosen being determined by the coverage of the records. Consequently many of the topics studied could only be examined for limited periods of time; this drawback is compensated for to some extent by the amount of information that could be recovered for each individual.

The procedure adopted, briefly, was as follows: an alphabetical name index of all householders listed in the 1622 token book, a comprehensive and detailed listing of inhabitants, was constructed and as many sources as was practicable were linked to each listed individual. Each document so linked was transcribed and each individual reference transferred onto a separate card. Consequently it was possible to refer back to the original document where necessary.[21] In this way biographies were constructed for each individual householder resident in 1622. The main classes of records used in this process were the sacramental token books for the Boroughside 1584 to 1643; the baptism, burial and marriage entries in the parish register, between 1580 and 1660; the vestry minutes between 1582 and 1628; manorial records dated between 1617 and 1639; calendared assize indictments for the period 1603 to 1625; local and national taxation assessments; records of poor relief administration; churchwardens' presentments; the reports of the searchers for inmates; the returns of new buildings and divided tenements and the wills of all those resident in the parish at death between 1620 and 1660. It was also found to be necessary to construct name indexes of those Boroughside householders resident in 1609, 1618, 1620, 1624 and 1631 in order to exploit fully certain classes of records and to overcome problems of turnover and mobility. It should be noted however, that a number of classes of records used in reconstructions of village life were not extant for early seventeenth-century Southwark, the most serious losses being those of the records of the Archdeaconry of Surrey and the early seventeenth-century Surrey Quarter Sessions files.[22] Nonetheless such losses, although serious, are mitigated by the survival of a number of particularly informative records not usually found in rural areas, such as the long series of sacramental token books, the official surveys of inmates,

---

[20] See Wrightson and Levine 1979: ix–xi; Macfarlane 1977: *passim*.

[21] A procedure recommended in Wrightson and Levine 1979: x; Macfarlane 1977: 87–9.

[22] For a list of records available in rural areas see, Macfarlane 1977: 42–6; Wrightson and Levine 1979: ix–x. The loss of the Southwark ecclesiastical records is noted in R. Houlbrooke, *Church Courts and the People During the English Reformation 1520–70*, Oxford, 1979, p. 256. For the loss of the quarter sessions records see, D. Johnson, *Southwark and the City*, London, 1969, p. 234.

divided tenements and the poor and early seventeenth-century vestry minutes. The survival of such records reflects in part the greater sophistication of parochial administration in early Stuart London compared to the less formal structures found in rural parishes.[23]

It is not intended to adopt a biographical approach to the study of the Boroughside but a brief résumé of one individual biography indicates the scope of the coverage of individual lives that can be achieved by the methods employed in the present study. Ralph Babington entered the Boroughside in the late sixteenth century and he lived in Chequer Alley off the east side of the Borough High Street until his death in 1628. At the time of his arrival he was a married man. Babington remarried following the death of his first wife Elizabeth in 1618, and again following the death of his second wife Barbara in 1626. In 1622 Babington's household consisted of his current wife, his only surviving son Thomas and six servants. Babington was a vintner by trade and a member of the Haberdashers' Company. He was, to judge from his taxation assessments, relatively wealthy being assessed at sixpence per week for the poor rate in 1622 and on six pounds worth of goods in the subsidy assessment of the same year. Like many other inhabitants of the Boroughside, Babington was prosecuted for offences in the manorial courts, once in 1620 for entertaining guests at unlawful hours and again in the same year, for 'that he suffereth a hanging board to hang upon the outside of his window to the annoyance of passengers'. As one of the wealthier householders he was elected to the vestry of St Saviour's in 1609 and acted as an assistant to the governors of the local grammar school. Babington did not own the freehold of his dwelling house but held the property in 1617, from one Mrs Harrison, a widow in Mark Lane, London. Although in some ways Babington is an atypical Boroughside resident, notably in the length of time he spent in the district, the biographical details recovered in his case can be duplicated for many other inhabitants. For all householders in 1622 the following information is known: sex, marital status, residential location, local offices held, level of taxation assessment, the presence of adult servants in the household and whether the household was in receipt of poor relief. For the majority of householders their occupation, residential movements and landlord can also be reconstructed. Other listings dating from the early seventeenth century supplied important additional information on household size and structure. It is noteworthy, in fact, that the research method adopted achieved a coverage which generally matches, and occasionally exceeds, that achieved in rural areas. Thus, for example, the occupations of 69% of Boroughside householders were recovered, compared to the ideal

---

[23] Thus the vestry as a formal body did not emerge in Terling, Essex, until after the Restoration, Wrightson and Levine 1979: 104.

figure of 75% for rural areas put forward by Macfarlane. Furthermore every householder could be placed in a specific geographical location, something which has not proved possible in recent village studies.[24] Moreover hitherto unexplored areas, such as religious behaviour and urban social relations, could be quantified and illustrated with suitable case studies drawn from the name indexes.

1.3 The setting: the Boroughside district of St. Saviour's, Southwark

Fig. 1.1 sets out the geographical location and number of parishes in Southwark in the first half of the seventeenth century. Stow included St Mary Magdalen, Bermondsey, in his description of Southwark and more recently Brett-James has asserted that Southwark was divided into *nine* parishes which were St Saviour's; St George's; St Thomas's; St Olave's; St Mary Magdalen, Bermondsey; Christchurch; Lambeth; Newington; and Rotherhithe.[25] In fact between 1540 and 1670 there were only four parishes within Southwark proper and this was recognised in the compilation of the London Bills of Mortality. The four parishes of Southwark lay in the liberties of the City of London (see Fig. 1.1).[26] St Saviour's, Southwark, was located on the south bank of the River Thames between London Bridge and Lambeth Marsh. To the east lay St Olave's which ran from the bridge to Bermondsey. To the south of St Saviour's and St Olave's lay the parishes of St Thomas's and St George's. The parish of St Saviour's was divided into three administrative districts: the Clink, Paris Garden and the Boroughside, the location of the intensive area study. St Mary Magdalen, Bermondsey, was technically an outparish and did not lie within the liberties of the City of London. Lambeth, Newington and Rotherhithe were all 'distant' parishes. In 1671 the parish of Christchurch was carved out of the parish of St Saviour's from the Paris Garden district.[27]

The map further clarifies the various civil jurisdictions at work in seventeenth-century Southwark. This is not the place for a detailed account of the workings of local government but several salient points should be borne in mind.[28] The extent of the City's jurisdiction in Southwark in the

[24] Macfarlane estimated that 80% of individuals could be, in ideal circumstances, placed in a particular house, see Macfarlane 1977: 133–4.

[25] See, J. Stow, *A Survey of London*, London, C. L. Kingsford (ed.) 2nd edn, Oxford, 1971, 2, p. 53; N. G. Brett-James, *The Growth of Stuart London*, London, 1935, p. 405.

[26] Finlay 1981: 171.

[27] M. D. George, *London Life in the Eighteenth Century*, London, Peregrine edn, 1966, p. 406.

[28] For the most recent, and seminal, work on the government of Southwark see, Johnson 1969: 292–304, 317–29 and *passim*. See also, Rendle 1878: 3–11; Valerie Pearl, *London and the Outbreak of the Puritan Revolution*, London, 1961, pp. 28–9; S. and B. Webb, *English Local Government from the Revolution to the Municipal Corporation Act: The Manor and the Borough*, London, 1908, 1, 572n; H. E. Malden (ed.), *The Victoria History of the Counties of England, Surrey*, London, 1967, 4, pp. 135–40.

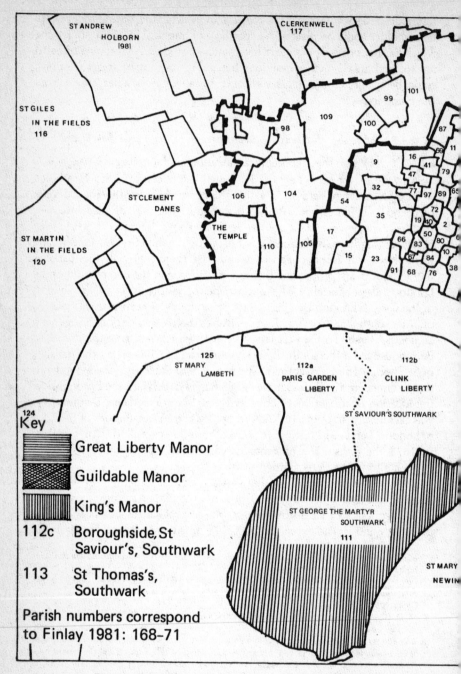

Fig. 1.1. Map of manorial and parish boundaries in Southwark

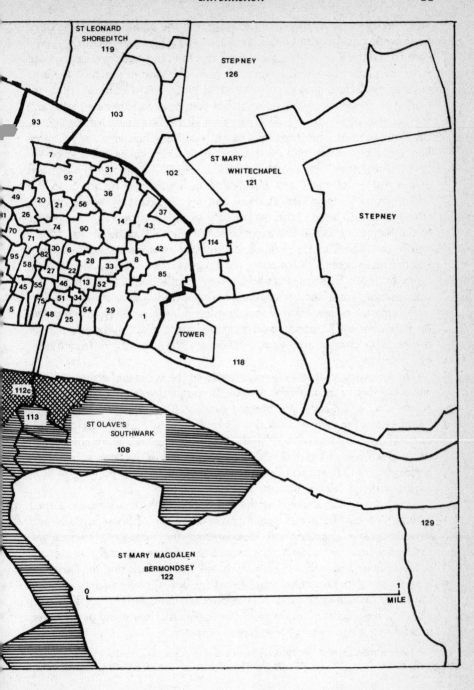

ST LEONARD
SHOREDITCH
119

STEPNEY
126

93

103

7

31

102

ST MARY
WHITECHAPEL
121

STEPNEY

92

36

49

20

21

56

37

26

14

43

70

74

90

114

71

30

6

42

95

82

28

8

85

58

33

27

22

45

55

46

13

52

75

51

34

5

48

25

64

29

1

TOWER

118

112c

113

ST OLAVE'S
SOUTHWARK

108

129

ST MARY MAGDALEN

BERMONDSEY
122

0   1
                                                                        MILE

early seventeenth century was delineated by the boundaries of the three Southwark manors. The Guildable Manor had long been under the City's control and the King's Manor and the Great Liberty Manor were purchased from the Crown by the City in 1557. Since the date of purchase the area covered by all three manors constituted the Bridge Ward Without. The ward consisted, therefore, of the Boroughside district of St Saviour's parish and the parishes of St Olave's, St George's and St Thomas's. Districts *outside* the boundaries of the three manors such as the Clink and Paris Garden liberties, Bermondsey and Newington lay within the jurisdiction of the Surrey authorities. The 1630s seem to have been an important watershed in the history of the City's jurisdiction in Southwark. Before 1635 the Alderman of Bridge Ward Without had been a relatively active official; afterwards much less so. This decline coincided with a growth in the power of the Surrey justices at the expense of the City authorities in the 1630s. Before then the City had held regular quarter sessions in Southwark and had been responsible for collecting central government taxation in the area. From the 1630s Surrey justices took over the collection of Ship Money and responsibility for a number of routine administrative tasks.[29]

In terms of ecclesiastical jurisdiction the Boroughside lay in the parish of St Saviour's. The parish lay within the deanery of Southwark, part of the Archdeaconry of Surrey, in the diocese of Winchester in the province of Canterbury.[30]

The following chapters give an account of the social and economic lives and behaviour of the inhabitants of the Boroughside district of St Saviour's, Southwark in the early seventeenth century. They examine this society therefore at a time when London was growing rapidly and absorbing about one eighth of the survivors of all those born in England. More Englishmen and women were to experience metropolitan life in the later seventeenth century but in the period under study London recruited its population from a truly national catchment area.

This book will examine how the inhabitants of the Boroughside earned a living, the distribution of wealth and poverty and of household size and structure. Later chapters will look beyond the household to examine residential patterns, housing, the ownership of property and the exercise of local power and authority. The study will end by analysing the particular type of social organisation represented by Boroughside society and the institutions which underpinned it. Before examining such topics, however, a basic demographic question should be answered. How many people lived in Southwark in the early seventeenth century?

[29] Johnson 1969: 151 and 235–7. Local government is treated in more detail in Chapter 10 below.
[30] J. S. W. Gibson, *Wills and Where to Find Them*, Chichester, 1974, pp. 128–9.

2

The demographic background

The demographic record forms an important backdrop to a study of the conditions in which the inhabitants of Southwark lived and worked. Such information enables us to look at such environmental measures as population density and to appreciate the effects of population movements on the local economy, administration and society. Furthermore an examination of the seasonal distribution of baptisms and burials throws valuable light on the annual tempo of life in pre-industrial Southwark.

Although it is well known that the population of London grew rapidly in the late sixteenth and seventeenth centuries it has also been established recently that it grew at different rates in different areas of the capital and that the impact of infant mortality and epidemic disease varied according to the socio-economic composition of each district.[1] It does not follow, therefore, that Southwark shared in the demographic experience of the rest of the capital. Indeed it has been claimed that Southwark's population did not grow significantly in the early seventeenth century.[2] If this were true it might indicate that the social problems sometimes associated with rapid growth in other parts of London were less pressing in Southwark.[3] The extent to which Southwark's population was affected by the rhythm of the seasons might also have differed from the experience of the inhabitants of the wealthier city parishes. Southwark's demographic experience must therefore be investigated directly.

[1] For recent estimates of London's population, see, Finlay 1981: 51, 60–2, 101–8; Wrigley 1967: 44; I. Sutherland, 'When was the Great Plague? Mortality in London, 1563 to 1665', in D. V. Glass and R. Revelle (eds.), *Population and Social Change*, London, 1972, pp. 308–10. For demographic variation within the capital see also, Finlay 1981: 60–2, 101–8; P. Slack, 'Mortality crises and epidemic disease in England 1485–1610', in C. Webster (ed.), *Health, Medicine and Mortality in the Sixteenth Century*, Cambridge, 1979, pp. 48–52; B. Shearer, 'Expanding suburbs', paper presented to Conference on London Economic and Social History 1500–1700, 27 June 1981. For London's impact on the national population see, Wrigley and Schofield 1981: 166–70.

[2] See, Brett-James 1935: 116–17, 406; Pearl 1961: 13.

[3] See, A. L. Beier, 'Social problems in Elizabethan London', *Journal of Interdisciplinary History* 9 (1978), 203–21.

13

2.1 Population estimates for Southwark 1547–1678

Fortunately three major sources used by historians to estimate population totals cover part or all of the four parishes which made up late sixteenth- and early seventeenth-century Southwark. The details for each parish are listed in Table 2.1. The 1547 Chantry certificates survive for St Saviour's and St George's. These returns supply totals of 'houselynge people' who can be confidently identified as communicants, that is those persons in a parish eligible to take communion.[4] The second source is the 1603 survey of communicants, returns from which survive for St Olave's, St Thomas's and St Saviour's, Southwark.[5] In addition to the problem of calculating the proportion of the total population covered by these sources, both sets of figures are rounded totals rather than precisely calculated censuses, which introduces a further element of imprecision.[6] Lastly, Gregory King's count of the number of householders in each parish in 1678, itself based on non-extant hearth tax returns has also survived.[7] In addition to these sources a population census made in London in 1631 has survived for the Bridge Ward Without.[8] To calculate population estimates for Southwark from each of these sources requires certain assumptions to be made about the demographic structure of Southwark's population.

It is difficult to estimate population totals from the number of householders because household size varied considerably between rural and urban areas and within London itself.[9] In 1695 mean household size in London ranged from 3.9 in Smithfield to 7.6 in St Gabriel, Fenchurch.[10] Because of such variations local historians should not borrow missing demographic information from national figures.[11] It is fortunate, therefore, that a survey of the Boroughside for 1631 can be used to calculate both household size and the proportion of the population under the age of communion in St Saviour's, Southwark.

The population count of 1631 followed Privy Council concern over a possible food shortage in London. In April 1631 the Council wrote to the

---

[4] For the chantry certificates see, Wrigley and Schofield 1981: 563–6; T. Craib (ed.), 'Surrey chantries', *Surrey Archaeological Collections* 25 (1912), 18–19; C. J. Kitching (ed.), *London and Middlesex Chantry Certificate 1548*, London Record Society 16, 1980, pp. ix–xxxiv.

[5] British Library, Harleian Ms 595.250. See, Wrigley and Schofield, 1981: 569.

[6] Kitching 1980: xx.

[7] Gregory King, 'L.C.C. Burns Journal', reprinted in P. Laslett (ed.), *The Earliest Classics: John Graunt and Gregory King*, Farnborough, 1973, pp. 38–9.

[8] See, Finlay 1981: 173; G.L.R.O. P92/SAV/219.

[9] R. Wall, 'Regional and temporal variations in English household structure from 1650', in J. Hobcraft and P. Rees (eds.), *Regional Aspects of British Population Growth*, London, 1979, p. 103.

[10] P. E. Jones and A. V. Judges, 'London population in the late seventeenth century', *Economic History Review* 6 (1935), 58–62.

[11] See, Wrightson and Levine 1979: 45.

Table 2.1. *Sources for estimating population totals of Southwark parishes 1547–1678*

Parish	Communicants 1547[a]	1603[b]	Households 1678[c]
St George's	921		1370
St Saviour's	1900	4232	2020
St Olave's	—	5002	2976
St Thomas's	—	301	1220
Christchurch	—	—	

Note: The 1603 returns are defective for St George's, Southwark. Only 190 (possibly an error for 1900) communicants and 100 'non communicants' are noted.
Sources: [a] Craib 1912: 18–19.
[b] British Library, Harleian Ms 595.250. Totals include, 'recusants' and 'non communicants'.
[c] King 1973: 38–9.

Lord Mayor to find out how much corn was needed to provision London for a year.[12] In July 1631 the Lord Mayor sent a precept to the Alderman of the Bridge Ward Without ordering a population count and this was then passed on to the parochial authorities.[13] The returns placed the total population of the Bridge Ward Without at 18,660.[14] The 1631 count has hitherto been considered inaccurate largely because its method of compilation is not known.[15] In view of this it is interesting that the method by which the 1631 count was taken in St Saviour's is known. The churchwardens of the Boroughside sent in their return, 'a view what number of men, women and children are inhabiting within the said parish in the Boroughside aforesaid', in which they certified 'there the full number of 3578 persons whereof are 2428 communicants'.[16] In fact the churchwardens had taken the survey around April 1631 using the sacramental token book of that year as a basis. The number of persons in each household was entered to the left of the name of each household head in the book. At the end of the book a memorandum recorded that there were communicants 'in toto' 2428 and 'of other persons 1150 so in the whole number persons in the Boroughside 3578'.[17] In fact due to an error in the addition there were 3708

---

[12] For the background to this count see, E. M. Leonard, *The Early History of English Poor Relief*, Cambridge, 1900, p. 188; Finlay 1981: 72–3; Pearl 1961: 120.
[13] G.L.R.O. P92/SAV/176, a copy of the reply to this precept.
[14] See, George 1966: 318–19; *City of London: Schedule C: Population of the City of London in A.D.1631*, Report of the City Day Census, 1881, pp. 129–30.
[15] Sutherland noted that 'there was probably a substantial under-enumeration' but Finlay has stated that the 'totals seem to agree with other estimates of the population of London'. Sutherland 1972: 307–8; Finlay 1981: 73.
[16] G.L.R.O. P92/SAV/176.   [17] G.L.R.O. P92/SAV/219.

persons in all. The book listed 966 householders, and consequently the mean household size was 3.8.

The actual accuracy of the 1631 count therefore depends on the comprehensiveness of the communicant listings.[18] It is known that few, if any, householders were omitted from these annually compiled lists of communicants. However the listings did not include those not entitled to receive communion in that year.[19] Consequently non-parishioners, such as most lodgers, inmates and guests were not counted. Only the more permanent lodgers and inmates who had achieved settlement were listed.[20] The 1631 survey thus omitted much of the 'floating population' of the Boroughside. To estimate the size of this floating population at any one point in time is complicated by its relatively high turnover.[21] In the Boroughside between October 1594 and September 1595, in six searches, 68 householders were detected as lodging 123 inmates but on average each search turned up 20 householders lodging 41 inmates, equivalent to only about 2% of the total population at that date.[22] Such a figure does not include the inhabitants of the inns, and lodgers attached to higher status households, examples of which occasionally appear in the burial and baptism registers. An arbitrary correction factor might inflate the population by 10% to account for the floating population, although this must have been subject to considerable seasonal fluctuations.[23]

The churchwardens of St Saviour's, therefore, were drawing a distinction between the household and the 'houseful' (which is the household plus lodgers).[24] Fortunately today's historical demographers draw a similar distinction so that it is possible to compare the mean household size in the Boroughside with other data in order to assess its plausibility (see Table 2.2). The mean household size of 3.8 in the Boroughside is clearly of the correct order of magnitude, resembling that found in the poor parish of St

---

[18] Sutherland 1972: 302, suggests that the 1631 count under-enumerated the population because a proportion of residents fled from the minor plague outbreak of that year. The Boroughside listing of householders shows no such evacuees.

[19] See, H. S. Wilson (ed.), *Constitutions and Canons Ecclesiastical 1604*, Oxford, 1923, no. XXVIII.

[20] A listing of communicants in Romford in 1562 also omitted temporary residents, Marjorie K. McIntosh, 'Servants and the household unit in an Elizabethan English community', *Journal of Family History* 9 (1984), 8.

[21] D. V. Glass, 'Notes on the demography of London at the end of the seventeenth century', in D. V. Glass and R. Revelle (eds.), *Population and Social Change*, London, 1972, pp. 280–2. The 1695 listing may also have omitted a proportion of the floating population, Jones and Judges 1935: 47.

[22] For these searches see, G.L.R.O. P92/SAV/1315. The population was estimated from the number of householders listed in the 1598 sacramental token book, G.L.R.O. P92/SAV/190.

[23] For the seasonal fluctuations in London's population, notably with the law terms see, D. M. Palliser, *The Age of Elizabeth. England Under the Later Tudors 1547–1603*, Harlow, 1983, p. 210; Fisher 1948: 43.

[24] Wall 1979: 103; N. Goose, 'Household size and structure in early Stuart Cambridge', *Social History* 5, 3 (1980), 364; A. L. Beier, 'The social problems of an Elizabethan country town: Warwick, 1580–90', in P. Clark (ed.), *Country Towns in Pre-industrial England*, Leicester, 1981, p. 60.

Table 2.2. *Household and houseful size in pre-industrial England*

	National sample 1650–1749[a]	Southampton 1695[b]	London 1695[b]	St Anne, Blackfriars 1695[c]	St Mildred, Poultry 1695[c]	Boroughside 1631[d]
Mean household size	4.2	3.8	4.4	3.7	5.2	3.8
Mean houseful size	4.5	4.0	6.1	7.4	7.2	(4.2)
Attached lodgers	0.3	0.2	1.7	3.7	2.0	(0.4)

Sources: [a] R. Wall, 'The household: demographic and economic change in England 1650–1970', in R. Wall (ed.), *Family forms in Historic Europe*, Cambridge, 1982, p. 497.
[b] Wall 1979: 103.
[c] D. V. Glass (ed.), *London inhabitants within the walls 1695*, London Record Society 2, 1966, p. xxvi.
[d] See discussion in text pp. 14–18.

Anne, Blackfriars. The estimated number of lodgers however is low when compared to the figures for London. This could reflect the temporal differences in the listings, local variations, or an underestimation of the lodging population.

The 1631 Boroughside evidence provides data with which to calculate population totals for other areas of Southwark at this and later dates. Using the 1631 evidence in this way involves the assumptions that the size of the floating population, household size and the proportion of the population under sixteen remain constant over time. Another source of imprecision is that household size as calculated from the Boroughside district, one of the wealthiest in Southwark, may, in fact, have been smaller in poorer districts causing an overestimate of population size in such areas. Despite such drawbacks, however, the totals so arrived at supply useful estimates of the numbers of people inhabiting the Southwark parishes in our period.

The 1631 count makes it possible to make an accurate estimate of the proportion of the population under the age of communion. Sixteen was the age specified for first communion in the 1604 canons and is usually assumed to have held for the rest of the country in the seventeenth century.[25] In the early seventeenth century the meagre data available for St Saviour's, Southwark, suggests that the parish conformed to the official age qualification. Age at first communion was between fifteen and sixteen years of age.[26] In the Boroughside in 1631 the population count shows that 1280 individuals out of 3708 or 34.5% were under the age of communion. Interestingly this proportion is very close to the Cambridge Population Group's recent estimate of the national total. Using their technique of 'back projection' they calculated that in 1601, 35.0% of the nation's population were under sixteen.[27] Contrary to what one might have expected from an urban area, the proportion of Southwark's population under sixteen years of age may not have been radically different from the rest of the country. To estimate the total population from the 1603 returns the number of communicants in each parish was multiplied by a factor of 100/(100–34.5). Each resulting figure was then inflated by 10% to allow for the floating population (see Table 2.3).

The multiplier derived from the 1631 count has less validity for the 1547 chantry returns since there is considerable evidence that age at first communion increased substantially in the sixteenth century. Wrigley and Schofield take age ten to be the minimum age of the 'houselynge' people

[25] Wilson 1923: no. CXII; Wrigley and Schofield 1981: 569. See also S. J. Wright, 'Family life and society in sixteenth- and early seventeenth-century Salisbury', Leicester (1982), pp. 9–11.
[26] In the Boroughside in 1622 forty-two households contained children of communicable age. The ages of thirteen of the latter were recovered from the baptism register of St Saviour's. The children's ages were distributed as follows 15(2), 16(3), 17(3), 18(1), 19(1), 20(2), 30(1).
[27] Wrigley and Schofield 1981: 569.

Table 2.3. *The population of Southwark 1547–1678*

Parish	1547	1603	1631	1678
St George's	1349–1548	[3,125]		5,727
St Olave's	[3652–4189]	8,418	16,447	12,440
St Thomas's	[271–310]	507		[1,326]
St Saviour's	2783–3191	7,123	[9,271]	[12,218]
Total	[8055–9238]	19,173	25,718	31,711

Note: Brackets indicate an estimated figure. In 1678 the parish of Christchurch has been added to that of St Saviour's.
Source: Table 2.1, discussion in text pp. 18–20.

in 1547.[28] Using the latters' estimate that 24.9% of the total population was under ten in 1546 a range of population totals has been calculated for St George's and St Saviour's, Southwark in 1547 on the assumption that age at first communion was between ten and sixteen years of age and that consequently the proportion of the population omitted from the totals of communicants lay between 24.9% and 34.5% (see Table 2.3). As before the final totals were inflated by 10% to allow for the floating population.

Where data for individual parishes was not available (see Table 2.1) gaps were filled in by estimating the missing figures from the relative sizes of each parish as calculated from the annual totals of baptisms, that is assuming that the number of baptisms from a parish is a guide to its size relative to its neighbours. Unfortunately, before 1640, the baptism registers of all four Southwark parishes are only extant consecutively between 1615 and 1627 and these have had to be used in default of an earlier series. Thus between 1615 and 1627 St George's, Southwark, contributed 16.3% of the total number of Southwark baptisms. Since we know the total population of the other three parishes in 1603 it is possible to reach a figure for St George's by multiplying the former total by 16.3/(100–16.3) (see Table 2.3). Similarly between 1615 and 1627 St Olave's and St Thomas's supplied 48.7% of all the baptisms in the Southwark parish registers. The aforementioned calculations have fairly wide margins of error since the methods adopted assume that the growth rates of the parishes were constant over time and that their birth rates were constant. It is hoped, however, that the results are accurate enough to establish the general order of magnitude.

[28] Wrigley and Schofield 1981: 565. Age at first communion may have been as low as eight in the early sixteenth century, see, R. Smith, 'Population and its geography in England 1500–1730', in R. A. Dodgshon and R. A. Butlin (eds.), *An historical geography of England and Wales*, London, 1978, pp. 199–204; J. Cornwall, 'English population in the early sixteenth century', *Economic History Review* 2nd ser., 23 (1970), 32. See also, Kitching 1980: xx.

The 1631 total of 18,660 persons included only that part of Southwark within the Bridge Ward Without and consequently omitted the two western liberties of St Saviour's parish. The Boroughside district, that part of St Saviour's within the Ward, contained 44% of all communicants in the parish in 1624, and this proportion has been used to estimate the total population of the whole parish in 1631.[29] To calculate the population of the remaining three parishes the population of the Boroughside has been subtracted from the 1631 total and the latter inflated by 10%. To arrive at population totals for the Southwark parishes in the late seventeenth century the number of households in 1678 has been multiplied by the 1631 mean household size of 3.8 and the result inflated by 10% to allow for the floating population. Gregory King's figures combine the parishes of St Thomas's and Christchurch, Southwark (carved out of St Saviour's in 1671). The relative size of each parish has been estimated from the relative total of baptisms produced by each parish 1673–80. In that period Christchurch produced 1053 baptisms compared to 368 from St Thomas's (see Table 2.3).[30]

However approximate they may be the importance of these population estimates is that they correct the impression left by Brett-James and others of population stagnation and relatively modest size. Barnes has stated that in 1590 Southwark consisted of a 'modest conglomeration of houses on the right bank'.[31] Another author has written that in the mid seventeenth century, when the population of St Saviour's exceeded 9000, the parish 'was still a small and pleasant spot'. Such mistaken assertions have perhaps been due to the false impressions left by the map evidence and the incomplete returns of new buildings.[32] In fact in 1600 Southwark contained 10% of the entire population of the City of London, and in the early seventeenth

[29] For the 1624 token book see, G.L.R.O. P92/SAV/213.

[30] The returns for the 1676 Compton census also survive for the four Southwark parishes. In general the figures for each of the Southwark parishes confirm that the population of Southwark continued to expand in the later seventeenth century. Unfortunately problems of interpretation (whether the totals given refer to communicants or the total population is not known) make direct comparison with King's figures difficult. If the figures *are* communicants then they suggest that King's totals *underestimate* the total population of Southwark by about 14%. It seems very probable, however, that some of the Southwark returns, notably the figures for St Olave's, refer to the total population of the parish. The raw totals for the Southwark parishes are as follows: St Saviour's 9200; St Olave's 12,000; St George's 2600; St Thomas's 1000. If these figures represent communicants, using a multiplier derived from Wrigley and Schofield 1981: 570, and applying a 10% adjustment for the floating population gives the following totals: St Saviour's 13,372; St Olave's 17,442; St George's 3779; St Thomas's 1454. I would like to thank Dr Anne Whiteman of Lady Margaret Hall, Oxford for the raw Southwark figures and for her helpful commentary on them. See also, Wrigley and Schofield 1981: 570; E. A. O. Whiteman, 'The census that never was: a problem in authorship and dating', in E. Whiteman (ed.), *Statesmen, Scholars and Merchants: Essays in Eighteenth Century History Presented to Dame Lucy Sutherland*, Oxford, 1973, pp. 1–16.

[31] T. S. Barnes, 'The prerogative and environmental control of London building in the early seventeenth century: the lost opportunity', *California Law Review* 58 (1970), 1335; Brett-James 1935: 116–17.

[32] Florence Higham, *Southwark Story*, London, 1955, p. 125. See also, Ida Darlington, 'The Reformation in Southwark', *Proceedings of the Hugenot Society of London* 19 (1955), 66.

century 13·5% of all baptisms listed in the London bills of mortality occurred in Southwark.[33] It was in fact the second biggest urban area in England, surpassing in 1603 its nearest provincial rival, Norwich, by over four thousand.[34]

2.2 Topography and population density

The relatively reliable map of Morgan in 1682 shows that the large population of Southwark did not fill the giant parishes to capacity (see Fig. 2.1).[35] In common with many other suburbs of London, Southwark contained considerable areas of open ground.[36] St Olave's contained Horsleydown Field and other open ground in the Maze.[37] About half (144 acres out of 282) of St George's consisted of St George's Fields, used mainly for pasture in the seventeenth century and intersected with ditches and ponds. In 1621 a strip system of agriculture was still in use and common grazing rights survived there. In St Saviour's some 58 acres in the Clink liberty were taken up by Winchester Park, chestnut trees from which were used in the rebuilding of London after the Great Fire.[38] Gardens, such as the Pike Garden, bear gardens, orchards and fishponds were also sited in the liberty.[39] The parliamentary surveyors reported that 'at the time of our survey [we] found the said fishponds stored with one hundred pike fish and eighty carps'. In the seventeenth century, in the relatively densely populated Boroughside, trees grew along Counter Lane and in the College Churchyard and occasionally blocked the local sewerage system. As late as 1656 Hugh Knightly, citizen and woodmonger, wished to be buried 'as near as conveniently may be to the elm trees in the college churchyard'.[40] In the

---

[33] Compare the totals given in Table 2.3 with that in Finlay 1981: 51. Between 1615 and 1627 the four Southwark parishes produced 13,694 baptisms compared to 101,390 produced by the city, its liberties (including Southwark) and the outparishes listed in the bills of mortality, ibid., 156.

[34] P. Clark and P. Slack, *English Towns in Transition 1500–1700*, London, 1976, p. 83.

[35] See the generally optimistic account of Morgan's work in Phillipa Glanville, 'The topography of seventeenth-century London', *Urban History Yearbook* (1980), 79–83.

[36] For a general topographical description of seventeenth-century Southwark see, Brett-James 1935: 407–10; Stow 1971: 2,52–69. For other open spaces in London see, M. Power, 'The east and west in early modern London', in E. W. Ives, R. J. Knecht and J. Scarisbrick (eds.), *Wealth and Power in Tudor England: essays presented to S. T. Bindoff*, London, 1978, p. 169; Brett-James 1935: 444–73.

[37] For much useful information on Southwark topography see, Malden 1967: 4, 126–62; Ida Darlington (ed.), *St George's Fields: the Parishes of St George the Martyr, Southwark, and St Mary Newington*, Survey of London 25, London, 1955; Ida Darlington (ed.), *Bankside – the parishes of St Saviour and Christchurch Southwark*, Survey of London 22, London, 1950. For the medieval period see the fascinating information painstakingly pieced together in Martha Carlin, 'The urban development of Southwark c. 1200–1550', Toronto (1983), passim.

[38] Darlington 1955a: 39–50; Darlington 1950: 44–65; Malden 1967: 4, 147.

[39] See, M. S. Guisseppe (ed.), 'The parliamentary surveys relating to Southwark', *Surrey Archaeological Collections* 14 (1899), 60–4; Carlin 1983: 58–78.

[40] P.C.C. Wills Register 140 Berkeley; J. Strype, *A Survey of London*, London, 1720, vol. 2, p. 28; G.L.R.O. SKCS 33.

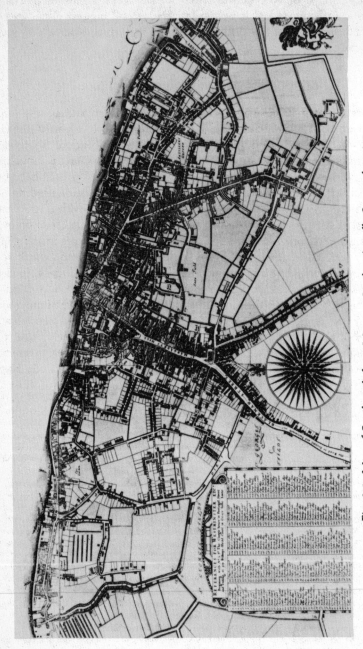

Fig. 2.1. Map of Southwark from Morgan, *London Actually Surveyed...1682*

mid-seventeenth century Paris Garden liberty included a 50-acre meadow, 30 acres of pasture and an acre of woodland. In 1655 it was said to contain twenty gardens and twenty orchards.[41]

New building was restricted by another topographical feature. Southwark lay in the Flood Plain of London. Nowhere in the district did the land lie more than 25 feet above the ordnance datum (a line conventionally sited 12.5 feet below high water level).[42] Some parts of Southwark, such as a large part of Paris Garden, lay below high-water level. Consequently a series of ditches and embankments was required to prevent regular flooding of the liberty. Drainage was accomplished by networks of these ditches which ran into sewers that were emptied into the Thames at low tide.[43] Despite the efforts of the Commissioners of Sewers to keep the embankments and ditches in good repair both Paris Garden and neighbouring St George's Fields remained badly drained and swampy.[44] The marshy ground in Paris Garden caused the subsidence of the parish church, built there in 1671, and in the early eighteenth century it was noted that 'the graves both within and without the church were filled with water as soon as dug'.[45] St George's Fields still contained bogs in the early nineteenth century.[46] In the sixteenth and seventeenth centuries Paris Garden and its surrounding areas were subject to regular flooding. This sometimes occurred when a tide mill erected on the ditch that surrounded all three sides of that liberty took too much water into its mill pond at high tide which then overflowed 'whereby the grounds called the Princes Meadows and divers other lands houses and grounds and likewise the highways are overflowed and surrounded to the great annoyance and damage of the landholders and other the King's liege People'.[47] Inadequate drainage, blocked sewers and poorly maintained embankments caused flooding in other parts of Southwark at high tide. In 1630, for example, St Olave's Street in eastern Southwark was totally inundated.[48]

Difficult building conditions in Southwark meant that population settle-

[41] Darlington 1950: 97–8; Carlin 1983: 37–57.
[42] See, H. Ormsby, *London on the Thames*, London, 1924, pp. 17–28; N. J. Barton, *The Lost Rivers of London*, Leicester, 1962, p. 15.
[43] W. Ingram, *A London Life in the Brazen Age. Francis Langley 1548–1601*, London, 1978, pp. 84–7, 214–20.
[44] Darlington 1950: 96; Malden 1967: 4, 131; Darlington 1955a: 40; Ida Darlington, 'The manorial and parish records of Southwark', *The Genealogists Magazine* 2, 13 (1954), 439–40. For the Commissioners of Sewers' efforts see also G.L.R.O. SKCS 19–40; British Library Add. Ms 34112.
[45] Malden 1967: 4, 159; Ida Darlington, 'The manorial and parish records of Southwark cont.', *The Genealogists Magazine* 2, 14(1954), 477.
[46] Malden 1967: 4, 132. See also the comment made by Rendle and Norman 1888: 340, 'As we saunter along, mentally picturing the past, we cannot but observe the swampy and offensive state of this district.'
[47] G.L.R.O. SKCS 28. See also, Ingram 1978: 84–6; Carlin 1983: 42. For a tide mill in East London see, Power 1978a: 29–46.   [48] G.L.R.O. SKCS 30.

Table 2.4. *Population density in Southwark. Households per acre in 1678
and in the City and its liberties 1638*

District	Acres[a]	Households[b]	Households per acre
St Thomas's 1678	9	310	34.4
St George's 1678	282	1,370	4.9
St Olave's 1678	116	2,976	25.6
St Saviour's 1678	200	2,930	14.7
Total	607	7,586	12.5
East London 1664[c]	4909	14,185	2.9
City within the walls 1638[d]			40.9
In the Liberties[d]			30.5

Sources: [a] *British Parliamentary Papers: 1851 Census of Great Britain, Population 6*, Shannon, Ireland, 1970, 386–93.
[b] King 1973: 39.
[c] Power 1972: 243.
[d] Finlay 1981: 168–72.

ment was more restricted than population density figures might suggest (see Table 2.4). If the simple acreage of each parish is taken into account, Southwark parishes were relatively lightly populated in 1678 compared to the London parishes north of the river forty years earlier. By the same measure Southwark was, in the later seventeenth century, more densely populated than the sprawling suburbs of East London. Within Southwark itself the western parishes, St Saviour's and St George's were less densely populated than the eastern parishes of St Olave's and St Thomas's. However, such a method of calculating population density is subject to local distortion and does not measure the actual densities in the *residential* areas in each parish. Southwark's topography in fact resembled that of East London suburbs, where densely populated residential areas lay adjacent to considerable areas of open ground and contrasted to that of the city parishes within the walls whose high density of households per acre reflected the absence of significant areas of open ground.[49]

---

[49] For problems of population density figures see, Jones and Judges 1935: 63; Shearer 1981: 3–5; M. Power, 'East London housing in the seventeenth century', in P. Clark and P. Slack (eds.), *Crisis and Order in English Towns 1500–1700: Essays in Urban History*, London, 1972, pp. 242–4. For maps of the residential areas of London see, Finlay 1981: 58; Brett-James 1935: 78, 242, 406; G. Rudé, *Hanoverian London: 1714–1808*, London, 1971, p. 9.

2.3 Population movements

As is apparent from Table 2.3 the population of Southwark participated in the rapid growth experienced by the whole of London between 1550 and 1700. Assuming that the estimates are accurate enough to reflect the general order of magnitude, Southwark's population grew at a slightly slower pace than the whole of London. Between 1550 and 1600 the population of London increased by about 186% compared to between 108% and 138% in the same period in Southwark. Thereafter between 1600 and 1650 the population of London grew by 100% compared to only 65% in Southwark between 1603 and 1678.[50] To examine this demographic expansion in more detail aggregative analysis of the four Southwark parish registers was carried out.

Only St Saviour's, the register of which commences in 1538, has a long, unbroken series. St Olave's, commencing in 1583, has no extant parish register for the years 1628 to 1639 inclusive; the register of St George's, commencing in 1602, has a gap between 1651 and 1653 inclusive and is defective for much of the Commonwealth period. Christchurch, Southwark, was included in the total for St Saviour's 1671–80. The parish register of St Thomas's does not commence until 1615.[51] Totals of baptisms and burials are presented graphically in Figures 2.2–5, and to facilitate their interpretation quinquennial average totals of christenings are presented in Table 2.5. Index scores for each quinquennium have been calculated using the period 1616–20 as base 100.[52]

The table shows that the parishes of Southwark exhibited different patterns. The baptisms for St Olave's exhibit a marked rise beginning in the 1590s and continue rising steeply until the 1620s when they drop away (see Fig 2.2). The annual totals of baptisms must have recovered however since they resume in 1640 at a high level but then rapidly fall away during the Civil War and Commonwealth period and never again reach their pre-war totals. The baptism series for St George's (Fig. 2.3) beginning in 1602, fluctuates considerably but a gradual upward movement can be discerned which ceases in 1642. As in St Olave's the baptism levels in St George's did not thereafter reach their pre-war totals. The number of baptisms in St Thomas's exhibit gradual upward movement in the early seventeenth

[50] Finlay 1981: 51.
[51] See, G.L.R.O. P92/SAV/356a, 3001–3004 (St Saviour's); P92/CTC/1/1, P92/CTC/55/1 (Christchurch); P71/OLA/9–11 (St Olave's); P71/TMS/1358A, 1358B, 1359 (St Thomas's). The parish register of St George's is kept in the parish church and is not available for prolonged study. I would like to thank Mr J. W. Pinder, churchwarden, for collecting the aggregative data for this parish. For the aggregative method see, D. Eversley, 'Exploitation of Anglican parish registers by aggregative analysis', in E. A. Wrigley (ed.), *An Introduction to English Historical Demography*, London, 1966, pp. 44–95.   [52] Finlay 1981: 53.

Table 2.5. *Quinquennial average totals of baptisms from the Southwark parish registers 1538–1680*

Period	St Saviour's			St Olave's			St George's			St Thomas's			Southwark	
	Average	N[a]	Index	Average	N	Index	Average	N	Index	Average	N	Index	Average	Index
1538–40	102.5	(2)	28											
1541–45	106.6	(5)	29											
1546–50	103.8	(4)	28											
1551–55	94.5	(2)	26											
1556–60	106.5	(4)	29											
1561–65	142.8	(4)	39											
1566–70	144.4	(5)	39											
1571–75	145.0	(5)	39											
1576–80	192.4	(5)	52											
1581–85	215.0	(5)	58	231.0	(2)	47								
1586–90	239.2	(5)	65	245.0	(5)	50								
1591–95	245.4	(5)	66	265.8	(5)	54								
1596–1600	258.6	(5)	70	305.4	(5)	63								
1601–05	289.2	(5)	78	362.8	(5)	74	171.3	(3)	95					
1606–10	312.8	(5)	85	412.8	(5)	85	162.8	(5)	91					
1611–15	353.2	(5)	96	444.2	(5)	91	163.2	(5)	91	33	(1)	95	993.6	93
1616–20	369.6	(5)	100	488.2	(5)	100	179.6	(5)	100	34.8	(5)	100	1072.2	100
1621–25	363.6	(5)	98	473.2	(5)	97	175.6	(5)	98	35.4	(5)	102	1047.8	98
1626–30	418.2	(5)	113	448.5	(2)	92	189.8	(5)	106	44.2	(5)	127	1100.7	103
1631–35	458.6	(5)	124	—	—	—	205.8	(5)	115	50.2	(5)	144	—	—
1636–40	469.2	(5)	127	659.0	(1)	135	206.0	(5)	115	55.4	(5)	159	1389.6	130
1641–45	452.0	(5)	122	590.6	(5)	121	190.6	(5)	106	53.6	(5)	154	1286.8	120
1646–50	402.0	(5)	109	494.2	(5)	101	129.0	(5)	72	26.6	(5)	76	1051.8	98
1651–55	433.6	(5)	117	497.4	(5)	102	165.5	(2)	92	26.4	(5)	76	1122.9	105
1656–60	461.4	(5)	125	539.2	(5)	111	128.3	(4)	71	17.8	(5)	51	1146.7	107
1661–65	506.0	(4)	137	537.3	(4)	110	168.0	(3)	94	29.6	(5)	85	1240.9	116
1666–70	498.5	(4)	135	555.6	(5)	114	156.0	(5)	87	52.6	(5)	151	1262.7	118
1671–75	531.4	(5)	144	477.8	(5)	98	179.4	(5)	100	48.6	(5)	140	1237.2	115
1676–80	537.0	(5)	145	517.6	(5)	106	200.8	(5)	112	45.8	(5)	132	1301.2	121

Note: [a] N = Number of complete years. Index: 1616–20 = 100.
Source: For St Saviour's, St Olave's, St George's and St Thomas's, see discussion in text, p. 25.

century to be checked again by the outbreak of Civil War; thereafter the totals did not recover until after the 1665 plague (see Fig. 2.4). The annual totals of baptisms in St Saviour's are particularly useful since, constituting an unbroken series from 1540, they enable the general course of population growth in Southwark to be outlined. Both Table 2.5 and Fig. 2.5 show that baptism levels remained constant between 1540 and 1560 and then rose to a plateau between 1560 and 1575. After 1575 continuous upward movement took place, with one pause in the early 1590s, until a mid-1620s trough. Thereafter the annual totals of baptisms continued to increase until the Civil War, fell away during the Commonwealth period, to recover and exceed their pre-war levels during the Restoration period.

Generally speaking the trend of the annual totals of burials was similar to that of baptisms in St Saviour's (see Fig. 2.5). Burials, like baptisms, remained (except in crisis years) at a plateau until the 1570s when they began a steady upward increase, in line with the known population growth, flattening out after 1626. Unlike baptisms there is a suggestion that burials remained, outside crisis years, relatively constant throughout the 1630s. They fell in the 1640s, began a steady recovery in the last quinquennium of the Interregnum and continued to rise until the end of the period.

If it is assumed that the baptism rate only fluctuated within narrow limits then the annual totals of christenings will be a fair guide to the course of population growth.[53] Information about vital rates of this sort is very difficult to come by. However, Table 2.6 supplies tentative evidence that the number of baptisms per marriage may have changed over time, increasing from 2.04 in the period 1566–80 to 2.43 in 1581–1600, falling back in the first two decades of the seventeenth century to 2.25 and rising to 2.59 in the period 1621–40. The very large numbers of events on which this exercise is based (which exceed the *combined* totals of the ten parishes used in the most recent study of London's population) do imply that these differences are real and not a product of random fluctuation.[54] Unfortunately, however, the baptism/marriage ratio is a product of too many demographic variables to make it a reliable indicator of changes in the underlying birth rate.[55] Nonetheless a rise in the birth rate might provide one explanation for the differences in growth rates which are apparent from a comparison of the population estimates for St Saviour's in 1603 and 1631 (see Table 2.3) and the average quinquennial totals of baptisms for that parish in 1601–5 and 1631–5 (see Table 2.5). The estimated population totals suggest an increase in population of 30.2% in this period while the average totals

[53] Ibid., 56; Wrigley and Schofield 1981: 174–6. See also their estimates of the crude birth rate calculated from back projection, pp. 528–35. Between 1571 and 1641 the long term quinquennial crude birth rate fluctuated between 31 and 34 per thousand. *Annual* fluctuations could be much more violent, ibid., 320–4.   [54] Finlay 1981: 57–60.

[55] Wrigley and Schofield 1981: 189–91.

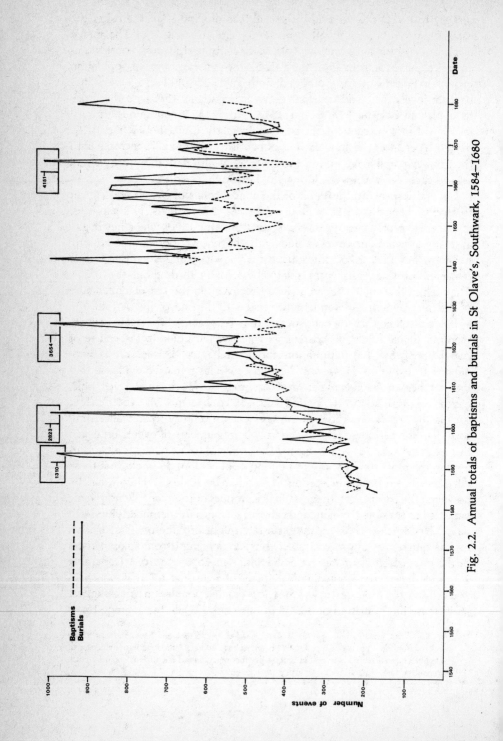

Fig. 2.2. Annual totals of baptisms and burials in St Olave's, Southwark, 1584–1680

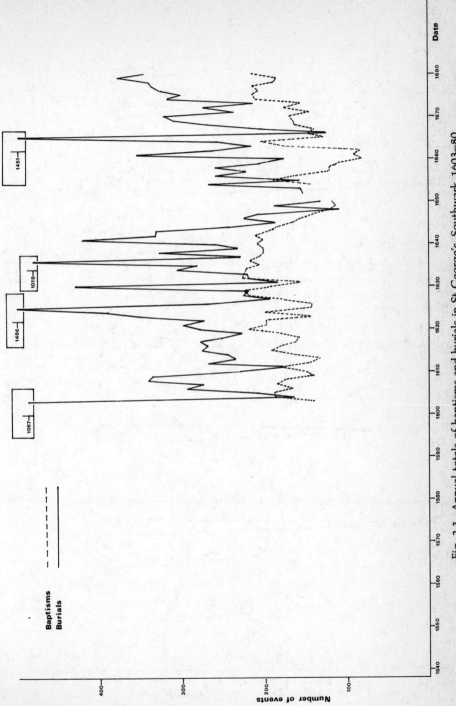

Fig. 2.3. Annual totals of baptisms and burials in St George's, Southwark, 1603–80

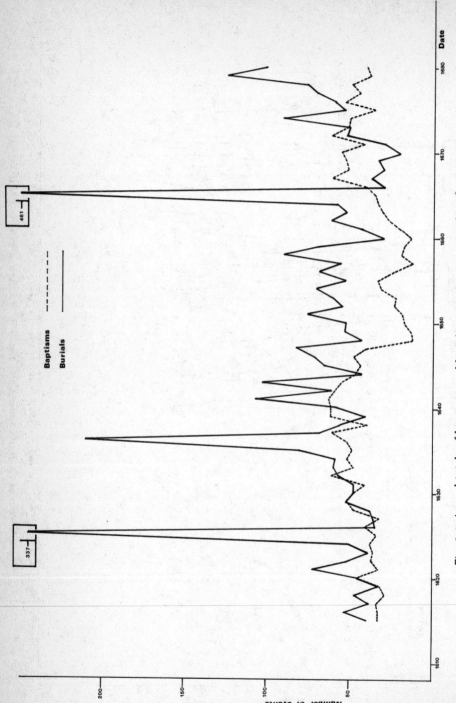

Fig. 2.4 Annual totals of baptisms and burials in St Thomas's, Southwark, 1615–80

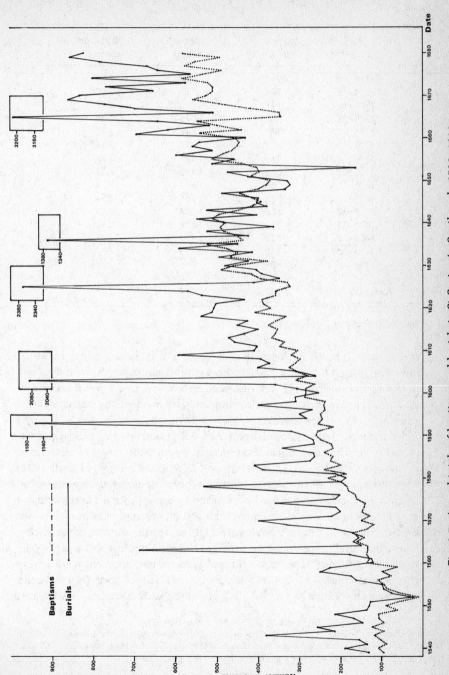

Fig. 2.5. Annual totals of baptisms and burials in St Saviour's, Southwark, 1539–1680 and Christchurch, Southwark, 1671–80

Table 2.6. *Quinquennial baptism/marriage ratios in St Saviour's Southwark, 1566–1640*

Period	Number of marriages	Number of baptisms	Baptisms per marriage
1566–70	359	722	2.01
1571–75	384	725	1.89
1576–80	441	962	2.18
1581–85	456	1,075	2.36
1586–90	485	1,196	2.47
1591–95	581	1,227	2.11
1596–1600	453	1,293	2.85
1601–05	654	1,446	2.21
1606–10	668	1,564	2.34
1611–15	756	1,766	2.34
1616–20	866	1,848	2.13
1621–25	732	1,818	2.48
1626–30	828	2,091	2.53
1631–35	850	2,293	2.70
1636–40	887	2,346	2.65
Total	9400	22,372	2.38

Source: St Saviour's parish register.

of baptisms suggest an increase of 58.6%. If it is assumed that baptisms under-registered births by 7% then this conflict could be resolved by a rise in the birth rate from 43 per thousand in 1601–5 to 53 per thousand in 1631–5. A rise of some sort is also suggested by the baptism/marriage ratios calculated for these periods. Jones and Judges, who also compared independently derived population totals with numbers of baptisms (uncorrected for birth under-registration), found a very wide range of birth rates, ranging from as low as 22 per thousand (unknown in England until 1921) to as high as 76. Birth rates as high as 50 per thousand are beyond what might be expected in a closed population in pre-industrial Europe and are at the limits of biological tolerance.[56] However, urban populations were not closed. High and rising birth rates are a known feature of cities experiencing heavy immigration of young adults. This has been put forward as a possible reason for the very rapid rate of population growth apparently shown by the annual totals of baptisms given in the bills of mortality in early seventeenth-century Norwich.[57] It is possible that St Saviour's, like the rest

[56] Jones and Judges 1935: 58–63; Wrigley and Schofield 1981: 174.
[57] Penelope Corfield, 'A provincial capital in the late seventeenth century: the case of Norwich', in P. Clark (ed.), *The Early Modern Town*, London 1976, p. 235; Finlay 1981: 56; Penelope Corfield, *The Impact of English Towns 1700–1800*, Oxford, 1982, pp. 107–8.

of London was experiencing immigration of a similar sort. Evidence presented in Chapter 6 suggests that, as expected, the age structure of Southwark's population favoured young adults and that, compared to provincial England, there were fewer individuals over forty-five years of age. Furthermore it seems probable that Southwark householders also tended to be on average *younger* than their rural counterparts, with more household heads under forty-five years of age. Furthermore it seems that there was an unusually *high* proportion of married couples heading households in the Boroughside compared to provincial England. Whatever the possible fluctuations in the birth rate it is unlikely that the annual totals of baptisms do more than slightly exaggerate the *course* of population change, particularly since the long term movements of burials in St Saviour's followed the same general trend as baptisms before 1640.

Another objection to the use of baptism totals for tracing the course of population growth is that the efficiency of parochial registration changed over time. Failures in parochial registration explain the double trough in baptisms and burials in St Saviour's in 1552, the impact of the Commonwealth Registration Act a similar trough in 1653, and the dislocation caused by the 1665 plague explains the defective recording of baptisms in 1665–6.[58] Under-registration, notably of baptisms, during the Commonwealth period explains the falling off in observed vital events after 1642 in both Southwark and London, following the collapse of the administrative machinery of the Anglican church and the growth of religious dissent.[59] The survival of such dissent after the Restoration retarded the recovery of parochial registration.[60] The registration experience of Southwark after 1640 adds more weight to the arguments of those who doubt the accuracy and usefulness of London's parish registers in the later seventeenth century. In Southwark between 1631 and 1678 the population is estimated to have grown by about 23%, but between 1636–40 and 1676–80 the average quinquennial totals of baptisms for the whole of Southwark *fell* by 6.4% (compare Table 2.3 and Table 2.5). After the mid seventeenth century, therefore, it seems likely that the annual totals of baptisms are no longer accurate guides to the course of population growth.[61] For this reason the course of that growth has not been examined in detail after this date. The aforementioned problems of interpretation reinforce the value of the independently estimated population totals for Southwark in Table 2.3.

[58] For defective parochial registration in England see, Wrigley and Schofield 1981: 23–32; D. Woodward, 'The impact of the Commonwealth Act on Yorkshire parish registers', *Local Population Studies* 14 (1975), 16–17.

[59] See, Sutherland 1972: 291–2; Finlay 1981: 23; J. Graunt, *Natural and Political Observations...Made Upon the Bills of Mortality*, London, 1662, reprinted in P. Laslett (ed.), *The Earliest Classics: John Graunt and Gregory King*, Farnborough, 1973, pp. 30–2.

[60] Noted in Glass 1966: xxxvi; Glass 1972:282–5; Finlay 1981: 33; Wrigley and Schofield 1981: 89–102.   [61] Finlay 1981: 103–4; Sutherland 1972: 291–2.

The results of the aggregative analysis of baptisms serve to confirm that the population of Southwark increased considerably between the mid-sixteenth and mid-seventeenth centuries. The rate of population growth, as suggested by the quinquennial averages, varied from parish to parish. Thus between 1611 and 1640 the average number of christenings increased in St Saviour's by 32%, in St Olave's by 48%, in St Thomas's by 67% but in St George's by only 26%. Overall in this period the number of baptisms in Southwark increased by 40% compared to a figure of 55% for the City of London and its liberties.[62] The annual totals of baptisms in St Saviour's suggest that the most rapid rate of growth took place in the last quarter of the sixteenth century. Between 1571–5 and 1596–1600 the average number of baptisms increased by 78% but between 1596–1600 and 1621–5 by only 40.6% (see Table 2.5). Available figures suggest that, at this date, Southwark's population was growing at a much faster rate than the parishes within the city walls.[63] Between 1580 and 1640 ten parishes within the walls increased their combined total of christenings by 47% compared to an increase of 118% in St Saviour's in the same period. Since Southwark's growth compared to all of London in the bills of mortality was slower, this must have meant that it was being outstripped by the even faster expansion to the east and west of London.[64]

Another feature of Figures 2.2–5 is that the annual totals of burials regularly outnumbered that of baptisms. An examination of this phenomenon in a little more detail in Table 2.7 shows the baptism–burial shortfall in St Saviour's, Southwark, for the period 1538–1640. The actual difference between the total of baptisms and that of burials could be exaggerated by the greater under-registration of births compared with deaths. The length of the birth–baptism interval as well as simple omission means that it is likely that baptisms under record the true number of births, although, since this interval was relatively short, the shortfall was not particularly serious. The short interval between death and burial makes it unlikely that significant numbers of burials escaped registration.[65] Table 2.7 supplies alternative figures for the natural increase in population based on Finlay's figures for Allhallows, London Wall, which show that baptisms under registered births by some 7%.[66] This table also shows regular birth deficits with the exception of the period 1626–35 which displays a modest surplus. Since it has been established that the population was in fact increasing, the impetus

[62] Finlay 1981: 156.
[63] Ibid., p. 56.
[64] Ibid., p. 62; Shearer 1981: 23.
[65] Wrigley and Schofield 1981: 166; Finlay 1981: 23–43; B. M. Berry and R. S. Schofield, 'Age at baptism in pre-industrial England', *Population Studies* 25, 3 (1971), 453–63.
[66] Finlay 1981: 31.

Table 2.7. *Natural increase in St Saviour's, Southwark, 1538–1640*

Period	Baptism–burial shortfall	Birth–burial shortfall assuming that baptisms under register births by 7%
1538–40	−118	−103
1541–45	−616	−579
1546–50	−323	−289
1551–55	−111	−89
1556–60	−449	−415
1561–65	−607	−558
1566–70	−552	−502
1571–75	−504	−453
1576–80	−521	−454
1581–85	−480	−404
1586–90	−236	−152
1591–95	−1,360	−1,274
1596–1600	−251	−161
1601–05	−1,873	−1,771
1606–10	−608	−499
1611–15	−398	−274
1616–20	−582	−452
1621–25	−2,591	−2,464
1626–30	+57	+203
1631–35	−82	+78
1636–40	−818	−653
Total	−13,023	−11,265

Source: St Saviour's parish register. These totals include all defective years.

for growth must have been due largely to immigration. Immigrants would have been required both to replace those who had died and those who moved out of the parish. In the early seventeenth century over a ten-year period in the Boroughside district of St Saviour's the overall persistence of householders was 43% with mortality accounting for rather less than half of this turnover (see below, Chapter 8). The volume of immigration in St Saviour's parish must have been subject to considerable annual fluctuations and have been particularly heavy following plague crises.[67] Some idea of the scale of immigration at the local level can be gauged from the sacramental token books which supply annual listings of householders. In 1636 the arrival of 28 newcomers was recorded in an area occupied by 615 householders in the previous year, so that 4.5% or one householder in 22

[67] Ibid., p. 111.

had been in the locality for less than a year. The impact of immigration found administrative expression in the routine complaints made by the churchwardens of St Saviour's that the numbers of poor increased daily and in the appointment from the late sixteenth century of two officials for searching out inmates and preventing the settlement of newcomers.[68] Population turnover with all its social consequences and the problems of assimilating newcomers is treated in detail in subsequent chapters.

In the absence of more detailed demographic information about the population it is not possible to say for certain that the baptism (or birth)–burial shortfall represents a natural decrease in the population (i.e. that the death rate exceeded the birth rate) since immigrants who died in the locality would have had their burials recorded but not their baptisms. There is some evidence that, in the wealthier parts of seventeenth-century London, although not in the poorer, Londoners may have been capable of replacing themselves.[69] Another point that calls for comment in Table 2.7 is the modest surplus of births produced in the parish in the period 1626–35. As noted above this was a product of the levelling off of burials after 1626 and an increasing number of baptisms. This period also returned the highest ratio of baptisms per marriage in the early seventeenth century (see Table 2.6) which suggests that the surplus might be a product of temporarily higher birth rates following the 1625 plague epidemic. It might also, of course, have been caused by lower death rates or a combination of both.[70] A slackening of immigration might also have helped to produce this surplus by reducing the number of immigrant burials in the annual totals.[71]

---

[68] See for example the records of their appointment in the vestry minutes. G.L.RO. P92/SAV/450, 17 August 1606, 11 August 1601, 15 January 1592, 6 July 1618 and their reports, P92/SAV/ 1314–15, 1422–3. See also Helen Raine, 'Christopher Fawcett against the inmates', *Surrey Archaeological Collections* 6 (1969), 79–85. In the sense described here the searcher for inmates seems to have equated 'inmates' broadly with 'poor immigrants', whether newly arrived single persons inhabiting another person's household or whole families occupying rooms in another person's house. The use of the term made by these local officials should be distinguished from that elsewhere in the text where 'inmate' refers to individuals contained within another person's household who were neither identifiable kin, servants or lodgers (the latter possessing a more formal paying relationship to the household). For the considerable semantic confusion surrounding this term see, Goose 1980: 362–3.

[69] Finlay 1981: 133–4; Valerie Pearl, 'The capital per caput', *Times Literary Supplement* (22 January 1982), 72. See also the debate on this subject between Finlay and Sharlin; R. Finlay, 'Natural decrease in early modern cities', *Past and Present* 92 (1980), 169–74; A. Sharlin, 'Natural decrease in early modern cities: a reconsideration', *Past and Present* 79 (1978), 126–38; A. Sharlin, 'A rejoinder', *Past and Present* 92 (1980), 175–80.

[70] Recent research has suggested that in pre-industrial England birth rates were strongly negatively associated with extreme fluctuations in the death rate. Marriages increased following mortality crises and there is some European evidence that age at marriage fell after such crises. Wrigley and Schofield 1981: 354, 348–55; Finlay 1981: 60; M. Flinn, *The European Demographic System 1500–1820*, Brighton, 1981, pp. 20–1, 34, 54.

[71] Immigration to London did begin to slacken in the mid seventeenth century during a period of population stagnation in England, Finlay 1981: 63; Wrigley and Schofield 1981: 166–70.

The annual totals of burials in all the Southwark parishes underwent considerable fluctuation from year to year. All parishes, where the registers are extant, exhibit enormous peaks in 1593, 1603, 1625, 1636 and 1665, caused by outbreaks of plague in London.[72] St Saviour's also exhibits major plague crises in 1543 and 1563; both years have been identified as years of crisis mortality in London.[73] Furthermore secondary peaks can also be observed in some Southwark parishes in 1578, 1581–2, 1597, 1609 and 1641.[74]

One of the problems often encountered in single-parish studies is that of sample size. In many cases the annual totals of vital events are too small for any clear pattern to be readily apparent and random fluctuations often explain annual variations in the numbers of observed vital events.[75] This is less of a problem here since, with the exception of St Thomas's, the Southwark parishes were very large. Consequently we can be confident that the larger peaks in mortality and the general trends are not a product of random variation. Nevertheless it is difficult to be similarly confident about the secondary fluctuations in mortality and the smaller peaks and troughs observed in the baptisms. Perhaps the best method by which to identify the effects of local random fluctuation is to compare the demographic experience of St Saviour's with the rest of London in order to isolate unusual years. By this method it should also be possible to assess the extent to which Southwark shared in the demographic regime of the capital. Accordingly Figures 2.6 and 2.7 plot the annual totals of baptisms and burials in St Saviour's against the totals given in the London bills of mortality between 1604 and 1650. The totals in the London bills have been scaled down by a factor of 20.[76]

What is particularly striking is that St Saviour's, demographically speaking, was very much part of the capital. The movements in the annual totals of christenings were almost identical in the early seventeenth century showing a steady upward movement interrupted by a trough in the 1620s and a falling off in levels after the outbreak of the Civil War. The only significant difference between the two areas is that the levels in St Saviour's did not fall as rapidly after the outbreak of the Civil War as they did in the City as a whole. The pattern of the annual totals of burials demonstrates,

---

[72] The presence of plague in Southwark was noted by contemporaries in 1603, 1625 and 1636, Malden 1967: 4, 128. For plague in London see also, Sutherland 1972: 287–320; Finlay 1981: 111–32; F. P. Wilson, *The Plague in Shakespeare's London*, Oxford, 1927; M. F. and T. H. Hollingsworth, 'Plague mortality rates by age and sex in the parish of St Botolph's Without Bishopsgate, London, 1603,' *Population Studies* 25 (1971), 131–46.

[73] See, Slack 1979: 14–43. The plague of 1563 is thought to have been the most severe, in terms of relative mortality, of all the sixteenth- and seventeenth-century outbreaks, Sutherland 1972: 300.

[74] Both 1578 and 1641 were identified as plague years in Southwark, Malden 1967: 4, 128.

[75] Eversley 1966: 57; Wrightson and Levine 1979: 45–6.

[76] For a similar exercise see, Finlay 1981: 53–6.

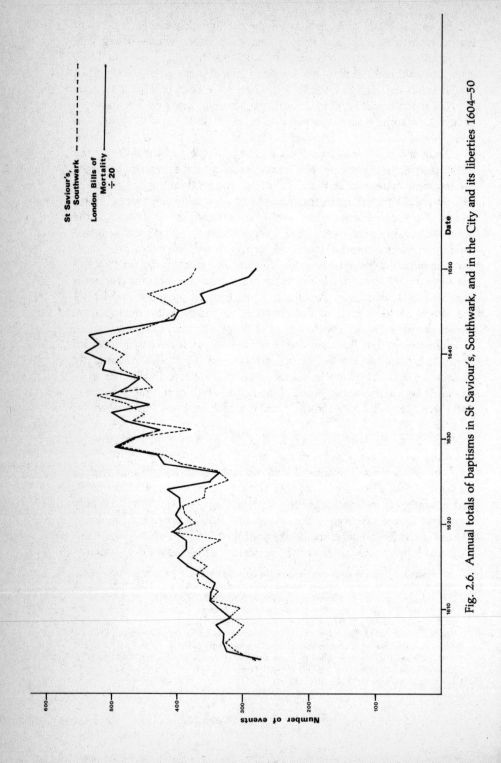

Fig. 2.6. Annual totals of baptisms in St Saviour's, Southwark, and in the City and its liberties 1604–50

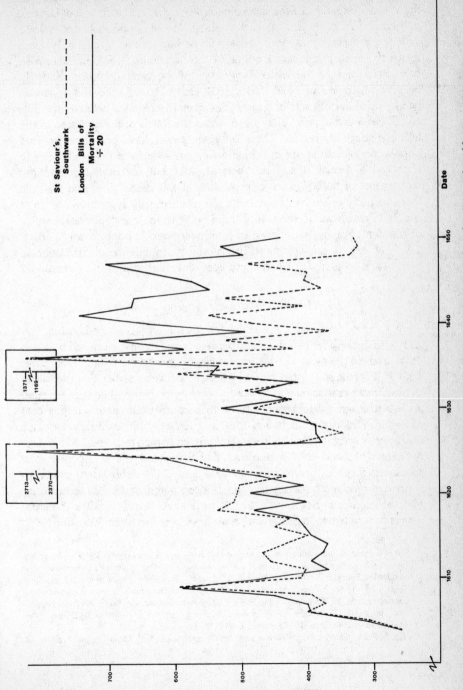

Fig. 2.7. Annual totals of burials in St Saviour's, Southwark, and in the City and its liberties 1604-50

perhaps to an even greater degree than that observed for christenings, that St Saviour's experienced the same demographic pattern as the rest of London in the first half of the seventeenth century. The burial peaks in 1609, 1625 and 1636 show up in both areas and perhaps more significantly even relatively small jumps and troughs in the burials in St Saviour's seem to have been part of the wider experience of the capital. Hence relatively insignificant peaks in 1618, 1630, 1632, 1634, 1638, 1641 and 1647 can be identified in both sets of figures. The main discrepancy between the bills and St Saviour's appears after 1636, when the levels of burials listed in the bills are relatively higher. These differences may have been due to rapid population growth in the eastern and western suburbs of the capital. Finlay observed a similar divergence between the bills of mortality and the movements of burials in ten city parishes at this date.[77] It is also possible that mortality levels in St Saviour's were abnormally high between 1612 and 1614 compared to the rest of London. With these exceptions the unity of the demographic experience of Southwark and London is noteworthy. To what extent can we relate the mortality experience of St Saviour's, Southwark, to periods of social and economic hardship in the metropolis?

2.4 Mortality, disease and hardship 1590–1640

As yet there is no real wage series for seventeenth-century London.[78] A rise in the real wages of London carpenters is said to have occurred between 1600 and 1670, most of the improvement, however, dating from after 1650.[79] It can be suggested, from the little evidence available, that the wages of Southwark craftsmen and labourers were much higher than those in rural areas at the same date, perhaps more than compensating for a higher cost of living in the capital. Between 1580 and 1629 the Phelps Brown Hopkins wage series suggests that southern building craftsmen received 12*d* per day; between 1613 and 1627 it is known that Southwark tilers, carpenters and plumbers received from between 20*d* and 24*d*. After 1629 southern craftsmen received between 12*d* and 16*d* compared to the 24*d* received by their colleagues in Southwark. In the early seventeenth century therefore wages for craftsmen in Southwark may have been between 50% and 100%

---

[77] Ibid., p. 53.

[78] For the sixteenth and eighteenth centuries respectively see, S. Rappaport, 'Social structure and mobility in sixteenth-century London', *London Journal* 9 (1983), 125–31; L. D. Schwarz, 'The standard of living in the long run: London, 1700–1860', *Economic History Review*, 2nd ser., 38, 1 (1985), 24–41. For national estimates of real wages and the problems associated with their construction see, H. Phelps Brown and Sheila V. Hopkins, *A Perspective of Wages and Prices*, London, 1981, pp. 1–105; D. Woodward, 'Wage rates and living standards in pre-industrial England', *Past and Present* 91 (1981), 28–46; Rappaport 1983: 125–31.

[79] Valerie Pearl, 'Change and stability in seventeenth-century London', *London Journal* 5 (1979), 34, n. 59.

higher than those in Southern England. Labourers fared nearly as well; between 1580 and 1626 Phelps Brown suggests a daily wage of 8d per day, compared to the 14d received by Southwark labourers in 1613. Between 1626 and 1639 when southern labourers were paid between 8d and 10d Southwark labourers were still receiving 14d. After 1639 when the wages of the former rose to between 10d and 12d per day the latter were receiving 16d in 1641. Wage labourers were apparently paid from between 33% and 75% more in Southwark than in the southern counties of England in the early seventeenth century.[80] There is, however, little data currently available on the differential cost of living in the capital and surrounding areas. The comparative price of wheat sold in London and other parts of Southern England indicates that, certainly by the 1640s, differences between prices in the capital and elsewhere were narrowing as the marketing and communications network in the south improved. In 1640–9 only in Cambridge did the lower price of wheat (36% more expensive in London) offset the lower wage levels in that town significantly. Only 17% separated Oxford wheat prices from those in London.[81] However we need to know a great deal more about purchasing power in the capital before social and economic conditions there can be compared convincingly to those in provincial England. More needs to be known too about the sources of income available to Londoners, of employment levels and economic behaviour in the capital. The following chapter will look in detail at some of these topics.

In the absence of an index of movements in the cost of living, one way of identifying years of particular hardship in the capital might be to identify years when the price of the basic necessities of life – food and fuel – were unusually high, when trade depressions hit the capital or when such periods overlapped. Such hardship, if it had a significant impact, would be expected to show up in higher mortality among the poorer sections of the population hit by malnutrition or low temperatures. Recent research on late Elizabethan and early Stuart England suggests that national mortality rates *did* rise when the harvest was poor and grain prices high but that the effects were geographically restricted. Arable areas with access to grain and good communications, such as the south and east of England, were rarely affected

---

[80] Wages for Southwark artisans are contained in bills and accounts, see, G.L.R.O. P92/SAV/83, 1580, 1585, 1595. For Southern England see, Phelps, Brown and Hopkins 1981: 11. Hutchins estimated that between 1600 and 1650 wages in London rose twice as fast as those in the countryside. Her evidence, from the accounts of building work carried out around the Tower of London, may well understate the true level of wages paid. Wages in Southwark and in the city parish of St Michael Cornhill ran at a higher level than those paid by the Crown for Royal Works. See, B. L. Hutchins, 'Notes towards the history of London wages', *Economic Journal* 9 (1899), 599–605.

[81] See, P. Bowden, 'Agricultural prices, farm profits and rents', in J. Thirsk (ed.), *The Agrarian History of England and Wales 1500–1640*, 4, Cambridge, 1967, pp. 614–15.

by harvest failure, unlike the more remote pastoral north.[82] As we shall see too, mortality also rose in periods of unusual cold in winter in provincial England. The effect of winter temperatures on mortality levels was immediate but only in years of extremely high wheat prices did mortality levels rise contemporaneously.[83] Keeping warm and getting adequate food were not always achieved in provincial England. What evidence have we for identifying periods of hardship in the capital and how far were increases in mortality associated with them?

For the late Elizabethan and early Stuart period we have the price of coals delivered to Westminster School and the maximum retail price of a four pound wheaten loaf allowed by the London Assize.[84] In the early seventeenth century in London bread was the staple food of the poor and coal the most important domestic fuel.[85] The period 1590–1640 has been selected for detailed study in order to compare coal prices (data for which is only available from 1585 to 1639) and bread prices. In order to identify short-term fluctuations in the prices of coal and bread, annual figures were compared to a nine-year moving average of prices (see Figures 2.8 and 2.9). Significant fluctuations have been arbitrarily defined as those exceeding the moving average figure by 5 % or more. Figures 2.10 and 2.11 present the annual fluctuations of coal and bread prices against the annual totals of burials in St Saviour's, Southwark.

Only in 1597 is there a convincing link between burials in St Saviour's and social and economic hardship in London. This was a year in which dearth-related mortality was spread over much of the country.[86] The small peak in burials in 1597 came after a four-year period (1594–7) of very high bread prices; 1595, for which no data exists, is thought to have been the worst year of shortage in London since the late fourteenth century.[87] The

[82] See, Wrigley and Schofield 1981: 356–401, 645–93; R. S. Schofield, 'The impact of scarcity and plenty on population change in England 1541–1871', *Journal of Interdisciplinary History* 14, 2 (1983), 286–91.

[83] Wrigley and Schofield 1981: 398–9.

[84] These are printed in B. R. Mitchell and Phyllis Deane, *Abstract of British Historical Statistics*, Cambridge, 1962, pp. 479, 497. See also, A. Appleby, 'Nutrition and disease: the case of London, 1550–1750', *Journal of Interdisciplinary History* 6 (1975), 1–22.

[85] Appleby concluded that in times of grain shortage the poor had little alternative foodstuffs to which to turn and that consequently bread prices were an accurate guide to nutritional levels, Appleby 1975: 6. The rising imports of coal to London were replacing the more expensive wood as a domestic fuel in the later sixteenth and early seventeenth century, Wrigley 1967: 58. For the resultant air pollution see, W. H. Te Brake, 'Air pollution and fuel crises in pre-industrial London, 1250–1650', *Technology and Culture* 16 (1975), 337–59.

[86] Although felt particularly severely in the pastoral north, parishes in the Home Counties, Southern and parts of Eastern England including Surrey, Essex and Middlesex also suffered crisis mortality in 1597–8. Apart from the years 1544–5, 1557–9 and 1727–30 the 1597–8 crisis was the most widely experienced in England, Wrigley and Schofield 1981: 653–72; A. Appleby, *Famine in Tudor and Stuart England*, Liverpool, 1978, pp. 109–45.

[87] Pearl 1979: 25.

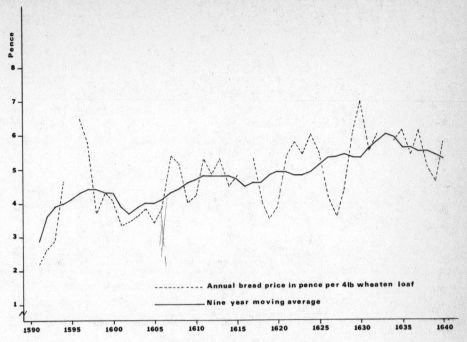

Fig. 2.8. London bread prices 1590–1640

1597 mortality peak was not caused by an increase in plague; the bills of mortality only returned 48 plague victims in that year.[88] Fuel prices, too, were higher than average in 1595–6.

Apart from 1597, years of high bread prices 1607–8, 1611, 1613, 1617, 1621–4, 1629–30, 1632, 1635, 1637 and 1640 were not associated with any significant mortality peak. The same lack of association is apparent from a comparison of fuel prices, significantly high in 1613–16 and (overlapping with high bread prices) in 1606–8 and 1630. Thus, for example, more individuals died in 1634 than in 1630 *despite* the latter year's high bread and fuel prices. In 1630 bread prices were 32.1% and fuel prices 7.5% above normal but both were slightly *below* normal in 1634. In 1631, as we have noted, concern for the capital's food supply had provoked a City-wide census and at the same period a number of parishes in Southwark were requesting that subsidised fuel should be provided for the poor.[89]

The relative immunity, in terms of mortality, of the inhabitants of St Saviour's in the early seventeenth century to these periods of social and economic hardship is the more surprising when the deleterious effects of

---

[88] Finlay 1981: 155. Appleby also identified dearth-related mortality in London in 1597, Appleby 1978: 137–9.   [89] See G.L.R.O. P92/SAV/1471.

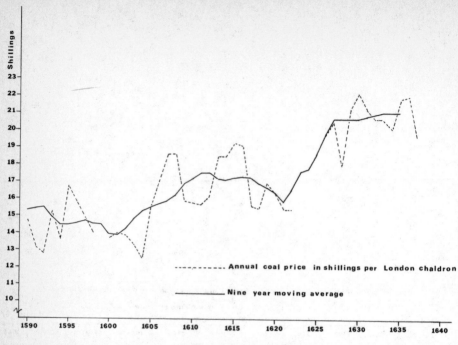

Fig. 2.9. London coal prices 1590–1640

depressions in the cloth industry are also considered. It is not possible to measure changing levels of employment in all occupational groups with the statistics available for early seventeenth-century London. What data we have relate mostly to the nation's principal export, the cloth trade. This trade, particularly sensitive to dislocation in both home and overseas markets, played an important role in the economy of the capital and large numbers of persons found employment within its various branches.[90] Major slumps in the cloth trade have been identified in the years 1603, 1625–6 (both

[90] In the mid sixteenth century 40% of London's freemen, something like 27 to 30% of the total adult male workforce, belonged to cloth related companies. It has been suggested that the proportion of the population employed in the cloth trade may have decreased from this period as the economy of the capital diversified, but there is, as yet, no evidence to support this suggestion. See, Rappaport 1983: 122–5; Beier 1978: 212; J. Patten, *English Towns 1500–1700*, Hamden, Conn., 1978, pp. 184–7. The problems involved in studying London's occupational composition and the inadequacy of our present knowledge are discussed in the following chapter. For the fortunes of the cloth trade see, B. Supple, *Commercial Crisis and Change in England 1600–42*, Cambridge, 1959, pp. 1–194; W. R. Scott, *The Constitution and Finance of English, Scottish and Irish Joint-Stock Companies to 1720*, Cambridge, 1912, 1, pp. 64–220; J. D. Gould, 'The trade depression of the early 1620s', *Economic History Review*, 2nd ser., 7 (1954), 81–90; D. W. Jones, 'The "Hallage" receipts of the London cloth markets, 1562–c. 1720', *Economic History Review*, 2nd ser., 25 (1972), 567–87; F. J. Fisher, 'London's export trade in the early seventeenth century', *Economic History Review*, 2nd ser., 3, 2 (1950), 151–61; G. D. Ramsay, *The English Woollen Industry 1500–1750*, London, 1982.

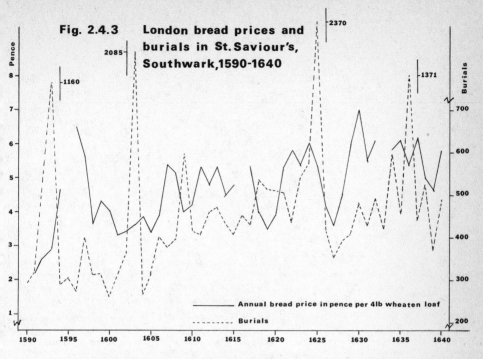

Fig. 2.4.3 London bread prices and burials in St. Saviour's, Southwark, 1590–1640

Fig. 2.10 London bread prices and burials in St Saviour's, Southwark, 1590–1640

caused by temporary dislocation of the London markets in times of severe plague outbreaks) 1607–11, the early 1620s and 1629–30.[91] Despite the fact that these depressions in the cloth trade often coincided with years of high bread and fuel prices (such as 1607–8, 1621–3 and 1629–30) there was little sign that whatever hardship was experienced in these years was transmitted to heavier mortality in St Saviour's. In 1622 – the worst year of the 1620–4 depression when London clothworkers were said to be being forced to emigrate – burials in St Saviour's *fell* markedly.[92]

The effects of the cycle of trade depressions on any one part of the capital can, however, be overstressed. The vulnerability of St Saviour's to such depressions would depend on the proportion of persons actually employed in the textile industry. This question is treated in the following chapter. Some trade depressions, too, were of relatively short duration, and the wealth of London merchants may have enabled them to shield their workforce from

[91] Jones 1972: 587; Supple 1959: 15, 25–6, 39–46, 52–7, 99, 117–18, 258; Fisher 1950: 153; Scott 1910–12: 1, 166–85, 193–9.   [92] Supple 1959: 57.

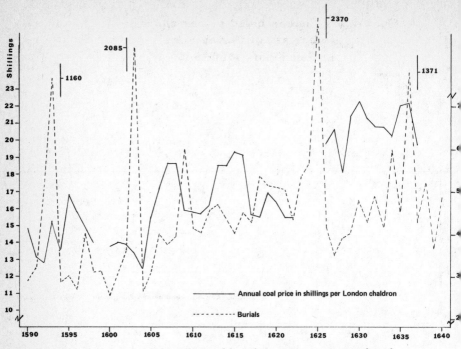

Fig. 2.11. London coal prices and burials in St Saviour's, Southwark,
1590–1640

extreme distress by stockpiling unsold cloth and maintaining employment.
Moreover contemporary sources also suggest that it was cloth-producing
areas such as the West Country or East Anglia, rather than the capital, which
were hit hardest by dislocations in the industry.[93] Above all, not all branches
of the cloth trade suffered alike in the early seventeenth century. The period
saw the gradual erosion and stagnation of the old broadcloth industry from
a peak in 1614, accelerated by the disaster of the Cockayne Project
(1614–17).[94] Other branches of the cloth industry were more buoyant. The
trade in the 'New Draperies' was little affected by the currency manipulations
in the Northern European markets which so depressed the broadcloth
industry in the 1620s. The former continued to expand (with a hiccup in
1630–1) throughout the early seventeenth century. London merchants also
benefited from the growing re-export trade that, by 1640, equalled the value
of all non-textile shipments.[95]

[93] Supple 1959: 10, 26, 44, 51, 53, 55–7, 117–18, 136; Scott 1910–12: 1, 194; Ramsay 1982: 23–31,
   51–7.
[94] Supple 1959: 31–50, 136–53; Fisher 1950: 152–5.
[95] Supple 1959: 153–62; Fisher 1950: 152–9.

The mortality peaks in St Saviour's therefore, with the possible exception of that of 1597, were caused by diseases – notably plague, but also possibly smallpox – which were *not* triggered by sudden deteriorations in living standards but were 'autonomous'. The 1634 peak in burials, noted above, may have been caused by the first recorded epidemic of smallpox in London.[96] As Appleby has established, the plague outbreaks which caused the significant mortality peaks in 1592–3, 1603, 1609, 1625 and 1636 occurred outside periods of social and economic hardship in the capital.[97]

A recent work has warned against overestimating the importance of the role of plague crises in contributing to the severe mortality in London.[98] As we have seen such plague crises show up as seismic leaps in the burial registers and troughs in the baptism levels. However the rapidity with which the annual totals of vital events reached and surpassed their pre-plague levels suggests that the losses caused in such outbreaks were quickly replaced. Plague is thought to have been a disease that fell especially heavily on the poor and consequently it might be supposed that St Saviour's and the other relatively poor parishes of Southwark would have suffered exceptionally heavily from plague compared to the wealthier city parishes.[99]

In order to examine the relative severity of plague crises the number of burials in plague years was compared to the average number of burials in the five years immediately preceding each plague crisis.[100] This measure, known as the crisis mortality ratio, is a far from perfect technique since its size depends not only on the severity of plague mortality but also on the level of 'background' or normal mortality which cannot be assumed to have been constant. A high ratio could mean either that plague was exceptionally severe or that normal mortality was unusually low. Conversely a ratio that declines over time could imply that the severity of plague was declining or that normal mortality rates were rising. Nonetheless the measure does at least indicate the relative importance of plague as a cause of death and enables us to compare its impact in Southwark with other parts of London.[101] Bearing the aforementioned reservations in mind Table 2.8. suggests that the impact of plague varied across time and space in Elizabethan and Stuart London. Plague in Southwark never had the impact that it apparently had on peripheral and extra-mural parishes (Allhallows, London Wall, and St

[96] The London bills of mortality record 1354 smallpox victims but only one case of plague in 1634, Appleby 1975: 14, 20.   [97] Appleby 1975: 8–19.

[98] Ibid., pp. 112–19. See also, T. R. Forbes, 'The changing face of death in London', in C. Webster (ed.), *Health, Medicine and Mortality in the Sixteenth Century*, Cambridge, 1979, p. 127.

[99] Power 1978b: 184–5; Finlay 1981: 121; Slack 1979: 48–9; P. Slack, 'The local incidence of epidemic disease: the case of Bristol 1540–1650', in P. Slack (ed.), *The Plague Reconsidered*, Local Population Studies Supplement, 1977, pp. 49–62.

[100] The year immediately preceding the plague year, often itself exhibiting above average mortality, was excluded from the calculations, Finlay 1981: 117.

[101] For the antecedents of this method see, ibid., p. 119; Slack 1979: 25.

Table 2.8. *Crisis mortality ratios in Southwark and London parishes*

Parish	1563[a]	1603	1625	1665
St Saviour's, Southwark	4.2	6.6	4.8	5.8
St George's, Southwark	—	4.1[b]	5.2	6.0
St Olave's, Southwark	—	8.7	6.5	6.1
St Thomas's, Southwark	—	—	7.0	8.9
St Mary, Somerset	8.0	4.4	5.2	6.7
Allhallows, London Wall	9.1	10.3	10.1	10.1
St Botolph, Bishopsgate	—	8.9	9.7	—
St Peter, Cornhill	8.0	6.6	4.4	4.2
St Michael, Cornhill	6.1	5.5	5.7	4.4
St Vedast, Foster Lane	7.5	6.3	5.7	3.3
Allhallows, Bread Street	4.3	3.8	2.7	2.1

Note: [a] Normal deaths taken as average of period 1559–62.
[b] Normal deaths taken as average of period 1605–7.
Source: Finlay 1981: 117–21 and Southwark parish registers.

Botolph's Bishopsgate). Up to and including 1625 the crisis mortality ratios of the Southwark parishes fall into the range experienced by the parishes within the city walls. The Southwark parishes, together with the poor riverside parish of St Mary Somerset, did not, however, exhibit the progressively declining ratios of the wealthier city parishes. The ratios increased over time in St Thomas's and St George's, declined in St Olave's and fluctuated in St Saviour's. In 1665 Southwark crisis mortality ratios resembled that of St Mary Somerset and were markedly higher than those of the wealthier central city parishes. This adds some weight to the views of those who have noted that plague was becoming concentrated in the poorer peripheral areas of the capital in the seventeenth century.[102] Interestingly, according to Table 2.7, without the 1636 plague the whole period 1626–40 would have returned a surplus of births over burials.[103] The demographic impact of plague in London requires further study. Within Southwark plague crises, and notably those of 1603 and 1625, seem to have had a greater impact in eastern Southwark (St Olave's and St Thomas's) than in western Southwark (St Saviour's and St George's).

The fact that Southwark's crisis mortality ratio never equalled that of the two peripheral parishes could have been related to Southwark's proximity to the river which may have increased the level of background mortality from waterborne infections, as it may also have done in St Mary Somerset, thereby artificially reducing the crisis mortality ratio.[104] That eastern

[102] Ibid., pp. 50–1; Finlay 1981: 120–1; Sutherland 1972: 302.
[103] For the effects of plague on population growth see Finlay 1981: 112; Flinn 1981: 22, 54–64.
[104] Finlay 1981: 121. But see Pearl, 1982: 72.

Southwark suffered more severely from plague than western Southwark might be connected to its higher population density (see above Table 2.4); plague is a disease known to flourish where rat and man are in close proximity. Recent studies, however, have found little correlation between population density and the impact of epidemic disease in London.[105] Furthermore it might be that the large areas of swampy ground in western Southwark further increased the level of background mortality from diseases such as malaria. A correlation between the incidence of fever and proximity to marsh was noted in Bethnal Green in the eighteenth century.[106] In the early nineteenth century the term 'Borough Ague' was used at Guy's Hospital to describe the fever prevalent in the Southwark marshland.[107]

2.5 The seasonal distribution of births and deaths

It is known that the seasons had a distinctive effect on the annual pattern of life and death in rural England in the pre-industrial period.[108] Temperature extremes increased mortality in provincial areas and the later winter months were the period of highest seasonal mortality.[109] Exceptionally severe winters were recorded in London in 1608, 1615 and 1622 when it was stated that the 'winter is so severe that 270 or 280 die weekly in London'.[110] Furthermore much employment in London, particularly in those occupations followed by the poorer sort, is known to have followed a seasonal rhythm. In the eighteenth century some elements of the building trade were said to suffer four to five months of unemployment during winter. In winter lack of dry weather prevented the dressing and dyeing of cloth. Tailors were also prone to seasonal unemployment.[111] It seems likely, therefore, that the winter months would have been a period of severe hardship for many of the poorer inhabitants of Southwark. Furthermore since the inhabitants of the Southwark parishes were relatively poor compared to those of many city parishes, it might be that they exhibited an idiosyncratic seasonal

---

[105] Finlay 1981: 122; Appleby 1975: 19. For the contrary view see, Power 1978b: 184–5; Beier 1978: 203–21.

[106] See, M. Dobson, '"Marsh Fever" – the geography of malaria in England', *Journal of Historical Geography* 6, 4 (1980); George 1966: 106.

[107] W. Ewart, 'On the decrease of ague and aguish affections in London', *Journal of Balneology and Climatology* 1 (1897), 34, 39.

[108] Wrigley and Schofield 1981: 285–313; D. Palliser, *Tudor York*, Oxford, 1979, pp. 116–18; R. A. Finlay, 'The population of London 1580–1650', Cambridge (1977), pp. 137–9, 181–2.

[109] Wrigley and Schofield 1981: 293–8, 384–401; Palliser 1979: 117.

[110] See E. Howes, *Annals, or, a General Chronicle of England…Continued…Unto the End of…1631*, London, 1631, pp. 1023 and 1034; *C.S.P.D., 1619–23*, 134.66.

[111] George 1966: 262–3; G. D. Ramsay, 'Industrial discontent in early Elizabethan London: cloth-workers and merchant adventurers in conflict', *London Journal* 1 (1975), 239; L. D. Schwarz, 'Income distribution and social structure in London in the late eighteenth century', *Economic History Review* 32 (1979), 259.

distribution of baptisms (or conceptions) and burials. The study of the seasonality of vital events might thus enable comparisons to be drawn between rural and urban experiences.

In order to look at seasonality the monthly totals of vital events in St Saviour's were totalled and converted to an index figure. This was done by calculating the expected number of vital events that would have occurred randomly in the particular month, allowing for the different number of days in each month (February being treated as 28.25 days). The index figure measures the extent to which the vital events in each monthly total differ from the expected total which is represented as 100.[112] Comparable data for the whole of England and for London are also presented in Tables 2.9–10 and graphically in Figures 2.12–15.

The analysis of the seasonal pattern of burials and baptisms suggests that, despite differences in relative wealth and occupational structure, the demographic regime in Southwark was not markedly different from the rest of London. The pattern of seasonality evinced by both baptisms and burials (see Figures 2.12–13) was virtually identical in both areas. Baptisms peaked in late winter (January to March), fell to a trough in early summer (June to July), and rose steadily thereafter to the winter peak. Burials were at their lowest point during the winter months (November to March), reached a secondary peak in the spring (April), but achieved their main peak in summer and early autumn (August to October).[113] A small rise in London burials in January is not duplicated in St Saviour's.

The seasonality of baptisms in St Saviour's and London bears a close resemblance to the national pattern (see Fig. 2.14), although the national peak (between February and March) and the trough (June to July) are more exaggerated. If it is assumed that in the late sixteenth and early seventeenth centuries the average interval between birth and baptism was relatively short, as recent studies suggest, then the seasonal distribution of baptisms should be similar to that of births.[114] Consequently the seasonal distribution of baptisms will also resemble that of conceptions, offset by nine months as an average interval between conception and birth.[115] Conceptions in London therefore were at their highest between April and June, when mortality was low, and at their lowest between September and October, when mortality was at its highest.[116] It is possible therefore that conceptions

---

[112] See, H. Palli, 'The seasonality of marriage in Estonia', *Local Population Studies* 14 (1975), 51; Finlay 1977: 137; Wrigley and Schofield 1981: 286.

[113] For a similar pattern for the parish of St Botolph's, Aldgate, in the seventeenth century, see, Forbes 1979: 122.

[114] Finlay 1981: 24; Wrigley and Schofield 1981: 289–92.

[115] The period of gestation apparently varies somewhat so that the result will tend to blur the true pattern. There is here a further assumption that there was no pronounced seasonal foetal mortality, ibid., p. 291.   [116] Finlay 1977: 139.

Table 2.9. *Seasonality of burials in St Saviour's, Southwark, 1540–1649 (by month)*

	J	F	M	A	M	J	J	A	S	O	N	D
St Saviour's												
1581–1649	85	91	91	104	96	94	101	113	124	111	96	93
1540–99	79	82	91	100	97	89	92	113	136	125	104	94
1600–49	88	91	89	99	96	90	103	117	126	111	97	92
London [a]												
1581–1650	94	85	100	102	95	96	101	109	120	115	94	89
National sample [b]												
1540–99	107	111	121	120	99	87	81	89	92	97	97	99
1600–49	112	114	115	116	102	90	83	85	91	93	98	102

Sources: [a] Finlay 1977: 138.
[b] Wrigley and Schofield 1981: 294.

Table 2.10. *Seasonality of baptisms in St Saviour's, Southwark, 1540–1649 (by month)*

	J	F	M	A	M	J	J	A	S	O	N	D
St Saviour's												
1581–1649	107	108	111	98	94	90	89	99	100	97	104	103
1540–99	105	100	109	95	93	88	91	99	106	109	102	103
1600–49	108	111	110	96	94	90	89	99	100	96	105	103
London [a]												
1581–1650	109	107	108	99	95	87	92	96	100	100	103	103
National sample [b]												
1540–99	111	123	123	111	89	81	78	89	105	100	101	91
1600–49	110	125	124	112	92	82	77	88	97	100	99	97

Sources: [a] Finlay 1977: 181.
[b] Wrigley and Schofield 1981: 287.

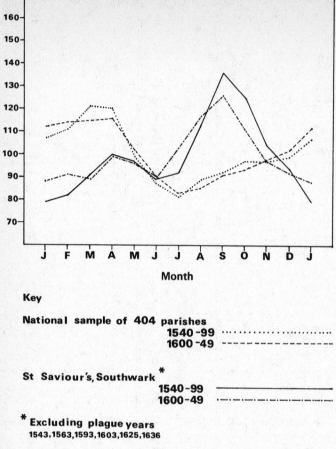

Key

National sample of 404 parishes
            1540 -99 ························
            1600 -49 — — — — — — — — — —

St Saviour's, Southwark *
            1540 -99 ————————————
            1600 -49 ·—·—·—·—·—·—·—·—·—

* Excluding plague years
  1543,1563,1593,1603,1625,1636

Fig. 2.12. Seasonality of burials in St Saviour's, Southwark, 1540–1649

were reduced by the unhealthy summer months in the capital, although in the countryside conceptions were at their lowest during August to November when burials were also low. Only 3.7% of the 404 parishes used in the national study of seasonality suffered their highest mortality in September and October. The existence of seasonality of baptisms in London also suggests that seasonal demands of agriculture may not be the full explanation of the national trough in conceptions.[117] A convincing explanation for the existence of similar patterns of seasonal conceptions in both the capital and rural England has yet to be put forward.

[117] Wrigley and Schofield 1981: 292–3.

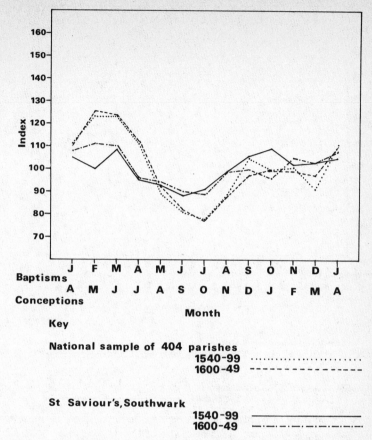

Key

National sample of 404 parishes
1540-99 ······················
1600-49 - - - - - - - - - - - - - -

St Saviour's,Southwark
1540-99 —————————————
1600-49 —·—·—·—·—·—·—·—·

Fig. 2.13. Seasonality of baptisms and conceptions in St Saviour's, Southwark,
1540–1649

The late summer peak in burials in the capital may have been caused by
the impact of plague, present even in non-crisis years for much of the
sixteenth and early seventeenth century (see Fig. 2.15).[118] Alternatively, it
has been suggested, diseases prevalent in the summer months such as
dysentery, may have been responsible.[119] The secondary peak in the spring
was possibly caused by diseases such as influenza.[120]

In order to examine this idiosyncratic pattern of mortality in greater detail

[118] If years of heavy plague mortality are included the monthly index of burials in St Saviour's, 1600–49,
runs as follows; J(72) F(74) M(74) A(83) M(82) J(84) J(117) A(163) S(161) O(116) N(94) D(79).
See, Finlay 1977: 139; Forbes 1979: 122–3.
[119] Wrigley and Schofield 1981: 295; R. S. Schofield, 'Microdemography and epidemic mortality: two
case studies', in J. Sundin and E. Soderlund (eds.), *Time, Space and Man: Essays in Microdemography*,
Stockholm, 1979, pp. 55–6.   [120] Finlay 1977: 139.

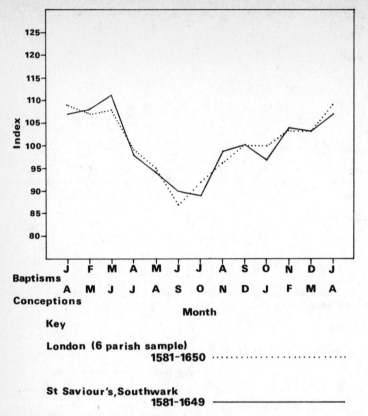

Baptisms
J F M A M J J A S O N D J

Conceptions
A M J J A S O N D J F M A

Month

Key

London (6 parish sample)
1581-1650 ······················

St Saviour's,Southwark
1581-1649 ————————

Fig. 2.14. Seasonality of baptisms and conceptions in St Saviour's, Southwark, and London, 1581–1650

it is helpful to make some sort of distinction by age at burial. In St Saviour's this can be done by exploiting the fact that the parish register invariably labelled the dead as 'man', 'woman', 'boy', 'girl', 'servant', 'child' and 'crisam' (here used to mean either an unbaptized infant or one dying within one month of birth). Accordingly the number of children and 'crisams' were counted separately. The run of years most suitable proved to be the period 1606–24. Table 2.11 therefore supplies the seasonal index of burials of the youngest members of the population and that of the adult and adolescent. Infant and child burials in St Saviour's peaked in the summer months (July–September) and were low in winter. Child burials in late sixteenth- and early seventeenth-century Ludlow and in Geneva followed the same pattern.[121] In the period 1606–24 infant and child burials contributed 48.9%

[121] R. Schofield and E. A. Wrigley, 'Infant and child mortality in England in the late Tudor and early Stuart period', in C. Webster (ed.), *Health, Medicine and Mortality in the Sixteenth Century*, Cambridge, 1979, pp. 89–91; Wrigley and Schofield 1981: 295.

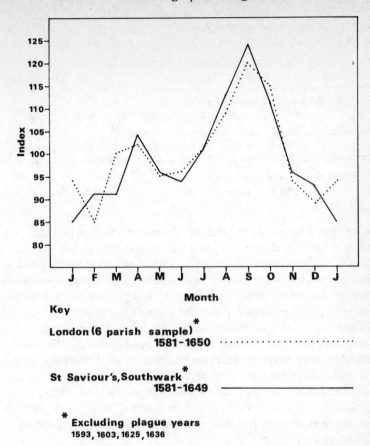

Key

London (6 parish sample)*
1581-1650 ·······················

St Saviour's, Southwark*
1581-1649 ————————————

* Excluding plague years
1593, 1603, 1625, 1636

Fig. 2.15. Seasonality of burials in St Saviour's, Southwark, and London,
1581–1650

of all burials in St Saviour's and 53.5% of all those in September. This
suggests that dysentery may, as suggested, have been an important cause
of the overall summer peak in burials since it is a disease known to
particularly affect young children. Demographers distinguish two components within infant mortality, namely the endogenous component, that is
deaths resulting from an internal defect of child or mother, and the
exogenous component, those deaths caused by external environmental
factors. It has also been found that endogenous deaths occur usually within
one month of birth.[122] It follows from this therefore that endogenous infant
deaths will follow a different seasonal pattern from exogenous infant and

[122] Schofield and Wrigley 1979: 73–82; E. A. Wrigley, 'Births and baptisms. The use of Anglican
baptism registers as a source of information about the numbers of births in England', *Population
Studies* 31, 2 (1977), 281–312; Finlay 1981: 25–37.

Table 2.11. *Seasonal distribution of burials of children and infants and adults and adolescents in St Saviour's, Southwark; 1606–24 (by month)*

J	F	M	A	M	J	J	A	S	O	N	D	Total
Children (includes children, infants and crisams)												
83	91	80	87	91	104	112	125	136	107	93	91	4015
Adults and adolescents (includes men, women, boys, girls, servants)												
101	86	97	115	98	85	94	99	113	106	106	101	4197

Note: The year 1609, a plague year, has been excluded.
Source: For method of calculating this seasonal distribution, see discussion in text, pp. 53–5.

child mortality. The parish register of St Saviour's makes precisely this distinction between endogenous infant deaths and exogenous infant and child mortality. The entries of the form 'Smith son of Robert Smith a crisam' refers to infants dying before baptism and 'Charles Smith a crisam' to infants dying within a month of birth. Consequently it is possible to examine the seasonal pattern of each (see Table 2.12). As can be seen 'child' and endogenous infant deaths display markedly different seasonal patterns. While child and exogenous infant deaths continued to peak in the summer months endogenous infant mortality, as one would expect was allied closely with the seasonal pattern of baptisms, although the jump in endogenous infant mortality in September cannot solely be explained by the modest August peak in baptisms. Perhaps deaths in childbed peaked in September, one of the worst months for adult mortality, and added to the crop of endogenous infant burials.

Since exogenous infant and child deaths were combined in the exercise this also indicates that exogenous infant mortality in Southwark cannot have followed a very different seasonal pattern to that of children which may suggest that infants faced similar exposure to infected food and drink and that, therefore, weaning took place early, in marked contrast to the pattern found at Ludlow.[123] Early weaning is biologically consistent with the short intervals between births reported for seventeenth-century London.[124] In the absence of the younger members of the population adult and adolescent burials still reached a modest, possibly plague-related, peak in September and also one in April. This April peak, whether or not caused by influenza, consisted of a disproportionate number of the older elements of the population.

It is particularly difficult to explain the fact that burials reached a trough

[123] Schofield and Wrigley 1979: 90.   [124] Finlay 1981: 146.

Table 2.12. *Seasonal distribution of burials of children and endogenous infant mortality (by month)*

J	F	M	A	M	J	J	A	S	O	N	D	Total
Children (includes exogenous infant mortality)												
73	81	70	85	100	107	118	139	142	118	89	78	2791
Endogenous infant mortality												
106	114	104	92	72	97	97	93	122	81	101	120	1224
Seasonal distribution of baptisms 1606–24												
108	112	109	99	85	88	90	104	96	99	102	109	6352

Note: The year 1609 has again been excluded.
Source: For method of calculating this seasonal distribution see discussion in text, pp. 55–6.

in the winter months, since, as we have seen, contemporaries did associate severe winters with high mortality and winter was the peak mortality period in rural England, (although John Graunt considered that autumn was an 'unhealthful season' in London).[125] Furthermore even during winters of known hardship, such as that of 1608, no significant rise in burials took place in St Saviour's.

The lack of correspondence between high mortality and the winter period is the more remarkable since it can be demonstrated from poor relief payments that the season was indeed the time of greatest economic hardship. In 1608, when the Thames froze over, the Lord Mayor distributed £200 among poor watermen, and the Overseers of the Poor in Paris Garden noted in their accounts for that year a separate distribution of money 'among the poor...in the time of the hard frost'.[126] College pensioners received extra payments in cold weather in 1621–2. Figure 2.16 shows the average number of householders receiving extraordinary poor relief per week every month in 1621–2 in the Boroughside district of St Saviour's, Southwark. More householders received payments during the winter months (December to March) than at any other time.

One of the reasons for the apparent lack of correlation between periods of hardship (whether caused by low winter temperatures or by rising food and fuel prices and upsurges in unemployment discussed in the previous section) and mortality may be that, using aggregative analysis, it is only possible to measure the number of burials, and that diseases and ailments

[125] Graunt 1973: 41.
[126] *C.S.P.D. 1603–10*, 31, 31 January 1608; P. Norman (ed.), 'The accounts of the Overseers of the Poor of Paris Garden, Southwark, 17 May 1608–30 September 1671', *Surrey Archaeological Collections* 16 (1901), 70.

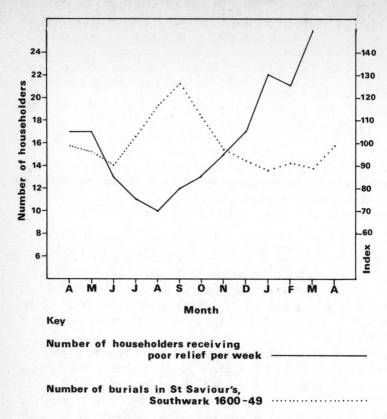

Key

**Number of householders receiving
poor relief per week** ————————

**Number of burials in St Saviour's,
Southwark 1600-49** ·····················

Fig. 2.16. Average number of householders in the Boroughside receiving
extraordinary poor relief per week 1621–2

not resulting in death, however debilitating, would not show up in the
seasonal pattern. The length of an illness may have blurred the effect of
seasonality and sudden deteriorations in living conditions.[127] It is also
possible that the administration of poor relief was indeed capable of
offsetting hardship with free distributions of fuel and cash payments.[128]

This survey of the demographic character of Southwark has established
that it was a large urban area containing, at the beginning of the
seventeenth century, about one in ten of London's total population, but that
nonetheless the inhabitants also had access to considerable areas of open

[127] Wrigley and Schofield 1981: 398–400; Appleby 1975: 7.
[128] See, Pearl 1979: 4–5; Appleby 1978: 139; Valerie Pearl, 'Social policy in early modern London',
in Valerie Pearl, H. Lloyd-Jones and B. Worden (eds.), *History and Imagination: Essays in Honour of
H. R. Trevor-Roper*, London, 1981, p. 124; K. Lindley, 'Riot prevention and control in early Stuart
London', *Transactions of the Royal Historical Society*, 5th ser., 33 (1983), 116–17.

ground. It has also been found that there were something like three times as many people living in Southwark in the 1630s than there had been eighty years earlier. What sort of society had been produced by these population changes? How had housing been affected by a trebling in population density? What kind of institutions gave structure to the lives of the inhabitants and influenced their behaviour? Moreover the fact that in Southwark the winter months were not associated with high seasonal mortality as was the case in rural England indicates that its inhabitants were less vulnerable to winter hardship than were their rural counterparts. The inhabitants of St Saviour's were much more affected by high summer temperatures than by low winter ones. In the early seventeenth century, too, the population of that parish was not directly affected by sudden deteriorations in living conditions in the capital caused by fluctuations in employment levels and rises in the prices of basic commodities. It will therefore be important to investigate how the inhabitants of Southwark earned a living, since it seems possible that the local economy worked in such a way as to bolster individual economic circumstances against periods of social and economic hardship by reducing individual dependence on any one source of income.

3

Earning a living in early seventeenth-century Southwark

The task of reconstructing the occupational profile of one part of London is made the harder by the absence of comparative information for the rest of the capital. The immense physical size of London and the daunting nature of the task involved has restricted work on its occupational make-up. Unlike many towns and cities in pre-industrial England there is no single central source for occupations available. In particular, Freemen's registers (i.e. registers of individuals taking up the freedom of a town or city), which have been used to delineate the occupational structures of some provincial towns, are not extant for London before the later seventeenth century and their representativeness depends on the (as yet unknown) proportion of the adult male population who took up the freedom in later Stuart London.[1] Because of this historians have been forced to nibble at the edges of the problem, either by studying one particular city company or by concentrating on a specific geographical area. Since comparative material is lacking, such studies can give us no real idea of the relative importance of an occupation to the whole of London.[2] Sampling by parish or ward has its drawbacks too, since

[1] See, for example, J. F. Pound, 'The social and trade structure of Norwich 1525–75', in P. Clark (ed.), *The Early Modern Town*, London, 1976, pp. 129–47; J. Patten, 'Urban occupations in pre-industrial England', *Transactions of the Institute of British Geographers*, n.s., 2 (1977), 296–313; J. Pound, 'The validity of the freemen's lists: some Norwich evidence', *Economic History Review*, 2nd ser., 34 (1981), 48–59; D. V. Glass, 'Socio-economic status and occupations in the City of London at the end of the seventeenth century', in Clark (ed.), *The Early Modern Town*, 227–30; J. R. Kellet, 'The breakdown of gild and corporation control over the handicraft and retail trade in London', *Economic History Review*, 2nd ser., 10 (1958), 383. A damaged register book of the freemen of the City of London does survive for the years 1551-3, see G. D. Ramsay, 'The recruitment and fortunes of some London freemen in the mid sixteenth century', *Economic History Review*, 2nd ser., 31 (1978), 526–40.

[2] For recent work on London occupations see, Glass 1976: 216–32; Power 1978a: 36–43; Forbes 1980: 119–32; Beier 1978: 211–14; D. Cressy, 'Occupations, migration and literacy in East London 1580–1640', *Local Population Studies* 5 (1970), 53–60; East London History Group, 'The population of Stepney in the early seventeenth century', *Local Population Studies* 3 (1968), 39–52. These studies also tend to assign occupations to categories which are not comparable.

occupational groups were not spread evenly across the capital. The little that is known of London suggests that certain occupations were often grouped together in specific zones. Hence the concentration of alien silkweaving in Bishopsgate and Spitalfields, dyeing close to the Thames, and gunsmiths around the Tower.[3] Occupations could also be grouped in certain streets: booksellers and stationers in Paternoster Row, and butchers in St Nicholas Shambles and Eastcheap. Though there is evidence that within the City street-specific occupational zoning was beginning to disintegrate in the seventeenth century, it cannot be discounted.[4] The position is further complicated by the unwillingness of historians to agree as to what area the term 'London' actually refers. Is London the City within the Walls, the City and Westminster, or the whole area contained in the bills of mortality? In reality, Langton writes, London was 'two cities in the seventeenth century', namely the government and royal court at Westminster and the City with its commerce and trade; a definition which ignores many of the poorer outlying suburbs which may have had 'quite distinct occupational quarters'.[5]

The occupational profile of the capital then will only be appreciated fully when the trades and crafts located in every district have been identified. Reconstructing the occupational structure of Southwark, which as we have seen contained a significant proportion of the total population of the capital, will in itself be an important step towards this goal.

Little too is known of local employment patterns in the capital. The occupational structure of an urban area will have an important bearing on local employment patterns and the distribution of economic power. Some manufacturing concerns are known to have employed relatively large numbers of people. In 1607 one London brewery had a wage roll of £687 per year. If one assumes that every employee worked every day of the year except Sundays for 16d per day then this wage bill would represent the annual employment of about 33 persons.[6]

To count the numbers recorded as following individual occupations might well give a misleading impression of how the inhabitants of Southwark earned a living. As one author has recently pointed out, 'it is

---

[3] For occupational zoning in London see, Pearl 1961:15–16; Clark and Slack 1976:67–8; Patten 1978:184–8.

[4] Reddaway 1963:189. The Butchers' Company was attempting to prevent butchers setting up shop outside the official shambles, P. E. Jones, *The Butchers of London: a History of the Worshipful Company of Butchers of the City of London*, London, 1976, pp. 71–149.

[5] See, Shearer 1981; J. Langton, 'Industry and towns', in R. A. Dodgshon and R. A. Butlin (eds.), *An Historical Geography of England and Wales*, London, 1978, p. 193.

[6] See, J. L. Archer, 'The industrial history of London 1603–1640 with special reference to the suburbs and those areas claiming exemption from the authority of the Lord Mayor', London (1934), p. 41; S. Rappaport, 'Social structure and mobility in sixteenth-century London', paper presented to the Conference on London History, London, 27 June 1981, p. 16.

the economic behaviour of individuals which must be examined and then aggregated in much greater detail if we are to get a true picture and better interpretation of occupational structures'.[7] Even if the potential earnings of the various occupational groups could be assessed such an approach neglects alternative sources of income.[8] This is a particularly important topic since there are those who believe that most urban dwellers lacked such alternatives and were consequently more vulnerable to trade depression and the effects of the seasons.[9] Evidence from the previous chapter suggests that, in fact, periods of such social and economic hardship did not cause rises in mortality in St Saviour's in the early seventeenth century. How strong was the financial safety net in seventeenth-century Southwark?

3.1 Trades, crafts and professions in Southwark

3.1.1 The economic geography of Southwark
Apart from the relative wealth of its inhabitants the occupational make-up of any particular area of London will reflect local employment opportunities such as the presence of large institutions or government offices, the proximity of major road arteries or open ground, whether or not the area had access to the riverside, and if so whether it was upstream or downstream from London Bridge. The occupational character of an area would also be influenced by the presence of aliens with occupational specialisations and by the effectiveness with which economic regulations were implemented by local government.[10]

Looking at these influences we would not expect Southwark as a whole to be an occupationally homogenous area. The parish of St Georges's contained three major prisons (the White Lyon, Marshalsea and King's Bench) and St Thomas's the hospital of the same name. Southwark market was held four days a week in the main street within the Boroughside. Playhouses and bear gardens operated in the Clink and Paris Garden liberties.[11] The main highway to Surrey and Sussex ran through the Boroughside and the parish of St George's, while the road to Kent bisected

---

[7] Patten 1977:311.

[8] Ibid., pp. 301–2; Sybil Jack, *Trade and Industry in Tudor and Stuart England*, London, 1977, pp. 45–6; Woodward 1981:39–45.

[9] J. Pound, *Poverty and Vagrancy in Tudor England*, London, 1971, p. 81; Woodward 1981:43.

[10] For the influence of location on occupational structure in London, see, Herlan 1977a:15; Beier 1978:213; Archer 1934:23–82.

[11] In the 1620s there was one bear garden in the Clink, and the Hope theatre (also sited in the Clink) doubled as another. Other playhouses sited in the Clink and Paris Garden were the Globe and the Swan. The Rose theatre, sited in the Clink, had been demolished in 1606; Malden 1967:4, 133–4; R. Ashton, 'Popular entertainment and social control in later Elizabethan and early Stuart London', *London Journal* 9 (1983), 3–19.

St Olave's.[12] City jurisdiction did not extend to the Clink and Paris Garden liberties and even within their area of jurisdiction small pockets existed claiming special privilege and exemption, such as Montague Close, the Rules of the King's Bench and the Mint.[13] As we have seen Southwark contained a substantial amount of open ground. St Olave's and St Saviour's were both riverside parishes. St Olave's covered the south bank of the Thames downstream to Bermondsey while St Saviour's ran one mile upstream to Lambeth. As a suburb Southwark may also have been affected by the traditional banishment from the City of particularly noxious and dangerous occupations although this should not be overstressed. Limeburning and dyeing are known to have taken place within the city walls in the early seventeenth century and in 1633 highly inflammable pitch, tar and resin was being stored in Thames Street.[14]

The proportion of 'aliens', that is immigrants from nations other than England and Wales (in London mostly from France and the Low Countries), resident in Southwark fits in with a recent estimate for the whole of London which suggests that it was low by the early seventeenth century, the large numbers of alien immigrants that had arrived in the late sixteenth century having, through death, intermarriage or naturalization, been assimilated into the population.[15] Table 3.1 expresses the number of alien householders listed in the 1618 returns as a percentage of the estimated number of households in 1603. Since the population of Southwark increased substantially between 1603 and 1618 the percentages exaggerate the size of the alien community. It is clear that alien settlement was not distributed uniformly across Southwark. Eastern Southwark (St Olave's and St Thomas's) was more densely settled than the west. In St Thomas's something like one in six households contained alien immigrants. In these latter two parishes therefore alien immigrants were still present in significant numbers.

Wealth too was distributed unevenly between the different areas of Southwark. A crude measure of relative wealth has been taken to be the proportion of householders contributing to the 1601 subsidy assessment.

---

[12] For the main road arteries of London see, J. A. Chartres, 'The Capital's provincial eyes: London's inns in the early eighteenth century', *London Journal* 3 (1977), 29.

[13] For jurisdictional problems in Southwark see below, Chapter 10.

[14] See, Pearl 1961:16, n. 25; N. Wallington, *Historical Notices of Events Occurring Chiefly in the Reign of Charles 1*, R. Webb (ed.), London, 1869, vol. 1, p. 19.

[15] See, R. E. G. Kirk and E. F. Kirk (eds.), *Returns of the Aliens in the City and Suburbs of London from Henry VIII to James I*, Hugenot Society Publications 10, 1907, vol. 3, pp. 218–29; Finlay 1981:67–8; Irene Scouloudi, 'Alien immigrants into and alien communities in London, 1558–1640', *Proceedings of the Hugenot Society of London* 16 (1938), 33. For the size of the London French Calvinist Church in the 1650s see, R. D. Gwynn, 'The Distribution of Hugenot refugees in England, II: London and its environs', *Proceedings of the Hugenot Society of London* 22 (1976), 523. For the assimilation of Dutch immigrants in seventeenth-century Colchester see, N. Goose, 'The "Dutch" in Colchester: The economic influence of an immigrant community in the sixteenth and seventeenth centuries', *Immigrants and Minorities* 1, 3 (1982), 272.

Table 3.1. *Distribution of alien households in Southwark in 1618*

Parish	Number of households in 1603	Number of alien households in 1618[a]	%
St Thomas's	121	21	17.4
St Olave's	2004	87	4.3
St Saviour's (Clink and Paris Garden)	950	15	1.6
St George's	744	11	1.5
St Saviour's (Boroughside district)	746	8	1.1
Total	4565	142	3.1

Note: Number of householders estimated from population totals given in Table 2.3 divided by 4.2. The Boroughside has been assumed to contain 44% of the parish of St Saviour's, as it did in 1624.
Source: [a] Kirk 1900–7: 3, 218–29.

The number of householders in each parish was estimated from the 1603 population totals (see above, Table 2.3) using the mean houseful size of 4.2. The parish of St Saviour's was divided into the Boroughside district and the two liberties of the Clink and Paris Garden. Table 3.2 demonstrates that St Thomas's was the wealthiest parish in Southwark in 1601, and that the Boroughside was ranked second with 18.9% of its householders assessed for the 1601 subsidy. The liberties of the Clink and Paris Garden were the poorest districts in Southwark with only 9·5% of the householders there contributing to the 1601 subsidy.

It is immediately apparent from the literary sources available that the Boroughside was an important business and trading centre. The Borough High Street was on the main thoroughfare between Kent, Surrey, Sussex and London. Stow wrote that from the Marshalsea on the east side of the High Street 'be many fair Inns for receipt of travellers'.[16] A petition of 1618 made the same point:

a place of great receipt of people and trade...tradesmen in the Borough and upon London Bridge...have their greatest utterance of their wares, in term time, by such as lodge and guest in the common Inns...the innkeepers and tradesmen (which live by the help of one another) are the ablest persons in the place...for the payment of subsidy and fifteens to his Majesty.[17]

[16] Stow 1971:2, 62.
[17] Printed in W. H. Hart, 'Further remarks on some of the ancient inns of Southwark', *Surrey Archaeological Collections* 3 (1865), 195. The first part of the petition is taken from Stow's *Survey*.

Table 3.2. *Wealth distribution in Southwark parishes 1603*

Parish	Estimated number of householders 1603[a]	Number of subsidy payers 1601[b]	Percentage of householders paying subsidy
St Thomas's	121	35	28.9%
St Saviour's (Boroughside district)	746	141	18.9%
St Olave's	2004	264	13.2%
St George's	744	77	10.4%
St Saviour's (Clink and Paris Garden)	950	90	9.5%

Notes: [a] Parish totals from Table 2.3 above, divided by 4.2. It has been assumed that as in 1624 the Boroughside district of St Saviour's contained 44% of the total population of the parish.
[b] P.R.O. E179/186/377.

The Borough High Street, wrote Strype, attracted substantial tradesmen 'as being so great a thoroughfare...makes it to be very well inhabited by tradesmen of repute, with buildings answerable...' The Boroughside was particularly well endowed with large inns such as the George 'very large and of a considerable trade'. In contrast, the part of the main street that ran into the poorer district of St George's was, though 'well resorted unto, not of so good a trade as the Borough, nor is so accommodated with Inns....'.[18] The Boroughside's trade was boosted by the market held in the main High Street, with stalls along the west side of the street from the Bridgefoot to the Counter 'where the leather is sold'.[19]

3.1.2 Occupational structure

The analysis which follows of the occupational structure of the Boroughside is based on the linkage to the householders listed in the 1622 sacramental token book of all sources supplying occupational information, the most important of which were baptism entries in the parish register. The other principal sources were manorial records, victuallers' recognisances of 1620 and wills of householders who were known to be present in 1622.[20] The

---

[18] Strype 1720:2, 10–25.

[19] Ibid. See also Malden 1967:2, 335.

[20] For the manorial records see, C.L.R.O. Presentments of the jurors of the King's Manor 1620 and 1624 – Southwark Box 2; Great Liberty 1622 – Southwark Box 4; Guildable Manor 1620 and 1624 – Southwark Box 2. The victuallers' recognisances are in P.R.O. E180/140. Wills used are discussed in Chapter 9. A small number of occupations were found in the State Papers, sacramental token books and poor relief records listed in the manuscript bibliography.

Table 3.3 *The occupational structures of the Boroughside 1622, the whole of St Saviour's parish (1618–25), St Olave's parish (1604–23) and the Clink and Paris Garden liberties (1619–25)*

	Boroughside 1622		Clink and Paris Garden liberties 1619–25 (baptisms)		St Saviour's, Southwark 1618–25 (baptisms)		St Olave's, Southwark 1604–23 (burials)	
Agriculture	12	1.8%	16	1.5%	28	1.5%	16	1.0%
Building	30	4.6%	30	2.8%	61	3.3%	138	8.5%
Production and retailing of food and drink	195	29.7%	136	12.9%	331	17.8%	238	14.7%
Retail of clothing and household goods	44	6.7%	29	2.8%	75	4.0%	54	3.3%
Transport and unskilled labour	70	10.7%	493	46.7%	627	33.7%	314	19.4%
Professional	37	5.6%	37	3.5%	80	4.3%	57	3.5%
Industry:								
Textiles	59	9.0%	79	7.5%	157	8.4%	413	25.6%
Clothing	53	8.1%	51	4.8%	110	5.9%	93	5.8%
Leather	80	12.2%	72	6.8%	163	8.8%	110	6.8%
Rope	3	0.5%	1	0.1%	8	0.4%	2	0.1%
Soap	7	1.1%	8	0.8%	18	1.0%	4	0.3%
Wood	22	3.4%	32	3.0%	63	3.4%	116	7.2%
Metal and Glass	39	5.9%	45	4.3%	93	5.0%	47	2.9%
Miscellaneous	6	0.9%	27	2.6%	46	2.5%	14	0.9%
Total	657		1056		1860		1616	

Source: For the method of construction of this occupational breakdown see discussion in text, pp. 65–8.

baptism register was searched as far back as 1590 for individuals resident in 1622. The biggest number came from the period 1619–25 and here the parish clerk's notebook proved useful, since it supplied addresses for every baptism.[21] A small number of occupations were also recovered from the burial register of St Saviour's. A large proportion of Boroughside householders turned up in more than one source. Despite these aids the result will inevitably include a few wrong linkages, and some bias against the non-will-makers, the childless and the highly mobile will remain.[22] There will also be a slight over-representation of occupations peculiar to manorial records, in particular victuallers.

The occupational structure presented is that of adult male householders since occupations are only given consistently for this group. Table 3.3 lists the occupations of 637 male household heads and also includes those of eleven married men listed in the token books as members of households headed by women and the occupations of a further nine men inhabiting households headed by other men. This approach has the advantages of dealing with a sample from a known population and ensuring that the results can be compared to other data linked to the same list. Nevertheless there is a demonstrable bias against the poor in the overall coverage of occupations achieved by this method. Although 91.4% of the occupations of the male poor-rate paying household heads were recovered, the coverage for those householders unable to pay at even the lowest rate was 70.2%. The latter figure, however, compares favourably with the only other study of London occupations based on household listings.[23]

The occupations were grouped into broad categories, following the system devised by Armstrong.[24] Food and drink production was made a separate category and transport and unskilled labour brought together as one category. The occupations that make up each category have been listed below.[25] As Patten among many others has pointed out, any such system

---

[21] G.L.R.O. P29/SAV/406. Between March 1619 and September 1625 the notebook listed 2640 baptism entries, of which the following is a typical example, '22 May 1621 Robert Saunders son of Edward a fruiterer shipyard'. For a description of the notebook and the circumstances surrounding its composition see, W. Caldin and H. Raine, 'The plague of 1625 and the story of John Boston, parish clerk of St Saviour's, Southwark,' *Transactions of London and Middlesex Archaeological Society* 23 (1971), 90–9.

[22] Only 14 out of 657 occupations were derived solely from wills.

[23] Glass took a sample from the 1692 poll tax which only supplied occupations for 49% of the adult males listed. Of 841 individuals whose occupations were not stated 89% were taxed at the lowest rate compared to only 37% of those given occupations, Glass 1976:224.

[24] See, E. A. Wrigley, 'The changing occupational structure of Colyton over two centuries', *Local Population Studies* 18 (1977), 16–17; W. A. Armstrong, 'The use of information about occupation', in E. A. Wrigley (ed.), *Nineteenth Century Society*, Cambridge, 1971, pp. 191–253.

[25] *Agriculture*: gardener – 5; husbandman – 1; yeoman – 6. *Building*: bricklayer – 5; carpenter – 6; glazier – 2; joiner – 10; mason – 3; painter – 1; plumber – 1; plasterer – 2. *Production and retail of food and drink*: Apothecary – 4; baker – 16; brewer – 10; brewer's servant – 12; butcher – 50;

is fraught with problems and inevitably certain occupations can be placed in more than one category.[26] The occupational structure of the Boroughside was compared to that of the rest of St Saviour's parish and the whole parish compared to that of its eastern neighbour St Olave's. Since the baptism entries in the parish clerk's notebook supply both occupations and addresses a separate occupational structure for the Clink and Paris Garden districts can be constructed by abstracting and indexing all entries relating to the two liberties. The occupational structure of the whole parish of St Saviour's was constructed by indexing all baptism entries between 1618 and 1625 and that of St Olave's by abstracting all the burial entries, which invariably supply occupations, for all adult males between 1604 and 1623. Such an approach has drawbacks. Comparison between the occupational information contained in baptism entries with that in burials is not exact since the former might be expected to be biased towards younger married men whilst the latter would over-represent the old. Burial information would also be distorted if death rates differed between occupational groups, and baptisms would be similarly affected by differential occupational fertility. Furthermore when a period of years is looked at rather than one point in time, then individuals who died or moved away and were then replaced, by a son or other successor in the same occupation, might be over-represented. A family business might in this way appear as two or even three separate practitioners.[27] Despite such biases, however, the methodology adopted should enable broad differences between the occupational structures of these areas of Southwark to be identified. The large number of occupations involved decreases the risk of any serious distortion (see Table 3.3).

cheesemonger – 10; cook – 2; distiller – 1; fishmonger – 5; fruiterer – 3; grocer – 17; poulterer – 1; salter – 2; tobaccoseller – 2; vintner – 5; victualler – 45; sauceman – 3; innkeeper – 7. *Retailing of clothing and household goods and dealing*: 'brasell seller' – 1; chandler – 13; haberdasher – 7; inkseller – 1; linendraper – 4; ironmonger – 3; mousetrap seller – 1; pedlar – 2; tinker – 1; tallowchandler – 3; merchant-tailor – 2; whitster – 1; stationer – 2; upholsterer – 1; woollendraper – 1; huckster – 1. *Professional*: attorney – 3; barber – 4; barber-surgeon – 4; falconer – 1; musician – 1; schoolmaster – 2; scrivenor – 5; usher – 1; central government official – 3; local government official – 6; gentleman *et sim* – 7. *Transport and unskilled labour*: barrowman – 1; collier – 1; carman – 8; carrier – 1; carter – 1; hackneyman – 1; horsecourser – 1; labourer – 4; ostler – 6; porter – 33; tapster – 1; sailor – 5; servingman – 2; waterman – 5. *Industry*: *textiles*: clothworker – 6; dyer – 9; dyer's servant – 1; feltmaker – 2; fustiandresser – 1; embroiderer – 1; weaver – 37; threddier – 1; tapeweaver – 1. *Clothing*: pointmaker – 1; boddicemaker – 2; girdler – 4; hosier – 1; tailor – 45. *Leather*: bellowsmaker – 1; currier – 2; glover – 16; leatherdresser – 1; saddler – 8; shoemaker – 52. *Rope*: hempbeater – 2; ropemaker – 1. *Soap*: soapboiler – 4; soapboiler's servant – 1; starchmaker – 2; *Wood*: cooper – 10; sawyer – 4; shipwright – 1; turner – 1; woodmonger – 6. *Metal and Glass*: cutler – 9; goldsmith – 4; guilder – 1; gunmaker – 1; grinder – 1; locksmith – 1; pewterer – 4; pinmaker – 1; sheergrinder – 2; smith – 11; potter/glassmaker – 4. *Miscellaneous*: basketmaker – 3; dicemaker – 1; spectaclemaker – 1; saltpetremaker – 1.

[26] Patten 1977:301–10; Wrigley 1977b:17–18.
[27] For a discussion of such drawbacks see, Wrigley 1977b:12; Beier 1978:211–14; D. Avery, 'Male occupations in a rural Middlesex parish', *Local Population Studies* 2 (169), 29–30.

There were major differences between the occupational structures of the Boroughside and the two liberties of the Clink and Paris Garden.[28] The production and retailing of food and drink which was the biggest occupational category in the Boroughside, accounting for 29.7% of all recovered occupations, came a poor second in the Clink and Paris Garden with only 12.9% of individuals so engaged. There were two main reasons for this difference. The commercial traffic running along the Borough High Street attracted a large number of wealthy retailers to the Boroughside. Grocers and cheesemongers formed, for example, 13.9% of all occupations in the food and drink sector in the Boroughside. Conversely there were no cheesemongers at all in the Clink and Paris Garden, and only three grocers who made up only 2.2% of the food and drink sector there. Some of the wealthy retailers must have been particularly drawn to the Borough market, the existence of which probably explains the siting of a large shambles in the Boroughside.[29] As a consequence butchers made up 25.6% of the food and drink sector in the Boroughside compared to only 4.4% in the Clink and Paris Garden. The occupational structure of the Clink and Paris Garden liberties was dominated by an enormous transport and unskilled labour sector. This sector employed 46.7% of all occupations in the two liberties in contrast to only 10.7% in the Boroughside. This glaring contrast was caused by the heavy concentration of watermen in the Clink and Paris Garden. The 420 watermen made up 39.8% of all the occupations in the two liberties in contrast to the 0.8% found in the Boroughside. Few watermen lived in the Boroughside possibly because the area had only a small river frontage

---

[28] The occupations in each category in the Clink and Paris Garden were: *Agriculture*: gardener – 10; husbandman – 3; yeoman – 3. *Building*: bricklayer – 4; carpenter – 12; glazier – 2; joiner – 5; painter – 4; plasterer – 1; fencer – 1; brickmaker – 1. *Production and retail of food and drink*: baker – 15; brewer – 10; brewer's servant – 28; butcher – 6; cook – 5; distiller – 2; fisherman – 9; fishmonger – 7; fruiterer – 9; grocer – 3; tobaccomaker – 1; vintner – 7; victualler – 26; sauceman – 2; miller – 1; mealman – 2; 'cornmeat' – 1; comfitmaker – 1; vintner's servant – 1. *Retailing of clothing and household goods and dealing*: chandler – 14; haberdasher – 2; pedlar – 4; tinker – 2; merchant-tailor – 1; merchant – 1; whitster – 1; stationer – 1; woollendraper – 2; perfumer – 1. *Professional*: attorney – 1; barber – 1; barber-surgeon – 3; musician – 2; schoolmaster – 6; scrivenor – 2; gentleman *et sim* – 10; central government official – 6; lawyer's clerk – 1; player – 5. *Transport and unskilled labour*: carman – 5; labourer – 10; ostler – 2; porter – 20; tapster – 2; sailor – 13; servingman – 12; waterman – 420; bargeman – 1; lighterman – 2; bearwarden – 4; drayman – 2. *Industry*: *textiles*: clothworker – 9; dyer – 7; feltmaker – 3; fustian-weaver – 3; weaver – 46; tapeweaver – 7; cardmaker – 1; embroiderer – 1; silkman – 1; felmonger – 1. *Clothing*: piccadillmaker – 1; pointmaker – 1; boddicemaker – 2; girdler – 1; tailor – 41; hattrimmer – 2; hatbandmaker – 3. *Leather*: currier – 2; glover – 23; leatherdresser – 23; shoemaker – 18; tanner – 6. *Rope*: hempdresser – 1. *Soap etc.*: soapboiler – 1; starchmaker – 6; limeburner – 1. *Wood*: cooper – 11; sawyer – 7; shipwright – 11; woodmonger – 1; oarmaker – 2. *Metal and Glass*: cutler – 1; goldsmith – 2; smith – 29; pinmaker – 3; needlemaker – 2; glassmaker – 6; pikemaker – 1; nailor – 1. *Miscellaneous crafts*: basketmaker – 22; maskmaker – 1; jackmaker – 2; brushmaker – 1; lastmaker – 1.

[29] See, Strype 1720:2, 10.

and was close to London Bridge. The presence of playhouses and bear gardens in the Clink and Paris Garden may have encouraged watermen to congregate in the liberties since they provided a great deal of custom. The capacity of the Swan and Globe theatres has been estimated at three thousand persons each.[30] Watermen petitioned for the speedy reopening of Henslowe's playhouse following its temporary closure, as part of anti-plague regulations, in 1593.[31] Not surprisingly the removal of several companies of players from Southwark to Middlesex in the early seventeenth century was said to have caused considerable hardship among watermen.[32] It might also be that watermen preferred to settle in an area outside the city's jurisdiction in order to avoid impressment in the city militia.[33]

Manufacturing industry seems to have been numerically more significant in the Boroughside than in the other two liberties. Some 40.9% of all occupations were engaged in manufacturing in the Boroughside in contrast to only 29·8% in the Clink and Paris Garden. In particular only 6·8% of individuals in the two liberties were involved in the important Southwark leather industry, the major manufacturing centre of the pre-eminent London leather trade, compared to 12.2% in the Boroughside. Locational and jurisdictional differences determined that the components of the industry were divided sharply between the two districts. Shoemakers, who preferred to live close to their customers, were far more numerous in the Boroughside making up 65.0% of the leather industry there in contrast to only 25.0% in the Clink and Paris Garden. The traffic along the Borough High Street also attracted saddlers who formed 10% of the leather industry in the Boroughside, but were totally absent from the Clink and Paris Garden. The two liberties attracted the more noisesome elements of the leather industry such as leatherdressing, banned from the city since the reign of Edward IV, an activity that formed 32% of all those in the industry, and tanning, which required a water supply and river transport, that made up 8%.[34]

As might be expected the occupational structure of St Olave's and St Saviour's also showed marked differences. St. Saviour's, being upstream of London Bridge, had no docking facilities for large ships and therefore had

[30] Malden 1967:4, 133–4; Ann J. Cook, *The Privileged Playgoers of Shakespeare's London, 1576–1642*, Princeton, 1981, pp. 175–9, 190–2; Ashton 1983:16, n.9.

[31] The petition is printed in W. Young, *A History of Dulwich College*, London, 1889, vol. 2, p. 13.

[32] Cook 1981:191; J. Taylor, *The True Cause of the Watermen's Suit*, in *All the works of John Taylor, the Water Poet*, London, 1630, facsimile edn, Menston, 1973.

[33] Watermen claimed exemption based on their traditional service at sea in time of war. See a petition from watermen claiming exemption from taxation for furnishing soldiers, P.R.O. SP16/92.

[34] For the leather industry in London and Southwark see, Malden 1967:2, 329–41; L. A. Clarkson, 'The leather crafts in Tudor and Stuart England', *Agricultural History Review* 14 (1960), 26–7; L. A. Clarkson, 'The organisation of the English leather industry in the late sixteenth and seventeenth centuries', *Economic History Review*, 2nd ser., 13 (1960), 252–3; G. Unwin, *Industrial Organisation in the Sixteenth and Seventeenth Centuries*, 2nd edn, Oxford, 1957, p. 128.

few maritime connections compared with its downstream neighbour St Olave's. Sailors therefore formed 15.3% of the transport and unskilled labour sector in St Olave's but only 3.0% in St Saviour's.[35] For similar topographical reasons shipbuilding and associated occupations, such as joiners, were important in St Olave's but less so in St Saviour's and explain why the wood industry made up 7.2% of occupations in St Olave's but only 3.4.% in St Saviour's. The concentration of watermen in St Saviour's was not duplicated in St Olave's. Watermen made up 25% of all occupations in St Saviour's but only 5% in St Olave's, the latter lacking both the drawing power of playhouses and possible jurisdictional advantages.[36] The occupational divisions between eastern and western Southwark are highlighted by the geographical distribution of textile manufacturing. Textiles occupied 26% of all occupations in St Olave's compared to only 8.4% in St Saviour's. Of all the trades in the textile sector feltmakers made up 16% of all occupations in St Olave's but only an insignificant 0.4% in St Saviour's. The latter concentration in eastern Southwark was said to have been determined by the need for cheap housing, an abundant water supply and open fields in which to dry wool. The swamps of western Southwark would hardly have met this last criterion.[37]

However, though it is useful to know the numbers of householders following different occupations, in fact the occupational structure, particularly of the Boroughside, was far more complicated than has so far been suggested. Indeed relying on a single source, as most studies of London occupations have done, leads to an acceptance of vague terminology that gives no clue as to the real economic behaviour of the individual concerned.[38] However, by using more than one source and matching these to a known population it becomes apparent that many individuals were assigned more than one occupation. Individual householders, whose residence is known from the sacramental token books, were often assigned differing occupations. Thus Richard Bailey, resident in Axe Yard between 1619 and 1622, as both the token books and addresses in the baptism entries in the parish clerk's notebook confirm, was described twice as a porter and once as a guilder. The phenomenon of multiple occupation tells us much more about individual economic behaviour in the seventeenth century.[39]

Related occupations were frequently ascribed to one individual. Hence

---

[35] Another source highlights this occupational division. In a 1629 muster of all seamen under the Port of London authorities St Olave's supplied 109 but St Saviour's none at all, P.R.O. SP16/135/130.

[36] A 1629 muster of watermen also illustrates the concentration of watermen in St Saviour's. In the muster St Saviour's supplied 706 watermen, 29% of all those called up by the Port of London; St Olave's supplied only 171, P.R.O. SP16/135/4.

[37] Archer 1934:64; Pearl 1961:15; Unwin 1957:128; Malden 1967:2, 359–63.

[38] Glass was forced to accept labels such as 'tradesman' and 'merchant', Glass 1976:224–63.

[39] Wrightson and Levine 1979:22–3.

an individual could be variously described as woodmonger or wharfhinger, shoemaker or cobbler, tanner or leatherdresser, waterman or lighterman, and so on. The wealthier sort were rarely assigned more than one occupation. Some sources sometimes supplied honorary titles instead of an individual's true occupation. Hence one John Crowder, cheesemonger, was also described as a 'merchant-taylor' in the parish register of St Saviour's. Moreover the wealthier inhabitants tended to use company titles in their wills that did not always reflect their true occupations. In other cases where different occupations are recorded for the wealthier inhabitants they often reflected a real change in that individual's circumstances. Hence William Batty, described as a tailor in the parish register between 1596 and 1609, is known to have rebuilt the Green Dragon Inn; his will accordingly labelled him as an innholder and the manorial records as a victualler. Hugh Hassall, described in April 1616 as a victualler, was called an innkeeper in May 1617. This coincided with the beginning of his residence at the Queen's Head.[40] Occupational changes associated with economic diversification can also be picked up. Henry Fawcett, a wealthy High Street butcher in 1622, was described as a grazier at the death of his wife in 1657.[41]

It was particularly among the poorer inhabitants that occupational labels tended to become blurred. Amongst the humbler inhabitants similar occupations were often interchangeable: silkweaver and tuftaffeta weaver, chapman and pedlar, brewer's servant and victualler, sawyer, carpenter and cooper, smith and grinder and so on. In a slightly different fashion occupational labels possibly associated with high social standing were sometimes adopted by the poor, perhaps in an attempt to enhance their social position. John Wrallings was described as a pedlar and chapman, but also as a chandler; and one James Clough, a minor retailer of sorts, was variously described in the baptism records as porter and costermonger but also as a chandler, grocer and apothecary.[42] Amongst the unskilled the terms used to describe their occupations were interchangeable. Labourers were also described as porters, ostlers, tapsters, husbandmen, carmen, draymen,

---

[40] The sacramental token book of 1616 shows Hassall moving a few dwellings along the east side of the High Street and records an increase in the number of communicants in his household from five to nine, G.L.R.O. P92/SAV/205.

[41] For other examples of such diversification see, Jones 1976:100–3; R. Grassby, 'The personal wealth of the business community in seventeenth-century England', *Economic History Review*, 2nd ser., 23 (1970), 222–3; Patten 1977:301–2; Wrightson and Levine 1979:23; P. V. McGrath, 'The marketing of food, fodder and livestock in the London area in the seventeenth century with some reference to the sources of supply', London (1948), 153–70.

[42] It is possible that Clough was either a ticket porter, handling the goods of the Grocers' Company, or employed by the Tackle House Porters to handle merchants' goods, and that this resulted in his adoption of a number of different occupational labels, Valerie Pearl, private communication. See also, G. Unwin, *The Gilds and Companies of London*, 3rd edn, London, 1938, pp. 359–60; McGrath 1948:102–16.

chamberlains and servingmen. One Henry Ducklyn was therefore described as a labourer, servingman and chamberlain; Richard Beldam as a servingman, labourer, horsekeeper, husbandman and victualler. Unskilled labourers seem often to have adopted the occupation of their most recent employer. Henry Packwood described himself as day labourer, porter and plasterer, and John Stanfield as labourer, tapster and plasterer. It is also amongst the poorer sort that individuals with radically different occupations are found. Hence Stephen Edgitt was described as a porter and glover and Nicholas Needham, porter and silkweaver. From the twenty or so cases available it is clear that this usually involved at least one unskilled occupation, a phenomenon duplicated in the Essex village of Terling studied by Wrightson and Levine.[43] Multiple occupations such as this reflect the underemployment that affected the poorer members of society and the casual nature of much of the work, with such individuals turning to many different tasks to make ends meet. Few skilled occupations were duplicated by one individual.

3.1.3 Marketing and local economic regulation

The surviving presentments and ordinances of the Southwark manorial courts, supplemented by other material, shed some light on the ways in which individuals functioned in the local economy. Those inhabitants of the Boroughside who marketed foodstuffs and household goods did so in several distinct ways. For the retailer or producer-retailer a particularly important outlet was the shop. No quantitative information on the extent of shop possession is available but all the signs are that shop ownership on both sides of the High Street was almost universal.[44] A survey of twelve main street dwellings reveals that all possessed shops of varying size, from the 320 square feet of Christopher Collinson, saddler, to the more modest 189 square feet of Christopher Fawcett, shoemaker.[45] The shop of Drew Stapley, grocer, a few dwellings along from Collinson's was a substantial 720 square feet. Many of these main street dwellings also possessed extensive storage space which might indicate economic activity on a considerable scale. All the dwellings surveyed contained a cellar and often 'a vault'. Richard Wright, grocer, known to have dealt wholesale, had by these means 845 square feet of storage space beneath his house.[46] The larger dwellings could have warehouses attached. Drew Stapley's house contained 'one warehouse 2 stories high' with a floor area of 364 square feet. It was the normal practice for individuals to live on site, though there are

[43] Wrightson and Levine 1979:23.
[44] For the growth of shopkeeping in seventeenth-century London see, McGrath 1948:52.
[45] See a book of surveys of property belonging to St Thomas's Hospital, G.L.R.O. HI/ST/E105.
[46] In September Wright and his partner Felix Hunt, another local grocer, were examined by the Privy Council for taking away '5 tons of currants' from a warehouse in Dice Alley without paying the customs duty on them, P.R.O. SP16/158/21.

occasional references to shops being let to under-tenants who lived elsewhere in the Boroughside.[47] The traffic along the High Street must have resulted in a significant turnover for many of these shopkeepers, perhaps on a par with the turner and shopkeeper in East Cheap who regularly took between three and seven pounds per day.[48] High Street shops may have represented a considerable capital investment. The cost of setting up a shop in seventeenth-century London has been estimated at £100. Thomas Cullum, draper, invested £130 in setting up shop in Gracechurch Street, London, in 1622.[49]

In the absence of a permanent shop buying and selling might also take place in the market held in the Borough High Street. Markets were held on Monday, Wednesday, Friday and Saturday. They lasted until 2 p.m. from Michaelmas to Shrovetide and until 3 p.m. from Easter to Michaelmas. Market time was officially ended, or 'raised', by the Bailiff ringing the market bell.[50] As part of a general extension of London's market facilities Southwark's meal market was improved in the early seventeenth century. In 1605 it was enlarged by one half. In 1619 a clock was set up in the market place, perhaps symbolic of a new desire to regulate and measure the working day.[51] The following year the market site was ordered to be substantially refurbished. Part of the site was to be paved, the bellhouse and pillory removed, and benches in the meal market repaired and extended.[52]

On market days the stall was an important retailing outlet for both outsiders and Boroughside inhabitants. To avoid traffic congestion the manorial courts carefully regulated the siting of stalls. Stalls were not to be set on the east side of the Borough High Street nor on the west side of the meal market. Butchers were forbidden to keep stalls 'between the meal market and the bridgefoot'.[53] Stalls were also let out to Boroughside inhabitants. In particular, minor retailers from side-streets sought to set stalls

---

[47] The 1643 land tax assessed St Thomas's Hospital for shops that it owned on the High Street P.R.O. E 179/257/22. Separately rented shops existed elsewhere in London, see, Finlay 1981:172; Reddaway 1963:186.

[48] Wallington 1869:1, xxiv.

[49] R. Grassby, 'Social mobility and business enterprise in seventeenth-century England', in D. H. Pennington and K. Thomas (eds.), *Puritans and Revolutionaries: Essays in Seventeenth-Century History presented to Christopher Hill*, Oxford, 1978, p. 366; A. Simpson,' Thomas Cullum, draper, 1587–1664', *Economic History Review*, 2nd ser., 11, 1 (1958), 21.

[50] See, C.L.R.O. Presentments of the jurors of the Guildable Manor: Market Orders 1624, Southwark Box 2; Johnson 1969: 304.

[51] C.L.R.O. Rep. 34, f. 176. For the significance of clocks see D. Palliser, 'Civic mentality and the environment in Tudor York', *Northern History* 18 (1982), 86–7. For much fascinating information on London markets see McGrath 1948:9–116, 332–4.

[52] C.L.R.O. Rep. 34, f. 304.

[53] Since the Boroughside butcher's shambles with its shops was sited in exactly this place this order probably reflected an ordinance of the city authorities that stalls rented by city butchers should not be placed in a manner prejudicial to the Southwark butchers, Jones 1976:134.

in main thoroughfares. Thus Nathaniel Drury, cobbler, who lived by the church in 1621, was presented by the jurors of the Guildable Manor in 1620 for that 'he annoyeth the street and for hanging shoes out beyond the edge of his stall to the annoyance of his neighbours and passengers'. The space occupied by a stall was therefore delimited. The placing of stalls was also strictly controlled.[54]

Those inhabitants unable to erect a stall simply hawked their wares in the street. Many such individuals were recognised as performing a specific economic role in the local economy and efforts were made by the manorial courts to keep itinerant 'pedlars, tinkers, fishwives, herbwives and sauce-wives' on the move. It was further laid down that 'no person that useth to buy any fish at Billingsgate shall set down with these fish in the street in any place but shall cry the same about the streets after the ancient manner'. Herbwives were prevented from 'sitting' on Tuesdays and Thursdays. Fishwives were charged on penny for 'standing all the week' but other less favoured itinerant retailers were charged one half penny per day for standing, the same fee charged for the erection of a stall.[55] A number of Boroughside inhabitants were presented for illegal retailing. One Christopher Pinkney, resident in Goat Yard and variously described as porter, carman and sawyer, was presented at the Guildable court in 1620 for 'setting wares in the street' and four years later at the same court a butcher, Thomas Swinbourne, who lived off the main street, was presented for 'standing at Chaingate to sell meat'. Itinerant fruiterers tended to inhabit the Clink and Paris Garden liberties, outside the jurisdiction of the Southwark manorial courts, rather than the Boroughside.[56]

The restrictive marketing regulations enforced in the manorial courts were often broken and frequently evaded by many Boroughside inhabitants. A large number of manorial ordinances were designed to enforce the restrictions on trading during Lent and on Sundays. Individuals who possessed defective weights and scales and those who broke the assize of bread and ale were presented in large numbers in the manorial courts in the 1620s. However the Bailiffs complained in 1618 that they were unable to collect the fines and were making a loss on their office.[57] The long mechanically written lists of offenders for 'annoyances', defective scales and victualling offences could well indicate formal registration rather than

---

[54] Stalls were arranged in a particular order. Hence, 'the country wives which sell pound or dish butter shall be placed next the bridgefoot, next to them those which sell fresh fish or Thames fish', etc. C.L.R.O. Presentments of the jurors of the Guildable Manor: market orders, Southwark Box 2.

[55] For fees see, 'A particular of the fees taken in the Fayre Borough Court and Compter of Southwark by Thomas Foster now Bailiff', P.R.O. E163/18/18. For the accepted role of fishwives in the capital's economy see, McGrath 1948:189.

[56] In the occupational breakdowns above there are nine fruiterers listed in the two liberties compared to only three in the Boroughside.   [57] Johnson 1969:191.

efficient regulation. Another indication that enforcement of the manorial ordinances was less than total is that offenders were prosecuted regularly for the same offences, with ever-increasing fines. Hence, for example, 'Richard Kellet, Broker, formerly presented by divers Leets for setting forth wooden ware and other things into the street' was tried yet again in the King's Manor in 1624. It is also clear that the jurors were openly ignored. In 1622 Humphrey Baker, innholder, was presented by the jurors of the Great Liberty Manor for

that he obstinately refused to bring forth and show unto the Jury sworn by this court, his weights and scales, whereby it may well be conceived that they may be defective wherefore in regard of his obstinate and irregular behaviour in that behalf being contrary to the ancient orders laws and customs of this court... [amerced] 13s 4d.

Such recalcitrance is all the more significant since it comes from the more substantial, economically active inhabitants.[58]

It seems likely that, by the early seventeenth century, in some occupations actual trading practice habitually ran contrary to the 'ancient customs' of the manorial courts. Virtually all the Boroughside victuallers and bakers infringed the assize of bread and ale from 1620 to 1624. Rapid resale of produce brought in by other inhabitants or by country people ('regrating') also seems to have been widespread. Butchers were especially liable to presentment for such practices. Hence, for example, 'William Wright of St Saviour for buying a dead calf in the market of William Abell, butcher' (another local inhabitant) 'and selling the same again in the same market'. There is some evidence, too, that Boroughside retailers openly resented the economic competition represented by the influx of 'country people' during market time. John Skargill, cook, was explicitly presented by the jurors of the Guildable Manor in 1639

for often times disturbing of country people and others coming to the market within this manor with victuals and other provisions in the market time by throwing down and spoiling of their goods and hindering their sale thereof to the great prejudice of the market and the ill example of others.[59]

Abuses of this sort were widespread in all the London markets at this time.[60] The need to avoid irksome market regulations was increasingly driving individuals to trade in inn yards and private houses in London and the nation in the seventeenth century. This well-documented function of the urban inn

---

[58] See below, Chapter 10.1. C.L.R.O. presentments of the jurors of the Great Liberty Manor 1622, Southwark Box 4.
[59] C.L.R.O. Southwark Box 2.
[60] C.L.R.O. Rep. 39, f. 18b. See also Jones 1976:99.

ran contrary to the laws of the London markets.[61] A market order of the Guildable Manor stated in 1624 that no 'persons buy any provisions in any Inn or private warehouse but in the open market'.[62] The Boroughside inns were well equipped to rival the market. Most innkeepers kept scales and balances in their yards, a fact recognised by the King's Manor jurors who, in 1624, attempted to regulate their use, ordering 'that they keep Beams and scales in their yards that they have their measures sealed by the Clerk of the market and chained with a chain, that every traveller may have the full measure of their cattle'. The Boroughside inns were also the headquarters of provincial carriers. Thus 'To the George in Southwark come every Thursday the Carriers from Guildford, Wonersh, Goudhurst, and Chidding-fold in Surrey, also thither come out of Sussex (on the same days weekly) the Carriers of Battle, Sandwich, and Hastings'. The seven Boroughside inns were said to serve carriers from parts of Kent, Sussex, Surrey and Hampshire.[63]

The manorial courts were not particularly concerned to regulate manu-facturing and only did so explicitly in connection with fire, pollution and transport ordinances. The dressing of 'flax, hemp or tow' was forbidden before 4 a.m. and after 9 p.m. unless in 'close lantern' and 'except the room be sealed all over one inch at the least with lime and hair'. Felmongers, leatherdressers and lutestringmakers were forbidden 'to carry any green skins or strings of guts in the streets' before 6 a.m. and after 8 p.m. and no leatherdresser, feltmaker or dyer was to wash 'felt, skins or cloth...in the common sewer or millpond except after half ebb tide and spent and after end of ebb or going out of water'.[64] As the comparison between the occupational structures of different areas of Southwark has shown, leatherdressing, feltmaking and hempdressing were almost totally absent from the Boroughside, and in fact the bulk of the manufacturing activity regulated by manorial ordinances must have taken place in eastern Southwark.[65]

[61] See, for example, McGrath 1948; 10–40; Archer 1934:159; Chartres 1977a:25–7; A. Everitt, 'The English urban inn 1560–1760', in A. Everitt (ed.), *Perspectives in English Urban History*, London, 1973, pp. 104–10.

[62] C.L.R.O. Southwark Box 2. Trading in inns was prohibited by an Act of the Corporation of London in 1663, see, Kellet 1958:382; McGrath 1948:39–40.

[63] J. Taylor, *Carrier's Cosmographie*, London, 1637, pp. 18–19. Note an entry in the parish clerk's notebook, '19 January 1621 John Parsons carrier of Guildford killed', G.L.R.O. P92/SAV/406. Links between certain districts and particular inns survived into the nineteenth century, Chartres 1977a:31. See also, J. Chartres, 'Road carrying in England in the Seventeenth Century: Myth and Reality'. *Economic History Review*, 2nd ser., 30 (1977), 73–94.

[64] C.L.R.O. Presentments of the jurors of the Guildable manor 1624, market orders, Southwark Box 2.

[65] The degree to which London gilds and companies regulated Southwark industry requires detailed investigation. Much of Southwark industry was located in areas within the City's jurisdiction and some companies, such as the Curriers', Cordwainers', Coopers' and Weavers', were exercising some control over Southwark craftsmen, Johnson 1969:310–13.

3.1.4 *Large scale enterprises*

The occupational structure presented above (Table 3.3) conceals the existence of a number of relatively large-scale business enterprises in the Boroughside, which could have significantly affected the social and economic structure of that district. Any definition of 'large scale' is bound to be arbitrary but one rough measure might be all households listed as containing six or more adult servants in the 1622 token book.[66] Using such a measure seven households, for which we have occupational information, operated large-scale enterprises of which four were manufacturing concerns. Most manufacturing concerns in the Boroughside therefore were based on the classic pre-industrial pattern of domestic, small-scale production.[67]

Thomas Overman operated a large soaphouse, converted from private housing in the early seventeenth century. Overman lived at the Three Crowns a 'mansion house...formerly divers tenements and now one worth £50 per annum. Being a soaphouse of his own'.[68] He was one of the biggest soapboilers in London, capable of producing 550 tons of soap per year, a quarter of the total output of the new Company of Soapmakers in 1637–8. Earlier, in 1601–2, Overman was said to have required 2000 barrels, 2000 kilderkins and 2000 firkins for use in his business. He is known to have been shipping soap to Kings Lynn in 1606. In 1622 Overman lived with his mother-in-law, who was listed as the household head, kept eleven servants and was rated at the maximum 40s. per year, more than 9d. per week, in the 1621–2 poor rate assessment. Overman's business centred round a partnership, based on close kin links, with the Bromfield family, important local property owners and, like Overman, soapboilers.[69] Another large manufacturing concern was that of Michael Nichollson, brewer and member of the Grocers' Company. Like Overman he lived with his mother-in-law, widow of a rich local brewer and also listed as household head, and kept eight servants. Nichollson brewed beer and supplied it to various outlets. We know that he supplied ale and beer to a Newington victualler in his own casks on a considerable scale.[70] The activity from this and similar activities caused him to be fined 39s. by the jurors of the Guildable Manor in 1620 for 'annoying the streets with drays and casks'. Nichollson contributed 5d. per week to the poor rate in 1622. John Watts, citizen and

[66] G.L.R.O. P92/SAV/211.
[67] D. C. Coleman, *The Economy of England 1450–1750*, Oxford, 1977, p. 71; P. Laslett, *The World We Have Lost*, 2nd edn, London, 1971, pp. 1–2; Unwin 1957:3.
[68] G.L.R.O. P92/SAV/1336.
[69] R. G. Lang, 'London's aldermen in business: 1600–1625', *Guildhall Miscellany* 3 (1971), 256; Malden 1967:2, 402–4. For a short biography of Edward Bromfield, Lord Mayor of London 1636–7, and his involvement with the Soap Monopoly, see, Pearl 1961:293–4; Unwin 1938:321–3.
[70] P.R.O. REQ2/304/22, 'Beer and ale to the value of £51 15s in all'.

brewer, ran another large-scale brewhouse with his co-resident brother-in-law. Watts contributed 5*d.* to the poor rate and employed nine servants. The other large-scale manufacturing establishment was a bakery run by John Marshall, citizen, whitebaker and tallowchandler. Marshall kept eight servants and, like Overman, paid the maximum poor rate. Though Marshall did not maintain an extended household he had, as we shall see, extensive kin links in the Boroughside.

The only establishments that employed servants on a similar scale to these manufacturers were some of the High Street inns. John Gilding at the George employed eight servants and paid 4*d.* per week to the poor rate; Hugh Hassall at the Queen's Head paid 12*s.* a year, just under 3*d.* per week, and maintained ten servants, and Humphrey Baker at the Spur Inn paid 4*d.* per week to the poor rate and kept seven servants. The personal wealth of the innkeepers was often considerable. Hugh Hassall (died 1623) left bequests totalling over £800. Like most Boroughside property, inns were leased by the innkeeper and other local inhabitants sometimes owned the freehold.[71]

However, though the number of 'on site' servants is some indication of the scale of these establishments it is not the whole picture. One reservation is that it is impossible to distinguish between the domestic servant and the resident working employee. The criterion of scale adopted excludes other substantial manufacturers. It is known, for example, that the biggest alien dyehouse in London was sited in the Boroughside. Daniel Tiberkin, who both dealt in silk and dyed it, had run up debts totalling over one thousand pounds in 1624. Between 1592 and 1611 he had been repeatedly brought before the Court of Exchequer for using the illegal logwood dye and had altogether been fined in excess of £2000. Tiberkin lived with two married sons-in-law, one also a dyer and the other the usher of the local grammar school, three servants and a related inmate, and was rated at 6*d.* a week for the poor rate.[72]

3.1.5 Economic relations between households
Previous studies of London's occupational structure have been impressed by the 'long list of occupations serving the society'.[73] In fact though many occupations were recorded (in the Boroughside 657 adult males followed 111 different occupations), the labels used to describe them are inadequate. Rarely, if ever, is an individual's position within any particular occupation

[71] The deed to the Queen's Head inn was owned by Gregory Franklin, a High Street saddler, in 1624. See, P.C.C. Will Register, 73 Byrde; G.L.R.O. Archdeaconry of Surrey Will Register, 25 Yeast. See also Chartres 1977a:28.
[72] See, P.R.O. REQ2/388/9;SP14/137/10; Kirk 1900–7:3, 218–19; Malden 1967:364–5.
[73] Glass 1976:224.

given in pre-industrial source material. This deficiency means that the basic division in the early modern economy between master and employee is hidden. Such occupational labels fail to reveal the important economic links between households in seventeenth-century London.

In this connection it is worth noting that many industries in London known to have had relatively large-scale practitioners, notably breweries and inns, were represented in the Boroughside.[74] Such concerns maintained a network of dependent households in related occupations in the neighbourhood and some of these relationships can be reconstructed from unusually detailed baptism and burial entries in the parish clerk's notebook.[75] A number of individuals who were identified as heads of household in the 1622 token book were clearly economically dependent, though their employer cannot be identified with confidence. Hence Richard Morgan, a householder in Horsehead Alley, was described as a 'baker's servant' as also was one Derrick Langton living in Christofer Yard. In the same way William Twitty was labelled as a 'soap-boiler's servant', one Francis Richards as a 'dyer's servant' and other similar cases could be quoted. It is probable that brewers were particularly likely to be at the centre of a network of dependent householders.[76] 'Brewer's servants' lived as separate householders professing a trade which was economically dependent on a local brewer. Hence, for example, Richard Clothier, brewer's servant, headed a household on Parkside in 1622. When his son Thomas died in 1625 he was described as 'Mr Nichollson's servant's child', implying that Richard Clothier was the servant of Michael Nichollson, the wealthy brewer. Many brewer's servants maintained a victualling house and were presented for this in the manorial courts. Apart from acting, presumably, as outlets for their brewer's beer such individuals were often given labels that suggested that they performed other functions. Hence Isaac Fowlds, living at Axe Yard Gate, was described as a victualler in 1617 but as a 'brewer's clerk' in 1621. Large bakeries may well have maintained similar dependent households. Two householders, Edward Wrallings and John Harman, lived near a bakery in Windmill Alley off the High Street in 1622. At their deaths in 1625 both were described as servants of a wealthy baker living nearby.

Many of the 'dependent' occupations recovered were of a relatively unskilled nature. This is especially true of ostlers. Though ostlers were attached to specific inns or taverns they did not necessarily live on site as part of the innkeeper's household. Hence, for example, Robert Frith, 'ostler

---

[74] For other examples of 'large-scale' soapboilers, brewers and dyers see, J. U. Nef, 'The progress of technology and the growth of large-scale industry in Great Britain, 1540–1640', in E. M. Carus-Wilson (ed.), *Essays in Economic History*, London, 1954, 1, 103–4; Archer 1934:141; Malden 1967; 2, 382–4; P. Clark, *The English Alehouse, a Social History 1200–1830*, London 1983, pp. 107–8.
[75] G.L.R.O. P92/SAV/406.   [76] Forbes 1980:127.

at the Talbot', maintained a separate household across the street from the inn in Fishmonger Alley as did another of his colleagues, one Thomas Whittingslow. The economic influence of some establishments may well have extended to informal control over their local retail outlets.[77] In particular innkeepers and victuallers, as well as those explicitly labelled as brewer's servants, provided an outlet for local brewers. By the early seventeenth century most English victuallers were being supplied by brewers rather then brewing their own, a development stemming from the supplanting of easily brewed ale by the less readily manufactured beer in the sixteenth century.[78] Victualling houses were also dependent on bakeries for supplies of bread. Consequently local bakers were presented when their bread sold in local victualling houses infringed the assize of bread. Hence Rowland Marsh, baker, was presented in 1638 for 'that his bread sold at the house of one Thomas Booth, victualler, of St Saviour's was underweight.[79]

The examples of dependency involving the keeping of victualling houses suggest that an 'alternative economy' may have existed from which the inhabitants of Southwark, from all ranks of society, could have supplemented their income.

3.2. An alternative economy: income supplements

The sources of income available to Southwark inhabitants included the total household income and not just that of adult males whose activities are the most frequently documented. Amongst the poorer sort, working wives made an important, though unquantifiable, contribution to the income of the household. Charles Phythian-Adams has recently pointed out that in early sixteenth-century Coventry during the day many adult males would have worked outside the family home.[80] As in Coventry so in St Saviour's wives were often required to represent absent husbands. It was wives who actually received poor relief payments from the Overseers of the Poor and, as we shall see, they were responsible for arranging short-term loans from neighbourhood pawnbrokers. A woman could play a significant part in her husband's business. In 1638 were presented: 'Robert Lambert...and his wife

[77] See, P. Clark, 'The alehouse and the alternative society', in D. H. Pennington and K. Thomas (eds.), *Puritans and Revolutionaries: Essays in Seventeenth-Century History presented to Christopher Hill*, Oxford, 1978, pp. 52, 71; Jack 1977:112–13; Clark 1983a:101–3.

[78] It was therefore, rare, in Southwark, for an individual to be professing the occupations of both brewer and victualler. See, Clark 1983a:101–6; Archer 1934:51.

[79] C.L.R.O. Presentments of the jurors of the Guildable Manor 1638; Southwark Box 2. A royal proclamation of 1605 allowed bakers to sell bread to victuallers and innkeepers at a discount, see, R. R. Steele (ed.), *Bibliotheca Lindesiana: A Bibliography of Tudor and Stuart Proclamations 1485–1714*, Oxford, 1910, 1, 116; Clark 1983a:132–3.

[80] C. Phythian-Adams, *Desolation of a City*, Cambridge, 1979, pp. 88, 96.

for buying and engrossing a quarter of a cartload of peas…and selling them again in the same market'. It is also clear that women indulged in economic activity unrelated to their husbands' occupations. In 1620 William Keyes, a smith, was fined 50s. 'for that his wife being a common forestaller of the market taketh in butter and such like commodities at her door of the country people as they came to town before the same be carried into the market and selleth it again'.[81] The manorial records recognised the wife as a retailer. As we have seen, the manorial courts regulated the activities of herbwives, fishwives and saucewives as well as their rural counterparts, 'the country wives which sell pound or dish butter'. Wives also indulged in baking or spinning to swell the household income. In neighbouring St Olave's an alien tailor's wife was called a 'Dutch baker'; of an alien weaver's wife it was written that 'her profession is a baker'. Other wives were described as seamstresses, tuftaffeta weavers, silkweavers and one housewife in St Saviour's as a buttonmaker.[82] Women also took in washing, acted as nurses and performed the duties of midwives. Testators occasionally bequeathed small sums of money to their nurses. An anti-plague order of 1609 for the Clink liberty laid down that

no woman Inhabitant of this liberty which live by washing…or keeping women in childbed. Or such as keep houses visited…be suffered to bring home any manner of persons visited, any clothes, beddings or other things to the endangering of their neighbours.[83]

The contribution made by children to the household income can only be guessed at. It is clear from the poor accounts that too many children were a financial burden. However beyond a certain age and until they went into service or apprenticeship a child was capable of bringing in some money. A female child of about eight years of age was referred to in a memorandum made by the churchwardens in 1626: 'Remember Mottlyes child kept in Christofer Yard it is said…that it can get 2 shillings a week making bonelace justified by Stockman's wife and yet is not well kept.'[84] The older a child the more it could earn. Richard Cliff, carpenter, charged the vestry 8d. per day in 1621 for the work of his fourteen-year-old son John. This compares with fourteen pence received by a labourer and 2s. by a carpenter.[85]

Over and above the activities of wives and children, households and

[81] C.L.R.O. Presentments of jurors of Guildable Manor 1638, Southwark Box 2; Presentments of the jurors of the King's Manor 1620, Southwark Box 2,

[82] G.L.R.O. P92/SAV/1315; Kirk 1900–7:3, 218.

[83] Young 1889:2, 30. For other references to female labour in towns see, Phythian-Adams 1979:87–8, 92; Clark 1983a:82–4; J. F. Pound (ed.), *The Norwich Census of the Poor 1570*, Norfolk Record Society 40, 1971, pp. 16–17 and *passim*; Alice Clark, *Working Life of Women in the Seventeenth Century*, London, 1982 edn, *passim*.   [84] G.L.R.O. P92/SAV/215.

[85] Details from the accounts of the College of the Poor 1621–2, G.L.R.O. P92/SAV/1582. For wage levels see also P92/SAV/1585,1589,1595 and some tradesmen's bills, 81–3, 682.

individuals turned to a wide range of other activities to supplement their income. In rural England one such was the keeping of an alehouse, often an informal, transient and unlicensed operation.[86] However, the manorial records make it clear that, in seventeenth-century Southwark, the function of the alehouse was performed by a more formal establishment, the victualling house. Many victuallers, in addition to drink, sold foodstuffs such as bread and cooked meat. Victualling houses were local institutions only a step down from taverns, were custom built and passed from one tenant to another, often keeping the same name. Apart from the difficulty of raising the capital required the Southwark victualler faced a large number of legal sanctions. Victuallers were presented in the manorial courts for selling ale and beer in unlawful measures and in the ecclesiastical courts for selling the same commodity in time of divine service. Licensing of victuallers in England was tightened up in the early seventeenth century. Consequently in the second decade of the seventeenth century Boroughside victuallers were being required to enter recognisances to observe the prohibition on consumption of meat during Lent, and in the 1630s were being licensed by the Lord Mayor.[87] For these reasons Southwark victuallers were, as we shall see, often fairly well off and in terms of relative wealth ranked with butchers, chandlers and salters. Their social ranking in Southwark appears to have been rather higher than that of victuallers in provincial England.[88] Given all this it is not surprising that alehouse-keeping was not the supplement to the income of the poor that it was in provincial areas. In Terling for example 'alehouse-keeping was an employment involving many of the poor', often following the advent of old age and loss of earning power.[89] In the Boroughside, however, only eleven individuals of all those whose occupations have been recovered kept victualling houses whilst professing an unrelated occupation. Hence, for example, Thomas Goodhand, described as a barber surgeon in 1608, was keeping a victualling house in 1622. Only five of these eleven were making no contribution to the poor rate. Furthermore, like the situation in rural England, women rarely kept such establishments. Only seven out of 54 individuals (13%), in the Boroughside entering victualler's recognisances in 1620 were female. Since there were some 135 female-headed households in the district in 1622 only one female in nineteen ran such an establishment.[90]

[86] For the transient nature of many provincial operations see ibid., pp. 72–3, 85–7.

[87] See, P.R.O. E180/140; G.L.R.O. P92/SAV/1320. See also Clark 1983a:166–76; McGrath 1948:22.

[88] Clark 1983a:74–7.

[89] Wrightson and Levine 1979: 23. See also, Clark 1938a:80–2; Clark 1978:52–3; P. Slack, 'Poverty and politics in Salisbury 1597–1666', in P. Clark and P. Slack (eds.), *Crisis and Order in English Towns 1500–1700*, London, 1972, p. 173.

[90] P.R.O. E 180/140. Clark found that between 6.6% and 10.3% of alehousekeepers were female, usually widows, Clark 1983a:78–9. For the view that widows were 'often alehousekeepers' see, Clark 1978:53. For alehousekeeping in London see also, Power 1978a:40; Schwarz 1979:257; Ashton 1983:10–13.

Employment in minor parish or manorial office, however, was a recognised method by which the aged, poor and infirm could support themselves. Hence, for example, one John Clove, described as a cook in 1601, petitioned the vestry in the 1630s, stating that by becoming 'a common watchman...he lived without being chargeable to the parish so long as he was able to undergo that pains'.[91] Oliver Lee, described as an ostler in 1593 and a shoemaker in 1595, was appointed one of the four bearers by the vestry in 1621, a duty which included looking 'to the gutters of the church'. Lee was described as a bearer at his death two years later. Such posts were partly charitable and possessed the attractions of subsidised accommodation and a regular income.[92] A few ablebodied individuals discarded their occupations in favour, as it were, of a career in local government.

Some individuals from all ranks of society supplemented their income by keeping livestock. Anchor Kitchin, baker, living in an alley off the main High Street, was presented in the Guildable manorial court in 1620 for 'suffering poultry to go abroad'. James Corde, a poor cobbler and hackneyman living in Horsehead Alley, was presented 'for that he keepeth hogs to the great annoyance of the inhabitants'. However, most of the individuals presented for keeping hogs followed middling to high status occupations such as butcher, victualler, starchmaker, chandler and, most common of all, innholder. Hogs were not merely kept in yards or allowed to wander the streets: in 1637 two householders in Ship Yard were fined for 'keeping of hogs in a cellar'. The jury of the Sewer Commission was also forced to present the owners of hogs when the animals, doubtless seeking to enliven their diet, endangered the common sewer.[93]

Some of the poorer Boroughside inhabitants earned money by taking in unwanted children. The large numbers of wealthier London-born children put out to wet-nurse has attracted comment and a few of these were sent to the Boroughside.[94] Far more important and widespread, however, was the nursing of abandoned children. The churchwardens paid certain householders to keep orphaned or unwanted children born in the Boroughside, a practice duplicated in rural areas. Eight householders were receiving

[91] G.L.R.O. P92/SAV/764.
[92] G.L.R.O. P92/SAV/450, 6 December 1621. The charitable nature of such posts is indicated by the following entry in the minutes: '24 April 1615, it is ordered that Richard Brownrigg shall be admitted to be one of the church officers to attend at the vestry door at every vestry holden, in regard of Old Sellwood's impotency and that he shall be allowed xxs per annum nevertheless Old Sellwood's wages shall not be abridged'.
[93] C.L.R.O. Presentments of the jurors of the Great Liberty Manor 1637, Southwark Box 2; G.L.R.O. SKCS 33, 40. See also, Rendle 1878:125, 226. Livestock was also kept in sixteenth-century York, Palliser 1982:88.
[94] Finlay 1981:146–8. Hence, '1 August 1620 William Page a nurse child ground and bell xvjd', G.L.R.O. P92/SAV/406.

such payments in 1622.[95] The sums paid were tailored to suit the age of the child and the financial circumstances of the household involved. Evidence for the private nursing of children is not as easy to come by. A few cases were turned up by the searcher for inmates but these probably represent the tip of an iceberg of unknown size. The small numbers found reflect the difficulty of detecting incoming children rather than their scarcity. The case of Widow Gray indicates that private nursing may have been relatively organised and even points to some middleman activity:

Widow Gray in Green Dragon Yard having taken in a strange child to keep not above three months old, [and] neither knew whose child it was, nor what his name was that delivered the child to her. But said a shoemaker in Fleet Lane helped her to it. So I went with her to the man, at last she spied him in the shop, so demanding whose child it was: a great while he would not tell us, but said she had undertaken to keep it and that she had a month's wages beforehand.[96]

In rapidly expanding Stuart London one of the most important sources of supplementary income came from the heavy demand for accommodation. The large inns could not meet all this demand and therefore the taking in of lodgers was a very important by-employment. Lodging as a source of income for urban inhabitants has been noted in pre-industrial towns and cities. According to Adam Smith, letting lodgings was a 'great industry' in eighteenth-century London and a particularly important 'by-industry' of London shopkeepers.[97] In the late seventeenth century each household in the capital contained on average 1.7 lodgers.[98] Those keeping lodgers in the Boroughside in 1622 can be detected from baptism records, entries in the 1622 token book and from the reports of the searcher for inmates. From these sources 70 households, 7% of the total number in the Boroughside in 1622 can be shown to have kept 'lodgers' between 1618 and 1625. Since the sources give a far from complete coverage this figure should be seen as a minimum estimate of those who were sometimes able to increase the household income in this way.[99] Those keeping lodgers seem to be divided into two distinct groups. Of the 26 households lodging married couples in 1622, 65% contributed to the poor rate. Of the 44 households which lodged widows and unmarried females only 14% made any contribution to the poor rate. Such differences probably stem from the number of rooms

[95] G.L.R.O. P92/SAV/1400.

[96] G.L.R.O. P92/SAV/1423. See also Raine 1969:79–85.

[97] Beier 1981:61; Goose 1980:379–80; Clark 1978:55; Pound 1971b:15; I. Roy and S. Porter, 'Social and economic structure of an early modern suburb: the tything at Worcester', *Bulletin of the Institute of Historical Research* 53, 128 (1980), 203; George 1966:100; L. D. Schwarz, 'Social class and social geography: the middle classes in London at the end of the eighteenth century', *Social History* 7, 2 (1982), 169–176.   [98] Wall 1979:103.

[99] This figure includes only those households containing specifically labelled lodgers, since this label indicates a formal paying relationship. Inmates have not been counted.

available and the social standing of the lodgers in question. All ranks of society took in lodgers. The better-off inhabitants tended to lodge individuals of similar or higher status to their own. Hence the wife of William Stitch, gentleman deceased, gave birth at the house of William Ward, goldsmith. Edward Payne, 'gent', stayed with Richard Yearwood, grocer. Among the wealthiest inhabitants kinship sometimes linked lodger and householder. As has been noticed elsewhere widows were particularly likely to take in lodgers.[100] Furthermore certain householders seem to have kept informal lodging houses. In 1595 it was reported that 'Thomas Dawkyn in Pepper Alley lodgeth his father-in-law a poor man...lately come forth of the country, he lodgeth sundry young men and women.'[101]

The middling and upper ranks of society were able to benefit from the widespread practice of dividing houses to provide extra accommodation. Despite government hostility and repeated proclamations against this, landlords, their lessees and their undertenants continued to exploit the demand for cheap accommodation. It is somewhat difficult to quantify this practice satisfactorily but, as is suggested below, subdivision may have accommodated much of the population increase between 1580 and 1630. There was also considerable profit to be made from the conversion of business sites such as bakehouses or inns, into cheap housing. The courtyards of some Southwark inns were similarly developed. Some of the wealthiest householders had invested heavily in local property often on a scale which must have provided the major slice of an individual's income. Hence Richard Wright, grocer, built the Three Tun tavern worth £26 a year as well as leasing tenements and stables in Ship Yard. Nicholas Newton, innholder, leased both Christofer Yard and Goat Yard from absentee landlords and received over £200 per annum from his hundred or so tenants.[102]

In fact wealthier London inhabitants often had some financial interest in both urban and rural property and those in Southwark were no exception.[103] Steven Brightling, tailor, owned three properties in Tunbridge Wells, and another in Hadlow, Kent. George Payne, grocer, owned a crane at Brenchley and property in Brasted, Kent. He also owned land in Gracious Street, London, and the house of John Burbage in St Saviour's.[104] Since the main source for this information is wills no attempt has been made to

---

[100] Sylvia McIntyre, 'Bath: the rise of a resort town, 1660–1800', in P. Clark (ed.), *Country Towns in Pre-Industrial England*, Leicester, 1981, pp. 217–19. See also Anderson 1971:46.

[101] G.L.R.O. P92/SAV/1315.

[102] G.L.R.O. P92/SAV/1331, *passim*. For the erection of tenements in the capital's inns see also, Chartres 1977a:27.

[103] See, R. G. Lang, 'Social origins and social aspirations of Jacobean London merchants', *Economic History Review* 27 (1974), 28–47; Grassby 1978:358–9.

[104] G.L.R.O. Archdeaconry of Surrey Will Register, 360 Yeast; P.C.C. Will Register, 88 Clarke.

quantify urban property holdings. It is clear that property was often settled before a willmaker's death, and the absence of references to it cannot be taken to imply that an individual did not actually possess any. Probably much of the land held by these individuals was inherited and in fact it may tell us more about an individual's origins than about his investment in real estate. In this connection it is noticeable that much of the property referred to lies in Surrey, Kent and Sussex which could have formed a major part of the catchment area from which Southwark drew its immigrants. Whatever its origins, property-holding of one sort or another was widespread amongst the wealthiest inhabitants of the Boroughside. For example, Richard Yearwood, grocer, rated at 40s. per year, in his will disposed of tenements in the neighbouring parish of Bermondsey, property in Lingfield, Surrey, a tenement and orchard in Frindsbury, Kent, and a manor and farm in Burstow, Surrey. This was in addition to his 'leases in friends names' and his undisclosed ownership of Green Dragon Yard in the Boroughside.[105] Altogether 73% of those rated at 5d. or more in the poor rate assessment of 1621–2 held some form of property other than their dwelling house and this is certainly a minimum figure. In their ownership of property the wealthy Boroughside inhabitants were only copying the example of more illustrious London counterparts. It has been shown recently that 84% of Jacobean aldermen held property other than their dwelling house.[106]

3.3 *Making ends meet: borrowing and charity*

3.3.1 *Borrowing*
Far from being able to supplement their income from property or by-employments many householders were forced to resort to borrowing and charity to make ends meet. Pawning personal property was practised widely by Southwark inhabitants as a short-term financial expedient. This safety net was not unique to Southwark; pawnbroking is known to have occurred in other towns and cities at this time and was widely practised in the capital. London pawnbrokers were the subject of royal proclamations which attempted in vain, to enforce the keeping of registers. In the late sixteenth century, at a time when there were said to be 'about 500 [individuals] in London which do take pawns and yet are no brokers', a scheme for public pawnshops was proposed.[107] Petitions sent into the vestry make routine references to pawning. Hence Thomas Clifford, shoemaker, asked for a loan

---

[105] P.C.C. Will Register, 98 Audley.   [106] Lang 1974:40.
[107] Registry offices had been erected in London and Westminster by Elizabeth I. Pawning was the subject of several Acts of Common Council, see, Steele 1910:1, 190, no. 1613; British Library Lansdowne Ms 351.18–23; Clark 1978:56; Clark 1983a:229; B. A. Holderness, 'Credit in a rural community 1660–1800', *Midland History* 3, 2 (1975), 96; T. Wilson, *Discourse upon usury*, R. H. Tawney (ed.), London, 1925, pp. 92–9.

of 19s. 'whereby he may redeem some things he hath pawned and set himself on work'. A decrepid old widow complained that she had been unable to maintain herself except by 'selling and pawning all that ever she hath'. To support his wife and three children Thomas Moore, glover, pawned the greatest part of that little goods he had'.[108] The parish authorities sometimes acted as pawnbrokers. The poor accounts for Paris Garden refer to 30s. 'which was lent unto widow scott upon a pawn which is a gold ring, which ring remaineth in the chest'.[109] Many of the poorer Boroughside inhabitants must have been indebted to their better-off neighbours who, in addition to their professed occupations, operated as pawnbrokers. The inventory of the possessions of an almswoman sold after her death refers to 12s. received for 'a gold ring being pawned' and £3 5s. 'received for pawns of Thomas Southwood'.[110] In 1596 the churchwardens presented one John Cleaborough, baker and subsidy man, 'for taking excess usury of Jonas Crowcher above £10 in the hundred'. The case is a good illustration of the mechanism of pawnbroking:

Elizabeth Crowcher says that she borrowed of John Cleaborough 24s. upon a gown and taffety apron and had [to pay] for the use of this money 8s. for three quarters of the year and 4d. for making of the bill, and when she came to redeem her goods her apron was worn out for which she refused to receive her goods, thereupon Jonas Crowcher husband to the said Elizabeth...did arrest him to the borough court...[but] then Cleaborough did remove it to Westminster Jonas being then pressed at sea [and] could not follow it, so Cleaborough recovered 8s. more of him for damage.[111]

We are particularly fortunate that the records of one Southwark pawnbroker have survived. Phillip Henslowe, gentleman, theatrical entrepreneur and property owner lived in the Clink liberty of St Saviour's, Southwark, from the late sixteenth century until his death in 1614. He served on the St Saviour's vestry and held a variety of local offices in the Clink liberty. More interesting, for our purposes, than his various theatrical connections are the miscellaneous lists of pawns taken that survive scattered amongst the pages of his 'diary'.[112] Although the records have some drawbacks they offer an unique insight into the mechanics and scale of pawnbroking in late sixteenth-century London.

Henslowe's diary contains references to pawnbroking between 1593 and 1596. To look at his pawnbroking in detail the loans made between January 1594 and March 1595 have been grouped together. This has been done

---

[108] G.L.R.O. P92/SAV762, 773, 776.   [109] Norman 1901:80.
[110] G.L.R.O. P92/SAV/815. For female pawnbrokers see, Clark 1982:28–9.
[111] G.L.R.O. P92/SAV/521.
[112] R. A. Foakes and R. T. Rickert (eds.), *Henslowe's Diary*, Cambridge, 1961, pp. xxi–xxiii, 106–21, 141–62, 253–62.

because in this period every month is covered. Pawns taken in 1593 have been excluded because the plague epidemic of that year might have unduly distorted the pattern of lending. It should be noted that even in the chosen period the records may be incomplete as to the number of loans. Nonetheless it may be significant, given the seasonality of hardship in London, that twice as many loans were taken out in January 1594 as in any other month of the year. Between January 1594 and March 1595 no less than 278 separate loans were made, representing the loan of the considerable sum of £269 8s. 6d. Pawnbroking was a freely available credit facility.

It is clear from the lists of pawns taken that Henslowe's pawnbroking was carried out frequently via agents such as his nephew Francis or miscellaneous females like 'Mrs Grant', 'Goody Watson' and 'Anne Nokes'. For this reason the names and addresses of most of Henslowe's clients are unknown to us. What is clear is that, of those that are listed, most were women, presumably running the household finances, much in the manner of their nineteenth-century emulators.[113] Furthermore the clientele ranged over the social scale from the occasional member of the aristocracy, such as 'my Lord Burte', to humble local inhabitants such as 'the midwife's daughter' or 'the woman which sells herbs in the market'. It is sometimes possible to identify local clients among the householders listed in the 1593 token book. Thus the 'Jude Merrecke' who borrowed 11s. 4d. on a woman's gown 'guarded with velvet' on 29 September 1594 was probably the 'wid Merryeke' listed on page eleven of the 1593 token book.[114]

Most of the loans made by Henslowe were for sums of less than 30s. (see Table 3.4). Only fifty-nine loans were for 30s. or more (21.2%). Very small sums, less than 5s., were unusual: only 29 (10.4%) were made of 4s. or less. It is clear that, as in the nineteenth century, credit obtained from these short-term loans was expensive. As we have seen Elizabeth Crowcher was charged 8s. for eight months on a 24s. loan or one shilling a month representing an (illegal) annual rate of 50%. Henslowe's rates were comparable. In 1594 memoranda against some of the loans indicate that interest payments ranged from between 8d. to 14d. a month on sums ranging from 2s. 6d to 33s. 2d. As noted in nineteenth-century studies borrowing very small sums was particularly expensive and may explain why they were relatively uncommon. Lower rates of interest than these were apparently charged by pawnbrokers in late seventeenth-century London.[115] Rates varied presumably according to the nature of the pawn and the likelihood of prompt repayment.

---

[113] For pawnbroking in the nineteenth century see, Melanie Tebbut, *Making Ends Meet: Pawnbroking and Working-Class Credit*, New York, 1983, pp. 37–67 and passim.
[114] Foakes and Rickert 1961:259; G.L.R.O. P92/SAV/244.
[115] Clark 1983a:229; Tebbut 1983:8–9.

Table 3.4. *Pawnbroking records of Phillip Henslowe, January 1594 – March 1595*

Sum of money lent in shillings	Number of loans	Total amount lent in shillings	%
100s +	7	820	15.2
90–99	0	0	0
80–89	1	80	1.5
70–79	3	210	3.9
60–69	6	364	6.8
50–59	0	0	0
40–49	17	685.7	12.7
30–39	25	773.5	14.4
20–29	47	971.7	18.0
10–19	96	1124	20.9
1–9	76	359.7	6.7
Total	278	5388.6	

Source: Foakes and Rickert 1961: 118, 144–62, 253–60.

The security left for these loans was, as it proved to be in the nineteenth century, mostly articles of clothing (see Table 3.5). This category includes pieces of material and offcuts ('remnants') as well as cloaks, suits, gowns, lace, hosiery and so on. Something like 62.2 % of all loans were secured solely on such articles.[116] A typical transaction of this type ran as follows; ' 13 february lent upon a violet coloured cloth cloak with a velvet cape and faced with serge of goodwife whitcares for ...Xs.' Some of the clothing pledged was clearly of high quality and must have been worn by persons who were (or had been) comfortably off. Nonetheless sums of money could also be raised from more humble garments. A joiner borrowed 10s. in March 1595 on security of his doublet and hose, Goody Haryson received 2s. 6d. for her '2 coarse smocks' and one individual borrowed 18d. 'upon a pair of old fustian breeches'. As one would expect clothing only required on special occasions, such as mourning gowns, or for limited periods was offered for security. In particular children's wear appears. In October 1594 'lent goody Watsones upon ij bibs for a child & their falls 3s.'. On three occasions in 1594 childbed linen was used to secure loans.

Most household goods left as pawns were articles of bedlinen, sheets, rugs, curtains, napkins and tablecloths. Furniture seems to have been rare: only once was a 'featherbed and a bolster' amongst items pawned. House-

---

[116] Clothing formed three quarters of all pawns in the nineteenth century, Tebbut 1983:33.

Table 3.5. *Pawns left with Henslowe, January 1594 – March 1595*

	Number of loans	%
Clothes (includes material, hats, gloves etc.)	173	62.2
Household goods (notably linen)	34	12.2
Plate (mostly rings)	32	11.5
Clothes and household goods	30	10.8
Clothes and plate	5	1.8
Clothes, household goods and plate	1	0.4
Household goods and bible	1	0.4
Unsecured loans to agent	2	0.7
Total	278	

Source: Foakes and Rickert 1961: 118, 144–62, 253–60.

hold implements such as 'a pair of tongs and a fire shovel' or a mortar and pestle were also the exception rather than the rule. Plate left as security was usually in the form of rings, sometimes memorial or wedding rings. On 26 November 1594 Henslowe 'lent Mrs Comber upon her wedding ring which hath this posey god hath appointed I am content' 10s. Only once did a bible provide material rather than spiritual comfort: lent 'upon a bible and x pieces of linen…of goody haryson at xs'. Industrial raw material was also uncommon. Apart from pieces of cloth the only occasion it was left as security was on 18 May 1594 when 5s. was lent 'upon 5 pounds of flaxen yard'. Most of these securities were sewn or wrapped up in sheets or cloth. Henslowe appears not to have been offered or to have taken bulky furniture, working tools, industrial raw material or perishable goods. Presumably storage facilities were limited while the loss of tools and raw material would (as in the case of Thomas Clifford) have prevented a client earning any sort of income at all.

The availability of pawnbroking has some important implications for the household finances of the Southwark inhabitants. The ability to take out loans provided a means by which householders, both rich and poor, could bridge periods of financial difficulty. The fact that useful sums of money could be borrowed on the security of goods might also tell us something about the way the inhabitants viewed their material possessions. It has been said, for example, that the meticulous listings of personal belongings found in the wills of the villagers of Terling, Essex, reflected their 'owner's pride'; such possessions were 'the outward and very visible sign of success'. In Southwark, however, such possessions were also realisable assets, to be pawned when circumstances demanded and willmakers may well have been

as conscious of their value as proud of their accumulation.[117] Thus when
Joan Bosse left her former maid 'my best gown and my best red petticoat,
my great brass pot, and my hoop gold ring which cost me 18*s* or
thereabouts' and to her nine-year-old godson 'my best featherbed, 2 feather
bolsters, 2 pillows, 2 pillowbeers [a] pair of sheets, a covering and a rug
blanket with curtains and vallence' the bequest should be seen in the material
value of the bequeathed items. Bosse was concerned to bequeath realisable
assets to her godson rather than to give him his own private featherbed.[118]

3.3.2 Poor relief
As we have seen the occupations followed by adult males were by no means
the only possible sources of income open to their families. However there
came a point (or points) in many individuals' lives when economic
depression, age or sickness prevented work, when death or desertion meant
the loss of the male income-earner and when stocks of pawnable goods were
exhausted. In the last resort such householders fell back on various forms
of poor relief to make ends meet.

By the 1620s the system of parochial poor relief in the Boroughside had
become a complex three-tiered structure, each administrative body being
responsible for the disbursement of different sources of income to distinct
categories of poor. Two bodies, the Warden of the General Poor and the
Warden of the College Almshouse, were both responsible to the vestry of
St Saviour's, while the Overseers of the Poor were responsible to the Surrey
Justices. Prior to the 1620s the administration tended to blur these divisions.
The system of poor relief described below probably dated from the vestry
order of 1616 which specified that 'the overseers of the poor shall pay only
the other poor which are no Collegers, and that two several books shall
be made one for the Collegers and the other for the other poor and weekly
taxations'.[119]

An unusual feature of the parochial system of poor relief in St Saviour's
was the institution known as the College or Hospital of the Poor. The
College was founded in the late sixteenth century, a period when a large
number of almshouses were founded by London benefactors.[120] In the 1620s
the institution was administered separately by a specially nominated warden
and funded by property endowments. It principally served the Boroughside
district of the parish; twelve of the sixteen inmates were to be drawn from
the area. Each member of the College was to be nominated by the
churchwardens, the vestry, overseers, constables and ministers. Throughout

---

[117] Wrightson and Levine 1979:38–9; Tebbut 1983:14–16.
[118] Archdeaconry of Surrey Will Register, 218 Peter.
[119] G.L.R.O. P92/SAV/450, 15 April 1616.
[120] W. J. K. Jordan, *The Charities of London 1480–1660*, London, 1960, pp. 139, 146, 158.

the early seventeenth century the institution was run (with some minor administrative changes) according to the ordinances and statutes laid down by the founder, Thomas Cure in 1584.[121] The College pensioner received the large sum of twenty pence per week plus free fuel, bread and accommodation in the institution. In addition extra payments were made to the inmates 'at sundry times as Easter, Christmas, in cold weather and when some of them were sick and paid to keepers to attend and look to those that were sick'.[122] Despite the general debilitation of most of the inmates it was nevertheless envisaged that their dependence on the College pension should not be total; they were therefore expected to 'labour daily on the working days according to their ability of body and former manner of honest life' on pain of fines and expulsion. Membership was normally for life unless a pauper married or was expelled for bad behaviour. College pensioners were normally chosen from the ranks of the ordinary parish pensioners, following an ordinance of the founder, and this served to lighten the burden placed on the resources of the Overseers of the Poor by removing some of the most desperate cases from their books. To decide on the order of election those admitted were to be classed according to 'degree' of poverty. The degrees reflect an awareness of the 'life-cycle' nature of poverty.[123]

In addition to the College, St Saviour's also possessed the normal apparatus of poor relief administered by the Overseers of the Poor. Temporary hardship was alleviated by weekly cash payments to the 'extraordinary' poor. Poverty occasioned by long term causes such as old age, widowhood or desertion might qualify for a parish pension — a regular weekly payment. Such payments to the 'ordinary poor' were accounted separately from the 'extraordinary' payments. The distinction drawn between the regular pension and more irregular payment was a common feature of early seventeenth century poor relief in London. As in city parishes the sums paid were adjusted to meet individual circumstances.[124] Pensioners might also qualify for free accommodation in a parish almshouse. The administration run by the Overseers of the Poor was funded principally by the proceeds of the annual poor rate, which accounted for 70% of the total sum disbursed, the balance being made up from collections at the communion table, fines for disorders in church and the occasional legacy. Most of the latter were administered by the Warden of the General Poor although on occasion he passed small legacies to the Overseers for

---

[121] For the ordinances of the College see, G.L.R.O. P92/SAV/1529. For its accounts see, P92/SAV/1577–83, 1596. See also Jordan 1960:113; Rendle 1878:184–5; Taylor 1833:96–7.
[122] G.L.R.O. P92/SAV/1582.
[123] G.L.R.O. P92/SAV/1529. For the urban life-cycle see Chapter 6.
[124] See Pearl 1981:123–4; Herlan 1977a; 25–8; Herlan 177b:179–99.

disbursement. Major endowments were jointly administered by the Overseers and the churchwardens. The accounts of the Warden of the General Poor suggest that the contribution of the poor rate to the relief of the poor was greater than that of private charity in the early seventeenth century. In 1627 the Warden received £96 11s. 5d. from legacies and endowments compared to the £127 14s. raised from the parishioners six years before. Poor rates therefore formed perhaps 57% of the total sum disbursed, a proportion similar to the 54% calculated for the London parish of St Dunstan in the West between 1639 and 1650 but very different from the 7% estimated by Professor Jordan, on altogether inadequate evidence, for the nation as a whole.[125] Nonetheless the reaction against Jordan should not be overdone. The impact of private charity clearly added significantly to the relief of poverty. The charity established by Henry Smith in the 1630s worth £28 per year clothed over thirty Boroughside paupers annually.[126]

The subject of urban poor relief can only be truly understood in the context of the many ways in which individuals actually earned a living, as described above. It would be quite wrong to imply that parish poor relief was the only income available to those who received it. In early Stuart Salisbury poor relief payments, for those in receipt of them, formed between 32·8% and 60·0% of the income of married couples and solitary

---

[125] See, G.L.R.O. P92/SAV/1400, 1401; Herlan 1977a:24. The 7% figure calculated by Jordan was arrived at by comparing the total income from charitable endowments listed in wills (mostly from the Prerogative Courts) and a miscellaneous collection of local documents covering ten selected counties in England in 1650 to the total income raised from poor rates in *all* of the overseers' accounts found by Jordan covering the *whole* country. This procedure has no validity at all. When Jordan restricted his analysis to a comparison of endowments and poor rate assessments in *only* those parishes with *extant* accounts he produced a figure of 25%. Jordan seems to have believed that those parishes leaving surviving evidence of regular poor rate collection were, by definition, exceptionally poor and thus not representative of England as a whole. Throughout he made the indefensible assumption that the dating and number of overseers' accounts that he was able to consult (in the 1950s) represented both the actual number of parishes collecting poor rate and the timing of such collections. Record survival does not equal original record incidence and figures based on such an assumption are quite valueless. In a footnote Jordan himself admitted as much; 'the figures we have used for amounts raised for poor relief are limited to the amounts set out in the overseers' accounts which we have found. These figures are necessarily incomplete, so any attempt to project them by computation to the whole of England would be pointless', see, W. J. K Jordan, *Philanthropy in England 1480–1660*, London, 1959, p. 141, n. 1. For Jordan's methodology see ibid., pp. 22–30, 128–41. For the debates over this and other aspects of Jordan's findings see also Herlan 1977b:179–85; Herlan 1977a:13–14; W. G. Bittle and R. T. Lane, 'Inflation and philanthropy in England: a re-assessment of W. K. Jordan's data', *Economic History Review*, 2nd ser., 29 (1976), 203–10; J. F. Hadwin, 'Deflating philanthropy', *Economic History Review*, 2nd ser., 31 (1978), 105–17; D. C. Coleman, 'Philanthropy deflated: a comment', *Economic History Review*, 2nd ser., 31 (1978), 118–20; J. D. Gould, 'Bittle and Lane on charity', *Economic History Review*, 2nd ser. 31 (1978), 121–3; W. G. Bittle and R. T. Lane, 'A re-assessment reiterated', *Economic History Review*, 2nd ser., 31 (1978), 124–8.

[126] For Henry Smith's charity see, G.L.R.O. P92/SAV/1760–81. See also, Jordan 1960:117–22. For a list of charitable endowments in St Saviour's see, *Parliamentary Accounts and Papers 16 Charities, session 8 February 1898–12 August 1898*, LXVII, 1898, pp. 523–641.

householders respectively.[127] How comprehensive was the poor relief system in the Boroughside?

The parish authorities certainly implied that the number of householders dependent on their efforts was considerable. In the early seventeenth century they claimed that 'there be very many poor people who receive a great *part* [my emphasis] of their maintenance from the petitioners [the vestry of St Saviour's]'.[128] They went on to claim that readiness to resort to charity was almost universal and deplored the resultant 'scrounger' mentality:

Many of these householders being artificers and able in time of health to maintain themselves by their labour if the accompt be made public and they know anything in stock, they will leave their vocation and hang upon the parish...this will maintain idleness, and to make from £3 subsidy men to crave alms. For we can speak by experience that some men well able to work and having good occupations to live by being reproved for idleness and ill-husbandry, and demanded what they would do with wife and children when age and sickness cometh, their answer hath been the parish shall keep them.[129]

In 1631 the churchwardens of the Boroughside went as far as to make the extravagant claim that, *excluding* pensioners, 'there are...to the number of 600 families which are relieved at certain times when it is thought most needful'.[130] However, this latter claim was designed to impress the Privy Council rather than to report the objective truth. Fortunately it is possible to make more careful and realistic estimates of the scope of parish poor relief from the surviving accounts of the Overseers of the Poor.

The accounts of the Overseers of the Poor for the year 1621–2 list seventy-one pensioners out of 958 householders, 7.4% of the total in 1622. The number of pensioners seems to have remained fairly constant over time. In 1631 there were said to be seventy-two (out of 966 householders or 7.5%) and seventy in 1633.[131] In 1621–2 a further thirty-eight households, 4.0% of the total number in the Boroughside at that date, received one or more extraordinary payments. All in all therefore 109 households or 11.4% of the total in 1622 received sums of money from the Overseers of the Poor. Poor relief was not an important source of income for households headed by men. From our sample of male householders with recovered occupations only 1.7% were receiving a weekly pension, with another 3.2% receiving extraordinary payments in 1621–2. Significantly, female-headed households were far more likely to receive such payments. Of all the households in 1622,

[127] Slack 1972: 175. For poor relief in Tudor and Stuart towns and cities see also, Patten 1978:190–1; Pound 1971b:passim; P. Slack, C. Phythian-Adams, Penelope Corfield and Rosemary O'Day, *The Traditional Community under Stress*, Milton Keynes, 1977, pp. 92–100; Beier 1981:45–86; Palliser 1979:275–7; A. D. Dyer, *The City of Worcester in the Sixteenth Century*, Leicester, 1973, pp. 165–72.
[128] G.L.R.O. P92/SAV/802.   [129] G.L.R.O. P92/SAV/790.
[130] G.L.R.O. P92/SAV/1467   [131] G.L.R.O. P92/SAV/1467–8, 1400.

34% of those headed by females received some form of poor relief as opposed to only 5% of those headed by males.

The payments distributed to the Boroughside poor were intended only as income supplements. This can be deduced from the overseer's accounts which show that many of the sums paid out were very small. In 1621–2 householders receiving extraordinary relief received an average sum of 7*d.* per week for only twenty-one weeks of the year. The sums ranged in size from only 2*d.* per week (14.6% of all payments) to one shilling or more (22.7% of all payments). The more regular parish pensions were worth an average 9*d.* per week and went to the recipients forty-eight weeks of the year. Parish pensions cost more than six times the amount of money expended on the extraordinary poor: in 1621–2 pensions cost £151 14s. 4d. compared to extraordinary payments of £24 6s. 6d.[132] The sums distributed should be seen in the context of London wage rates. In the 1620s a labourer was paid 14*d. per day*, more than most parish pensioners received in a week.[133]

It is probably incorrect therefore to see the various poor relief mechanisms as anything more than institutional attempts to bridge the gap between the income and expenditure of poor households when it became necessary. Only the College pensioners could be said to be near total dependence on their pension. The 'effectiveness' or ability of parish poor relief to cope with poverty must be judged with this point in mind. Certainly the number of households relieved and the size of the sums disbursed bear comparison with some city parishes at this period and indicate that the administration of poor relief was as effective as that found elsewhere in London. In most city parishes the amounts of 'dole' varied from 1s to 6s per month (equivalent to 3d to 1s 6d per week), sums duplicated in the Boroughside. As we have seen 7.4% of Boroughside householders received a pension compared to between 2% and 5% in two city parishes. It may also be significant that the proportion of those considered to be in need and receiving relief in the Boroughside was similar to that in Norwich *after* that city had, apparently successfully, reorganised its poor relief administration in the later sixteenth century.[134]

It is particularly difficult to assess adequately the total flow of relief to the poor. Unfortunately there are not even complete lists of individuals who received payments from the Warden of the General Poor. Furthermore informal charity and extra-parochial donations must have augmented the

[132] G.L.R.O. P92/SAV/1400.

[133] See the wages in surviving bills, G.L.R.O. P92/SAV/82, 83. In 1641 a labourer employed by a bricklayer working on the College of the Poor received 16*d.* per day, G.L.R.O. P92/SAV/1585.

[134] See Pearl 1981:123; Herlan 1977a:32. Some 47% of the Boroughside poor were receiving relief compared to 46% of those in Norwich, Pound 1971b:19–21.

efforts of the Overseers of the Poor. In addition one-off payments, such as gifts and collections were occasionally distributed among the poor. Many of the one-off payments, however, cannot have had much impact on the regular flow of money since they were designed to alleviate periods of particular hardship such as severe winters and plague epidemics.[135] The lot of many poor Southwark families must have been eased by the winter fuel provided regularly by the city authorities in the early seventeenth century.[136] Private legacies would have provided some fortunate recipients with a windfall but cannot have played a large part in the income of most households. More significant to some individuals may have been the receipt of a company pension. John Norgate, a Boroughside stationer, able to contribute to the poor rate in 1621–2, is known to have received a charitable payment from the Stationers' Company in 1636.[137] Perhaps the most difficult source of poor relief to pick up is that of begging. All that can be said is that miscellaneous references suggest that informal charity of this sort was sought and that inhabitants of the Boroughside indulged in it. In 1619 two inhabitants of Christopher Yard in the Boroughside testified that 'Millaine's [a poulterer's] wife having but one eye and going with a staff did live by begging, and with Agnes Cooper alias Shell [an inmate] did daily beg together.'[138]

3.4 A local economy

Southwark, therefore, possessed a distinctive occupational geography in the early seventeenth century. St Olave's in eastern Southwark was an important centre of textile manufacture whilst the two liberties of St Saviour's were dominated by watermen. The Boroughside of St Saviour's also had a distinctive occupational structure in which the food and drink sector was most important. Jurisdiction as well as topographical factors were responsible for these differences in Southwark's occupational geography. Within the local economy of the Boroughside retailing took place from shops and market stalls and there is some evidence that other trading practices by-passed customary marketing techniques. Although most manufacturing took place in small domestic units, there were some relatively large-scale enterprises sited in the Boroughside whose owners could have exercised significant economic influence over networks of dependent employees. The extent of such networks can only be guessed at.

---

[135] Thus the vestry recorded a gift of £50 sent by the Lord Mayor for plague stricken poor following the epidemic of 1603, G.L.R.O. P92/SAV/450, 14 November 1603.

[136] See, G.L.R.O. P92/SAV/1468, 1398.

[137] W. C. Ferguson (ed.), 'The Stationers' Company Poor Book, 1608–1700', *The Library* 31 (1976), 47.

[138] G.L.R.O. P92/SAV/1421. For informal and extra-parochial charity, see also, Pearl 1981:123–4; Herlan 1977a:21.

However, it is clear that many Boroughside inhabitants were not dependent solely on their occupation in order to earn a living. A number of financial safety nets were available to Southwark inhabitants. The better-off householders of many different occupations invested in property and all ranks of society were able to earn money by taking in lodgers and other forms of financial diversification. In the last resort the poorer inhabitants supplemented their earnings from parish poor relief and by pawning their personal property to their wealthier neighbours. All in all something like a third of those householders not wealthy enough to contribute to the poor rate supplemented their income by one means or another in the 1620s.[139] Such households possessed a hitherto unsuspected resilience to economic depression and seasonal unemployment.[140] Within Southwark, the parish of St Saviour's (with only a small number of households involved in textile manufacturing) may have been less vulnerable to the depressions in the cloth industry discussed in the previous chapter. The social and economic resilience of the Boroughside district of that parish could have been particularly marked. The area not only possessed a small textile sector but also, compared with neighbouring districts, a relatively small proportion of householders following unskilled, low-paid occupations. No occupational group in the Boroughside was present in overwhelming numbers and consequently the district was not as liable to mass unemployment in times of seasonal hardship or economic depression.[141] That the Boroughside may have been in a relatively favourable socio-economic position compared to some other districts of Southwark must be borne in mind when looking at the social structure and distribution of power in the area. Moreover the availability of short-term credit reinforces the importance of the possession of material wealth to the Southwark householder. The possession of goods, particularly clothing if Henslowe's accounts are representative, could be seen as a crude index of the ability to ride out times of financial hardship. How was wealth distributed among the Boroughside inhabitants?

[139] Of 664 households not assessed for the poor rate 109, mostly those headed by women, received some form of charity, 50 kept lodgers at one time or another and at least 40 were involved in nursing, kept livestock or held paid local office.
[140] For the alleged vulnerability of the urban wage-labourer see, Jack 1977:46; Pound 1971a:81; Woodward 1981:43.
[141] Textile manufacture occupied only 8.4% of adults in St Saviour's (9% in the Boroughside) compared to 25.6% in St Olave's, Southwark. The proportion of individuals in the transport and unskilled labour sections in the early seventeenth century was as follows, (see Table 3.3), Boroughside — 10.7%; Clink and Paris Garden liberties — 46.7%; St Olave's, Southwark — 19.4%.

4

Wealth and social structure

4.1 Society and social groups in London

It has become a truism that the predominant feature of English society in the sixteenth and seventeenth centuries was social inequality and that social stratification 'the inequalities that arise from the organisation of people in society' was commonly recognised and described by contemporary commentators.[1] Individuals such as Sir Thomas Wilson or William Harrison conventionally devised hierarchical social rankings in order to classify society's members. Such schemes normally referred to adult males and excluded all women. These pictures of society tended to focus particularly sharply on the higher social groups, reflecting the social perspective of the author, and often lumped the lower strata together, so that finer social gradations that may have existed among these groups are lost.[2]

The social stratification of seventeenth-century rural society seems to be well established. Within village society social stratification was determined largely by wealth. Social status, an individual's ascribed position or standing in that society, and participation in positions of authority followed the same pattern. Furthermore the occupational descriptions: yeoman, husbandman and labourer, did indeed broadly correspond to real social and economic differences in village society.[3] However this is not to say that wealth did not overlap between these social groups, that they were discrete social

---

[1] M. Drake and Pauline Hammerton, *Exercises in historical sociology*, Milton Keynes, 1974, p. 11; Palliser 1983: 61–77; K. Wrightson, *English Society 1580–1680*, London, 1982, pp. 17–38; D. Cressy, 'Describing the social order of Elizabethan and Stuart England', *Literature and History* 3(1976), 29–44; Vivien B. Elliott, 'Mobility and marriage in pre-industrial England', Cambridge(1978), pp. 24–8.

[2] Cressy 1976: 31–4; Elliott 1978: 26–8; Wrightson 1982: 22. See also, G. A. Kerby, 'Inequality in pre-industrial society: a study of wealth, status, office and taxation in Tudor and Stuart England with particular reference to Cheshire', Cambridge (1983), pp. 1–39, 445–8.

[3] Wrightson 1982: 35; Wrightson and Levine 1979: 103; D. Cressy, *Literacy and the Social Order*, Cambridge, 1980, pp. 126–7.

'estates' or that they did not encompass considerable regional variation.[4]
It is then perhaps symbolic that the 1533 Act of Apparel, widely publicised
in repeated proclamations, divided English society according to income
levels rather than the social classifications of unpublished contemporaries.[5]

Delineating the social stratification of urban society has proved more
difficult. One of the principal difficulties has been that, unlike village society,
occupational labels of the sort analysed in the previous chapter are not
adequate guides to an individual's position within the social structure.
'Without intensive local research it is rarely possible to assign a precise
economic and social standing to a man described by a trade.'[6] Wealth is
clearly seen as important. In towns among 'crafts and trades a certain
hierarchy existed, based largely, it would seem, upon the relative wealth
of their practitioners'.[7] Factors other than wealth, however, are thought to
have affected the possession of power and social status. Many commentators
have argued that the citizenry or freemen were a distinctive and superior
social group.[8] How did Londoners view their own society?

John Stow included in his *Survey of London* an anonymous tract, *An
Apologie of the Cittie of London*, seemingly written in the early 1580s, which
includes a description of London society.[9] The author of the *Apologie* divided
the capital's society into three groups: merchants, handicrafts men and
labourers (see Table 4.1). Of the merchants group the 'navigation' group
were termed merchants in 'common speech' and the rest retailers. The chief
part of these retailers consisted of those who sold goods brought in
wholesale by the merchants, such as mercers, grocers, vintners, haberdashers
and milliners. These functional occupational groups were distinguished by
different levels of wealth. In the first place came merchants (here meaning
those involved in overseas trade) and some of the chief retailers. In the
second or 'mean' (i.e. intermediate) place were the majority of the retailers
and all handicrafts men. The 'lowest room' was assigned to the labourers.
'The private riches of London resteth chiefly in the hands of the merchants
and retailers, for artificers have not much to spare and labourers have need
that it were given unto them.'[10] Furthermore the author went on to give

[4] Wrightson 1982: 33–8; Kerby 1983: 25–39; Cressy 1976: 38–42; Cressy 1980: 125–8; J. D.
Marshall, 'Social structure and wealth in pre-industrial England', paper presented to 139th Annual
Meeting of the British Association for the Advancement of Science 31 August–7 September 1977,
pp. 20–30.
[5] N. B. Harte, 'State control of dress and social change in pre-industrial England', in D. C. Coleman
and A. H. John (eds.), *Trade, Government and Economy in Pre-Industrial England*, London, 1976,
p. 137.
[6] Cressy 1976: 37. See also, Elliott 1978: 29–40; Cressy 1980: 139–41.
[7] Wrightson 1982: 36; Dyer 1973: 174–7; Palliser 1983: 134–45.
[8] Dyer 1973: 181–3; Pound 1981: 52–3; Palliser 1979: 147–8; Wrightson 1982: 36; Rappaport
1983: 110–13; A. M. Dingle, 'The role of the householder in early Stuart London c.1603–1630',
London (1974), pp. 13–25.   [9] Stow 1971: 2, 207–11.   [10] Stow 1971: 2, 209.

Table 4.1. *The social stratification of London c. 1580*

Name	Description
1 Merchants	(a) 'Navigation' i.e. overseas trade
	(b) 'Invection' i.e. importing and supplying rest of nation.
	(c) 'Negotiation' i.e. shopkeepers or retailers.
2 Handicrafts men or artifiers	'do excercise such arts as require both labour and cunning', goldsmiths, tailors, haberdashers, skinners...
3 Labourers and hirelings	'Porters, watermen and carmen.'

Source: Stow 1971: 2, 207–11.

a rough estimate of the sizes of these three groups. The handicrafts men 'do far exceed the rest', the labourers were the next most numerous and the merchants were the smallest numerical group. So, the *Apologie* concluded 'the greater part' of Londoners 'be neither too rich nor too poor, but do live in the mediocrity'.

There are obvious difficulties with this social analysis. Firstly the gentry and the professions are not allocated any place in London society at all. Secondly the author was unable to allocate trades to his categories satisfactorily. Haberdashers appear as both handicrafts men and retailers. As noted above trade descriptions alone are not adequate pointers to social position in urban society. The dating and perspective of the document are further drawbacks. The *Apologie* was written explicitly to defend London 'to some objections that then were made against the growing greatness thereof' and consequently paints a rosy picture of the City's social stability, wealth and value to the nation. Furthermore the *Apologie* was written *before* the great expansion of the London suburbs and may be describing that society before an influx of immigrant poor. It is interesting to note that one author has been struck by the finding that in 1638 in '*the City and its liberties* the ordinary Londoner had average means by the standards of the time, being neither especially wealthy nor poor'.[11] Wealth, (if it can be measured according to some objective criterion), and its relationship to the practice of various trades or crafts was clearly an important element in the stratification of London society.

It is also noticeable that the *Apologie* did not made a social distinction between the citizenry and the unfree. This omission might well reflect the ubiquity of citizenship in London in the middle of the sixteenth century.[12] It might also reflect its general irrelevance to social stratification. Logic

[11] Finlay 1981: 79.   [12] Rappaport 1983: 109–14.

would suggest that membership of city companies and citizenship would serve to enhance individual power through company office and greater economic opportunities. However it is possible that some trades did not require company membership or citizenship for successful practice, and power and influence might be available in the parish or ward administration. in some provincial towns citizenship varied widely between different occupational groups.[13] Clearly we need to identify the role that citizenship played in Boroughside society. However, attaining the position of house-holder, essentially the first stage in gaining social power and responsibility, could be achieved outside the citizenry.

It is worth emphasising that pre-industrial urban society can be seen as an aggregate of households. Contemporaries were more or less agreed that households were the primary social unit and consequently addressed their moralistic advice specifically to them.[14] Householders were held to be responsible for the religious disciplining of those under their charge. 'A good and careful householder so ordereth and frameth his household, so as it may manifestly appear, that it is indeed the house of a faithful Christian, and that he himself is as a Pastor over his family, that he instructeth it in good and godly discipline, by a continual exercise in godliness.'[15] Between 1550 and 1600 around one hundred catechisms were published explicitly for household use and visitation articles were addressed specifically to household heads.[16] Householders were also responsible for the social disciplining and welfare of all family members including servants and apprentices.[17] In London only householders served in local office, received parish poor relief and paid local taxation.[18] What proportion of Southwark inhabitants ever reached even this lowly social position and how was the household affected by the possession of wealth?

For those apprenticed to a London company it is undeniable that length of service and subsequent attainment of the freedom of the city was an important factor governing age at marriage, and consequent attainment of the position of householder. Most men were forbidden to marry within the

[13] Pound 1981: 52–3.

[14] R. L. Greaves, *Society and religion in Elizabethan England*, Minneapolis, 1981, pp. 291–326; Felicity Heal, 'The idea of hospitality in early modern England', *Past and Present* 102(1984), 77; Palliser 1983: 61; Wrightson 1982: 68.   [15] Greaves 1981: 292.

[16] Greaves 1981: 295; Dingle 1974: passim; W. P. M. Kennedy, *Elizabethan Episcopal Administration*, Alcuin Club Collections 27, London, 1924, vol. 3, pp. 344–6; K. Thomas, *Religion and the Decline of Magic*, Harmondsworth, 1978, p. 190; W. Nicholson (ed.), *The Remains of Edward Grindal*, Parker Society, Cambridge, 1843, p. 169.

[17] Greaves 1981: 301–22; S. R. Smith, 'The ideal and the reality: apprentice-master relationships in seventeenth-century London', *History of Education Quarterly* 21(1981), 449–60; Lindley 1983: 120–1.

[18] Pearl 1979: 15–18; Dingle 1974: passim; J. Boulton, 'The social and economic structure of early seventeenth-century Southwark', Cambridge(1983), p. 226, n.16. For office-holding in London see also, Alice E. McCampbell, 'The London parish and the London precinct 1640–1660', *Guildhall Studies in London History* 2,3(1976), 107–24.

terms of an apprenticeship and the mean age at marriage of men married by licence in London (twenty-eight) is the same age at which they achieved the freedom of the city.[19] There are some problems with this seemingly simple link between length of apprenticeship and age on marriage. First it is known that, in the mid-sixteenth century, only 41.1% of apprentices actually completed their terms. Nearly half of all enrolled apprentices 'simply abandoned their training'; were they making unlawful marriages and setting up house in the capital and its suburbs? Secondly, in the mid-sixteenth century (before the rapid population growth of London), two-thirds of the adult male workforce were thought to have been freemen; are we to suppose that the remaining non-freemen remained unmarried, celibate and were part of other men's households? The point here is that although all freemen may (given survival) have become householders it does not follow that, therefore, all householders were freemen. This problem derives from a certain semantic confusion. Dr Pearl has pointed out that in the sixteenth century the term householder, strictly meaning a freeman of a company who had become a master, became synonymous with 'housekeeper' which is the householder in the modern sense.[20] Furthermore it should not be thought that age on marriage of London men was exceptionally high. Age at first marriage for male Londoners seems to have been slightly *lower* than that found in a national sample. In the early seventeenth century mean age at first marriage for London men was 27.6 years compared to 28.1 in a national sample.[21] Apprenticeship was, after all, only an institutionalized form of the service common in rural areas. As in rural areas it was the time needed to save up enough money to set up an independent household which was the crucial factor in determining age at marriage, and which delayed entry into that honourable estate both in the capital and in the countryside for, on average, a similar period.[22] There was certainly no automatic and universal transition from apprenticeship to marriage. Thomas Cullum remained as a paid employee within his master's household after his apprenticeship had expired.[23] At what age did individuals attain the position of householder in seventeenth-century Southwark?

The previous chapter described in essence how wealth flowed into Boroughside households. Household income was earned via skilled or unskilled labour, the profits of selling or dealing, the provision of services, from investment in property and from secured loans or charitable payments.

[19] Rappaport 1983: 118; Vivien B. Elliott, 'Single women in the London marriage market: age, status and mobility, 1598–1619', in R. B. Outhwaite (ed.), *Marriage and Society. Studies in the Social History of Marriage*, London, 1981, pp. 82–4.
[20] Pearl 1979: 15; Rappaport 1983: 117–19.
[21] E. A. Wrigley and R. S. Schofield, 'English population history from family reconstitution: summary results 1600–1799', *Population Studies* 37(1983), 162. See also Finlay 1981: 139.
[22] Flinn 1981: 28; Wrightson 1982: 68–70.   [23] Simpson 1958: 19–20.

Household wealth, as distinct from income, was of course not solely determined by household activities since it might have been supplemented from family inheritance. Furthermore accumulation of wealth depended on the outgoings or expenses of each household. This chapter looks at how wealth was distributed within Boroughside society and later chapters go on to look at how possession (or lack) of it affected the social status and power of the members of that society.

4.2 Taxation, wealth and poverty

To date the published work on London's wealth distribution has been beset by a number of shortcomings, some of which are common to studies of other pre-industrial towns and cities. The most basic of these is that the whole area of the metropolis is not covered by a single source. Hence Glass's pioneering work related only to the city parishes within and without the walls; approximately the same area was covered by the sources used by Finlay, Jones and Herlan.[24] Unfortunately, therefore, the distribution of wealth in peripheral and populous areas of the capital such as Westminster, Southwark, Stepney and Whitechapel has not been systematically examined for the seventeenth century.[25] More seriously most previous studies of the distribution of wealth in London have concentrated on the 'social articulation' of the capital i.e. the spatial distribution of wealth and poverty, rather than on the spread of wealth within individual parishes. Glass's study could only divide up the householders into those who paid surtax and those who did not.[26] Although such a method provides a relatively accurate measure of social articulation, it cannot detect the finer gradations in the distribution of wealth that must have occurred at the parish level and which no local study can afford to neglect. Only Finlay has looked beyond the geographical spread of wealth and has made an attempt to examine its social distribution. Finlay constructed a picture of social articulation similar to that of Glass but also went on to examine, 'the range of wealth in some parishes in greater detail'. His study of eight city parishes revealed in all that 'although there were wide variations between the wealthiest and poorest London inhabitants, there were many householders of middling wealth, neither rich nor poor, who lived in parishes between the centre and periphery'.[27] However, the distribution of wealth obtained by Finlay rests on the assumption that individuals occupying houses of low value were all

---

[24] See Glass 1966: ix–xxxviii; Finlay 1981: 77–82; E. Jones, 'London in the early seventeenth century: an ecological approach', *London Journal* 6, 2(1980), 123–33; R. W. Herlan, 'Social articulation and the configuration of parochial poverty in London on the eve of the Restoration', *Guildhall Studies in London History* 2, 2(1976), 43–53.

[25] For published work on eighteenth-century London which includes such areas see, Schwarz 1982: 167–85. See also Shearer 1981.

[26] Glass 1966: xx–xxv.   [27] Finlay 1981: 79–81.

in fact 'poor'. There is some evidence to suggest that, in Southwark and elsewhere, house values did not necessarily correspond closely to levels of wealth.[28] Unless sources for wealth distribution can be tested against other material supplying similar information there is a danger that the interpretation will be too subjective.

Valerie Pearl has recently chided the new school of urban historians for their philosophy of 'gloom and doom' and this same attitude could be said to colour their picture of urban wealth distribution.[29] Certain areas of common ground have emerged within this school. The distribution of wealth in pre-industrial towns was pyramidal with a small number of individuals owning most of the taxable wealth. Below this group was a somewhat larger number of 'comfortably-off' individuals and below this was the very broad base of the pyramid made up by the poor.[30] However, the actual size and nature of the 'poor base' may have been exaggerated by those writers who make the assumption that all non-taxpayers were 'poor' and that even those taxed below a certain level fall into the same category. In particular the work of Hoskins on the 1524–5 subsidy and his conclusion that 'fully two-thirds of the urban population in the 1520s lived below or very near the poverty line' has been especially influential.[31] Thus, using the 1524–5 subsidy assessment for Norwich, Pound, like MacCaffery in Exeter, found one-third of the population too poor to pay at even the lowest assessment. Adding this group to the lower tax brackets Pound reached the conclusion that 60% of the population were 'poor or very poor'. He went on to contrast his findings with the 1576 subsidy assessment and a poor rate assessment of the same date and found that some 40% of the householders paid the subsidy, 20% only the poor rate and 40% nothing at all. Those householders paying only the poor rate or nothing were among those identified by Pound as comprising the 'poor or very poor' group discovered in 1524–5.[32]

Recently, however, Phythian-Adams has questioned previous interpretations of the distribution of wealth as shown by the 1524–5 assessments, noting that, 'the truly vulnerable layer of society...was very much smaller than has been normally assumed'.[33] Given such reservations it is vital that when reconstructing the distribution of wealth in the Boroughside from

[28] In Southwark a few wealthy individuals can be shown to have occupied houses similar in value to those occupied by people of substantially lesser means, Boulton 1983: 107, n.6. For the view that 'houses...are imperfect indicators of the wealth of their inhabitants', see Power 1978a: 33.

[29] Pearl 1979: 3.

[30] For the distribution of wealth in pre-industrial urban society see, Dyer 1973: 157–88; Clark and Slack 1976: 111–25; Palliser 1979: 134–44; Pound 1976: 129–47; W. T. MacCaffrey, *Exeter 1540–1640*, London, 1975, pp. 246–51; W. G. Hoskins, 'English provincial towns in the early sixteenth century', in P. Clark (ed.), *The Early Modern Town*, London, 1976, pp. 91–105.

[31] Hoskins 1976a: 101.   [32] Pound 1976: 132; MacCaffrey 1975: 249

[33] C. Phythian-Adams, K. Wilson and P. Clark, *The Fabric of the Traditional Community*, Milton Keynes, 1977, p. 34.

taxation assessments, the researcher should use other historical material to clarify the picture so produced.

Unfortunately, the standard sources commonly used by urban historians for reconstructing wealth distribution are not available for this period. Both the 1524–5 lay subsidy and the later seventeenth-century hearth tax assessments are incomplete and the 1695 Marriage Duty Act returns have not survived. The 1638 listing of rents and tithes did not extend to Bridge Ward Without.[34]

However, it is still possible to construct a picture of the relative distribution of wealth in the Boroughside by using the 1622 subsidy assessment and a surviving assessment for the poor rate for the years 1621–2. Both the subsidy assessment and the poor rate assessment were then linked to the householders listed in the 1622 sacramental token book for the Boroughside. In this way it was possible to look at a known population at one particular point in time.[35] It should be noted that the distribution of wealth so obtained may slightly understate the number of taxpayers in the Boroughside since the taxation assessments and the listing of householders were not compiled at exactly the same time. The poor-rate assessment was compiled in April 1621 and updated throughout that year. Consequently a small number of newcomers were added to the assessment but not allocated a specific rating; these have been classed as poor-rate payers (see Table 4.4). Similarly the 1622 subsidy assessment listed a number of individuals who arrived in the Boroughside after the 1622 token book had been compiled (in March of that year). Such drawbacks did not significantly affect the overall picture of the distribution of wealth. Five widows whose recently deceased husbands had been assessed for the poor rate were arbitrarily classified as poor-rate payers. Since assessments were often reduced or (occasionally) abolished their inclusion may not be fully justified.

Contemporaries, like most historians, knew that by the seventeenth century the subsidy assessment bore no relation to the *actual* wealth of the individual assessed. Underassessment, evasion and negligence were all cited in 1606 as a cause of the devaluing of the subsidies. The assessors it was claimed 'are contented to omit oftentimes persons of the best ability and do not present their names...If they do present them yet do they

34 For the 1524–5 lay subsidy see P.R.O. E179/184/154, 145, 173 and also J. Sheail, 'The regional distribution of wealth in England as indicated in the lay subsidy returns of 1524–5', London (1968) pp. 323–8. The hearth tax returns for Southwark do not include householders exempted from assessment. Those of 1664 are damaged. See, for example, P.R.O. E179/188/481, E179/258/7. For the 1638 tithe listing and the 1695 Marriage Duty Act returns see, T. C. Dale (ed.), *The Inhabitants of London in 1638*, London, 1931, p. iv; Glass 1966: ix–xlii.
35 For the 1622 subsidy assessment see, P.R.O. E179/186/407. For the 1621–2 assessment and the 1622 token book see, G.L.R.O. P92/SAV/1400, 211.

undervaluably tax them.'[36] Nonetheless in St Saviour's the subsidies do provide a means of identifying the *wealthiest* members in that locality. As we shall see contribution to that tax itself qualified the person assessed to a particular social and economic standing which was recognised in the parish.

There is good reason to think that the weekly poor-rate assessments were more sensitive to individual financial circumstances than those of the subsidy. The amount of assessment was not linked solely to a particular house in early seventeenth-century London.[37] Many householders' assessments were altered even though they remained in the same dwelling. Since the assessors were local parish officials they must have been aware of the ability of each individual to pay. Even apparently small alterations in individual assessments probably represent genuine changes. A dispute that arose over the assessment of one Widow Payne, which involved only one half penny a week, the lowest category of assessment, reached Star Chamber in 1613.[38] During the same case the voluntary element involved in each individual assessment was described in the case of one Widow Angell. Richard Wright, grocer, the Overseer of the Poor in 1613,

received directions from the churchwardens and others of the said parish to take notice of any new dwellers come into the said parish since the last taxation, and to gather of them what they would willingly and voluntarily contribute...and thereupon he went to the house of the said widow Angell which she had converted and used as an alehouse, and moved her what she would be contented to pay towards the relief of the poor and she voluntarily agreed to pay half a penny a week for so much she said she had paid where she dwelleth before...and thereupon this defendant entered her name into his book for the poor.

As with the subsidy so with the poor rate, contribution to such tax helped to build up local credit.

Local and more regular assessments taken for pressing local needs were not only more sensitive to levels of wealth than the subsidy rolls but also penetrated further down the social scale. In 1601 the vestry

agreed that the collectors constables and Overseers for the poor and the churchwardens shall first make collections within the parish of such as are no subsidy men and able to make payment to the Collection for a house of correction...And the residue which cannot be gathered of them to be gathered of the subsidy men according as they shall find the same will arise by the subsidy book upon the pound.[39]

Subsidy men were thus not the only inhabitants capable of paying tax. In 1609 an official in the Clink noted that the charge of the poor 'is chiefly

---

[36] See, 'Notes for taxations of subsidy in London', P.R.O. SP14/23.29. For a useful discussion of the subsidy assessment see, Kerby 1983: 109–29.

[37] Pearl 1981: 124–5.   [38] P.R.O. STAC 8/228/8.

[39] G.L.R.O. P92/SAV/450, 11 August 1601.

born by the subsidy men, with the help of some few others'. In 1599 the vestrymen of St Saviour's decided 'to gather money from subsidy men for soldiers. And shall gather also so much money of others that be no subsidy men as they can.'[40] What light does a systematic analysis shed on the range and sensitivity of local and national taxation assessments?

A comparison between the levels of assessment of subsidy men and poor-rate payers demonstrates that subsidy men were indeed the wealthiest group in Boroughside society and that they normally bore the brunt of taxation (see Table 4.2). With only two exceptions all householders assessed for the subsidy were also assessed for the poor rate. More significant is the fact that subsidy payers were drawn from the highest levels of poor rate assessments. Few of those paying 1d. per week and none of those paying ½d. were subsidy men. Subsidy men dominated the highest categories of poor-rate payers, 92% of all those householders ranked at 3d. or more were subsidy men as were 77% of those rated at 2d. Table 4.2 also supplies some evidence that the levels of subsidy assessment *did* broadly correspond to levels of wealth. Hence those in the lowest £3 category were assessed at a mean value of 1.9d., those in the £4 group at 3.0d., the £5 category at 3.9d., the £6 at 5.1d., the £7 at 4.0d., the £8 at 6.7d. and the £10 and £15 at 7.0d. However, subsidy assessments were less sensitive indicators of relative wealth. Each level of subsidy assessment was not related exactly to one corresponding poor-rate assessment but contained a range of values which overlapped between different categories. Thus most (92%) of the £3 men were assessed at between 1d. and 3d. with 32 (50·8%) at 2d. £4 men were rated mostly between 2d and 4d, 49% actually at the mean value of 3d. The foregoing does supply some encouraging evidence that levels of taxation assessment can be made to give a reasonable picture of the *relative* distribution of wealth at the top end of the wealth range.[41]

The taxation assessments reveal the familiar pyramidal distribution of wealth (see Tables 4.3, 4.4, 4.5). Only 148 households or 15.5% of all those resident in the Boroughside in 1622 were assessed for the 1622 subsidy. Within this group only thirty-four (3.6%) were assessed on goods worth £5 or more. The poor-rate assessments for 1621–2 and 1631 show a similar picture but reveal that the hierarchy of taxable wealth reached lower in the social scale than the numbers assessed in the subsidy would indicate. In 1621–2, 30.7% of householders were assessed to contribute weekly sums ranging from ½d. to more than 6d. Again few were assessed at the highest

[40] See, R. A. Foakes (ed.), *The Henslowe Papers*, London, 1977, vol. 2, p. 47; G.L.R.O. P92/SAV/450, 1 January 1599.

[41] For the value of the later sixteenth- and early seventeenth-century subsidy assessments in this respect see, Palliser 1979: 139–40; Kerby 1983: 19–22, 81–3, 144–5, 168; W. G. Hoskins, *Exeter in the Seventeenth Century: Tax and Rate Assessments 1602–1699*, Devon and Cornwall Record Society, 1957, n.s., 2, pp. xiii–xiv.

Table 4.2. *Comparison of subsidy assessment and poor-rate assessment in the Boroughside 1621–2*

Level of subsidy	Poor-rate assessment (pence per week)											
	0	Assessed	$\frac{1}{2}$	1	$1\frac{1}{2}$	2	3	4	5	6	+7	Total
£												
15											1	1
10											5	5
8										1	2	3
7								1				1
6							1	1	5	4		11
5		1					2	7	2	1		13
4	1					11	25	13		1		51
3	1	2		10	6	32	10	2				63
0	662	7	46	70	5	13	2	3	1	0	1	810
Total	664	10	46	80	11	56	40	27	8	7	9	958

Note: See notes to Tables 4.3 and 4.4.
Source: See discussion in text, pp. 106–8.

Table 4.3. *Distribution of wealth in the Boroughside from subsidy assessment 1622*

Amount of assessment	Number of households assessed[a]	Percentage of total households
£		
15	1	0.1
10	5[b]	0.5
8	3	0.3
7	1	0.1
6	11	1.2
5	13	1.4
4	51	5.3
3	63	6.6
0	810	84.6
Total	958	

Notes: [a] This column excludes five persons, members of extended households, who were assessed in addition to the household head. One person was assessed at £8, one at £6, one at £3 and two at £4.
[b] Includes one Commissioner of the subsidy whose actual assessment was not listed. Commissioners were normally rated at high levels.
Source: See discussion in text, p. 106.

levels – only twenty-four were assessed at 5d. per week or more, while 137 out of 294 (46.6%) were assessed at less than 2d. This latter distribution of wealth changed little over time. In 1631 some 32.5% of households were assessed, only twenty-five (2.6%) at 5d. or more and with 48.1% of all poor-rate payers assessed at sums of less than 2d. per week. Some 67.5–69.3% of all Boroughside households were not assessed for the poor rate at all.

It is clearly necessary to test the relative distribution of wealth that emerges from the analysis of taxation documents against independent sources. Are we to say that, following Pound, households who were assessed only for the poor rate, and not the subsidy, should be thought of as poor? Are those households unable to pay even the lowest category of poor rate the 'very poor'? We need independent evidence of the relative wealth of Boroughside householders.

Phythian-Adams used the keeping of servants as an independent measure of wealth in early sixteenth-century Coventry.[42] The same criterion can be

[42] Phythian-Adams *et al.* 1977: 34; Phythian-Adams 1979: 205–7.

Table 4.4. *Distribution of wealth in the Boroughside from poor rate assessment 1621–2*

Weekly assessment in pence per week	Number of households assessed[a]	Percentage of total households
+7d.	9	0.9
6d.	7	0.7
5d.	8	0.8
4d.	27	2.8
3d.	40	4.2
2d.	56	5.9
1½d.	11	1.2
1d.	80	8.4
½d.	46	4.8
Assessed amount not listed	10	1.0
0d.	664	69.3
Total	958	

Note: [a] Excluding four persons, members of extended households, who were assessed in addition to the household head. One was assessed at 5d., two at 2d. and one at a halfpenny.
Source: See discussion in text, p. 106.

used to test the wealth distribution in the Boroughside. Accordingly, the households listed in the 1622 token book as containing servants were matched to the 1621–2 poor-rate assessment (see Table 4.6). The numbers of households containing servants should be seen as minimum figures since the 1622 token book only lists those persons of communicable age. As has been noted elsewhere the employment of servants was clearly related to levels of wealth.[43] The higher the level of assessment the more likely a household would contain one or more servants. The substantial proportions of those households in the lower levels of assessment that contained servants indicates a certain level of prosperity and suggests that, contrary to Pound's interpretation, payers of the poor rate were not 'the poor'. It is also interesting that 12.7% of the non-rated households contained servants which suggests that poverty may not necessarily have been the lot of all such households.

An inventory of the household goods of a poor-rate payer reinforces the impression that this group was comfortably off. John Coleman, citizen and tallowchandler and a salter by trade, paid one penny to the poor rate in 1621–2 but did not contribute to the 1622 subsidy. He lived with his wife

[43] Servants, and household structure are treated in detail in the following chapter.

Table 4.5. *Distribution of wealth in the Boroughside from poor rate*
assessment 1631

Weekly assessment	Number of households assessed	Percentage of total households
+ 7d.	7	0.7
6d.	6	0.6
5d.	12[a]	1.2
4d.	19	2.0
3d.	46	4.8
2d.	73	7.6
1½d.	2	0.2
1d.	102	10.6
½d.	47	4.9
0d.	652	67.5
Total	966	

Note: [a] Includes one wealthy innkeeper, assessed at £5 in the 1629 subsidy, but omitted in the 1631 assessment, arbitrarily allocated a 5d. assessment.
Source: G.L.R.O. P92/SAV/219.

and two daughters on the east side of the High Street next to the White Hart Inn and kept one servant of communicable age, Giles. Coleman married in 1617 in St Saviour's Parish Church and died in the 1625 plague epidemic. His will reveals that he possessed 'land in East Grinstead held of deed dated from Queen Elizabeth's reign' which probably indicates his family origins. Apart from a 20s. bequest to the poor and 80s. in memorial rings, all his estate was left to his wife and children. The inventory of his household goods was made after the death of his wife in 1631.[44] Coleman's household goods were valued at £30 4s. Among these were pewter to the value of £3 19s. 2d. and two brass pots in the kitchen. Coleman's furniture consisted of, among other things, 'a drawing table, 6 joined stools, 6 cushioned stools', three standing bedsteads, three featherbeds and what has been described as 'an element of sophistication', a warming pan.[45] In the garret of his house was a 'man's gown to the value of 40 shillings'. If Coleman's case is any guide it would seem to be strong evidence that contribution to the poor rate indicated a reasonably comfortable standard of living. Unfortunately no other comparable inventories survive for the inhabitants of the Boroughside before 1660, but other independent measures of wealth can be used

[44] G.L.R.O. P92/SAV/817. For Coleman's will see P.C.C. Will Register 93 Clarke.
[45] Wrightson and Levine 1979: 38.

Table 4.6. *Poor-rate assessments of servant-keeping households 1622*

Weekly assessment	Number of households	Households with servants	Percentage
7d.	9	9	100
6d.	7	7	100
5d.	8	8	100
4d.	27	26	96.3
3d.	40	37	92.5
2d.	56	44	78.6
1½d.	11	9	81.8
1d.	80	49	61.3
½d.	46	17	37.0
Assessed amount unknown	10	7	70.0
Nil	664	84	12.7
Total	958	297	31.0

Source: See discussion in text, p. 111.

to test the validity of the distribution of wealth derived from the taxation assessments.[46]

The cost of burial was a fairly reliable test of individual economic standing. Burial duties are particularly likely to be a good test of relative wealth since individuals were given a burial commensurate with their local social standing.[47] 'Paupers' were buried at parish expense and hence rated 'nihil' in the parish clerk's notebook.[48] In 1623 the vestry granted the clerk an extra allowance 'for burials of poor people which leave not wherewith to pay for their burials'.[49] Above paupers were those individuals who left only enough money to pay for 'ground', normally 8d. for an adult. Above these were those persons who incurred extra charges for 'bell' and 'cloth'. Hence the family of Edward Harrison, not rated in the year of his death 1622, was charged 3s. 8d. for the cost of his burial: 1s. for ground, 8d. for

[46] An inventory of the goods of the parish clerk, who was exempt from assessment, was made in 1625; two inventories for College almswomen also survive, G.L.R.O. P92/SAV/815, 816, 1960. Inventories of the goods of a few Boroughside householders resident in 1622 but who died after 1660 can be found, listed by name only, in the P.R.O. See, for example, PRO B4/5184,1414.

[47] Sampson Cuthbert, sailor, in his will stated in 1624 that his burial should 'be such as becometh a christian man of my degree and calling', P.C.C. Will Register 124 Hele. For other references to the social distinctions in burial costs see, Marshall 1977: 32–5; Rendle 1878: 198–9, 225; C. Hill, *The Economic Problems of the Church*, London, 1971, pp. 168–9.

[48] G.L.R.O. P92/SAV/406.

[49] G.L.R.O. P92/SAV/450, 28 April 1623. In the aftermath of the 1625 plague the gravemaker complained that he 'was out of purse eleven pounds and fifteen shillings...considering the great abundance of the poor we then buried without any church duties', G.L.R.O. P92/SAV/782.

Table 4.7. *Burial expenses incurred by Boroughside householders 1622–4*

Cost of burial	Subsidy payers	Poor-rate payers	Not assessed	Total
20s. + (in the church)	9	4	1	14
5s.–10s.	5	3	3	11
3s.–5s.	1	7	15	23
1s.–3s.	—	2	17	19
4d.–1s.	—	—	9	9
Nothing (paupers)	—	—	21	21
Total	15	16	66	97

Source: See discussion in text, pp. 113–14.

cloth and 2s. for bells to be rung at his funeral. The wealthiest individuals opted for interment 'in the church' which cost a minimum of £1. The most expensive burials recorded for Boroughside inhabitants were incurred by two vestrymen and a wealthy widow who were interred 'in the Southquire' at a cost of £1 7s. 8d. each. It should be noted that the total cost of a burial was not fully recorded in the parish clerk's notebook. For example a bill for the interment of Richard Bird, vintner, in 1626 reveals that in addition to paying 10s. 2d. for ground, cloth and bell, his family was also liable to pay 3s. to the 'minister, clerk and sexton', 1s. 4d. to the bearers and 8d. to the gravemaker.[50] The burial duties paid by ninety-seven householders resident in 1622, who died between 1622 and 1624, have been compared to their 1621–2 poor-rate assessments (see Table 4.7).

The distribution of burial duties largely confirms the distribution of wealth obtained from the subsidy and poor-rate assessments. Of the fourteen householders buried in the church nine were subsidy payers and four poor-rate payers. The table also shows that there was some overlap in relative wealth between the three groups and underlines the existence of an economically self-sufficient group outside the rate-paying householders. Fifty-four per cent of all the householders not assessed in 1622 were still able to pay 1s. or more towards the cost of their burial. Only twenty-one householders were buried at parish expense. Clearly 'the poor' were not equivalent to 'non-rated' householders.

It seems likely, then, that the taxation assessments discussed above identify the wealthiest groups of householders but omit a substantial number of householders who possessed what may be termed 'adequate' income,

[50] G.L.R.O. P92/SAV/61

Table 4.8. *Summary of the distribution of wealth of households in the Boroughside, 1622*

Classification			
'Surplus income'	I Assessed for both subsidy and poor rate[a]		15.5%
	II Assessed for poor rate only		15.5%
'Adequate income'	III Households able to pay for own burial and occasionally keep servants		43%
'The poor'	IV Unemployed and sick	buried at	18.6%
	V Pensioners	parish expense	7.4%

Note: [a] Includes two householders assessed for the subsidy but not for the poor rate.
Source: See discussion in text, pp. 113–16 and Table 4.2.

being occasionally able to maintain servants and to leave something for their burial. We can put a figure to the number of households whose income was inadequate if we assume that individuals identified as 'poor' were equivalent to those whom the author of the *Apologie* described as those 'who have need that it were given unto them'. The 1618 survey of the poor listed 232 households as poor, 26% of the total number in 1618. This figure bears a significant similarity to the 21.7% unable to pay for their own burials. A similar percentage (26.8%) of households in the Clink liberty were, in 1609, described as 'very [poor] people widows and others, all being ready to take, and not one of them fit to give, of which number many do now receive relief of weekly pension…'[51] As noted in the previous chapter only about half of the Boroughside poor commonly received either a weekly pension or less regular payment. The proportion of pensioners in the population (7.4%) was only slightly higher than that found elsewhere in London and in other towns and cities in pre-industrial England.[52]

A 'middling' group of householders emerges from this analysis, not possessed of enough surplus income to contribute to local taxation but earning enough to maintain their families without assistance in normal years. This middling group has been identified in other studies. In Warwick in 1582, 44% of householders were said to be able to maintain themselves but unable to relieve others.[53] If, using the evidence of the 1618 survey, it is assumed that 26% of Boroughside householders were 'poor' in 1622 then that would imply that 413 householders (43%), were below the rate-paying category but above the poor. The existence of this middling group helps to explain

[51] Foakes 1977: 2, 47. For the 1618 survey see, G.L.R.O. P92/SAV/1465.
[52] See, Herlan 1977a: 32; Pearl 1981: 125; Slack 1972: 176.
[53] See Beier, 1981:58–9. See also, Finlay 1981:79–80; R. M. Smith, 'Fertility, economy and household formation in England over three centuries', *Population and Development Review* 7, 4(1981), 608.

Table 4.9. *Proportions of poor-rate paying householders in three London parishes and in the Boroughside*

		Percentage of householders paying poor rate
St Bartholomew by the Exchange	1638[a]	78.4%
St Margaret, Lothbury	1624[b]	67.0%
St Bride, Fleet Street	1687[c]	50.0%
Boroughside, Southwark	1622[d]	30.7%

Sources: [a] E. Freshfield (ed.), *The Vestry Minute Book of the Parish of St Bartholomew by the Exchange in the City of London 1567–1676*, London, 1890, pp. 132–3.
[b] E. Freshfield (ed.), *The Vestry Minute Book of the parish of St Margaret Lothbury in the City of London 1571–1677*, London, 1887, pp. 55–6.
[c] Pearl 1979: 33, n. 42.
[d] See Table 4.4.

how vigorously applied taxation might catch larger numbers of house-holders. The 1643 parliamentary tax caught 43% of all Boroughside householders.[54] In crisis years, such as plague outbreaks, members of this economically self-sufficient group might be pressed below the poverty line.[55] The distribution of wealth in the Boroughside has been summarised in Table 4.8.

It is difficult to compare the distribution of wealth in the Boroughside with other areas of London since there have been no studies based on proportions of subsidy and poor-rate payers. The simple proportions of poor-rate payers can be calculated for three London parishes (see Table 4.9). Clearly the Boroughside was relatively poor compared to the wealthy parish of St Bartholomew by the Exchange and the 'socially mixed' parish of St Margaret Lothbury. It may even have been ranked somewhere below the extra-mural parish of St Bride, Fleet Street.

Although the Boroughside may have been a relatively poor part of seventeenth-century London it clearly contained individuals of some substance. Since the occupations of many of these have been recovered it should be possible to determine how what wealth there was in the Boroughside was spread among the trades and craftsmen of the district.

In order to look at the distribution of wealth within the occupational structure, each occupation was ranked according to the average contribution of its practitioners to the poor rate (see Table 4.10). The ranking of occupations by wealth that is thus produced is easily criticised. Local officials,

[54] See P.R.O. E179/257/22.
[55] For this process see Beier 1981: 58–9; Slack 1972: 168–78; Pound 1971a: 25–6.

Table 4.10. *Occupations ranked by wealth in the Boroughside 1622*

	Average weekly contribution to the poor rate 1622	Occupation[a]
I	3d. or more	'Brasell seller', Grocer, Goldsmith, Gentleman, 'Horse courser', Innholder, Pewterer, Soapboiler, Tallowchandler, Vintner.
	2½d.–3d.	Merchant-tailor, Government official
II	2d.–2½d.	Dyer, Linendraper, Potter, Saddler, Upholsterer, Ironmonger.
	1½d.–2d.	Attorney, Baker, Brewer, Barber-surgeon, Cheesemonger, Glazier, Starchmaker, Woodmonger, Woollendraper, Saltpetremaker.
III	1d.–1½d.	Butcher, Chandler, Distiller, Salter Scrivener, Turner, Victualler, Haberdasher.
	½d.–1d.	Apothecary, Bricklayer, Cook, Husbandman, Hosier, Hempbeater, Huckster, Joiner, Mason, Sheergrinder, Spectaclemaker, Stationer, 'Sauceman', Tobaccoseller, Yeoman
IV	Less than ½d.	Basketmaker, Bellowsmaker, Barber, Brewer's servant, Barrowman, Boddicemaker, Cutler, Cooper, Carpenter, Collier, Carman, Carrier, Carter, Currier, Clothworker, Dicemaker, Dyer's servant, Fishmonger, Falconer, Feltmaker, Fruiterer, Fustiandresser, Glover, Gardener, Guilder, Girdler, Gunmaker, Grinder, Hackneyman, Embroiderer, Inkseller, Labourer, Leatherdresser, Locksmith, Mousetrapseller, Musician, Ostler, Porter, Painter, Plumber, Pedlar, Pinner, Poulterer, Plasterer, Local official, Ropemaker, Weaver, Schoolmaster, Smith, Shoemaker, Sawyer, Sailor, Soapboiler's servant, Servingman, Shipwright, Tailor, Threddier, Tinker, Tapster, Tapeweaver, Usher, Waterman, Whitster.

Note: [a] For the number of householders in each occupation group, see above Chapter 3.
Source: See discussion in text, pp. 116–18.

such as the parish clerk, the schoolmaster and the usher of the local school, were exempt from assessment and a few individuals such as attorneys and government officials may not have been permanently resident. More seriously, the numbers involved in each occupation are often very small, giving rise to the risk of some distortion. Occupational categories often contained a wide range of wealth. Hence the bakers, ranked at level II, included both John Marshall, who contributed 40s. per year to the poor rate and one Derrick Langton who made no contribution at all. The table does however indicate that wealth was not distributed evenly among all occupational groups. Hence, for example, the total weekly contribution to the poor rate of *seven* innholders was slightly more than that of *seventy-eight* tailors and weavers (20.8d. and 19.3d. respectively). Moreover the numbers involved in any one occupational category bore little relation to the relative financial standing of its practitioners. The clothing, textile, and leather categories which employed some 29.3% of all the households in the Boroughside were clearly humble ones. For example, 65% of all those involved in the leather industry were shoemakers, 85% of those in clothing were tailors, and 63% of those in textiles were weavers. Those in the lowest levels of wealth distribution in the Boroughside tended to be craftsmen, manual labourers, and minor retailers such as pedlars and fruiterers. In contrast the upper echelons were filled with luxury retailers such as grocers, relatively large-scale manufacturers, such as dyers and soapboilers, highly skilled craftsmen, such as goldsmiths, or else they were innholders and professional men.

This ranking of trades suggests that the social stratification put forward by the author of the *Apologie* had some basis in reality in this suburb of early seventeenth-century London. Manual labourers, 'porters, watermen and carmen' were indeed in the lowest social and economic category. The high economic standing of wealthy retailers such as grocers, vintners and cheesemongers was also borne out. Handicrafts men or craftsmen said to be in 'the intermediate place' by the *Apologie* tended to occupy the lowest economic echelons but some were also found in higher groups. Potters found their way into a high ranking and turners, bricklayers, joiners and masons exhibited modest wealth. The importance of wealthy manufacturers, such as soapboilers, dyers and brewers, in Boroughside society was a feature not described in the *Apologie*. Such manufacturers may have been concentrated in the suburbs of the capital so that the author of the *Apologie*, more concerned perhaps with the social order in the city proper, overlooked them.

Although this ranking of occupations by wealth may be a useful *general* social classification it cannot be used to predict any particular individual's social and economic position with certainty. Each occupational label comprised a wide range of wealth, providing little clue to the position of members within any particular group. Thus the social position of James Todcastle, glover, here a craft ranked at level IV, living with his wife in an alley off the High Street and never assessed for any type of taxation is hardly comparable to that of Robert Buckland, also a glover, who lived on a thoroughfare with a wife and three servants, contributed 20s. per year to the poor rate, paid on £5 in the 1622 subsidy and had been a vestryman since 1613. Occupations, it would seem, in themselves carried no significant social prestige and were only more or less effective means of gaining wealth.[56]

Moreover so far as one can tell from the evidence discussed above wealth appears to have been distributed unequally among Boroughside households. Wealth, as we have seen, was associated with household structure; for example the wealthier the household the more frequently it contained servants. We now need to examine the size and structure of the Boroughside households. Was the association between wealth and household structure a simple one, as described above? Or were the poorer households, in addition to the burdens of underemployment, attempting to support large numbers of children? And what was the familial experience of female householders?

[56] Robert Buckland went on to endow three parish charities in St Saviour's, *Accounts and Papers 16* 1898: LXVII, 553–4.

5

Household structure and the household economy

Hitherto all that is known about household structure in Tudor and Stuart London derives from the evidence provided by the Marriage Duty Act returns of 1695.[1] Evidence from the Boroughside can be used to look for the first time at household structure in a part of London before this date.

It is possible, using the 1622 Boroughside token book, the 1618 survey of the poor and the 1631 population count to look at household size and structure in the area in the early seventeenth century. The 1622 token book lists each household, supplying the name and surname of the household head and their marital status (defined by the Latin *et uxor*). Following standard procedure the household head is taken to be the person listed first in each household entry.[2] Servants are identified by christian name and usually labelled as such. (In some of the larger households some servants were occasionally represented by dots when their names were not known.) Inmates and lodgers are identified by christian name and surname but are not usually labelled. Consequently some of these may, in fact, have been unlabelled servants. Children related to the household head are denoted as 'fil'. It was possible to identify some individuals as offspring or servants from other sources, notably wills and the parish register. The 1622 entry for Ralph Babington, vintner, is set out as follows:[3]

13.14	Ralph Babington *et ux[or]*
15.	Tho:fil
16.17	Barbara.Ellen ⎫
18.19	Prudence.Nicholas ⎬ Svts
20.21.	Robert.Christopher ⎭

---

[1] See, Glass 1966: ix-xlii; Jones and Judges 1935: 45–63; Wall 1979: 89–113.

[2] See, P. Laslett, 'The history of the family', in P. Laslett (ed.), *Household and Family in Past Time*, Cambridge, 1972, p. 86.

[3] For the token book, survey of the poor and 1631 population count used in the following analysis see, G.L.R.O. P92/SAV/211, 1465, 219 respectively.

120

The token book can be used to look at the household membership of all those over communicable age.[4] The 1618 survey listed poor households by street. All entries are of the form 'Richard Gosse, with his wife, plus 2 children'. The survey allows us therefore to look at the household structure of those considered, on some unknown criteria, to be the poorest inhabitants. The 1631 population count supplies material on the sex of the head of each household, its size and its poor-rate assessment. Wealth data is also available for the 1622 listing.[5]

In addition to the shortcomings of each listing the sources cover three different points in time. Consequently it has been assumed that the aspects of household structure discovered were not products of some unique demographic or economic crisis. How far, for example, was the 1631 population's household size and structure affected by the 1625 plague that killed something like 26% of the total population of the parish?[6] The effects of mortality crises, however, were part of the experience of living in the capital. Few generations before 1670 would not have experienced at least one major epidemic. Furthermore the rapid recovery in population that characteristically followed epidemics would also eliminate excessive distortion. Certainly the proportion of widows and single females heading households rose only slightly between 1622 (14.1%) and 1631 (15.6%).

The size of a household is determined partly by demographic factors outside the scope of this study. A number of studies have revealed or referred to the importance of mortality and fertility rates in determining household size.[7] Other significant determinants, however (such as the age at which children left home, chances of remarriage, the presence of servants) would be influenced by social customs that reacted to the harsh realities of household finances.

In the seventeenth century, and particularly among the poorer sections of society, the biggest single item of household expenditure was the provision of food. It has been estimated that in the late seventeenth century a poor family of five in the Essex village of Terling would have spent something like 76% of the household income on food alone. Joan Thirsk has recently put that proportion as high as 80%.[8] Clothing, too, was an

---

4 See above Chapter 2.   5 For the background to this count see above, Chapter 2.
6 The parish register reveals that something like 2370 persons died in the 1625 epidemic in St Saviour's. With a population of about 9200 in 1624 this represents a death rate of 25.8%. The figures given by Finlay suggest a rate of between 22.2% and 25.9% in London in this epidemic, Finlay 1981: 118. For plague in Southwark, see above Chapter 2.
7 See, for example, T. K. Burch, 'Some demographic determinants of average household size: an analytic approach', in P. Laslett (ed.), *Household and Family in Past Time*, Cambridge, 1972, pp. 91–102; Wall 1982: 493–512; Wall 1979: 90–3; R. Wall, 'The age at leaving home', *Journal of Family History* 3 (1978), 181–5.
8 Wrightson and Levine 1979: 40; Joan Thirsk, 'The horticultural revolution: a cautionary note on prices', *Journal of Interdisciplinary History* 14, 2 (1983), 300.

important item in the household budget. In Terling a further 14.6% was spent on the latter. Within wealthier households food was a proportionally less important item in the total household expenditure but was nonetheless a considerable burden. Between 1632 and 1641 'diet' formed on average 43% of the 'expenses' of Thomas Cullum, a wealthy London draper. Similarly, a London bakery was estimated (by the Whitebakers' company in 1619) to spend 38% of its total weekly outgoings on food. Clothing or 'apparell' cost Cullum another 11.3% a year.[9] The importance of these simple facts about household finances lies in the colour and weight they lend to statistics of household size since it might be expected that the number of persons in a household will be determined partly by the cost of their maintenance as measured by expenditure on food and clothing. Other major items of household expenditure such as fuel must have been less responsive to alterations in family size.

Wages for household servants, on top of their full board and lodging, were additional burdens on the finances of their employers. Thomas Cullum spent 9.5% of his expenses on this item in the 1630s. Hiring a female servant cost Edward Alleyn 6*d*. a week in 1618. Wages for servants occasionally concerned Boroughside testators. John Marshall, the baker keeping nine adult servants in 1622, in 1625 bequeathed that 'to all my menservants and womenservants that shall dwell with me at the time of my decease and perform obedient service to my Executrix, three months after my decease ...for their wages 40*s*. each'.[10]

The cost of maintaining family members must have been offset by their earning potential. As has been noted above, quite young children were capable of earning. Furthermore master craftsmen charged employers for the labour of their workmen.[11] Servants and apprentices were also needed to run businesses and serve in shops. They were an integral part of large labour-intensive manufacturing concerns like brewing and soapmaking and, much in the manner of those servants not resident in the employer's household, acted as ostlers, tapsters and chambermaids in the Boroughside inns. Domestic servants might be required to help run large houses or to act as status symbols. It might be useful to think of household size as the solution to a crude equation: the balance struck between the cost of maintaining an individual and the economic and social advantages of his or her presence to that household.

The 1631 survey reveals that the mean household size in the Boroughside was small, 3.8 (see Table 5.1.). This appears to have been typical of other

[9] See, Simpson 1958: 25; Young 1889: 2, 77; Cook 1981: 234–6.
[10] Simpson 1958: 25; Young 1889:2, 77. For Marshall's will see P.C.C. Will Register, 83 Clarke.
[11] For example of this see, Woodward 1981: 32–4, and for St Saviour's, G.L.R.O. P92/SAV/81, 82, 83, 1585, 682, 692.

Table 5.1. *Percentage distribution of households by size 1618 and 1631*

Household size	1618 survey of poor		1631 households not assessed for poor rate		1631 households assessed for poor rate		Total households 1631	
	N	%	N	%	N	%	N	%
1	46	19.8	86	13.2	7	2.2	93	9.6
2	45	19.4	173	26.5	19	6.1	192	19.9
3	42	18.1	157	24.1	60	19.1	217	22.5
4	45	19.4	119	18.3	58	18.5	177	18.3
5	30	12.9	62	9.5	55	17.5	117	12.1
6	15	6.5	29	4.5	35	11.2	64	6.6
7	8	3.5	15	2.3	33	10.5	48	5.0
8	1	0.4	8	1.2	17	5.4	25	2.6
9			1	0.2	12	3.8	13	1.4
10			1	0.2	7	2.2	8	0.8
11			1	0.2	4	1.3	5	0.5
13					2	0.6	2	0.2
16					2	0.6	2	0.2
17					1	0.3	1	0.1
19					1	0.3	1	0.1
21					1	0.3	1	0.1
Total	232		652		314		966	
Mean household size		3.2		3.2		5.2		3.8

Source: 1618 survey of poor households and 1631 token book. G.L.R.O P92/SAV/1465 and 219.

pre-industrial urban communities such as Coventry in 1523 (where mean household size was 3.7), early seventeenth-century Cambridge (4.1) and late seventeenth-century Southampton (3.8) and slightly larger than that found in the suburbs of Canterbury in 1563 (3.4). In rural England households were commonly slightly larger than in urban centres. A national sample of 100, mostly rural, communities found a mean household size of 4.8 although this was subject to considerable regional and temporal variation. In 1700 mean household size was 4.6 in Kent but only 3.9 in Wiltshire. Furthermore a smaller sample of households, based on listings of exceptional quality, dated between 1650 and 1749 recently found an overall mean household size of only 4.2[12] Mean household size in London north of the river in 1695 was

[12] Phythian-Adams 1979: 246; Goose 1980: 363; Wall 1982: 497; P. Laslett, 'Mean household size in England since the sixteenth century', in P. Laslett, *Household and family in past time*, Cambridge, 1972, p. 133; Clark 1983b: 69.

4.3, although this was subject to considerable variation according to the social articulation of the capital.[13] The experience of the Boroughside suggests that London's suburbs, like those of other towns and cities at this period, had on average fewer persons per household than in the wealthier central areas.[14]

The distribution of people among the Boroughside households appears to fall between the experience of other pre-industrial towns and cities. In 1631 some 9.6% of all Boroughside households consisted of persons living alone compared to 12–13% in late seventeenth-century Southampton, early sixteenth-century Coventry and Canterbury in 1563. Solitaries were, however, more common in Southwark than in London in 1695 (where only 5.8% of households were such), in early seventeenth-century Cambridge (6.2) and in England as a whole (5.7). Households containing six persons or more were more commonly found in the Boroughside than in the Canterbury suburbs but less so in all other areas. Only 17.6% of Boroughside households contained six persons or more in 1631 compared to 25% in later seventeenth-century London, 20.2% in late seventeenth-century Southampton and 33.2% in the country at large.[15] It should be noted that the experience of living in households of six persons or more was greater, and that of living alone smaller than the foregoing figures would suggest. Of the *total population* of the Boroughside only 2.5% lived alone, while 35% lived in households of six persons or more.[16]

As expected from the discussion of household finances and from research on other communities, those households considered poor or not eligible to be taxed were much smaller than their taxable neighbours. As in sixteenth-century Warwick and Norwich the households of the poor were typically small. In the Boroughside in 1618 'poor' household size was 3.2 compared to 3.0 in Norwich and 2.6 in Warwick in the later sixteenth century.[17] The mean household size of the poorer households found by the 1618 survey was identical to that of the non-rate paying householders in 1631 in the Boroughside. The rateable households were significantly larger, possessing a mean household size of 5.2. The distribution of households by size reveals that solitary households were a feature of the poor. Only 2.2% of rate payers lived alone compared to 13.2% of those not assessed in 1631 and 19.8% of the poor in 1618. Only 10.4% of poor households contained six persons or more in 1618 and 8.6% of those not assessed in 1631, compared to as

---

[13] Wall 1979: 103. For variations see Glass 1966: xxi–xxvii; Jones and Judges 1935: 58–62.

[14] Clark 1983b: 70; Goose 1980: 364–5; Phythian-Adams 1979: 306–15; Jones and Judges 1935: 61–2. For an exception to this rule see the relatively large mean household size (4.9) found in a Worcester suburb, Roy and Porter 1980: 207.

[15] See Goose 1980: 366; Clark 1983b: 69; Phythian-Adams 1979: 310; Laslett 1972b: 146. The figures for London and Southampton were calculated from the tabulated listings kept at the Cambridge Group. The parishes from each sample are those used in Wall 1979: 110.

[16] Calculated from figures in Table 5.1.   [17] Pound 1971b: 18; Beier 1981: 60.

Table 5.2. *Number of children in poor households 1618*

Number of children per household	Households headed by			
	Married couple	Single man	Single woman	Total
0	32	6	40	78
1	35	1	12	48
2	37	1	6	44
3	29		8	37
4	15		1	16
5	8			8
6	1			1
Total	157	8	67	232
Mean number of children	1.9	0.4	0.8	1.6

Source: 1618 survey of poor households, G.L.R.O. P92/SAV/1465.

many as 36.6% of the poor-rate paying households. The maintenance of a large household, not surprisingly, was the prerogative of the better off.

As Table 5.2 shows, poor households contained relatively few children. Each poor household contained on average only 1.6. Of those households with children (154) the figure was 2.3 comparable to the 2.1 for poor families in late sixteenth-century Norwich. Only nine households, 3.9% of the total, contained more than four children.

The high infant and child mortality rates that prevailed in seventeenth-century London partly explain the relatively small numbers of children found in poor households. Infant mortality rates in London are now known to have exceeded those found in rural England at this period. The difference is most marked in the poorest areas of early seventeenth-century London which displayed markedly higher rates than wealthier districts. In London infant mortality ranged from 161 to 204 infant deaths per thousand live births in the wealthier Cornhill district to as high as 271 to 318 in the poor parishes of St Mary Somerset and Allhallows London Wall. Throughout the seventeenth century provincial England recorded infant mortality rates of between 161 and 170 per thousand live births. Child mortality was similarly more severe in London than in rural areas. Not surprisingly children are known to have been relatively uncommon in late seventeenth-century London households compared to those of the nation at large.[18]

However the cost of maintaining children was also a factor in this scarcity.

[18] Pound 1971b: 18; Wall 1979: 105–6; Beier 1981: 60–1. See also, Slack 1972: 177. For infant mortality rates in London see Finlay 1981: 30, 102–4, and for those of 13 reconstituted parishes see, Wrigley and Schofield 1983: 177.

Feeding and clothing a London child was estimated to have cost £8 13s. 8d. per year in 1619, although poor relief accounts would suggest that poorer children could be maintained for considerably less. In 1621–2 the overseers of the poor maintained one foundling for £4 6s. 8d. per year.[19] The sixth and last 'degree' of poverty recognised by the founder of the college almshouse was that of the poor man or woman 'which is become overcharged with a burthen of children, which they cannot by their labour find and sustain'. Children were (and are) not only expensive but time-consuming. In the 1620s Elizabeth Brown, a deserted wife, asked for an increase in her parish pension 'or else to take from her, her youngest child, by reason whereof she cannot employ herself in that labour which the time affordeth'.[20] It is possible that the financial imperative forced the poor to *reduce* their household size as soon as possible, perhaps by farming out young children on kin or by compelling them to leave home at a relatively early age to go into service with wealthier households. The parish authorities, like those elsewhere, were similarly concerned to dispose of expensive foundlings. Thus a parish child, the overseer of the poor noted, was, 'to be put forth as soon as may be'.

The evidence that we have certainly suggests that, by the age of 16, most children had left home in the Boroughside. The 1622 token book lists only forty-two households (4.4% of the total) containing children of communicable age. A similarly small proportion of children of 16 or over were still at home in the households in the Canterbury suburbs in 1563. An early age on leaving home appears to be an early seventeenth-century *urban* phenomenon. Few comparable rural figures are available but in Cardington in the late eighteenth century between 32 and 58% of children aged 15 and above were still residing with their parents. In late seventeenth-century Swindon as many as 53% of children over 15 were still at home. In the nineteenth century 98% of children of Preston parents aged between 15 and 19 were residing at home.[21] Children rarely stayed at home after their mid-teens in the Boroughside but they were more likely to do so if they were fortunate enough to be members of wealthier households. Of the forty-two households containing adult children nineteen or 45.2% were assessed for the poor rate. Some 6.5% of all households assessed for the poor rate compared to only 3.5% of those not assessed contained children of communicable age in 1622. Only four households were able to maintain two adult children at home. The majority of adult children kept at home were female (of those whose sex can be determined thirty were female and only twelve male). Male children may have been awaiting succession to a

[19] G.L.R.O. P92/SAV/1400; Cook 1981: 23–5.   [20] G.L.R.O. P92/SAV/757, 1584.

[21] Clark 1983b: 72; Wall 1978: 181–190; R. Schofield, 'Age-specific mobility in an eighteenth-century rural English parish', *Annales de Démographie Historique* (1970), 261–74.

Table 5.3. *Size and wealth of households headed by women 1631*

Household size	Total headed by females	Rate payers	Poor rate assessment	Number of female householders in in each category of assessment
1	71	2	7d.+	0
2	29	4	6d.	1
3	21	7	5d.	1
4	18	9	4d.	1
5	8	3	3d.	1
6	2	0	2d.	6
7	1	1	1½d.	0
8	1	0	1d.	12
9+	0	0	½d.	4
			Nothing	125
Total	151	26		151

Source: 1631 token book. G.L.R.O. P92/SAV/219.

family business. John Simonds, son of Samuel the baker, who is listed as 'John fil' in his father's household in the 1622 token book made a will which illustrates his state of financial suspended animation. After making a number of bequests to kin and some charitable donations 'because I have no land' John entreated his father (his executor) to purchase property to fund John's bequests. No legacies made by John could be paid until after Samuel's death.[22]

As a comparison between Tables 5.3 and 5.1 makes clear, female headed households exhibited distinctive characteristics. Female headed households were, as other studies have shown, less likely to contribute to local taxation than their male counterparts. In 1631 female household heads formed 15.6% of all household heads but only 8.3% (26 out of 314) of those assessed for the poor-rate. Female household heads were only half as likely as men to be so rated; 26 out of 151 female householders were rated compared to 288 out of 815 households (35.3%) headed by men. Not only were women less likely to be assessed for local taxation than men but they were also far more likely to be living alone. Some 71 out of 151 female householders (47%) were solitaries compared to only 22 out of 815 (2.7%) of those headed by men. Even allowing for the absence of a husband, women were more likely to head small households. In 1631 the mean household size of those headed by women was only 2.2 compared to 4.1 for those headed by men. Only 4 of 151 female householders (2.7%) contained six

[22] G.L.R.O. Archdeaconry of Surrey Will Register 278 Yeast.

persons or more compared to 166 of the 815 (20.4%) headed by men. The parlous state of the female-headed household, in the absence of a male breadwinner, noted in other pre-industrial towns and cities and in some rural areas, was reflected in the size of their households.[23] It is understandable therefore that female householders were over-represented among those considered poor. In 1618, 67 of 232 poor households (28.9) were headed by women. Of these 40 were solitaries (see Table 5.2). As we have seen something like one third of all female-headed households in 1622 had received poor relief payments compared to about one in 20 of those headed by men. The solitary widow's position is described graphically in a 'humble petition' sent into the vestry by one Ann Tedder 'a poor aged widow' who was,

above three score and twelve years of age and past labour and hath nothing to live on but a pension of 8*d* a week and not able to pay any Rent for dwelling and destitute of friends to relieve her living in extreme need and misery. Wherefore she humbly beseecheth your worships in respect she is a lone woman and hath been long acquainted with Goody Coleman being now also a lone woman living in the College where there are two rooms with chimneys in them, that your worships will be pleased to suffer her to dwell in the house with the said goody Coleman.[24]

The burden of maintaining children is often recorded explicitly in the poor relief accounts and also frequently referred to in petitions. Thus Ann Jones, widow,

by reason of her late husband lying sick on her hands two years and in regard of her two small children which she hath had no means at all to relieve, except only her own labour, is now fallen into great extremity and want and likely to suffer most miserable calamity and affliction.[25]

Most households were headed by married couples (see Table 5.4). In 1622, 80.6% of all Boroughside households were headed by man and wife, with 14.1% headed by females and only 5.3% by widowers and single men. This pattern closely resembles that found in the suburbs of Canterbury in 1563 where 80.9% of all household heads were married couples, 18.5% widows and an insignificant 0.6% were single males. The proportion of female-headed households found in the Boroughside was similar to that found in London in 1700 (14.5%) but lower than that found in other pre-industrial urban areas where headship rates ranged from 17.0% in early seventeenth-century Cambridge to 27.7% in later seventeenth-century Southampton. Rural female headship rates too were higher than in London and its suburbs; Laslett found 20.5% of households headed by females in

[23] Smith 1981b: 607–8; Beier 1981: 60–1; Phythian-Adams 1979: 241–2.
[24] G.L.R.O. P92/SAV/784.   [25] G.L.R.O. P92/SAV/774.

Table 5.4. *Marital status of household heads in the Boroughside 1618–1631*

| | Percentage households headed by | | | |
	Married couples	Widowers, single men	Widows, single females	Total households
Boroughside 1622	80.6	5.3	14.1	958
Boroughside 1618	67.7	3.5	28.9	232
Boroughside 1631	84.4		15.6	966

Source: P92/SAV/1465; P92/SAV/211, 219.

his national sample although this was subject to considerable regional and temporal variation; in Kent in 1700 only 10.5% of households had female heads. Although fewer householders seem to have been female in the capital a similarly small proportion of single male householders (3.9%) seems to have been found in early seventeenth-century Cambridge and early sixteenth-century Coventry. This latter finding contrasts to the situation found in urban areas in the later seventeenth century, when the proportion of single male householders seems to have ranged between 10 and 15% and in rural areas between 9.3 and 17.0%. In London it was 11.4%.[26] The small proportion of single men relative to single female householders may well reflect differential male and female mortality and the slim remarriage chances of the poor widow.[27]

The relatively smaller proportions of females heading households in the Boroughside and the capital compared to elsewhere may be explained simply by higher adult mortality rates in London, but it could well be that local government policy towards females, known to be in a particularly vulnerable socioeconomic position, significantly reduced the numbers heading households. The majority of those inmates prevented from settling in the area in the early seventeenth century were single females.[28] A disproportionate number of widows were placed in the college almshouse or in the households of their neighbours. If the college pensioners alone are combined with the 1622 population, 14.9% of household heads would have been female.[29]

[26] Clark 1983b: 70; Goose 1980: 378; Phythian-Adams 1979: 202; Laslett 1972b: 78; Wall 1979: 105.

[27] Clark 1983b: 71; Finlay 1981: 130–1; Hollingsworth 1971: 145.

[28] Just over two thirds of all inmates and new settlers detected (and often ejected by the searcher for inmates were single women, mostly pregnant servants, G.L.R.O. P92/SAV/1422–3; Raine 1969: 79–85. [29] See, G.L.R.O. P92/SAV/210.

Less easy to explain, however, is the changing proportion of widowers and single men heading households over time in the seventeenth century. The lower proportion of widowers may reflect a surplus of females in the population which maximised the chance of remarriage. Certainly the local sex ratio favoured women in the Boroughside in 1622. Among household heads and spouses there were 823 males to 907 females, a sex ratio of 91 males to 100 females, this imbalance, like a similar one in sixteenth-century Canterbury, being caused by the number of female-headed households.[30] The predominance of males among the adult servant population raised the sex ratio of the total male population to 98:100. Local chances for remarriage then would seem to have slightly favoured men in 1622. The argument that simple availability was the predominant factor, however, is difficult to reconcile with the fact that, in London, as in other towns and cities, the seventeenth century saw an appreciable *fall* in the relative number of males in the population, which might lead us to expect an even *lower* proportion of single men heading households in the later seventeenth-century towns and cities, when the choice of female partners would have been even more extensive than in the earlier period.[31]

It may be the case that the rising proportion of single male householders was related to more subtle factors (such as the way in which the wifely role was defined), that may have lessened the impulse for men to make rapid remarriages. Certainly there is evidence that, in the country at large, the frequency of remarriage declined from the mid-sixteenth century and that the proportion of the population never marrying was smaller in the late sixteenth and early seventeenth centuries than it was in the late seventeenth century.[32] As well as the biological and biblical imperatives to marriage, testators in the Boroughside did occasionally leave evidence of companionship and love shared with wives. Some testators expressed wishes to be buried with (or as near as possible to) deceased wives and might leave declarations of feelings outside the conventional phrases of 'loving' or 'well beloved' wife. Richard Wright, a wealthy High Street grocer, declared at the end of his will that 'I desire God with my heart and soul to give his blessing withall and to make her life comfortable to her that she may enjoy

---

[30] Clark 1983b: 70.

[31] Finlay, measuring the sex ratio at burial of the total population, found a surplus of males in the population in the early seventeenth century, Finlay 1981: 140–2. See also, D. Souden, 'Migration and the population structures of later seventeenth-century provincial cities and market towns', in P. Clark (ed.), *The Transformation of English Provincial Towns*, London, 1984, pp. 150–61; Corfield 1982: 126. The distribution of males to females across London was, however, not uniform. Glass found, in 1695, some parishes, both rich and poor, with a surplus of men, Glass 1966: xxvii.

[32] The proportion of persons never married by age 44 was, apparently, between 147 and 174 per 1000 in the 1620s compared to a figure of 267 to 270 per 1000 in the 1690s, Wrigley and Schofield 1981: 258–65, 426.

his blessings to God's glory and her comfort'.[33] More significant may be the strong tendency for men of differing social standing to view women as unpaid nurses. For husbands with young children the death of a wife must have entailed rapid remarriage or the payment of a nurse. Poorer and older men required a nursing wife for their own sustenance. The vestry of St Saviour's recognised this function of wives in 1595 when it ordered that 'father Burgoyne should be placed, only for harbours [sake] and no otherwise, in one of the rooms belonging to father Lewys, the rather that the wife of Burgoyne might be helping to both the men'. John Acors, a bedridden porter, sent in the following petition which emphasises the point:

that your poor petitioner hath lain Beddered this 9 years and upwards and hath no ways or means to get a penny towards his relief, but lieth expecting the good hour of his releasement out of this vale of misery. But now so it is…that through some contentions that arose the stairs of your poor petitioners house was taken away whereby his wife is barred from his society, and comfort and hath been so barred this quarter of a year and upwards whereby he hath not that attendance and looking unto which a man in his case ought to have but is in great misery his bed having never been made since the taking away of the stairs, nor none ever been above with him, he being no ways able to help himself in regard he wanteth the society of a woman to keep him clean, as a man in his case ought to be kept being no ways able to administer help to himself. But is like to perish for want of looking unto, except your worships will be a means to provide their ways for him. May it therefore please your worships…to commiserate your poor petitioners estate, to be a means that he may be placed in [a] house wherein he may have the society of his wife to help and comfort him in this his extremity and also to keep him clean and sweet and to help to relieve him in this case of extremity.[34]

Loss of a wife therefore might threaten the very independence of the husband. Evan Reynolds, with his then wife, was listed as poor in 1618 and was receiving a pension of 8*d*. per week in 1621–2. His wife must have died subsequently because on 8 July 1621 pensioner Reynolds remarried. The 1622 token book, however, lists him as a solitary. This inconsistency is resolved by an entry in the vestry minute book of 19 January 1623 which records his admittance into the college almshouse. At this time Reynolds promised 'not to be unquiet or troublesome. And if his wife who is gone from him return to him that then he will leave the place willingly and of his own accord'. Sad to relate Reynolds died, still a colleger, in January 1626. Perhaps the rise in the proportion of single men heading households might be linked to the growing effectiveness of poor relief that reduced the need to marry or remarry. It might also be an early symptom of the more relaxed

---

[33] P.C.C. Will Register, 97 Alchin. For emotional content of this sort see also, Margaret Spufford, *Small Books and Pleasant Histories*, London, 1981, pp. 157–70; Wrightson 1982: 90–104.

[34] G.L.R.O. P92/SAV/450, 2 March 1595; P92/SAV/750.

urban mores thought to have prevailed in towns and cities in the eighteenth century.[35]

As noted above the token books listed only the more established inmates and lodgers. Only some 42 out of 958 households in 1622 can be shown to have contained individuals labelled as lodgers or individuals not apparently related to the household head. A similarly small percentage of inmates and lodgers were listed in Canterbury in 1563.[36] These latter inmates can occasionally be shown to be poor-law placements, usually widows taken in by better off neighbours. Thus, for example, one Widow Collier found within the household of James Rayner, a poor-rate paying householder, was in receipt of a parish pension in 1621–2.[37]

In the absence of large numbers of adult children and permanent lodgers and inmates it was the presence of servants that made the households of the better off larger than those of their poorer neighbours. This can be demonstrated by subtracting the number of adult servants from the total number of persons in each household in 1631 (see Table 5.1). In 1622, 119 servants were kept by 664 non-rated households and 480 by 294 rate payers.[38] If we assume that these proportions hold for 1631 then 314 rate payers would be expected to keep 513 adult servants and 652 non-rated households to keep 117. If these two latter totals are subtracted from the total number of persons in each group of households the effect of servants on household size can be appreciated. The mean household size of rate-paying householders, without adult servants, was 3.6 compared to 5.2 with them and that of the non-rated 3.0 compared to 3.2. Adult servants comprised 31.2% of all persons inhabiting rate-paying households compared to only 5.7% of all persons inhabiting the non-rated. Lower mortality rates, particularly infant and child mortality, and financial hardship may have been responsible for the remaining difference between the household size of the richer sort and their less fortunate neighbours. It should be noted, however, that our calculation only concerned servants of communicable age. There is occasional evidence of younger individuals acting as servants in the

[35] Corfield 1982: 108. It may be relevant here to note that, after the death of his wife in 1669, Samuel Pepys formed a lasting relationship with one Mary Skinner, with whom he was living at his death in 1703, an association 'never consecrated by marriage but accepted as respectable by all his friends', R. Latham and W. Mathews, *The Diary of Samuel Pepys*, London, 1970, vol. 1, p. xxxix. See also, H. J. Habbakuk, 'Marriage settlements in the eighteenth century', *Transactions of the Royal Historical Society*, 4th ser., 32 (1950), 24, n.1. Habbakuk quotes a contemporary who commented in the early eighteenth century 'I believe there are more bachelors now in England by many thousands than there were a few years ago; and probably also the numbers of them (and of single women of course) will every year increase.'

[36] Clark 1983b: 74. For definition problems, see Goose 1980: 379–80.

[37] G.L.R.O. P92/SAV/211, 1400.

[38] Number of servants is calculated from 1622 token book, G.L.R.O. P92/SAV/211. See below Table 5.6.

Table 5.5. *Age at burial of male servants in St Botolph's Aldgate,*
1584–1601

Age at burial	Number buried	%	Assumed death rate[a] per 1000	% in population in each age group
6–10	5	3.6	10.0	3.8
11–15	22	15.8	6.8	24.4
16–20	43	30.9	9.0	36.2
21–25	25	18.0	12.2	15.5
26–30	23	16.6	13.6	12.8
31–35	4	2.9	15.6	1.9
36–40	8	5.8	17.8	3.4
41–45	1	0.7	20.6	0.4
46–50	2	1.4	23.4	0.6
51–55	1	0.7	30.2	0.2
56–60	3	2.2	38.2	0.6
61–64	2	1.4	54.4	0.2
Total	139			

Note: The year 1593, a plague year, has been excluded.
Sources: Guildhall Library Ms 9234/2–7.
[a] Hollingsworth 1971: 144. Age groups do not correspond by one year.

households of the better off. Thus the parish clerk noted the burial of one
Richard Fox in August 1625 'Mr [Samuel] Simond's boy'. Thomas Alborne
buried in that same month was said to have been 'Dally's boy' and a certain
John Vinter 'Mr Bolt's boy'. An unknown number of younger servants may
have been living in the wealthier households.

What evidence there is suggests that servants in London were, on
average, older than their provincial counterparts. In St Botolph's, Aldgate,
when the burials of 139 males labelled as servants were recorded only 19.4%
were less than 16 years of age (see Table 5.5.). Numbers buried of course
may tell us more about death rates than about the relative size of age groups
among the servant population. However, the age-specific death rates
calculated by the Hollingsworths for St Botolph's Bishopsgate in 1601
suggest that the Aldgate figures do not greatly distort the true picture.
Death rates apparently lay between 6.8 to 10 per 1000 for those aged
between 10 and 20 and increased progressively as age increased, reaching
54.5 per 1000 for the 60–64 age group. Applying these death rates (which
may well be overestimates for those in their late teens and twenties) to the
numbers buried in order to get some estimate of the size of the population

at risk in each group, (Table 5.5) shows that, as expected, the burials exaggerate the size of the elderly servant group and underestimate the numbers in the younger categories.[39] This evidence suggests that in St Botolph's most servants (72%) were over 16 years of age. In Canterbury in 1563 only 41.4% were aged 16 or over.[40] One reason for this striking difference may well be the disproportionate number of adolescent immigrants taking up apprenticeships or service in London, which reduced the numerical significance of those Londoners who left home before the age of 16 to go into service of some sort in the capital. Perhaps more significantly it has been found that, in the later seventeenth century, longer distance migrants to towns tended to be older than those recruited from the immediate locality. Since a large percentage of London's apprentices were long-distance migrants in the early seventeenth century a reason for London's older servant population at this time emerges.[41]

It is certain that the term 'servant' embraces many individuals who were technically apprentices. Apprentices are never labelled as such in the 1622 token book even though the age at which most apprentices began in London (in the late teens and early twenties), and the length of apprenticeship, on average eight years, meant that most should have been listed if present.[42] The probable explanation is that, as other studies have noted, apprentices were simply designated as servants because both were in a dependent position obliged to take orders from the household head.[43] The terminological confusion is nicely demonstrated by two case studies from the Boroughside. At his death in 1625 John Turner, a High Street shoemaker, bequeathed his 'wearing apparel' to his 'apprentice' Edward Mason. Two days after the will was drawn up, however, Edward too was buried, being described by the parish clerk as Turner's servant.[44] The 1622 token book listed one Peter Sherley, a bricklayer, living on the High Street together with his wife and 'Hen: servant'. This is very probably the individual referred to in the records of the London Bricklayers' Company when Sherley's most recent apprentice was enrolled, in February 1620, 'Henry

---

[39] If the total number of servants in the Boroughside included 28% under 16 years of age then this, if their distribution among rich and poor households was the same as that of adult servants, reinforces the point made above that it was the presence of servants, rather than different mortality and fertility rates, which made rate-paying households larger than their poorer neighbours.

[40] It is probable that, since the Hollingsworths did not allow for the immigration of a large number of adolescents they underestimated the numbers present in the population at risk and consequently *overestimated* the normal death rate for those age groups, Finlay 1981: 129–30. For Canterbury see, Clark 1983b: 72.

[41] Finlay 1981: 66–7, 130; Clark 1979: 70–1.

[42] Rappaport 1983: 117; Elliott 1978: 199.

[43] Laslett defined the servant group as including apprentices. Laslett 1972a: 87. For this terminological grey area see, Goose 1980: 373–6; Glass 1972: 278–9.

[44] Archdeaconry of Surrey Will Register, 220 Yeast. For the notebook see G.L.R.O. P92/SAV/406.

Parsons son [of] Henry Parsons of Wooton Underhedge Gloucestershire clothier [to] Peter Cherley *civi et tiler et Bricklayer'*. Five years later the parish clerk recorded the burial of 'Henry Parsons Sherlye's man'.[45]

The keeping of servants, not surprisingly, tended to reflect the number of wealthy households in a community. In 1622 in the Boroughside 213 out of 294 rate-paying households (72.5%) contained one or more adult servants compared to only 84 out of 664 non-assessed households (12.7% – see Table 4.6). The proportion of Boroughside households containing *adult* servants (31.1%) compares to only 26.2% of those keeping servants *of all ages* in late seventeenth-century Southampton, 26.6% in late sixteenth-century Canterbury and 30.0% in late seventeenth-century Shrewsbury. The number of servant-keeping households in St Saviour's, was, if the unknown number of households keeping servants under 16 years of age is taken into account, perhaps closer to that found in early sixteenth-century Coventry (39.4%) or early Stuart Cambridge (35.2%). Most striking is the great contrast with London north of the river where some 58% of all households contained servants of all ages in 1695.[46] The relative poverty of the Boroughside district compared to the wealthier areas of London noted above, was reflected in the number of servants kept in each area.

Unlike late seventeenth-century London, however, servants kept in the Boroughside were more likely to be male than female. Of 571 servants whose sex could be determined from their christian name 315 were male and 250 female, a sex ratio of 123:100. In London in 1695 the servant group possessed a sex ratio of 85:100. This difference probably reflects the decline in the importance of apprenticeship as a means of recruiting immigrants to London that took place in the later seventeenth century.[47]

It is also clear that adult servants were rarely kept in large numbers in Boroughside households (see Table 5.6). In 1622, 599 servants were kept by 297 households, a mean group size of 2.0. Nearly half (48.2%) of all households keeping servants kept only one and a further 30.6% kept two. Consequently more than half the adult servant population were solitaries or had only one colleague. Only 6.1% of households keeping servants kept five or more but 21.4% of all adult servants came from these households. Interestingly, the sex ratio of the servant group rose with the number of servants per household. Solitary servants were more likely to be female (100 females to 76 males) but thereafter the sex ratio greatly favoured men (177 males per 100 females). The difference presumably reflects the restricted demand for and role of female domestics and the

[45] Guildhall Library Ms 3045/1.
[46] Clark 1983b: 73; Wall 1979: 106; Goose 1980: 374 (figures for servants and apprentices combined); Phythian-Adams 1979: 204.   [47] Finlay 1981: 141.

Table 5.6. *Number of adult servants kept in Boroughside households 1622*

Number of servants per household	Number of households	%
1	143	48.2
2	91	30.6
3	34	11.5
4	11	3.7
5	4	1.4
6	6	2.0
7	1	0.3
8	1	0.3
9	4	1.4
10	1	0.3
11	1	0.3
Total	297	

Source: G.L.R.O. P92/SAV/211.

financial imperative which ensured that, where large numbers of servants were kept, then they would be males more able to offset the cost of their maintenance.

The familial experience of Boroughside householders therefore was determined largely by wealth. The households of the poorer sort were commonly small, unlikely to contain large numbers of children and very unlikely to contain servants. The inferior social and economic position of women was reflected in the exceptionally small size of their households and their disproportionate representation among those classed as poor. Members of wealthier households (in 1631 something like 44% of the population lived in poor-rate paying households) were likely to experience the presence of at least one adult servant, although more than two would have been relatively unusual. It was largely the inclusion of servants that made the households of the wealthier sort larger than those of their poorer neighbours. Living without the love and companionship of a member of the opposite sex was an experience restricted mostly to women who formed the bulk of solitaries. In addition men were unlikely to be running a household without the aid of a spouse.

Little can be said about the way in which the household was seen by its members. The large households, not commonly found (such as those represented by the Southwark inns or breweries), were miniature worlds where fellow feeling between servants and master-servant relations were common parts of everyday experience. John Moorey 'yeoman', a married

servant apparently resident at the George Inn bequeathed his son £200
'which lieth in the hands of John Geldinge at the George...my master'.
Moorey went on to leave 10 shillings each to 'my master...and my Mistress
his wife' and two shillings to their children. He also bequeathed to James
'my fellow the doublet hose and Jerkin which I now wear and a pair of
hair coloured stockings' and to 'the rest of [the] servants in the house' two
shillings each.[48]

As a unit of socialisation the Boroughside household was commonly
small. In crude terms in 1631 some 966 heads of households controlled, at
least in theory, the lives and behaviour of 2742 dependent women, children
and servants. Individuals in this elementary position of social responsibility
formed a surprisingly high proportion of the population – some 26%, or
more than one person in four. Of these 84% were men. The influence of
females was lessened still further by their frequently precarious financial
position. Wealthier householders presided over larger family units. But the
distribution of power and authority in this urban society was more directly
related to the possession of wealth.

[48] Archdeaconry of Surrey Will Register, 271 Yeast.

6

Power, status and social mobility

6.1 Power and influence in the urban neighbourhood

As we have seen, the primary position of social power derived from an individual's position as head of household. This power, however, was restricted by the size of each unit. Opportunities to influence the lives and behaviour of others were much wider in a society where wealth was divided unequally. 'Formal' or 'institutional' power derived from membership of local administrative bodies is the one usually emphasised by social historians.[1] Possession of office of this sort gave individuals further influence over the social, economic and religious behaviour of their fellows. Before discussing the institutional aspects of individual power we should consider the *informal* opportunities to influence the lives of neighbours which derived from the unequal distribution of wealth discussed earlier. Unlike institutional power, however, evidence for the deployment of informal power is far less easy to come by. In a society where wealth was distributed unequally and where two thirds of all households had little money to spare, it is clear that those households which were able to do so might use surplus income as a means to power and influence. The ways in which money might be used in return for deference is a neglected form of informal social control in pre-industrial England.

One of the obvious means of converting wealth into a form of social capital was to provide dinners for neighbours. This practice was part of the tradition reflecting the ideas of social obligation that went with the possession of wealth. In return for the provision of food and drink the host received honour and influence. Although the poor were held in literature to be the prime recipients of this hospitality it seems to have been 'neighbours, tenants and social superiors' who were in practice the chief

[1] Dyer 1973: 197–202; Palliser 1979: 60–110, especially 78; Wrightson and Levine 1979: 104–6; Phythian-Adams 1979: 125–7; Pearl 1979: 15–18.

beneficiaries. In the city such hospitality was thought to be more selective and on a smaller scale than the rural norm.[2] Edward Alleyn, gentleman and vestryman of St Saviour's, was providing hospitality of this sort in the early seventeenth century. From the pages of his diary it is clear that he provided food and drink to neighbours, both to his social superiors and to those lower in the social order. Thus on 26 September 1619 Alleyn gave dinner to a High Street butcher, Henry Fawcett, 'there dined with us Mr Fawsset and his wife Colbrand's daughter'. Later that year Alleyn entertained 'Daggert his wife and 2 of his neighbours'.[3] Apart from providing dinners for neighbours, which the diaries make clear were reciprocated, Alleyn's wealth was deployed for more direct purposes. When Alleyn was employing workmen on 20 October 1617 he recorded that he had 'Given the Joiners to make them friends 6d.' Workmen too found themselves at his table. On visits to friends Alleyn often noted gifts to the servants of the house.[4]

Money of course could be converted into social capital in other ways. The ability to loan out money to neighbours or to employ them (described in Chapter 3) must not be forgotten as a source of power and influence. Furthermore investment in property might bring social deference as well as income. As the next chapter will show there are grounds for imagining that landlord–tenant relations were a potent social force in the district. A wealthy person would have also been faced regularly with demands from beggars and from neighbours in need. Wealth might also be used to endow a private charity which, separately administered by the parochial authorities, might advertise the donor's generosity. Those who held local office were only reinforcing the power and influence derived from the possession of wealth in an unequal society.

In order to discover which Boroughside householders participated in the local administration a detailed study of office-holding in the Boroughside was made. Those individuals listed in manorial records and the vestry minute book as holding office between 1618 and 1624 were linked to the names in the 1622 token book.[5] Tables 6.1 and 6.2 examine the proportions of those in each category of subsidy and poor rate assessment who held manorial or vestry office between 1620 and 1624.

It is clear that those householders who made no contribution to the poor

[2] See, Heal 1984: 66–93; Greaves 1981: 587–93.
[3] Young 1889: 2,175. The parish register reveals that Henry Fawcett, a High Street butcher, had married a certain Elizabeth Coleburne (a name interchangeable with Colbrand) in 1610.
[4] Young 1889: 2,54. For tips to servants see, 51, 78, 97, passim.
[5] Manorial offices include constables, jurors, aletasters, beadles, rakers, scavengers, collectors for the parish pumps, assirors (i.e. auditors) and the Bailiff. C.L.R.O. Presentments of the jurors of the Guildable Manor 1620–4, Southwark Box 2; Kings Manor 1620–4, Southwark Box 2; Great Liberty Manor 1622, Southwark Box 4. For the vestry minute book see, G.L.R.O. P92/SAV/450. For the scope of this local administration see below, Chapter 10.

Table 6.1. *Subsidy assessments of those householders holding manorial and vestry office 1620–4*

Level of subsidy assessment	Number holding manorial office 1620–24	Number holding vestry office 1622
£		
15		1
10		5
8		3
7		
6	3	7
5	3	2
4	18	1
3	15	1
Nothing	12	1
Total	51	21

Source: See discussion in text, pp. 139–40.

rate were almost totally excluded from local office. Only three out of 664 non poor-rate paying householders held some form of manorial or vestry office between 1620 and 1624. Even if ten watchmen and ten minor parish officials are included this would still indicate that only 23 out of 664 or 3.5% of the non poor-rate paying householders held any form of local office.[6] A distinction should be made, too, between paid and unpaid office. The offices held by poor-rate payers were unpaid and represented voluntary participation in local government. Most of the posts occupied by the non-rated householders were salaried and often involved manual labour. As we have seen, the watch and some minor parish offices were accepted alternative sources of employment for the old. It is also clear that the office of constable was not the humble post that it was in some rural areas of pre-industrial England. Constables were, in terms of relative wealth, typical manorial officials and, as befitted the incumbents of an office that was an essential stepping-stone to vestry membership, were fairly substantial householders.[7]

[6] Parish officers were the gravedigger, sexton, conductor, bearers, parish clerk, sidesmen, searchers for inmates, overseers of the poor and surveyors of highways.

[7] For the humble nature of rural constables see, Wrightson and Levine 1979: 104. See also, K. Wrightson, 'Two concepts of order: justices, constables and jurymen in seventeenth-century England', in J. Brewer and J. Styles (eds.), *An Ungovernable People*, London, paperback edn., 1983, pp. 26–32. It is probable that the most onerous task of the constable, the night watch, was often shoved off onto a paid deputy. An ordinance of the Great Liberty Manor in 1622 ran that 'We

Table 6.2. *Poor-rate assessment of householders holding manorial and vestry office 1620–24*

Level of poor rate assessment	Number holding manorial office 1620–24	Number holding vestry office 1622
d.		
+7		8
6	3	4
5		7
4	5	
3	13	1
2	13	1
$1\frac{1}{2}$	5	
1	6	
$\frac{1}{2}$	3	
Assessed but amount unknown	0	
Nothing	3	
Total	51	21

Source: See discussion in text, pp. 139–40.

Office-holding tended to follow the hierarchical distribution of wealth in the Boroughside (see Tables 6.1 and 6.2).[8] Hence 26.4% of all those rated at between 2*d.* and 4*d.* for the poor rate held office between 1620 and 1624 compared to only 9.5% of those rated between a $\frac{1}{2}d.$ and $1\frac{1}{2}d.$ Some 71.4% of those rated at £5 or more in the 1622 subsidy held some form of office between 1620 and 1624, and 88.0% of those rated at 5*d.* or more for the poor rate. Overall more than 1 in every 3 subsidy payers held some form of office between 1620 and 1624 as opposed to 1 in 62 non-subsidy payers. In the same way, 1 in 4 poor-rate payers held office compared to 1 in 221 non poor-rate payers. Payment of some form of taxation was therefore an essential qualification for local office-holding.

The breakdown of office-holding by wealth highlights the difference between vestrymen and their more humble brethren, the manorial officials. Only one householder held both vestry and manorial office at the same

ordain that from henceforth no Constable…shall at any time during his being in his office, hire or appoint any unsworn deputy to watch the night watch unless he or they be sick or out of town, but shall in their own persons keep their turns.' C.L.R.O. Presentments of the Jurors of Great Liberty Manor 1622, Southwark Box 4. For this practice elsewhere in London see, Lindley 1983: 119.

[8] For a similar wealth bias in London and Essex see, Dingle 1974: 108–9; McCampbell 1976: 116; Wrightson and Levine 1979: 104–6.

time and generally speaking the wealthy élite occupied the vestry while those at lower levels in the wealth distribution held manorial office. As befitted the wealth qualification all but two of the Boroughside householders elected to the vestry were assessed at £5 or more in the 1622 subsidy. Two individuals assessed below that figure had been substantial householders but had suffered a relative decline in their financial position with the onset of old age; Robert Harvard, assessed at 5*d.* in the poor-rate assessment was omitted from the 1622 subsidy roll. Apart from controlling the parochial administration, members of the vestry were invariably chosen as commissioners, collectors and assessors of the subsidy and frequently served on the assize Grand Jury. The local power and influence of the vestrymen was also increased by membership of the governing bodies of local institutions such as the Grammar School and St Thomas's Hospital.[9] A sign of the fact that social standing was linked to an individual's type of work only insofar as it brought in wealth is that in St Saviour's vestry bakers, glovers and butchers sat alongside grocers, gentlemen, cheesemongers and soapboilers. Occupations carried no particular social advantage *per se.*

It is possible that local power and influence were not the sole motives behind the competition for vestry places.[10] It is clear from the vestry minutes that membership brought with it considerable opportunities for lucrative business deals. Members of the vestry usually got first refusal of parish leases and were in an excellent position to benefit from parish property. The purchase of the rectory was particularly fruitful for John Bingham, who lent the Corporation of Wardens £600 at 8% annual interest for three years towards its purchase. In return for this service the vestry agreed to sell Bingham three acres of land in St George's Fields and three rural tenements 'called Tamhall'.[11] Other members of the vestry obtained similar benefits. Perhaps the most blatant piece of exclusiveness occurred when the vestry privately auctioned off the lease of a property called the Vine and Beerpot.[12] Not for nothing was the vestry known irreverently as

---

[9] Nineteen of the twenty–one Governors and Assistants of the Free Grammar School were Boroughside vestrymen, see, Minutes of the Governors of the Free Grammar School of St Saviour's 28 October 1619. See also R. C. Carrington, *Two schools, a history of the St Olave's and St Saviour's Grammar School Foundation*, London, 1971, pp. 21–33. A number of vestrymen such as Thomas Overman and Richard Yearwood, were governors of St Thomas's Hospital, G.L.R.O. H1/ST/E105, 23 March 1628.

[10] Vestry membership was eagerly sought after and there are few recorded cases of individuals refusing to serve. Parish politics probably explain why it was that Mr Dampord in June 1605, 'denied to take the same place upon him or to come into the Society'. John Kelleck resigned after two months service in December 1625 'being otherwise occasioned by reason of his Majesties service'. G.L.R.O. P92/SAV/450, 2 June 1605, 9 December 1625. For fining for local office in London see, Dingle 1974: 128; McCampbell 1976: 120–1.   [11] G.L.R.O. P92/SAV/450, 26 February 1611.

[12] G.L.R.O. P92/SAV/450, 26 September 1616. Some idea of the wealth of vestrymen can be gained from the sums bid at this auction. The bidding began with £600 offered by Edward Alleyn and ended at £840 from William Iremonger, ex-Bailiff and lawyer.

the 'sharing house' in the early seventeenth century.[13] In 1606 it emerged that elderly vestrymen of long service were occasionally granted leases at concessionary or nominal rents in recognition of their long service to the parish.[14] Given that the wealthy were able to translate their wealth into local office, precisely what power and influence did it provide over the lives of their neighbours?

The churchwardens, vestrymen and overseers of the poor gained considerable local power and influence from their control over the flow of poor relief.[15] It should be noted here that the machinery of poor relief was based partly on the personal fortunes of the office holders. Consequently when the outlay exceeded the income the overseers needed to draw on their personal wealth, although they would expect to be reimbursed. In 1621–2 'there resteth to Balance this Account to us the Overseers of St Saviour's £11 13s. 0d'.[16] Consequently those in receipt of poor relief must have perceived the money as coming directly from a local neighbour. It is probable that those able to deploy parish charity received in return deference. The standardised preambles in the petitions sent into the vestry might reflect the expectations of giver and receiver alike. The petitions were expected to address the vestrymen as 'your worships'. Petitioners also ended their request with a customary expression of gratitude. When the college almsmen petitioned for the payment of a legacy they added 'And your poor petitioners (as in Duty bound) shall daily pray for your worships Health and happiness long to continue.' Rose Cluff asked the vestry 'in all humility' not forgetting that 'for your worships favour the petitioner and child shall ever pray'. Roger Cotten if admitted to an almshouse 'shall during all that small remainder of their lives be bound forever daily to pray to the Allmighty for your worships long lives and Eternal felicities'.[17] The lower an individual in the social scale the more marked the loss of social and economic independence.

The college pensioners were subject to a rigorous godly discipline of the sort envisaged in mid seventeenth-century plans for a London workhouse.[18] The terms of the college ordinances reflect the radical protestantism followed by the vestry of St Saviour's and their implementation imposed the puritan 'reformation of manners' onto the miniature society of the

[13] Johnson 1969: 320.   [14] G.L.R.O. P92/SAV/793.

[15] For this aspect of poor relief see, Slack 1972: 185; J. Sharpe, 'Enforcing the law in the seventeenth-century English village', in V. A. C. Gatrell, B. Lenman and G. Parker (eds.), *Crime and the Law: The Social History of Crime in Western Europe Since 1500*, London, 1980, p. 115. See also Wrightson 1982: 57–61, 63–4.

[16] G.L.R.O. P92/SAV/1400.   [17] G.L.R.O. P92/SAV/749, 765, 769.

[18] See Valerie Pearl, 'Puritans and poor relief. The London workhouse, 1649–1660', in D. H. Pennington and K. Thomas (eds.), *Puritans and Revolutionaries. Essays in Seventeenth-Century History presented to Christopher Hill*, Oxford, 1978, pp. 218–26.

college. Poverty was not the sole criterion for admission into the college. The elected pauper was to be 'honest and godly…None but such as can say the Lord's Prayer, the Articles of the Christian Faith or belief and the ten commandments of God in English'. The vestry minutes make it clear that such examinations were carried out.[19] Once elected the social and religious behaviour of each pensioner was closely controlled. Prayers, especially composed by the Founder, were to be recited twice daily: each evening immediately after the shutting of the gates and each morning immediately before the opening, 'upon their knees with loud and audible voices' on pain of a 4*d*. fine for non-attendance. There was a chapel of prayer in the college but those able were expected to attend church services each Sunday, holiday, and every Wednesday, Friday and Saturday. Throughout the early seventeenth century the accounts of the college reveal that the inmates were regularly catechised by the parish clerk.[20] Moral injunctions prohibited tippling, begging, swearing and railing. Furthermore the college pensioners were to be physically and socially segregated. The doors of the college were locked at night and absences were prohibited on pain of a fine; licensed absences were restricted to four a year.[21] In addition, as was commonplace in seventeenth-century London, the college poor were to wear a badge so that they could be identified.[22] Discipline was reinforced by a scale of punishments and was applied to the breakers of most of the ordinances, 'for the first time lose 18*d*., for the second time a whole months pension…and for the third time…shall be deemed expulsed out of the said College forever'. No record of the fines has survived but the vestry minutes do record the expulsion of one James Bensted 'for his misdemeanours' in 1621.[23] It is a tribute to the strictness of the regime that despite the regularity and size of the pension, a number of persons refused to enter the college after their election or subsequently gave up their places.[24] It may be symbolic that entrance into the college effectively abolished householder status and in turn exerted a paternalistic discipline over those admitted.

Apart from controlling parish funds local office might serve to give the holder considerable executive power over his neighbours. Constables,

[19] Note for example the election of 'Richard Ashton, cobbler, who could say the Lord's Prayer the Creed and Ten Commandments was chosen by a general consent to be one of the College in place of Goodwife Patrick deceased'. G.L.R.O. P92/SAV/450, 27 July 1623. For the College ordinances see, P92/SAV/1529.

[20] 'Paid…the parish clerk…for one years catechizing the poor of the College…10s.' G.L.R.O. P92/SAV/1582. See also a book (written in the 1590s) by a minister of St Saviour's, T. Ratcliffe, *A Short Summe of the Whole Catechisme for the Greater Ease of the Common People of Saint Saveries Southwark*, London, 1620.

[21] G.L.R.O. P92/SAV/1529, 11. For similar segregation see, Slack 1972: 191.

[22] G.L.R.O. P92/SAV/1529, 13. See also Dingle 1974: 79; Pearl 1978: 225.

[23] G.L.R.O. P92/SAV/450, 30 September 1621.

[24] For examples of this see, G.L.R.O. P92/SAV/450, 27 February 1615, 13 June 1619, 8 May 1625.

manorial jurors, churchwardens and others could and did present their neighbours to various civil and ecclesiastical courts and might be involved in their physical detection and even arrest.[25] In addition the churchwardens determined the order of seating in the parish church, which was, as we shall see, an outward manifestation of social stratification. Lesser officials might be empowered to know the names of all individuals in another's household, to detect and physically eject newcomers and inmates and whip vagrants from the church door. Control over individuals was naturally highest among the vestrymen. Parish tenants could be evicted and parish pensions abated.

Next to controlling access to local courts the assessment and collection of local taxation was a further power conferred on some householders. This power could be displayed nakedly. During an internal dispute within the St Saviour's vestry in 1605 one Mr Humble, amongst other threatening speeches, explicitly avowed to the rest of the vestry 'that being a Commissioner [of the subsidy] he would raise a great many of them in subsidy'. Power of this kind might obviously be converted into political power. In May 1640 opposition to the levying of coat and conduct money took the form of the Boroughside assessors, men of the vestry, refusing to assess the parishioners.[26] The collector of the poor rate, assisted by the constable, seems to have had the power to make forcible entry into the houses of those reluctant to pay and could threaten imprisonment in the local jail or compter.[27]

6.2 Social status

The study of social status has attracted considerable attention from historians of late. Recent studies, using data on wealth and occupations, have searched for simple criteria by which individuals' position in society might have been determined and expressed.[28] As we have seen it can be demonstrated without undue difficulty that certain occupations were indeed more likely to have wealthy practitioners. It was the way in which this wealth was likely to be deployed that determined social status. Moreover it is difficult to abstract social status from its local context. Most individuals in seventeenth-century England were members of local 'communities' such as rural villages or urban parishes or wards and it is within this context that social status should be examined. Such a study is complicated by the 'extra local' pull of the gilds and companies of London, 'more work needs to be done on the social and occupational structure of the metropolis to determine

---

[25] For the involvement of the parishioners with these formal institutions see below Chapter 10.
[26] See P.R.O. SP 16/453/117.   [27] See P.R.O. STAC 8/228/8.
[28] Glass 1976: 216–32; Elliott 1978: passim; Cressy 1980: 118–41; Wrightson 1982: 17–38; Armstrong 1971: 198–203.

whether people identified themselves by livery company affiliation'.[29] What social and economic criteria determined social status in the Boroughside and how was it expressed?

So close was the link between status and wealth that contribution to the subsidy and to the poor rate was in itself used as an indication of status. Payment of such rates conferred 'good reputation' and a few petitioners to the vestry for alms therefore stressed their previous contributions to local taxation. John Clove petitioned that, 'so long as he was able [he] did relieve others and pay 2*d*. weekly and 3*d*. weekly for 30 years together towards the relief of the poor there and was in Queen Elizabeth's Reign £3 in the subsidy books'.[30] In a similar manner one Roger Cotten and his wife claimed to have been 'using themselves as becometh and paying and discharging the subsidies to his Majesty and all other duties to the poor of 2*d*. weekly and other both ordinary and extraordinary, as amply as any other there of his rank or fashion'.[31] Subsidy men also held (limited) political rights. In 1606, when the select vestry was seeking to oppose a parliamentary bill that aimed to increase the number of vestrymen, the vestry canvassed the views of the 195 subsidymen in the parish, 142 of whom duly certified 'under their hands...that they do not only desire any other course but do well approve of that which is now used'.[32]

The intimate links between social status, wealth and local office found visual expression in the order of seating in the parish church.[33] Vestrymen and their wives were accorded privileged seating. Women were placed according to their husband's social position; in 1610 the vestry ordered that 'the pews towards the south wherein the vestrymen's wives sit shall be made longer into the Aisle and that no men shall stand in that Aisle but only maid servants or other women kind'.[34] Below the rank of vestryman the amount of duty paid often determined individual placings, hence a memorandum against the name of George Belcher in the 1613 token book that 'he hath no pew and subsidy man £3'.[35] It is a measure of the importance which the inhabitants of the Boroughside attached to their pew placings that re-adjustments to the seating arrangements caused disputes with the churchwardens and legal action between parishioners. The churchwardens complained to the Bishop of Winchester in 1639 that 'the pew wherein one Mrs Ware sits and pretends to be placed is and hath always been a pew for women of a far better rank and quality than she and for

---

[29] Cressy 1980: 135.   [30] G.L.R.O. P92/SAV/764.
[31] G.L.R.O. P92/SAV/769.   [32] G.L.R.O. P92/SAV/793.
[33] For other examples of this see McCampbell 1976: 110; Wrightson 1982: 17; R. Gough, *The History of Myddle*, Harmondsworth, 1981, pp. 77–84; A. Heales, *The History and Law of Church Seats or Pews*, London, 1872, pp. 127–55; Hill 1971: 175–82.
[34] G.L.R.O. P92/SAV/450, 24 September 1610.
[35] G.L.R.O. P92/SAV/202.

such whose husbands pay far greater duties than hers'.[36] In fact women may well have been particularly liable to involvement in pew disputes due to changes in their local social status following remarriage. Robert Chambers' wife Marie went to extraordinary lengths to resist such reclassification; in 1634 she was presented to the church courts,

for refusing to sit in the pew where she is placed by the churchwardens and procuring a key to be made to the lock of that pew from whence she was removed without the leave of any of the churchwardens and striving to sit there still having been by them warned to the contrary and placed in another decent pew.[37]

Seating disputes also occurred between parishioners. Hence William Locke, a wealthy inhabitant of the Clink liberty, caused an inhibition to be served on the wife of William Crofts, cheesemonger, of the Boroughside,' for sitting in a pew in the church, that hath been otherwise appointed'. He also threatened Crofts with further action: 'I send notice unto you as a neighbour to wish her to forbear, otherwise I shall take such a course as will not be pleasing to you or any of those that advise her to do that she hath done'.[38]

Another way in which local standing might be displayed was through dress. As is well known official attempts to enforce sumptuary legislation, wherein certain articles of clothing were deemed suitable for particular social groups, were rarely enforced effectively in the sixteenth century and were repealed in 1604.[39] Nonetheless wealth and power was still reflected in dress. In the socially heterogeneous environment of seventeenth-century London dress may have assumed a particular importance as a means of displaying one's social rank to stranger and neighbour alike. That only London, in the 1560s and 1570s, made any serious effort to enforce Tudor sumptuary legislation may reflect the enhanced importance of personal appearance in that crowded and expanding city.[40]

In the Boroughside membership of certain institutions could be reflected in distinctive clothing. The beadles of St Thomas's Hospital, who regularly

---

[36] The administrative districts of the parish of St Saviour's were also reflected in these seating arrangements. The pews for Bankside inhabitants 'being for the most part all on the Northside of the body of the Church'. G.L.R.O. P92/SAV/520. For the effect of residence on pew placing see Chapter 10, below.

[37] Marie Chambers had been married previously to Richard Overman and thereby related to Thomas Overman, one of the vestrymen, and to the influential Bromfield family, G.L.R.O. P92/SAV/533.

[38] G.L.R.O. P92/SAV/409.

[39] See Harte 1976: 132–65; W. Hooper, 'The Tudor sumptuary laws', *English Historical Review* 30 (1915), 433–49. For a useful account of personal appearance see also, Latham and Mathews 1970–83: 10, 98–101. For local sumptuary legislation in Coventry see, Phythian-Adams 1979: 128–9.

[40] See Hooper 1915: 438–44; Harte 1976: 146–7. For efforts to control dress within London companies see, T. F. Reddaway, 'The livery companies of Tudor London', *History* 51, 173 (1966), 292. For personal appearance see also the excellent Margaret Pelling, 'Appearance and reality: barbersurgeons, the body and disease in early modern London', in A. L. Beier and R. Finlay (eds.), *The Making of the Metropolis* (forthcoming).

patrolled the Southwark streets, were dressed in a blue livery.[41] Liverymen of city companies were expected to attend company dinners or members' funerals in distinctive livery gowns. George Dalton, a Boroughside joiner, bequeathed his best livery gown to a neighbouring relative 'when he is called to be one of the liverymen of his company'.[42] Local officials were also expected to wear gowns on particular occasions. The vestrymen of St Saviour's were to don their gowns at colleagues' funerals and the governors of St Thomas's Hospital were to be fined for failing to wear similar clothing at governors' meetings.[43]

As noted above parish paupers were dressed to be identified as such. Members of the College of the Poor in St Saviour's wore a special badge. Thomas Cure the founder ordained in 1584, 'that every one of the poor of this College and every their children and servants shall daily wear upon their right shoulder the cognizance of the College provided for that purpose, and that so apparently that they may be discerned thereby wheresoever they shall be come'.[44] Robert Buckland, the wealthy glover, who also founded a local parish charity likewise ordered that each recipient should wear a badge comprising the initials 'R.B.'. In this Buckland was emulating one of the provisions of the charity established by Henry Smith, an important London philanthropist, which supplied clothing for Boroughside poor complete with red badges 'H.S.'. The nationwide charitable endowments made by Smith meant that the urban practice of publicly identifying local paupers was spread to many rural parishes before the practice was enshrined in national legislation in the later seventeenth century.[45]

Richness and variety of clothing not unnaturally reflected wealth. Wealthy Boroughside testators invested some of their surplus income in a diverse wardrobe. Many distinguished between their 'best' clothing reserved for festivals or holidays and everyday wear. Andrew Baxter, a wealthy victualler, bequeathed his brother 'my stuff suit of cloth and my cloth suit of clothes, my best hat, one pair of my best stockings, my best pair of garters, and the girdle belonging to the said suit' but left his cousin the 'suit of clothes which I usually wear in the weekdays'. Poorer individuals did not have these sartorial resources.[46] In a very real sense an altered personal appearance might itself lead to changes in one's ascribed social

---

[41] Eileen M. McInnes, *St Thomas's Hospital*, London, 1963, p. 29.
[42] G.L.R.O. Archdeaconry of Surrey Will Register, 369 Yeast.
[43] McInnes 1963: 44–5.
[44] G.L.R.O. P92/SAV/1529, 13.
[45] For details of Smith's and Buckland's endowments, see, *Accounts and Papers 16*, 1898: 523–641. See also Jordan 1960: 117–22; Wrightson and Levine 1979: 179. It seems therefore unlikely that Henry Smith was a 'local yeoman' of Terling or that the poor of Terling were 'singled out' and badged, ibid. See, also, Sharpe 1980: 115.
[46] G.L.R.O. Archdeaconry of Surrey Will Register, 286 Yeast. See also, Palliser 1983: 115.

standing. In seventeenth-century London you were, at first, what you appeared to be. The perils of this method of allocating social status were brought out by a petition to the vestry written by an aging widow in which she complained that her pension for keeping her son-in-law's child had been stopped 'for of necessity the petitioner must still keep the...child his father being unable though (through wearing an old black suit given him by a gentleman) the collectors suppose otherwise'.[47]

Local status received further public expression in burial ceremonial.[48] Vestrymen accompanied the corpses of their colleagues according to a precise ritual, the manner of which was set out by the vestry in 1621: 'when the vestrymen shall be requested to accompany the corpse of any vestryman or vestryman's wife to burial they shall first meet in the vestry in due time in their gowns and then afterwards go together to the house of the party that is to be buried'.[49] As we have seen, burial charges varied according to wealth. The length and number of bells tolled, the quality of the cloth laid over the corpse, the use or otherwise of a coffin and interment in the church were themselves public advertisements of local status. For the wealthier householders such duties were only a very small part of the total cost of interment. Small memorial gifts such as rings or gloves and charitable handouts took place at the funerals of the better off.[50] A form of wake also took place after the funeral, hence Hugh Knightly, citizen and woodmonger, 'do will the sum of £7 to be bestowed on my funeral and in the entertainment of such as shall accompany my corpse to the grave'. Such public displays of wealth smacked of popery to some of the more puritan-minded inhabitants. Joshuah Phinnies, soapboiler, was participating in a growing trend among certain sections of the Boroughside's wealthier inhabitants when he asked to be 'buried in decent manner and no mourning apparel nor scarfs nor ribbands to be given to any', although he still added that 'I do appoint to be expended on my funeral charges the sum of £30'.[51]

For the wealthy élite interment in the church could be followed by the erection of a public monument. The contemporary importance of such monuments is reflected in the space allocated to them in the works of John Stow and his successor John Strype. Strype noted a number of monuments erected by Boroughside inhabitants resident in 1622. Hence Robert

---

[47] G.L.R.O. P92/SAV/765. Samuel Pepys, wearing a plain hatband, in 1667 was mistaken for a servant, Latham and Mathews 1970–83: 10, 99.

[48] Thomas 1978: 718–22; Palliser 1979: 291; Jordan 1960: 87–90.

[49] G.L.R.O. P92/SAV/450, 6 December 1621.

[50] Memorial rings often carried appropriate insignia, note for example, William Potter, citizen and ironmonger, who left his brothers and sisters 10s. each 'for a ring each with a Death's Head', G.L.R.O. Archdeaconry of Surrey Will Register, 329 Stoughton. See also, Thomas 1978: 718; Jordan 1960: 90; Rendle 1878: 176.

[51] P.C.C. Will Register, 140 Berkeley, 336 Brent.

Buckland, the wealthy glover, erected a monument to his only son, John, who died in the 1625 plague epidemic. John Bingham, another vestryman, also had a monument erected to his memory after his death. Such monuments stressed the piety and good works of the deceased. Samuel Simonds who was a wealthy baker resident in Horsehead Alley in 1622, and became a vestryman in 1625, erected a monument to his son John on which was inscribed a list of John's charitable donations and a suitable epitaph.[52]

Considerable local social status derived from membership of the vestry. In fact, the members of the vestry were almost a 'society within a society'. William Ward, goldsmith, who became a member of the vestry in 1624, explicitly bequeathed £6 for a dinner to the vestry, 'of which society I am now a member'.[53]

The élite nature of vestry membership, already set out in public ceremonial and privileged seating in the parish church, was reinforced by the secrecy surrounding meetings, secrecy which was backed by rigorous penalties: in 1615 it was ordered that 'no vestryman [is] to persuade or openly discuss [the] choice of minister on pain of 40s. and exclusion from office'.[54] Within this miniature society seniority rather than social position conferred status. In a list of all the vestrymen made in March 1622, therefore, the vestry clerk began with the name of John Bingham (elected June 1594) and ended with the most junior member Nicholas Norman (elected September 1621).[55] Seniority was expressed in the vestry seating arrangements; in 1615 it was laid down that 'every one shall sit according to his election and coming into the vestry and not in order according to their rank and qualities'. The placings were reinforced by small fines: in 1621 Mr Dawson paid 4d. to the poor box 'for sitting out of his place'.[56]

It is clear, however, that city gilds and companies were an important 'extra-local' source of social prestige. A number of Boroughside householders proclaimed their citizenship and membership of city companies in a manner which suggests that membership of such groups conferred some status. By the 'custom of London', membership of a 'buying and selling' gild brought with it the freedom to practise any trade in the City.[57] In their wills a number of Boroughside testators preferred to be identified with such a company rather than simply by their true occupation. Hence in his will

[52] See Thomas 1978: 721; Strype 1720: 2, 8–16; Taylor 1833: 81–124; Rendle 1878: 157–96.
[53] P.C.C. Will Register 80 Byrde.
[54] G.L.R.O. P92/SAV/450, 21 February 1614.
[55] G.L.R.O. P92/SAV/450, 2 March 1622.
[56] G.L.R.O. P92/SAV/450, 24 August 1615, 29 August 1621. For similar codes of conduct elsewhere in London see, McCampbell 1976: 110.
[57] See, Pearl 1979: 8; Kellett 1958: 390; Ramsay 1978: 532; Ramsay 1975: 228; Unwin 1957:105; Elliott 1978: 368–71.

Ralph Babington styled himself 'citizen and haberdasher of London' rather than as a vintner.[58] In a similar fashion members of less exalted 'manual' gilds, who were more likely to follow the actual trade of that gild, also gave company membership in preference to simple occupational label.[59] Thomas Witcherly styled himself 'citizen and pewterer' in his will rather than simply 'pewterer'.[60]

It seems probable that, in the City and its liberties, citizens formed the majority of adult males in the late sixteenth and early seventeenth century. In the mid sixteenth century something like two thirds of the adult male workforce were freemen of the city. In the mid seventeenth century Valerie Pearl has estimated that three-quarters of all male householders 'in the City' were freemen. Within the City therefore freemen were not a privileged minority élite but were ubiquitous in the social order.[61] However such estimates neglect the population of the outparishes and distant parishes incorporated into the London Bills of Mortality in the early seventeenth-century. We do not know how many freemen chose to live *outside* the jurisdiction of the City in Westminster, Stepney, Whitechapel, St Martin-in-the-Fields and so on. Such areas came to include an ever-increasing proportion of London's population. If it is assumed that inclusion in the bills of mortality of these areas 'accurately reflected the growth of the townscape', then in 1605 the outparishes alone already contained something like 44,000 people – a quarter of the capital's population. By the mid seventeenth century the population of the City and its liberties may have been equalled by that of the areas beyond its jurisdiction. Calculations that fail to take this 'dilution factor' into account may seriously overestimate the proportion of householders who were also freemen of the City.[62]

It has become historical convention that large numbers of non-freemen settled in Southwark to escape the irksome economic controls of London's companies and gilds. Reddaway has perhaps best set out this orthodoxy. For company officials,

---

[58] G.L.R.O. Archdeaconry of Surrey Will Register, 465 Yeast.
[59] Pearl 1979: 8. In the early eighteenth century gild or company affiliation and actual occupation correlated closely in the smaller bodies, Kellett 1958: 390.
[60] P.C.C. Will Register 55 Harvey.
[61] Pearl 1979: 13; Pearl 1981: 117–18; Rappaport 1983: 112.
[62] Finlay 1981: 51–60, 155–7; Pearl 1979: 7. Valerie Pearl used a population of 200,000 in her calculations and divided this total by five to arrive at the number of households. This figure seems to refer to the City and its liberties only in the mid seventeenth century, ibid., p. 13. The population of London *including* the outparishes and distant parishes has been estimated recently at 391,000 and 456,000 in 1640. Without the distant parishes the figure is now thought to have been between 326,000 and 380,000 (Finlay 1981: 60). If we accept a total of 33,000 freemen living in the City, its liberties and the outparishes in 1640 (Pearl 1979: 31) then this would, assuming an equal geographical distribution across London, imply that between 43.4 and 50.6% of householders in the capital as a whole were freemen. The dilution factor is critical.

to spend a day going to Southwark or Westminster...was to pass beyond the civic boundaries into Surrey or Middlesex, into quarters where aliens abounded and where loyalty to the company and its benefits was largely replaced by dislike of irksome controls and suspicion as to motives. Payment of quarterage brought no obvious benefit to such men. The hall was not a familiar place where friends met and business was arranged.[63]

A more recent writer has written that for similar reasons 'a great many Southwark traders did not belong to London Companies and had no interest in doing so'.[64] This phenomenon is thought to have occurred despite the fact that from the mid-sixteenth century most of Southwark had been within the liberties of the City of London and many gilds and companies had jurisdiction in the area. Furthermore citizenship brought with it the important right to set up shop within the liberties of the city.[65] Information presented in Chapter 3 indicates that possession of shops was widespread among High Street dwellers. How many Boroughside householders were London citizens?

Satisfactory evidence by which to estimate the proportion of citizens in the Boroughside's population is hard to come by. Table 6.3 sets out the proportion of will-makers who styled themselves citizens of London in wills proved between 1622 and 1646. The table gives only the roughest of guides to the proportion of citizens. Not only do the figures assume a constant death rate for all social groups and make the unjustified assumption that absence of reference to a company reflects non-membership, but it is also clear that will-makers were not a representative cross-section of Boroughside householders. Comparison with the distribution of wealth demonstrates that will-makers were drawn from the wealthier members of the community.[66] Hence only 12 out of 550 or 2.2% of those male householders not contributing to the poor rate made wills between 1622 and 1646 compared to 14 out of 25 or 56% of those male householders paying 5*d.* or more. Table 6.3 will also be distorted by individuals whose poor-rate assessments changed significantly between 1622 and 1646. Despite such reservations the figures do indicate that citizenship was widespread among the wealthier groups. Hence 85.7% of all will-makers contributing 5*d.* or more to the poor rate in 1622 styled themselves as citizens of London. The table also suggests that there may have been a fairly close relationship between the possession of citizenship and wealth. Of those will-makers assessed at between 1*d.* and 4*d.*, 42% were citizens but of those assessed at $\frac{1}{2}d.$ or nothing at all only

---

[63] Reddaway 1966: 297.   [64] Johnson 1969: 313.

[65] McGrath 1948: 37; Johnson 1969: 310–13.

[66] See Chapter 9 below. For the wealth of will-makers see, R. T. Vann, 'Wills and the family in an English town. Banbury 1550–1800', *Journal of Family History* 4 (1979), 353–6; Wrightson and Levine 1979: 93.

Table 6.3. *Proportion of will-makers in the Boroughside describing themselves as citizens 1622–46*

Poor-rate assessment of will-maker in 1622	Number of will-makers	Number of will-makers describing themselves as citizens	%
d.			
+7	4	4	100
6	5	4	80
5	5	4	80
4	9	5	56
3	17	8	47
2	19	6	32
1¼	1	1	100
1	9	3	33
½	5	0	0
Nothing	12	3	25
Total	86	38	44

Source: See discussion in text, p. 152.

18% declared themselves as freemen. Another piece of evidence that citizenship was widespread among the wealthier inhabitants of the Boroughside is contained in the Holymote inquest of the Whitebakers' company 1622. There were sixteen bakers identified in the Boroughside in 1622, seven of whom were poor-rate payers. Six of these seven attended the inquest in December 1622.[67] In a similar fashion most Boroughside grocers, for which evidence survives, were members of the prestigious Grocers' company and a number served as wardens of that company.[68]

If the foregoing evidence suggests that a large number of the Boroughside's wealthier householders were also London citizens there is also some material to indicate that substantial householders were able to hold office and run large businesses outside the citizen body and an appropriate company structure. The relative stagnation of the Butchers' company in the later sixteenth century may be explained partly by the establishment of the large Butchers' shambles in the Boroughside, few of whose members belonged to that company.[69] Most of these High Street butchers kept

[67] For the record these were: William Stubbes; Richard Thickens; Anchor Kitchen; John Williamson; Henry Wilson; John Marshall. See the quest book of the Whitebakers' Company, Guildhall Library Ms no. 5181. Samuell Simonds, the only poor-rate paying baker not to attend, was a member of the associated Starchmakers' company.

[68] Richard Yearwood, warden 1626 and 1631; Drew Stapely, warden 1631; Richard Wright, warden 1633 and 1640. See W. Grantham, *List of the Wardens of the Grocers' Company (from 1345 to 1904)* 2nd edn., London, 1931, pp. 25–6.   [69] Rappaport 1983: 124.

servants, contributed to the local poor rate and the subsidy and served in local parish and manorial office. It may be of course that some of these individuals were members of other London companies, such as the tallow-chandlers or the skinners.

Membership of city companies received public expression in both burial ritual and church monuments. Fellow members were enjoined to attend the funerals of Boroughside inhabitants and money bequeathed to companies was often linked to this practice. John Bingham left £6 to the Saddlers' company 'for a supper at [my] funeral'. A more cautious Boroughside resident Thomas Witcherly bequeathed £4 to the 'company of pewterers if they come to my funeral'. Similarly Samuel Simonds left £5 to the Starchmakers' company for a dinner, and Gregory Franklin £4 to the Saddlers' company. John Marshall bequeathed £50 to the Tallowchandlers' company, 'whereof I am a brother', £30 of which was for the relief of 'poor brethren' and £20 for a dinner for the master, wardens and livery.[70] Some Boroughside householders were interred in the church underneath their company's arms. Hence John Simonds, the son of Samuel referred to above, lay under the Whitebakers' arms, and John Bingham under the Saddlers'.[71]

Not surprisingly, power and influence, like wealth, were distributed unequally in this society. Richer households controlled not only the members of their larger than average domestic units but also other householders in dependent social or economic positions. These social inequalities were advertised and reinforced by various forms of visual displays from tombs in the parish church to the paupers' badge. Dress and other forms of conspicuous expenditure also distinguished householders with money to spare from those who barely earned enough to make ends meet.

6.3 Social mobility: the urban life cycle

Social mobility can take different forms. Inter-generational social mobility has recently been studied by comparing the social status of fathers to the subsequent career choice of sons or the marriage partners of their daughters. Other studies have looked at the turnover within urban oligarchies and the role of immigration in replenishing them.[72] Indeed, social mobility is sometimes linked to geographical mobility, although details of both the subsequent fortunes and the social origins of the migrant are required in

[70] See P.C.C. Will Register 112 Clarke; 55 Harvey; 111 Sadler; 73 Byrde; 83 Clarke, respectively.
[71] Strype 1720: 2, 12–13.
[72] Elliott 1978: 343–72 *et passim*; W. G. Hoskins, 'The Elizabethan merchants of Exeter', in P. Clark (ed.), *The Early Modern Town*, London, 1976, pp. 148–67; MacCaffrey 1975: 257–68; Dyer 1973: 180–8; Palliser 1979: 127–34; Hoskins 1976a: 96; Clark and Slack 1976: 118–19.

order to assess fully the impact of each move.[73] It has recently been argued that parental influence played a significant role in determining the success or otherwise of London apprentices.[74] It is not possible, however, in the absence of information on the social and geographical origins of most Boroughside householders, to say anything about inter-generational social mobility.

Social mobility has tended to be defined as a single movement between two fixed occupational or social groups. Thus for example an individual would be said to have moved 'downwards' from draper to tailor or 'upwards' from husbandman to yeoman. Movement between such groups can be observed on the occasions of marriage, migration or apprenticeship.[75]

All studies of social mobility, however, are complicated by the fact that movement must have been continuous. Individuals did not necessarily maintain the same socio-economic status throughout their lives. A number of studies have recently noted the effect of aging and the life-cycle on individual social and financial circumstances.[76] Comparisons between the social position of a father and his son may be distorted by the different points in the life-cycle reached by each individual. It has been established, for example, that it could take ten years to establish a business in seventeenth-century London, consequently, 'a merchant who died young died poor'. Furthermore the insecurity of trade and the brittle credit networks could quickly undermine even substantial fortunes.[77]

For those whose occupations involved physical labour, earning potential must have lessened with age.[78] The constant physical strain meant that, according to Adam Smith, a London carpenter had only eight years of 'utmost vigour'. In medieval Coventry a capper's working life was said to have been over by the age of 50, although 60 was commonly taken to be the 'stylised age of decrepitude'.[79] What effects did the life-cycle have on the social and financial status of Boroughside householders?

It is possible, using a 1629 muster of watermen, to say something about the age at which individuals might expect to become householders. The age structure of the population of seventeenth-century London is very

---

[73] L. Stone, 'Social mobility in England 1500–1700', *Past and Present* 33 (1966), 29–33.
[74] Elliott 1978: 61; Rappaport 1981: 19; Ramsay 1978: 539. For other comments on paternal influence see Stone 1966: 38; Grassby 1978: 358; Lang 1974: 31–40; Smith 1973a: 195–205.
[75] Elliott 1978: 367. See also, Elliott 1981: 81–100.
[76] Elliott 1978: 369; Rappaport 1981: 2–25; Ramsay 1978: 534–40; Smith 1981b: 606–11; Phythian-Adams 1979: 91–5, 144–7; Grassby 1970: 221; P. Laslett, 'Societal development and aging', in R. H. Binstock and E. Shanas (eds.), *Handbook of Aging and the Social Sciences*, New York, 1976, pp. 87–116.
[77] Grassby 1978: 369; Grassby 1970: 223; Hoskins 1976a: 96.
[78] Herlan 1977b: 187; George 1966: 202; K. Thomas, 'Age and authority in early modern England', *Proceedings of the British Academy* 62 (1976), 38.
[79] George 1966: 203; Phythian-Adams 1979: 93; Thomas 1976: 35.

difficult to reconstruct in the absence of household listings supplying ages.[80] However, the 1629 muster supplies information about the ages of all those watermen enrolled. Watermen were liable to maritime service in time of war. Thames watermen were ordered to be pressed in April 1624, an order which was repeated in April 1627. The 1629 muster was entitled a 'Muster taken the second day of February 1628/9 of all the watermen belonging to the Port of London and the liberties thereof'.[81] The roll listed the residence, name, age, and number of previous voyages of each individual. Despite the fact that the trade of waterman involved strenuous physical activity there are grounds for believing that few individuals were excluded from the roll on grounds of physical debility or old age since even very old men, such as one John Callowhill of the Clink liberty, aged 80, were listed. Moreover it is clear from the acts of parliament that regulated the trade that apprentices and servants were expected to take sole charge of their masters' boats, in theory at least, two years after the commencement of their training. Old or infirm watermen could live off the labour of apprentices, servants or offspring without retiring from the profession altogether.[82] Nonetheless the possibility that some elderly watermen were not listed and that their numbers have been underestimated cannot be entirely ruled out.

In order to look at the ages of householders the names on the 1629 muster roll for Paris Garden were linked to those listed in the token book of that year for the same place.[83] Fortunately the token book was compiled at about the same time as the muster roll, in March 1629, so that the ages do not require adjustment. All in all 188 of the 424 male householders resident in Paris Garden in 1629 (44.3%) were listed in the muster roll. What follows therefore is an age profile of male householders belonging to the low status manual trade of waterman and consequently it may not reflect the age profile of some of the higher status occupational groups found in the Boroughside area. No waterman was under 17 years old, in line with the minimum age at which apprenticeships could be taken up.[84] As other studies have noted the age-reporting tended to favour numbers ending in zero. This tendency would not have significantly altered the profile of the age structure although it might have caused some overlap between adjacent age groups.[85]

---

[80] For a review of known household listings supplying age data for places in England before 1800 see, Laslett 1976: 100. For attempts to estimate the age structure of London's population, see, Finlay 1981: 83–91; Hollingsworth 1971: 133–44.

[81] *C.S.P.D. 1623–5*, 162.46; *C.S.P.D. 1627–8*, 61.22; P.R.O. SP16/135/4.

[82] For regulation of the Watermans' company see, H. Humpherus, *History of the Origins and Progress of the Company of Watermen and Lightermen of the River Thames 1514–1859*, London, 2nd edn, 1981, vol. 1, pp. 100–7, 159–61, 213–18 and *passim*.

[83] G.L.R.O. P92/SAV/305.   [84] *C.S.P.D. 1625–6*, 34.22.

[85] Hollingsworth 1971: 135; Finlay 1981: 124–6; Thomas 1976: 5.

Table 6.4. *Age structure of watermen and those becoming householders in Paris Garden, St Saviour's, Southwark, 1629*

Age group	Persons mustered in age group	Percent of age group who were householders	Householders in age group	Percent distribution of householders
17–19	20	5.0	1	0.5
20–24	112	7.1	8	4.3
25–29	52	48.1	25	13.3
30–34	35	80.0	28	14.9
35–39	31	87.1	27	14.4
40–44	40	85.0	34	18.1
45–49	23	100.0	23	12.2
50–54	16	100.0	16	8.5
55–59	8	100.0	8	4.3
60–64	14	100.0	14	7.5
65–69	3	100.0	3	1.6
70–74	1	100.0	1	0.5
Total	355		188	

Source: See discussion in text, pp. 155–6.

Table 6.4 supplies both the age distribution of male householders and also the proportion of each age group who were householders. It has been assumed that individuals mustered but not identified as householders were present in other watermens' households as servants or apprentices. The study confirms the views of those who have noted that attainment of this elementary social and economic responsibility took place in the late 20s.[86] Only one householder proved to be in his late teens and only nine were under 25. Some 112 out of 188 (59.6%) were in their 30s or 40s. By the age of 45 *all* male watermen had become householders; 80% had done so by their early 30s. Another point worth noting is that the distribution of ages of all mustered watermen shows a bulge in the number of men in their early 20s. This is in striking contrast to the age structure of the population estimated for St Botolph without Bishopsgate in 1601. If the Hollingsworths' figures for the age distribution of the total population are corrected by the age-specific sex ratios at burial to refer to the male population, they indicate that only 20.9% of those males in the age group 20–74 were in their early 20s compared to 30.1% among Paris Garden watermen. It may be that watermen were, as a group, unusually likely to maintain servants and apprentices, although their relative poverty vis-à-vis other occupational groups makes this seem unlikely. It is more probable that the skewed age structure is a product of the predominance of adolescent males who formed a large proportion of the capital's total annual imigration in the early seventeenth century, a point which the St Botolph figures did not allow for.[87] There also appears to have been an unusually large discrepancy between the numbers of men in their early 20s and the numbers in their late 20s. This may reflect limited economic opportunity (watermen were said to be severely underemployed in the 1630s) which discouraged them from following the trade and thus restricted the chances of setting up an independent household.[88] It may be that, as in some other trades and crafts in the mid sixteenth century, many of those in service or apprenticed to watermen did not subsequently settle or complete their training in the capital.[89]

Comparison with data from other towns and villages in pre-industrial England suggests that, although the *probability* for those in the younger age groups of setting up households was not always better and very often worse in the capital than elsewhere, *overall* male household heads were generally younger (see Tables 6.5–6.7). The chances of becoming a householder before the age of 30 were poorest in Paris Garden – only 20.1% of all male

---

[86] Elliott 1981: 185; Finlay 1981: 139; Rappaport 1983: 115–18.
[87] Hollingsworth 1971: 143–4. For this problem see also, Finlay 1981: 126–7, 130.
[88] See, for example, the complaints echoed in Taylor 1973: passim and also the same author's *The World Runnes on Wheels*, ibid., 232–44.   [89] Rappaport 1983: 117.

Table 6.5. *Age distribution of watermen in Paris Garden, St Saviour's, Southwark, 1629, and adult males in three pre-industrial settlements*

Age group	Paris Garden[a]		Lichfield 1695[b]		Stoke 1700[b]		Ealing 1599[c]	
	N	%	N	%	N	%	N	%
20–24	112	33.4	54	8.6	55	13.9	14	12.1
25–29	52	15.5	62	9.9	60	15.1	17	14.7
30–34	35	10.5	98	15.6	59	14.9	21	18.1
35–39	31	9.3	99	15.7	43	10.8	8	6.9
40–44	40	11.9	90	14.3	32	8.1	14	12.1
45–49	23	6.9	49	7.8	27	6.8	2	1.7
50–54	16	4.8	62	9.9	33	8.3	19	16.4
55–59	8	2.4	31	4.9	26	6.6	5	4.3
60–64	14	4.2	40	6.4	24	6.1	12	10.4
65–69	3	0.9	16	2.5	18	4.5	3	2.6
70+	1	0.3	28	4.5	20	5.0	1	0.9
Total	335		629		397		116	

Sources: [a] See Table 6.4 and discussion in text, pp. 155–6.
[b] Tabulated data from household listings, Cambridge Population Group.
[c] Laslett 1972a: 75–9.

watermen between the ages of 20 and 29 were household heads. Chances were slightly better in rural Ealing (22.6%) and markedly better in late seventeenth-century Lichfield (31.9%) and Stoke (33.9%).[90] For those who stayed the course in Southwark attainment of householder status was certain by the age of 45 which was not the case elsewhere. The males' overall chances of becoming a householder seem to have been lower in Paris Garden in 1629 than in rural Ealing (55.8% of all watermen over the age of 20 were householders compared to 60.3% in Ealing). It is likely that *competition* for householderships was a key factor in this situation. Something like 33.4% of all male watermen over 20 were in the 20–24 age group compared to between 7.8% and 12.1% in other areas. The immigrant faced considerable competition from his own age group. The universal attainment of the position of householder for all watermen over 45 (Table 6.6) contrasts greatly with the experience of other communities where there was often

[90] The data for Ealing can be found in Laslett 1972a: 75, 79. The listing has been published, see, K. J. Allison,' An Elizabethan village "census"', *Bulletin of the Institute of Historical Research* 35 (1962), 93–103. The data for Lichfield and Stoke-on-Trent has been taken from the tabulations kept at the Cambridge Group for the History of Population and Household Structure. For Lichfield see also, D. V. Glass, 'Two papers on Gregory King', in D. V. Glass and D. E. C. Eversley (eds.), *Population in History*, London, 1974, pp. 208–9.

Table 6.6. *Headship rates, percentage of adult males in each age group heading households*

Age group	Paris Garden watermen 1629	Lichfield 1695	Stoke 1700	Ealing 1599
15–19	5.0	0	0	0
20–24	7.1	27.8	14.6	7.1
25–29	48.1	35.5	51.7	35.3
30–34	80.0	79.6	83.1	66.7
35–39	87.1	77.8	97.7	37.5
40–44	85.0	90.0	96.9	71.4
45–49	100.0	87.8	96.3	100.0
50–54	100.0	90.3	93.9	89.5
55–59	100.0	90.3	100.0	100.0
60–64	100.0	72.5	83.3	83.3
65–69	100.0	81.3	88.9	66.7
70 +	100.0	60.7	95.0	0

Sources: See Table 6.5.

a significant fall off rate after the age of 60, as the elderly lost their positions as household heads. This could be explained either by a few elderly dependent watermen having, in fact, been omitted from the muster roll or by a greater ability of such persons to maintain their position as heads of household in the face of the aging process.

Among watermen, male household heads in Paris Garden were, as a body, *younger* than elsewhere – 18.1 % of households were headed by individuals under 30 years of age compared to between 8.1 % and 13.1 % in pre-industrial England (see Table 6.7). Elderly householders appear to have been less common. Paris Garden had the lowest percentage of householders over 45 (34.5 %) and Ealing the highest (51.4 %). Part of this could, of course, be an artifact caused by the omission of some elderly watermen from the original muster roll but high adult mortality rates in London, coupled with the pressure from young apprentices and servants capable of taking up places as they fell vacant, could also have played a part in producing this youthful bias.[91] What other evidence have we for the effects of aging in Southwark society?

One method of looking at the effect of getting older is to examine the process of 'pauperisation'. Poverty was a state that individual households could enter at different points in the life-cycle.[92] In the absence of detailed

[91] Higher adult mortality rates in London 'meant that only one-half of native Londoners had living fathers compared with three quarters of...immigrants', Rappaport 1983: 118.
[92] Slack et al 1977: 84; Beier 1981: 62; Smith 1981b: 606–11.

Table 6.7. *Percentage age distribution of adult male householders in Paris Garden and three pre-industrial settlements*

Age group	Paris Garden watermen 1629	Lichfield 1695	Stoke 1700	Ealing 1599
20–24	4.3	3.3	2.7	1.4
25–29	13.4	4.8	10.4	8.6
30–34	15.0	17.0	16.4	20.0
35–39	14.4	16.8	14.1	4.3
40–44	18.2	17.7	10.4	14.4
45–49	12.3	9.4	8.7	2.9
50–54	8.5	12.2	10.4	24.3
55–59	4.3	6.1	8.7	7.1
60–64	7.5	6.3	6.7	14.3
65–69	1.6	2.8	5.4	2.9
70+	0.5	3.7	6.4	0.0
Number of householders in each age group	187	459	299	70

Note: Paris Garden figures omit one 19 year-old householder.
Sources: See Table 6.5.

records of poor-relief payments over a long period of time, however, it is not possible to follow an individual's lifetime experience. Furthermore, as has been referred to above, many poor-relief payments were only intended as income supplements and were made to householders who were by no means entirely dependent on them. The remainder of this chapter seeks to identify the point in the life-cycle at which householders were likely to reach near total dependence on poor-relief payments. It was felt that the best means of achieving this aim was to look at those individuals admitted into the college hospital of the poor since its inhabitants received the largest weekly pensions and had reached the point where physical independence was virtually impossible.

The college 'degrees of admittance' recognised the life-cycle nature of poverty. In descending order of priority the degrees were: one who had 'become aged and which having before been a labourer is now past work'; the lame and sick; the blind; those 'despoiled of their goods and brought from riches to poverty by any sudden casualty'; the continually sick; and those families 'overcharged with a burthen of children'.[93] Need occasioned by accident or sickness, however, was usually relieved by loans, regular weekly pensions or one-off extraordinary payments rather than admission to the college.

[93] G.L.R.O. P92/SAV/1529.

Age-related pauperism was the usual reason for admission to the college hospital. Ten individuals chosen by the vestry, whose ages were given, were said to be between 62 and 92 years old.[94] Similarly those petitioning for college admittance were aged between 60 and 91.[95] Other petitioners referred to their 'decrepid old age' or 'age and weakness'. In particular blindness was often linked to old age, thus Susan Coleman 'near upon 80 years of age...is now past labour being full of aches and dim of sight'. Nicholas Purchase, '76 years of age and upwards...did so long as he was able, truly labour for his living, but his sight now, failing him, he is altogether unable to get any thing towards the same, being a very poor man destitute both of friends and means and his wife also blind'.[96]

Given that the over-sixties were the most likely age group to fall into near total dependency, how many persons were at risk? Estimates of the proportion of the population over 60 in pre-industrial England range from as low as 3.4% in late eighteenth-century Manchester to as high as 19.1% in the small village of Ringmore in 1698. Most estimates, however, lie between 5.9 and 10.6%. The most recent estimate put the proportion of the population over 60 in England to be between 7.9% and 8.9% in the first half of the seventeenth century.[97] Contemporaries, however, thought that London's age structure was significantly different from the country at large. John Graunt, the pioneer demographer, wondered 'why are there more old men in Countries than in London, *per rata*?', answering that the capital's unhealthy climate was the answer. Gregory King also believed that there were fewer old people in London (and in other towns) than in the countryside.[98] The evidence of the muster rolls also suggests that at least one part of London might have had proportionately fewer elderly persons in its population than the nation as a whole. The only attempt to establish the age structure of a seventeenth-century London parish estimated that some 5.5% of the population were over 60.[99] If the same proportion held for the Boroughside in 1631, when there was a population of 3708 (excluding the floating population), then 204 individuals would have been over 60 and in the age group likely to experience the greatest hardship.

---

[94] See, G.L.R.O. P92/SAV/450, 30 June 1616, 27 April 1617, 17 August 1620, 27 October 1622, 22 December 1622, 6 March 1625, 8 May 1625, 4 March 1627.

[95] See the following petitions: G.L.R.O. P92/SAV/1601, William Shawe (91 years of age); 753, James Bankes (80); 754, Thomas Bentley (60); 759, Widow Carlton (80); 764, John Clove (64); 766, Richard Coleman (79); 767, Susan Coleman (80); 769, Roger Cotten (70); 775, Rice Jones (74); 779, Nicholas Purchase (76); 784, Anne Tedder (72); 786, Margaret Wood (78).

[96] G.L.R.O. P92/SAV/779. See also Thomas 1976: 38–42.

[97] Laslett 1976: 100; Glass 1974: 208–16; Wrigley and Schofield 1981: 528. For the age structure of the poor in Norwich see Pound 1971b: 17.

[98] Graunt 1973: 279; King 1973: 46.

[99] Hollingsworth 1971: 144. Subject to the distortions produced by the migrant population, discussed above.

Table 6.8. *Sex of heads of families resident in the College of St Saviour's, Southwark, 1621–41*

Date	Male	Female [a]	% Female
1621	5	12	71
1628	2	14	88
1641	6	10	63
Total	13	36	74

Note: [a]Excluding wives. The 1621 list records the presence of four women with their husbands.
Source: G.L.R.O. P92/SAV/210, 1583, 1596.

Given that about 15 individuals from the Boroughside who were over 60 would also have been resident in the college hospital then some 7% of all those over 60 would have lived in the institution in 1631. In the Boroughside the elderly person's chances of ending his days in an institution were similar, if not greater, to those of the over 65s in mid-nineteenth-century England.[100]

The loss of independence represented by college membership was largely the experience of elderly females (see Table 6.8). Three listings of the inmates record names of heads of resident families. Between 1621 and 1641 three-quarters of those living in the college were elderly females. This female preponderance probably reflects both the poorer earning potential and social and economic position of female householders discussed in previous chapters and also higher mortality rates prevailing among elderly men who were thus more likely to die in harness, whilst still heading households rather than sinking into abject dependence. This lends a little more weight to the relatively high headship rates found among the Paris Garden watermen (see Table 6.6).

The aging process therefore greatly affected the possession of status in the Boroughside. As we have seen the elderly might with the onset of age have been forced to give up their position as household head and move into the college hospital. Those who ended up in the college would have been subjected to a harsh religious discipline and physically segregated from the rest of the population. Many of the elderly poor would have been distinguished by a pauper's badge and would have been buried at parish expense in a pauper's grave. Elderly persons were also distinguished in

---

[100] In England and Wales in 1851, 4.3% of all males over 65 and 2.3% of all females resided in workhouses, the figure in London was 8.3 and 8.7% respectively, see, D. W. Thomson, 'Provision for the elderly in England, 1830 to 1908', Cambridge (1980), p. 166.

speech, being termed 'father' or 'mother'; hence George Claverly living in the college in 1621 was described as 'father Claverly' in the accounts.[101]

Aging, however, as other studies have indicated, also brought with it a certain status.[102] Another characteristic of those seeking admittance into the college was their long period of residence in the parish of St Saviour's. Of the twelve petitioners who specified the length of time they had lived in the parish the shortest period cited was 22 years; on average each petitioner had spent 41.9 years in the district. Others had 'lived in the said parish from a child' or had been 'born in this parish and had lived here most of this time'.[103] Consequently the elderly were a source of oral tradition, being called in to settle boundary disputes within the parish. In this connection the college hospital acted as a convenient reservoir of experience. Hence Thomas Oliver 'one of the almspeople of the College...aged 94 years or thereabouts' was called upon to testify as to the origins of two small yards in 1622.[104] The status attached to great age also seems to have led to exaggerations in age-reporting in the early seventeenth century in St Saviour's. On 27 December 1603 was buried 'Alice Pinke a woman 112 years old'; five days later this feat was excelled by Lawrence Darby 'a poor man aged 115 years'. This local record survived until 28 January 1604 when the burial occurred of 'John Harnece a man gravemaker of the age of 126'.[105]

The examination of Boroughside society in this and the previous two chapters has established that, like pre-industrial society all over Europe wealth was distributed unequally. The possession of wealth increased the power and influence of householders both directly by qualifying them for local offices and indirectly through employment, hospitality and charity. The size and structure of these households was also linked to possession of wealth. Growing older, with consequent loss of income, brought corresponding loss of social power and might even lead to loss of the primary position of household head, achieved by a significant proportion of the population. Social status was advertised publicly in church seating, in dress, in funeral ceremony and was enhanced and reinforced by the power, influence and prestige deriving from local office and membership of city companies.

However, the household was only part of the social world of Boroughside inhabitants. With the exception of the particularly large household most individuals would have been forced to seek their social contacts outside its boundaries. Relations between parents and adult children of necessity

---

[101] G.L.R.O. P92/SAV/1582.
[102] Thomas 1976: 7–9; Phythian-Adams 1979: 93, 126.
[103] G.L.R.O. P92/SAV/751, 756, 758, 762, 764, 766, 768, 779, 780, 783, 784, 786.
[104] G.L.R.O. P92/SAV/499. For similar examples also see, Thomas 1976: 32; Phythian-Adams 1979: 93.
[105] G.L.R.O. P92/SAV/1301, burial register. See also, Thomas 1976: 32–3.

involved an extra-household dimension. Those individuals employed in building or transport would have spent a large proportion of their time away from home. Indeed any trade or manufacture involved contacts with employers, suppliers or customers. The household was only part of the wider world represented by the street and by the neighbourhood.

7

Residential patterns and property ownership

7.1 The urban environment of the Boroughside: a typology

Where people lived and who they lived next to are important topics in urban history because it is thought that such residential patterns reflected the social composition of urban areas and the ways in which individuals related to each other. Thus the social topography of the classic medieval town or city is said to have been distinguished by social mixing, where rich and poor lived in close physical proximity, perhaps living in streets dominated by one particular occupational group. This pattern underpinned a sense of community involvement, familiarity and belonging. Such social cohesion is thought to have broken down in the modern industrial city, marked as it was by physical segregation of social classes and distinguished by class rather than social solidarity, developed by people living close together with others of similar means rather than similar trades and crafts.[1] Occupational or social zoning then, if it existed, might have exercised an important influence on urban social relations in the Boroughside. By reconstructing the residential distribution of wealth and occupations other information about neighbourly interaction can be placed in its proper context.

An examination of where Boroughside households were located might also allow us to infer something about how they lived. We know, for example, that in terms of persons per acre Southwark was less densely populated than the city parishes north of the river, but can we say anything about residential housing density? How restricted was personal living space? To what extent did the wealthy and the poor inhabit different urban environments?

---

[1] See, M. Power, 'Hearths and homes in pre-fire London', paper presented at the Conference on London Social and Economic History, 27 June 1981, p. 18; Pearl 1979: 7; R. Dennes and S. Daniels, '"Community" and the social geography of Victorian cities', *Urban History Yearbook* (1981), 8. For the social topography of Medieval Coventry see, Phythian-Adams 1979: 166.

There has recently been a considerable volume of work done on the social and occupational geography of pre-industrial towns and cities.[2] For example, Langton found that the cities of Newcastle, Dublin and Exeter consisted of a wealthy central core surrounded by a poorer periphery. Similarly the City of London in the seventeenth century consisted of a wealthy central zone surrounded by a poorer riverside belt in the south and a ring of poor parishes to the north and east.[3] However, work on certain parts of London and on other towns and cities has gone some way to blur the relatively neat patterns produced by historical geographers. Individual parishes often contained a wide range of wealth and even wealthy parishes had some poor inhabitants. In the West End of London in the mid-seventeenth century there was 'a variety of distinct kinds of urban environment'.[4]

It is possible to distinguish four residential 'sub-districts' in the Boroughside in the early seventeenth century. Within an urban parish access to a thoroughfare was of considerable economic and social importance. Households located on thoroughfares would have been exposed to human traffic but in alleys and yards, usually possessing only one entry, non-residents might rarely have entered. In such places, therefore, exposure to strangers was far more limited than life in a crowded and expanding city like London would at first have suggested.[5] The classification of the 'sub-districts' depends to a great extent on the volume of traffic entering them.[6] The High Street was the chief thoroughfare and the most superior residential district. Access to this street meant access both to the market site and the considerable traffic passing in and out of London via the bridge. As we saw in Chapter 3, Strype praised its size, the wealth of its inhabitants and the quality of its buildings (see Fig. 7.1). Counter Lane and Foul Lane were both secondary thoroughfares that linked the 'New Rents' to the High Street. Strype noted that Counter Lane in 1720 was 'a street of pretty good

[2] See, J. Langton, 'Residential patterns in pre-industrial cities: some case studies from seventeenth-century Britain', *Transactions of the Institute of British Geographers* 65 (1975), 1–27; Dyer 1973: 177–9; MacCaffrey 1975: 250–1; Pound 1971b: 10; D. J. Hibberd, 'Urban inequalities: social geography and demography in seventeenth-century York', Liverpool (1981).

[3] Langton 1975: 7–11; Glass 1966: ix–xxxix; Finlay 1981: 77–82; Jones 1980: 124–5; Herlan 1976: 53; Power 1981: 1–18; G. Carr, 'Residence and social status', Harvard (1974).

[4] Power 1978b: 174; Dyer 1973: 178; Hibberd 1981: 152–5; Finlay 1981: 79–80; Pearl 1979: 7–8; Carr 1974: 84; Jones 1980: 126; Schwarz 1982: 170–2.

[5] See, J. Bourchet, 'Urban neighbourhood and community: informal group life, 1850–1970', *Journal of Interdisciplinary History* 11, 4 (1981), 625.

[6] The streets and alleys in each residential sub-district were classified as follows: *High Street*; east side and west side of main street; *Close and Pepper Alley*; Montague Close, Close and Pepper Alley; *Counter Lane*; Counter Lane, Foul Lane, Corner Brickhouse and Triangles; *Alleys and Yards*; Chequer Alley, Boarshead Alley, Ship Yard, Swan Alley, Three Crane Yard, Windmill Alley, Christopher Yard, Horsehead Alley, Axe Yard, Bell Yard, Fishmonger Alley, Goat Yard, Saints Alley, College Churchyard, Browns Rents, Castle Alley, Soap Yard, Collier and Sack Alley, Green Dragon Yard, Angel Yard, Chaingate Churchyard, Counter Alley, Fryingpan Alley. Power has attempted recently to distinguish residential 'types' in seventeenth-century London, see Power 1981: 8.

account, indifferent large and square with well built and inhabited houses having trees before the doors, which renders it pleasant'. The Close and Pepper Alley constituted a third district. The area was the only one in the Boroughside to possess a riverside frontage and in addition claimed exemption from certain jurisdictions, a situation which attracted a small Catholic population. The district was physically distinctive enough to be separately numbered in the 1622 token book, and as late as 1795 the Close gates were shut up every evening. Alleys and yards constituted a fourth type of environment. Running off the High Street, Strype noted many yards and back alleys 'of little account' and 'meanly inhabited'. Physically such alleys were narrow and hid from the passer-by the condition of the inhabitants within. Hence Windmill Alley was described as a 'dark entrance and narrow within but poorly inhabited and very ordinary buildings'.[7]

The four residential 'sub-districts' identified above have been represented in schematic maps of the Boroughside drawn from the sacramental token books. Each token book lists each household street by street. To clarify some topographical questions, such as the exact location on the maps of the hospital gate or Chaingate, the addresses supplied in the parish clerk's notebook were used.[8] In the cases where the token books omitted the name of an alley or yard, topographical information from other token books filled the gap. The earliest token books are the most deficient in this respect. The ground plan of each schematic map corresponded closely to the plan of the Boroughside given in the map of John Roque (see Fig. 7.1).[9] In 1622 the only topographical differences were that 3 Crown Court, a soaphouse at that date, was depicted as a residential area, and Castle Alley, between the Soap Yard and Browns Rents, was omitted by Roque. Lastly a new inn seems to have been constructed on the High Street between what was Goat Yard and Saints Alley in the later seventeenth century. Otherwise only some of the names of certain alleys and yards changed between the early seventeenth and mid eighteenth century.[10] The Close and Pepper Alley area is difficult to represent accurately and in this district the schematic map supplies only the most likely of several possible topographical interpretations.[11] Each

---

[7] Strype 1720: 2, 28–9; Rendle 1878: 227.

[8] G.L.R.O. P92/SAV/406

[9] See, J. Roque, *A Plan of the City of London and Westminster and the Borough of Southwark*, London 1746, reprinted in R. Hyde (ed.), *The A to Z of Georgian London*, Lympne Castle, 1981. Roque's map was preferred to that of Morgan (1682) because of the former's larger scale. A serious fire of 1676 in Southwark did not alter the ground plan of the Boroughside significantly, Rendle and Norman 1888: 152–4.

[10] Swan Alley became Black Swan Alley, Axe Yard became Axe and Bottle Yard, Browns Rents became Whore's Nest and Collier and Sack Alley became Kirby's Court. Goat Yard and Saints Alley are labelled as brewhouses.

[11] In particular, Green Yard, Angel Alley and Cock Alley depicted in Roque's map in the Close, cannot be identified confidently.

Fig. 7.1. The Boroughside in 1746, detail from Roque's, *Plan of the City of London*

block on the plan represents one household in one dwelling. Multiple membership of a household has only been represented when more than one member was allocated an occupation. The schematic maps accurately represent the relative position of contiguous neighbours but do not necessarily depict opposite neighbours. The dotted line between Counter Alley and the entry to Counter Lane represents adjoining dwellings the position of which has been distorted by the demands imposed by the schematic map (see Figures 7.2–7.4). The schematic format was chosen because, in the absence of comprehensive and detailed property surveys, it provided a reasonable representation of the relative location of each householder. By comparing schematic maps constructed for different dates a clear picture of the topographical development of each district can be drawn.[12]

7.2 Topographical development 1584–1635

The Boroughside seems to have been the most densely populated and developed area of Southwark as early as the thirteenth century. However, following the late fourteenth- and fifteenth-century fall in the national population, building in the area appears to have slackened. In the early sixteenth century a number of High Street buildings were said to have been derelict.[13] Similar signs of stagnation have been observed for early sixteenth-century Cheapside.[14] Although there are signs of an increase in building activity in the 1520s and 1530s in Southwark (a phenomenon not seen at this time in Cheapside) it is probable that it was not until the 1560s and 1570s that population pressure caused a really significant quickening of residential development.[15]

The way in which the Boroughside's topography developed after 1580 helps to explain the social and economic character of the district in the 1620s. Furthermore an account of this growth serves to correct an earlier incomplete account of the area's development. Brett-James used a 1638

---

[12] For plans based on property surveys see Power 1978a: 31; J. Langton, 'Late medieval Gloucester: some data from a rental of 1455', *Transactions of the Institute of British Geographers*, n.s., 2 (1977), 263–70. The schematic format was adapted from that used by Slack, see Slack 1977: 56–7. For the difficulties encountered in the production of such plans see, H. Carter, 'The map in urban history', *Urban History Yearbook* (1979), 19–20.

[13] Carlin 1983: 120.   [14] Keene 1984: 18–19.

[15] For the timing of population increase in Southwark, see above Chapter 2. There is, apparently, evidence for a 'lively demand' for property in Westminster in the early sixteenth century. It may be that much of the demand for property in Southwark in the latter period came from a few, wealthy, rather than numerous poor immigrants. Thus Chequer Alley, built between 1525 and 1550, was small and housed wealthy as well as some poor residents; Carlin 1983: 256–7; Keene 1984: 19. For the growth of London and attempts to restrict it see, Pearl 1961: 9–44; Finlay 1981: 56–9; Brett-James 1935: passim; R. Ashton, *The City and the Court*, Cambridge, 1979, pp. 168–71.

return of new buildings to estimate growth in Southwark in the early seventeenth century. The list, however, only records a number of buildings in St Olave's, Southwark, and Bermondsey. Building known to have taken place in the Boroughside in the early seventeenth century is omitted. Other historical sources can be used to give a more complete picture of the development of the area's topography.[16]

The physical development of the Boroughside can be examined using the topographical information supplied by the token books, supplemented by the returns of new buildings and of poor and divided tenements made in 1635 and 1637 respectively.[17] The 1635 return was entitled 'a certificate of all such new buildings as have been erected within the said parish so far as they know or can learn since the 2-year of the reign of our late sovereign Lord King James'. The return, made to the lord mayor by the churchwardens, was part of the campaign, initiated by the privy council in 1634, to raise revenue by enforcing the restrictions on building.[18] The city authorities ordered the taking of the 1637 survey in response to a demand for information on divided tenements made by the privy council in March of that year.[19] In fact the city authorities were already in the process of conducting a similar survey in an attempt to alleviate the hardship in the suburbs brought about by the effects of the 1636–7 plague epidemic.[20] The 1637 returns set out the numbers and ownership of all poor and divided tenements. The churchwardens identified those tenements recently chargeable to the parish and listed the amount each alley had cost the parish in plague relief since 'Pentecost last'. The surveys were subject to some omissions. Lessees were often reluctant to inform the compilers of the surveys of the rent they paid. More seriously some parts of the Boroughside were not covered in the survey and furthermore many tenements built or divided a long time before the compilation might have escaped notice. Despite such reservations the surveys contain valuable information about the physical growth of the Boroughside; the 1637 return supplies a brief potted history of many alleys and yards which is often confirmed by information from the token books.

To make possible a topographical comparison of the district at different points in time the above information was combined with that obtained from

[16] Brett-James 1935: 406–7. For the 1638 return see, P.R.O. SP16/408/65.

[17] G.L.R.O. P92/SAV/1336 and 1331. See also P92/SAV/1335, a rough note of householders keeping inmates.

[18] Barnes 1970: 1353–4. For a similar attempt in 1615, see, Pearl 1961: 19–20.

[19] Barnes 1970: 1353–4; Brett-James 1935: 116.

[20] See, *C.S.P.D.1636–7*, 343, 36–7. The returns were dated 25 January 1637 following a warrant dated 8 January, see G.L.R.O. P92/SAV/1330 and 1331. In response to a second warrant dated 17 March the information obtained from the January survey was summarised and a tabulated survey added, see, G.L.R.O. P92/SAV/1332 and 1333. Neat copies of these returns were made to the Privy Council, P.R.O. SP16/359/23.

Table 7.1. *The pattern of residential development in the Boroughside*
1584–1635

| Residential sub-district | Householders inhabiting each district | | | | | |
| | 1584 | | 1622 | | 1635 | |
	N	%	N	%	N	%
High Street	196	34.3	192	20.0	202	18.5
Close and Pepper Alley	50	8.7	106	11.1	106	9.7
Counter Lane	110	19.2	144	15.0	163	15.0
Alleys and yards	216	37.8	516	53.9	619	56.8
Total	572		958		1090	

Note: Percentages as a proportion of the total number of householders.
Source: Calculated from 1584, 1622, 1635 token books according to method discussed in
text, pp. 168–72. G.L.R.O. P92/SAV/186, 211, 227.

schematic plans of the Boroughside (constructed from the token books in
the manner described above) for the years 1584 and 1622 (see below Fig.
7.5 and 7.2). In the 1584 token book both the Counter Lane and Close
sub-districts are particularly difficult to reconstruct so that the map depicts
only the most probable topography. The 1635 token book was also broken
down into the number of householders resident in each sub-district in order
to exploit fully the information in the 1635 survey (see Table 7.1).[21]

The various residential sub-districts experienced different rates of growth
between 1584 and 1635. There was little if any increase in the number of
householders living on the High Street. Between 1584 and 1635 the number
of householders resident on the main thoroughfare increased by only 2%
compared to the overall expansion in the Boroughside of 91%. The building
activity that took place in the early seventeenth century on the High Street
did not increase the number of houses but took the form of piecemeal
rebuilding on old foundations. Hence for example Richard Humble erected
three 'tenements of timber on old foundations' on the west side of the High
Street in 1611 and Owen Jones built '3 Fair houses with brick upon old
foundations' on the street adjacent to Horsehead Alley in 1634.[22] The
impression that the High Street was built up as early as the late sixteenth
century is confirmed by a passage in Stow, who noted in 1598 'from the

---

[21] For the token books used see, G.L.R.O. P92/SAV/186, 227, 211.
[22] In 1616 Humble bequeathed £5 4s. per annum to the poor of the parish issuing out of the rent
of these tenements, Taylor 1833: 98–9; *Accounts and Papers* 16, 1878: 548. For an account of
Humble's business activities see, Lang 1971: 263–4; Higham 1955: 157–63.

Bridge straight towards the south a continual street, called Long Southwark, builded on both sides with divers lanes and alleys up to St George's Church'.[23]

Between 1584 and 1635 alleys and yards grew by 187%, the highest rate of growth of any residential sub-district (see Table 7.1). There were two phases in this expansion. Major conversions and redevelopment of large High Street properties into alleys and yards in the later sixteenth and first two decades of the seventeenth century and piecemeal building and subdivision thereafter. The progress of alley and yard construction is highlighted by a comparison between the schematic maps of 1584 and 1622 (see Figs 7.5 and 7.2). The token book evidence suggests that alleys and yards filled up with householders some five to ten years after the date of construction given in the 1637 survey. The construction of each alley has therefore been dated precisely from the appropriate token book.

Alleys and yards began to radiate outwards from the High Street in the later sixteenth century, and often took their names from the property from which they were converted. Hence the Bell Inn, kept by Richard Blower in 1584, was converted into Bell Yard shortly after that date. Windmill Alley was originally converted from a bakehouse run by one 'Simpson deceased'. The Christopher Inn was converted into tenements around 1590 and Goat Yard and Boarshead Alley were similarly developed between 1610 and 1612 from two brewhouses. The positions and occupiers of properties developed subsequently into alleys can be identified in the 1584 token book. Thus Richard Blower, innkeeper of the Bell, is listed heading a nine communicant household on the west side of the High Street in 1584.[24] After the first two decades of the seventeenth century no large alleys were constructed; indeed one small alley was demolished to make way for a soaphouse. Only Falcon Court, between Fishmonger Alley and Goat Yard and housing just seven households in 1635, was constructed after 1622. The subsequent growth in the alleys and yards was not accommodated by building. Only a little new building was reported in the 1635–7 surveys, mostly on old foundations. Horsehead Alley had had eleven tenements built there in 1618 and 1626 and in 1632 'three fair houses built with brick upon old foundations', and a few other alleys and yards underwent small-scale addition.[25]

The apparent contradiction between the continued growth in alleys and yards indicated by the token books (see Table 7.1) and the insignificant new

[23] Stow 1971: 2, 52.
[24] The sites of old inns can be identified in a 1542 map of Southwark, Rendle 1878: i–ii. See also, for a detailed account of Boroughside properties in the mid sixteenth century, Carlin 1983: 120–256.
[25] See, *Acts of the Privy Council of England 1617–19*, London, 1929, p. 172; Brett-James 1935: 14; G.L.R.O. P92/SAV/1336.

building is resolved by the widespread practice of subdivision. As in other pre-industrial towns and cities subdivision of houses into smaller dwellings provided a mechanism by which built-up areas could accommodate population growth.[26] There were a number of divided tenements reported in the late sixteenth century in the Boroughside but subdivision increased markedly in the seventeenth century. The 1637 returns of new buildings list the conversion of 78 tenements plus some stables and out-houses, into 207 dwellings since 1607. Most of the subdivision had taken place after 1622 and must have accommodated much of the population increase between that date and 1635. Subdivision seems to have been particularly widespread in the Counter Lane district. Despite a 48% increase in the number of householders in the district between 1584 and 1635 (see Table 7.1) the 1635 returns recorded little building activity. Both the 1637 schedule and the 1635 token book indicate extensive subdivision in the area.[27]

The Close underwent major redevelopments in the sixteenth and early seventeenth century. The Close and Montague House were originally the Priory of St Mary Overy. After the dissolution the cloisters of the Priory, 'the close' quickly filled with tenements. The conversion of large mansion houses and former monastic buildings into tenements was occurring all over the capital at this time. Montague House continued to be occupied by the heirs of Lord Montague until its conversion into tenements in 1612.[28] This redevelopment accounted for most of the expansion between 1584 and 1622. The slight fall in the number of householders in the sub-district between 1622 and 1635 fits in with what is known of its second redevelopment following the sale of Montague House and the Close to a local inhabitant in 1625. The new owner deliberately upgraded the area, it was reported, and as a result, 'tenements and buildings...are fewer in the number of houses by his new building than before, they having been formerly mean cottages and habitations for the poorer sort of people that crowded themselves there together...whereas now they are fit for men of

---

[26] See, Keene 1984: 15; Dyer 1973: 164–5; M. Reed, 'Economic structure and change in seventeenth-century Ipswich', in P. Clark (ed.), *Country Towns in Pre-Industrial England*, Leicester, 1981, pp. 118–19; M. Laithwaite, 'Totnes houses 1500–1800', in P. Clark (ed.), *The Transformation of English Provincial Towns*, London, 1984, p. 67.

[27] Between 1607 and 1637, 19 tenements were reported to have been converted into 45 dwellings, G.L.R.O. P92/SAV/1333. The 1635 token book seems to have distinguished householders living in divided tenements by placing them in open-ended brackets. According to this measurement 69 householders out of 163 resident in the Counter Lane district in 1635 or 42.2% inhabited divided tenements, G.L.R.O. P92/SAV/227.

[28] For accounts of the Close and Montague House see, Stow 1971: 2, 58–9; Darlington 1950: 43–4; Malden 1967: 4, 129; E. J. Davies, 'The transformation of London', in R. W. Seton-Watson (ed.), *Wealth and Power in Sixteenth-Century England; Tudor Studies presented to A. F. Pollard*, London, 1924, p. 307. See also, Pearl 1961: 18; Brett-James 1935: 101; Power 1972: 253–4.

better ability and do yield relief to the poor'. Unfortunately subdivision of tenements quickly followed this rebuilding and lessened the beneficial effects of the redevelopment. By 1637 it was reported that in Montague Close there were 'formerly 5 tenements made 3 and so let by Mr Bromfield and now 7 [and] 4 tenements made 2...and now 12'.[29]

The topographical development of the Boroughside must have had a significant impact on the occupational composition of the district as it would appear in the 1620s. In the late sixteenth and early seventeenth centuries a number of relatively 'large-scale' concerns, notably two High Street inns, a bakehouse and two brewhouses were converted into back alleys. Furthermore other 'occupation-related' buildings such as tallowhouses, slaughterhouses, stables and warehouses were sacrificed to meet population expansion. What did the social topography of the district, produced by this pattern of development, look like in 1622?

7.3 The social topography of the Boroughside

To establish the residential distribution of wealth at that date those householders assessed for the 1621–2 poor rate and the 1622 subsidy were identified on a schematic map drawn from the 1622 token book (see Fig. 7.2 and Table 7.2). The High Street was dominated by the wealthier inhabitants. Of the 192 households located on the High Street, 108 (56.3%) were subsidy payers and 57 (29.7%) were poor-rate payers. Only 14% of the householders on the High Street were not rated for either tax. The wealth of main street dwellers is an established topographical feature of pre-industrial London.[30] The wealth of the High Street was in sharp contrast to that of the other three sub-districts. Only 31.1% of householders in the Close and 20.1% of those in the Counter Lane area were assessed for some form of taxation. As one might expect alleys and yards were the poorest residential districts with only 13.4% of their inhabitants rated. A few of the smaller alleys were clearly superior 'social enclaves' of the sort identified elsewhere in London. Chequer Alley included two subsidy payers and three poor-rate payers among its six householders in 1622 and even one hundred years later was described as, 'small, but pretty well built and inhabited'.[31]

In this uneven distribution of wealth among the four sub-districts, poverty was related to the proportion of female household heads in each area. Some 20.0% of all household heads in alleys and yards were female compared to 7.6% in Counter Lane and in the Close and 6.8% on the High Street. This uneven residential distribution probably reflects the greater

---

[29] G.L.R.O. P92/SAV/1336, 1333.
[30] See Herlan 1977a: 16; Power 1981: 8. For a similar topographical feature in seventeenth-century Bristol, see, Slack 1977: 55.　　　[31] Strype 1720: 2, 29. See also, Power 1978b:180.

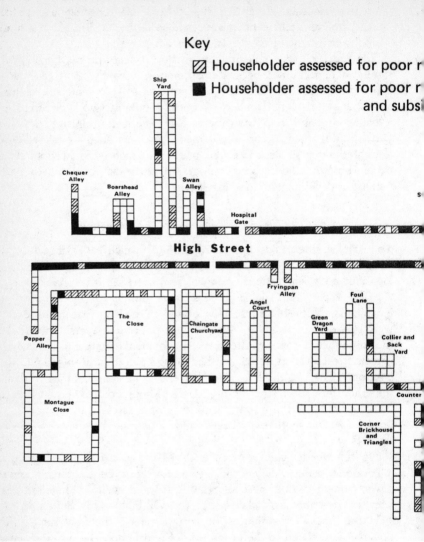

Fig. 7.2. Schematic map of the Boroughside showing the residential distribution of wealth in 1622

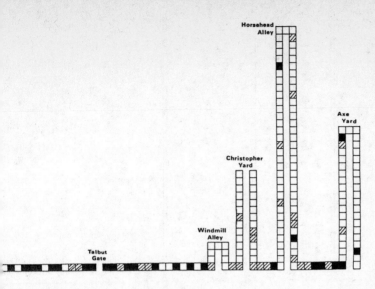

High Street

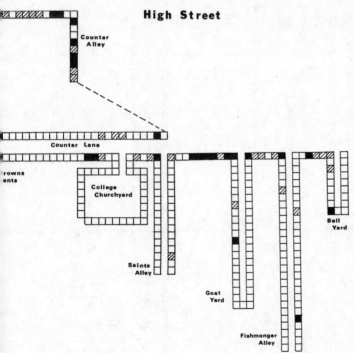

Table 7.2. *The residential distribution of wealth in the Boroughside 1622*

Residential sub-district	Number of households in each sub-district	Number of householders paying both subsidy and poor rate[a]		Number of householders paying poor rate only	
	N	N	%	N	%
High Street	192	108	56.3	57	29.7
Close and Pepper Alley	106	10	9.4	23	21.7
Counter Lane	144	9	6.3	20	13.9
Alleys and yards	516	21	4.1	48	9.3
Total	958	148	15.5	148	15.5

Note: Percentages expressed as the total number of householders in each sub-district in each tax category.
[a] Includes two householders assessed for the subsidy but not for the poor rate; both lived on the High Street.
Source: See discussion in text, pp. 168–70 and 175.

Table 7.3. *Residential distribution of female household heads 1622*

Sub-district	Number of households[a]	Number of female household heads[b]	
	N	N	%
High Street	192	13	6.8
Close and Pepper Alley	106	8	7.6
Counter Lane	144	11	7.6
Alleys and yards	516	103	20.0
Total	958	135	14.1

Sources: [a] See Table 7.2.
[b] G.L.R.O. P92/SAV/211.

poverty of female-headed households, especially those headed by widows, noted above. Widows also congregated in the poorer areas of seventeenth-century Cambridge (see Table 7.3).[32]

To carry the analysis a stage further the residential distribution of poverty was examined by linking the householders listed in the 1618 survey of the poor to those in the 1618 token book (See Fig 7.3 and Table 7.4).[33]

Poverty, like wealth, was distributed unevenly among the four residential sub-districts. The wealthiest area, the High Street, contained only two poor households in 1618 (1% of the total) compared to 18 (19.2%) in the Close and 23 (19.5%) in Counter Lane. Poverty was concentrated in the alleys and yards, 36.8% of whose households were considered poor in 1618. The residential pattern of poverty, however, was more complex than Table 7.4 suggests since it is apparent from the schematic plan that the poor crowded together in particular alleys and yards. Those on the east side of the High Street between Chequer Alley and Christopher Yard were better off than others elsewhere. Hence only 12.5% of the householders in Christopher Yard were poor and 17.8% in Ship Yard compared to such desperate areas as Axe Yard (51.3% poor) Green Dragon Yard (62.5% poor), Angel Yard (52.6% poor) and Saints Alley (48.3% poor). Such differences suggest that there were fine gradations in back street housing.

It is apparent that the 'social intermingling' observed in early seventeenth-century London and elsewhere also existed in the Boroughside.[34] There was

[32] Goose 1980: 378. See also preceding Chapter.

[33] The survey and the 1618 token book were compiled in April and March respectively. As a result 12 poor householders could not be found in the token book. G.L.R.O. P92/SAV/1465, 207.

[34] See above. A recent article has cast some doubt on the degree of social segregation in the nineteenth-century city, see, D. Ward, 'Environs and neighbours in the "Two Nations", residential differentiation in mid nineteenth-century Leeds', *Journal of Historical Geography* 6, 2 (1980), 133–62.

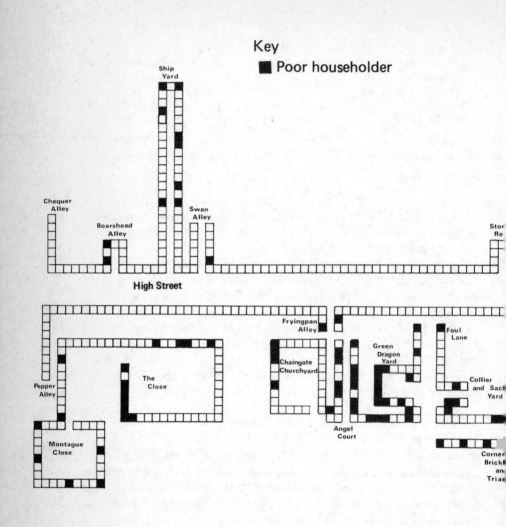

Fig. 7.3. Schematic map of the Boroughside showing the residential distribution of poverty in 1618

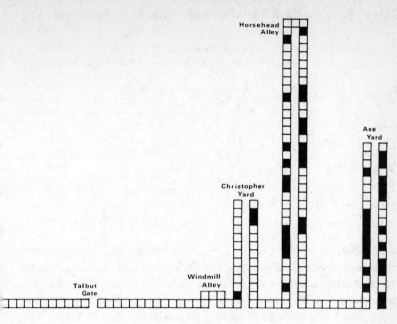

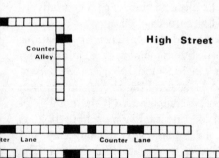

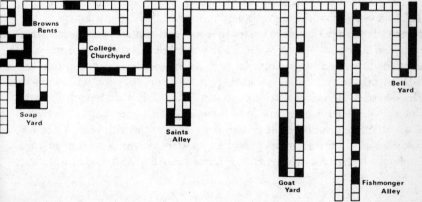

Table 7.4. *The residential distribution of poverty in the Boroughside*
1618

Residential sub-district	Number of householders in each sub-district	Number of householders described as poor	
	N	N	%
High Street	198	2	1.0
Close and Pepper Alley	94	18	19.2
Counter Lane	118	23	19.5
Alleys and yards	481	177	36.8
Total	891	220	24.7

Source: See discussion in text, p. 179.

no rigid social segregation. Although the majority of subsidy payers inhabited the High Street, 40 out of 148 (27 %) lived in the other sub-districts. This social mixing is even more marked when the location of poor-rate payers is considered (see Table 7.5). In both 1622 and 1631 only just over half of the poor-rate payers were located on the High Street and over 20% were located in alleys or yards. Many of these, of course, paid at relatively lower rates of assessment than their High Street neighbours.[35]

The impression of some social mixing and the existence of gradations within alleys and yards is reinforced by combining the information contained in two housing surveys taken in 1635 and 1637. A 1637 survey listed the number of 'poor tenements' in many of the alleys and yards in the Boroughside and these figures can be compared with the number of householders listed in the 1635 token book. It is clear that most householders inhabited 'poor tenements' since in alleys and yards inhabited by 414 householders in 1635 some 363 (87.7%) such tenements were reported. The 1637 survey gave brief general descriptions of this type of housing. The tenements in Ship Yard were 'all for the most part divided houses consisting of 1 and 2 rooms a piece'. The 32 tenements in Christopher Yard each contained two or three rooms. Rents for such tenements varied within the 40s. to 60s. a year range. The average rent for 70 poor tenements in Horsehead Alley was 40s. per annum while most Ship Yard tenements were 'let at 50s. or £3 a tenement' and those in Christopher Yard at between 40s. and 60s. a year. Back alleys and yards, as the schematic maps indicated also contained a small number of higher quality tenements. Christopher Yard contained 'other good tenements', Horsehead Alley also contained 'some

[35] See Chapter 4.

Table 7.5. *Residential location of poor-rate payers 1622 and 1631*

Residential sub-district	Number of householders paying poor rate 1622[a]		Number of householders paying poor rate 1631[b]	
	N	%	N	%
High Street	163	55.4	167	53.2
Close and Pepper Alley	33	11.2	39	12.4
Counter Lane	29	9.9	43	13.7
Alleys and yards	69	23.5	65	20.7
Total	294		314	

Source: [a] See Table 7.2.
[b] Calculated from 1631 token book, G.L.R.O. P92/SAV/219.

good' tenements. Of the 54 householders resident in Goat Yard in 1635 42 inhabited 'poor tenements.... consisting of 1, 2 and 3 rooms apiece some dwelling in cellars underground...which pay in all about £130 per annum'.[36] But the 1635 survey also revealed higher quality dwellings. In Goat Yard, of 22 tenements whose rents were listed, 14 were let at 50s., one at 80s., six at £5 and one at £8 per year.[37] It should be remembered that, in the local economy of the poor, the distinction between a 40s. and 60s. tenement may have been as significant as that between High Street houses worth £20 and £30 per year.

We can identify, then, distinct residential sub-districts in the Boroughside. The High Street was the wealthiest area with a high percentage of taxpayers, few female-headed households and an insignificant number of poor. The Close area would be ranked second with one third of its inhabitants paying some form of taxation and relatively few female household heads but with one in five households described as poor in 1618. In Counter Lane fewer individuals paid tax but otherwise the area resembled the Close. Alleys and yards were the poorest type of environment with one in three of their households described as poor and one in five headed by females; only one in eight paid any form of tax. This social topography, however, was marked by considerable internal gradations and a significant amount of social mixing. Some of the latter is explained by the residential distribution of trades and crafts between these areas.

The residential distribution of occupations has been examined by mapping the occupations of all male householders in 1622 onto a schematic plan (see Fig. 7.4 and Table 7.6). The residential coverage achieved was

[36] G.L.R.O. P92/SAV/1331.   [37] G.L.R.O. P92/SAV/1336.

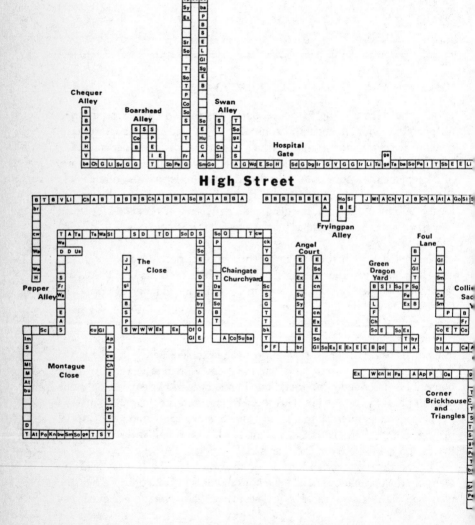

Fig. 7.4. Schematic map of the Boroughside showing the residential distribution
of occupations in 1622

For key to figure 7.4, see page 186.

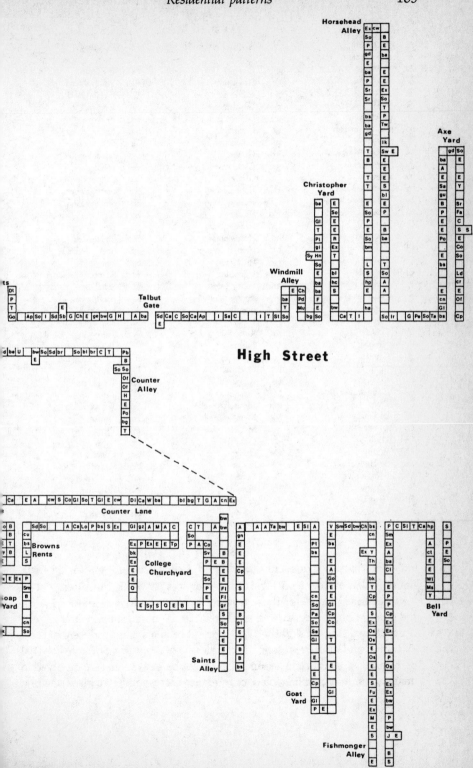

KEY to fig 7.4

A	Victualler	Fu	Fustiandresser	Pl	Poulterer
Ap	Apothecary	G	Grocer	Po	Potter
At	Attorney	Gl	Glover	Ps	Plasterer
B	Butcher	Go	Goldsmith	Pt	Pointmaker
ba	Baker	gd	Gardener	Q	Parish Official
bk	Basketmaker	ge	Gentleman	R	Ropemaker
bl	Bricklayer	gu	Guilder	S	Silkweaver
bm	Bellowsmaker	gi	Girdler	Sa	Salter
br	Barber	gn	Gunmaker	Sb	Soapboiler
bs	Brewer's servant	gr	Grinder	Sc	Schoolmaster
bu	Barrowman	gs	Glass seller	Sd	Saddler
bw	Brewer	gz	Glazier	Se	Saltpetremaker
by	Boddicemaker	H	Haberdasher	Sg	Sheergrinder
be	'Brasell' seller	Hn	Husbandman	Sh	Starchmaker
bg	Barber-surgeon	Ho	Hosier	Si	Scrivener
C	Cutler	ha	Hackneyman	Sm	Smith
Ca	Chandler	hc	Horsecourser	So	Shoemaker
Ch	Cheesemonger	hp	Hempbeater	Sp	Spectaclemaker
Co	Cooper	Hu	Huckster	Sr	Sawyer
Cp	Carpenter	I	Innholder	Ss	Soapboiler's servant
cb	Chamberlain	Im	Imbroiderer	St	Stationer
ch	Coachman	Ir	Ironmonger	Sv	Servingman
ci	Collier	I	Inkseller	Su	Sauceman
ck	Cook	J	Joiner	Sw	Shipwright
cm	Costermonger	Kn	Knight	Sy	Sailor
cn	Carman	L	Labourer	T	Tailor
cr	Carrier	Ld	Leatherdresser	Ta	Tallowchandler
ct	Carter	Li	Linendraper	Tp	Tapster
cu	Currier	Lo	Locksmith	Th	Threddier
cw	Clothworker	M	Mason	Ti	Tinker
D	Dyer	Ms	Mousetrap seller	Ts	Tobaccoseller
Di	Dicemaker	Mt	Merchant-tailor	Tu	Turner
Ds	Dyer's servant	Mu	Musician	Tw	Tapeweaver
Dt	Distiller	Of	Central and City Official	Us	Usher
E	Widow	Os	Ostler	U	Upholsterer
Ex	Single woman	P	Porter	V	Vintner
F	Fishmonger	Pa	Painter	W	Woodmonger
Fa	Falconer	Pb	Plumber	Wa	Waterman
Fl	Feltmaker	Pd	Pedlar	Wd	Woollen Draper
Fm	Flexman	Pe	Pewterer	Wi	Whitster
Fr	Fruiterer	Pi	Pinner	Y	Yeoman

uniformly high but unevenly distributed, falling from 89.4% for all male householders resident on the High Street to 76.7% for those resident in Counter Lane, 73.6% for those resident in alleys and yards and 72.5% for the male householders in the Close. As is noted in Chapter 3 the occupational sources slightly overrepresent retailers and producers of food and drink and underrepresent the childless. The accuracy of the residential patterns also relies on the assumption that, where persons were involved in manufacturing or retailing, place of residence corresponded to place of work.

Table 7.6. *Residential distribution of occupations 1622*

Occupational category	Residential sub-district			
	High Street	Close	Counter Lane	Alleys and yards
Agriculture	0	1	2	9
Building	4	4	8	14
Production and retail of food and drink	80	10	25	80
Retail of clothing and household goods	21	3	12	8
Professional	12	10	2	13
Transport	2	8	6	54
Industry:				
Textiles	0	21	7	31
Clothing	9	6	9	29
Leather	18	6	14	42
Rope	1	0	0	2
Soap	5	0	2	0
Wood	1	4	5	12
Metal and glass	13	2	11	13
Miscellaneous	0	0	1	5
Total	166	75	104	312

Source: See discussion in text, pp. 183–6. For the trades and crafts in each occupational category see Chapter, 3, note 25.

Although it is possible to cite a few Boroughside householders whose workplace (or shop) and dwelling house were separate, in general, as in the rest of London and other pre-industrial cities, such cases were rare.[38]

It is clear that occupations were not *rigidly* segregated. There was little sign that occupational groups congregated together in particular streets or alleys in the classic medieval fashion and as they still did in some parts of London.[39] The High Street between Chequer Alley and the Hospital Gate contained a baker, a cheesemonger, five grocers, a linendraper, a servingman, a tailor, a soapboiler, a pewterer, a smith, a goldsmith, a victualler, a woollendraper, a shoemaker and a haberdasher. Alleys and yards displayed similar occupational heterogeneity. Ship Yard contained a huckster, three tailors, two silkweavers, five shoemakers, a cooper, two porters, a sawyer, a sailor, a spectaclemaker, an ostler, a baker, two butchers, a labourer, a

[38] Power 1978a: 38; Finlay 1981: 81; Langton 1977: 272.
[39] See, for example, W. M. Stern, 'The trade, art or mistery of silk throwers of the City of London in the seventeenth century', *Guildhall Miscellany* 1,6 (1956), 27; Reddaway 1963: 181–206.

glover, a sheergrinder, a cutler, a victualler and a fruiterer. Only two areas of the Boroughside were dominated by particular occupations. The wealthy butchers were grouped into a large shambles sited on the west side of the High Street from the Bridgefoot to Fryingpan Alley. This topographical feature was referred to by Strype, who noted in 1720, that, 'the westside of the Borough being generally taken up by Butchers, there [is] a good shambles'.[40] However, even this shambles included a tailor, two cheesemongers and a shoemaker and was punctuated by the ubiquitous victualler. The riverside frontage of the Close and Pepper Alley gave them a unique occupational composition. All the Boroughside dyers were clustered in the sub-district, drawn to the water supply. Strype noted that the Bankside (of which Pepper Alley was technically a small part) contained many dyers 'seated for the conveniency of the water'. The riverside location also explains the concentration of watermen in Pepper Alley; Pepper Alley stairs were 'much frequented by watermen', reported Strype. The existence of loading and river transport facilities probably explains the heavy concentration of woodmongers in the Close. A 1605 survey listed two wharves in the Close, one of which was leased by Henry Williams, a wealthy woodmonger, still resident in 1622. Strype mentioned that Montague Close had 'a wharf for the loading of corn and other goods' and the survey of 1635 listed a woodyard.[41]

If the occupations in the Boroughside are grouped into broader functional categories it can be seen that the residential sub-districts possessed different occupational characteristics. Thus the High Street was dominated by the producers and retailers of food and drink who made up 48.2% of all occupations recovered in that area, compared to a quarter of those in alleys and yards and in Counter Lane (25.6% and 24.0% respectively). As one would expect only the thoroughfares had substantial numbers of individuals retailing clothing and household goods. In alleys and yards 17.3% of all occupations were drawn from the transport and unskilled labour sector and 13.5% from the leather industry. The leather industry equalled the retailing of clothing and household goods in the Counter Lane sub-district. If the occupational categories are grouped together as retailing and services (food and drink, clothing and household goods and the professions) and manual labour (agriculture, building, transport and industry) then the unique composition of the High Street becomes even more apparent. Some 68% of all occupations sited on the High Street involved retail or service compared to only 30.7% in the Close and 32.4% in alleys and yards where manual labour predominated. Interestingly, even the secondary thoroughfare

---

[40] Strype 1720: 2, 29. Butchers were commonly grouped in shambles in early modern cities, Jones 1976: 71–83; Palliser 1979: 168.
[41] Strype 1720: 2, 28; G.L.R.O. P92/SAV/1336, 664.

of Counter Lane was dominated by manual labour (62.5%) (see Table 7.6). Occupational zoning in districts and streets has also been observed both in other parts of London and in other pre-industrial towns and cities.[42]

The residential patterns also highlight the problems involved in attempting to simplify occupational labels under one heading. Some of the 'industrial' occupations must in fact have involved retailing. In particular saddlers, classified as labouring in the leather industry, almost invariably occupied the High Street, reflecting their service function, and similarly, within the metal industry, smiths were usually located on a thoroughfare.

The residential location of many occupational groups was interrelated with the social geography of the Boroughside. As one would expect, and as other writers have noted, resident on the High Street were the wealthier trades and the wealthier members of trades that were generally poorer.[43] Located most frequently on the same street were prosperous occupations such as grocers, soapboilers, innholders, vintners and cheesemongers. Less likely to be found there were less wealthy ones such as victuallers, brewers and chandlers. Some humble occupations such as carpenters, glovers and fishmongers were not to be found on the main street at all.

The location of some other relatively humble manufacturing occupations on the High Street is the effect of the wide range of wealth included within many occupations. Possession of street frontage must have indicated that individuals had achieved master status and were able to retail direct, possibly employing their more humble brethren in back alleys and yards. Hence shoemakers, ranked according to their wealth, at level IV, had 21.2% of their members located on the High Street. Similar social divisions explain the mismatching of cutlers who, although also ranked at level IV, had 44.4% of their members on the main street (see Table 4.10).

It is clear that a certain amount of the social intermingling was related to the industrial composition of the Boroughside. Some subsidy men were involved in manufacturing and were tied to a specific site. Hence of the ten subsidy payers in the Close five were dyers or woodmongers. Similarly a brewery explains the location of a subsidy man in Fishmonger Alley and a saltpetre manufacturer of one in Goat Yard.[44] Large bakeries operated by subsidy payers were sited in Horsehead Alley, Axe Yard and the Chaingate Churchyard. Two other subsidy men kept small inns in Boarshead Alley and Green Dragon Yard. The social topography of the Boroughside in 1622 showed some features of the district as it was forty years earlier.

---

[42] See Power 1981: 8–16; Glass 1976: 224–6; Langton 1977: 237–44; Langton 1975: 16–19; Hibberd 1981: 115.

[43] Langton 1975: 21; Power 1981: 16.

[44] For the activities of Hugh Grove, saltpetremaker, see, *Acts of the Privy Council of England 1629 May–June 1630*, London, 1960, p. 19.

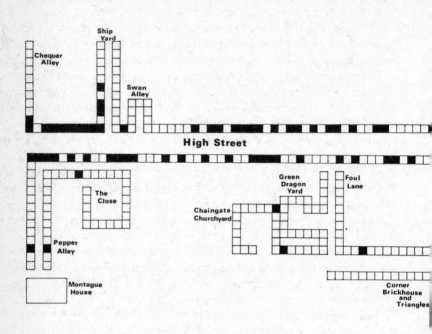

Fig. 7.5. Schematic map of the Boroughside showing the residential distribution of taxpayers in 1584

To examine the residential distribution of wealth in 1584 a taxation assessment was linked to the householders listed in the 1584 token book and those paying tax were identified on the schematic map (see Fig. 7.5). The assessment used was that made for the repair of highways in May 1583.[45] Householders were assessed to pay sums ranging from one penny to 20*d.* per week. In 1584, 121 out of 572 (21.2%) householders were identified as taxpayers compared to 15.5% of those resident in 1622 paying the subsidy. If the residential distribution of wealth in 1584 is compared

45 See G.L.R.O. P92/SAV/186, 1310.

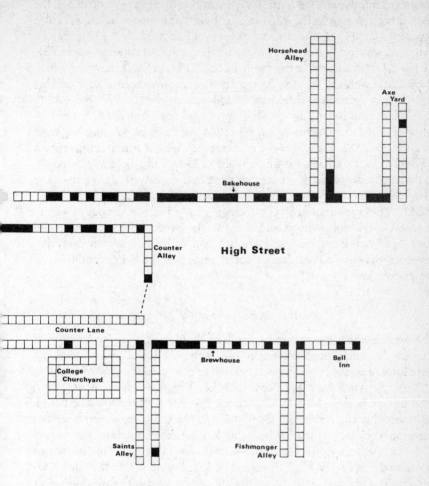

with 1622 (see Figures 7.2 and 7.5) little significant change can be observed. Taxpayers were concentrated on the High Street in both 1584 and 1622, although the proportion seems to have fallen between the two dates; 84.3% of all taxpayers lived on the High Street in 1584 compared to 73.0% of subsidy payers in 1622, but this might be only a distortion caused by comparing two different types of taxation assessment.[46] The conversion of large High Street properties must have caused the loss of a number of wealthy taxpayers. Thus William Derryck, owner of the Goat brewhouse

[46] For a similar view of the social composition of the High Street in Medieval Southwark see, Carlin 1983: 382.

converted into Goat Yard in the early seventeenth century, contributed the second highest sum in the 1583 tax.[47] Some social intermingling was also apparent in 1584; 15.7% of all taxpayers were located off the High Street. Large manufacturing concerns run by wealthy inhabitants were responsible for much of this pattern, as they were in 1622. Two of the taxpayers resident in the Close were the wealthy brewer John Smith, who headed an enormous twenty-two communicant household and was assessed at 20d. in the 1583 assessment, and Peter Johnson 'the dyer' who contributed 4d. in 1583. A number of the manufacturing sites in 1584 were still performing the same function in 1622. Hence John Peacock who headed a ten communicant household in the Chaingate Churchyard in 1584 and who contributed 4d. to the 1583 assessment, was occupying the bakery converted from the Lady Chapel of St Saviour's church which was occupied by Henry Wilson, baker, in 1622. The chapel, noted Strype disapprovingly, had been let out to 'Wyat, Peacock, Cleybrook, Wilson, all bakers'.[48] The effect of the subdivision and alley construction of the late sixteenth and early seventeenth centuries, however, did have a considerable social impact on the living conditions of the population.

7.4 *The urban environment of the Boroughside*

The way in which the physical growth of the Boroughside took place has considerable social implications. In 1584 some 34.3% of all householders were located on the High Street compared to only 20.0% in 1622 (see Table 7.1). At the same time the proportion of alley dwellers increased, from 37.8% of all householders in 1584 to 53.9% in 1622.[49] It should be noted, however, that the residential distribution of the *whole population* does not correspond closely to that of householders because household size varied with the relative wealth of each sub-district (see Table 7.7).[50] In 1631 mean household size on the High Street was 5.3, falling to 4.2. in the Close, 3.6 in Counter Lane and only 3.3 in the alleys and yards. The proportion of the total population resident on the High Street therefore was always greater than the number of householders. In 1631, 27.9% of the total population were living in High Street households compared to 47.5% in alleys and yards.

Unlike those areas of London where new building on open ground accommodated population expansion, such as parts of East London, the practice of subdivision led to a considerable reduction in personal living

---

[47] G.L.R.O. P92/SAV/1310.
[48] Strype 1720: 2, 10.
[49] For the relative number of alley dwellers in East London, see Power 1972: 242.
[50] See Chapter 5 on variations of household size by wealth.

Table 7.7. *The residential distribution of the population of the Boroughside* *1631*

Residential sub-district	Number of householders in sub-district		Total population of each sub-district		Mean household size
	N	%	N	%	
High Street	196	20.3	1036	27.9	5.3
Close	102	10.6	424	11.4	4.2
Counter Lane	137	14.2	488	13.2	3.6
Alleys and yards	531	55.0	1760	47.5	3.3
Total	966		3708		3.8

Note: The calculations omit the 'floating population'.
Source: Number of householders and total population in each sub-district calculated from 1631 token book, G.L.R.O. P92/SAV/219.

space in the back alleys and yards of the Boroughside.[51] Overcrowding, reported as early as 1595, was on the increase in the second and third decades of the seventeenth century. Symptomatic of this was the use of cellars as dwelling places and reports of families occupying one-room tenements.[52] This overcrowding was facilitated by the way in which such property was owned. Thus it was reported that Agnes Dallin, widow of a local bricklayer, owned a block of tenements in the Close and 'hath 9 several tenants there in 9 several rooms...which tenants as we are informed were put in by an underlessee of the said Dallyn and which she is willing to reform if she could get the tenants out'.[53]

The surveys of houses owned by St Thomas's Hospital suggest that, even on the High Street, social space was relatively restricted. The hospital surveyors often recorded the confusion brought about by the vague residential boundaries between properties. The surveyors were asked to remember when renewing a lease of a Mr Collinson's house that 'the rooms under Mr Perin's house opening into the yard...are not measured nor to be granted within the said premises'. Domestic rooms encroached directly on the hospital buildings. In 1635 one widow owned a house containing 'one chamber over part of Jonas Ward [of the hospital]'. The surveyors noted

[51] Power 1972: 258; Power 1978b: 182–3.
[52] G.L.R.O. P92/SAV/1315, 1331 passim. For cases of overcrowding in London see Beier 1978: 208; Power 1978b: 182; Brett-James 1935: 77–8.
[53] G.L.R.O. P92/SAV/1331.

that 'the rooms within the Ward being part of this house, we think fit should be pulled down'.[54]

These surveys also suggest that housing quality varied considerably on the High Street. Three-storey dwellings were immediately adjacent to those of four stories, frontages ranged from as little as 8 feet to as wide as 22. The houses, as was common in main streets in early modern towns and cities were long and thin, with relatively narrow street frontages, designed to maximise the number of households which had access to the commercial traffic of the High Street. Thus the house of Francis Grove, grocer, had a street frontage of 15 feet but it went back 56 feet. William Sledd, an ironmonger, possessed 10 feet of frontage, but his house stretched back 42 feet.[55] As was noted in Chapter 3 all these High Street houses possessed shops. The pressure on street frontages in the Boroughside does not seem to have been comparable to that in Cheapside, the premier retailing centre of London. In Cheapside most shop frontages were less than 6 feet wide reflecting the commercial buoyancy and importance of that district.[56]

The impression that High Street housing varied considerably in size and quality is reinforced too by the evidence of rent. Thus relatively modest housing such as the three-storey single chamber house occupied by one Widow Slow was held on a twenty-one year lease at £5 per year plus a £35 payment to the landlord on taking up the lease (entry fine). A similar but slightly smaller dwelling held by Christofer Fawcett, shoemaker, was held on a twenty-one year lease at £4 per year and a £20 fine. A few yards down the street from this dwelling Francis Grove, grocer, held a much larger property on a twenty-five year lease for £10 per year and a £100 entry fine. James Pollard, ironmonger, and a close neighbour of Grove, was also paying about £10 a year with a £120 fine. The range of wealth in this society was reflected in a concomitant spread of housing type and quality. Even the more modest High Street housing was, at least, twice as costly as the 40s. or 50s. tenements within the Boroughside alleys and yards. The margin between more superior back street housing and small High Street properties could be smaller or even non-existent. The one tenement rented in Goat Yard in the 1630s for £8 per year would have paid for Christopher Fawcett's High Street house at the same date.

Many houses, wherever they were sited, lacked basic social amenities. Only half of the fourteen properties surveyed possessed a kitchen, reminding us of the important social functions performed by local alehouses

[54] G.L.R.O. HI/ST/E105.
[55] G.L.R.O. HI/ST/E105. High Street inns had similarly narrow frontages. For similar pre-industrial buildings see, Chartres 1977a: 25–9; Rendle and Norman 1888: 124–30; Power 1972: 247–9; Laithwaite 1984: 67; M. Laithwaite, 'The buildings of Burford', in A. Everitt (ed.), *Perspectives in English Urban History*, London, 1973, p. 65.   [56] Keene 1984: 14–15.

and cooks.[57] Private houses of office (privies) were only mentioned in one property: Collinson had one eight by ten feet in his yard. Apart from warehouses attached to the larger properties specialised rooms were only referred to twice. Henry Clift, butcher, possessed a small slaughterhouse adjoining (conveniently) his kitchen and the house of his next-door neighbour George Idle, victualler, contained 'a shop or drinking house' abutting the High Street.[58]

7.5 *Landlords, tenants and the ownership of local property*

The influence of the urban landlord and the way in which urban property was held are important, but neglected, topics in the social history of seventeenth-century towns and cities.[59] The relationships between landlord and tenant could well have been an important social force. The contemporary pamphleteer Donald Lupton painted a colourful picture of landlord–tenant relations. The 'tenant-by-lease' had to ensure that 'New Year's Day must not pass over without a presentation of a gift. If the landlord be either rich, good, religious, or charitable he feasts their bodies ere Christmas run away.' The 'tenants-at-will' are 'continuous only upon their master's pleasure, their own behaviour, or ability...they must study how to please before they speak'. The landlord–tenant relationship might also produce more informal social activity. Edward Alleyn recorded 6*d*. spent on 'ale and wine at Corden's with the tenants' at the quarterly rent day on 9 April 1618.[60] The nature of house ownership also has important implications for the residential behaviour of householders; nineteenth-century studies suggest that immobility tended to be associated with owner-occupation.[61] The existence of any large-scale property holders could have influenced the topographical development of the Boroughside as Thomas Neale did in Shadwell. Furthermore the residential patterns (or absence of them) might well have been related to the pattern of property ownership. It is known that the occupational homogeneity of one London street was only preserved by the strict policy of the London company that owned it.[62]

The main sources for a study of property ownership in the Boroughside can be divided into two main classes. Information on freeholders is contained in a 1617 survey of the 'chief landlords' who held property in the three Southwark manors. The survey also listed the more substantial tenants of each landlord and covered most of the Boroughside area; it

[57] Clark 1983a: 133.   [58] G.L.R.O. HI/ST/E105.
[59] See Hibberd 1981: 456–7; Pound 1971b: 13–15; Langton 1977: 266–71; Reed 1981: 117–19.
[60] D. Lupton, *London and the Country Carbonadoed*, London, 1632, pp. 108–15; Young 1889: 2, 117–19.
[61] R. Lawton, 'Mobility in nineteenth-century British cities', *Geographical Journal* 145 (1979), 220.
[62] Power 1978a: 40–3; Reddaway 1963: 182–3.

omitted the Close district, a small part of the High Street, and the majority of the back alleys and yards. In almost all cases the tenants listed in the 1617 survey can be identified, in the same order, in the 1618 token book.[63] The identification of manorial freeholders was required so that those who failed to make suit to the court could be 'amerced', that is, fined. The freeholders named in the 1617 survey can also be identified in the lists of 'freeholders amerced' drawn up by the Southwark manorial courts.[64]

The growing importance of the landlord as a source of taxation generated a number of other property surveys. In common with other towns and cities in the seventeenth century efforts were increasingly made to enforce the landlords' financial responsibility for their poorer tenants. As early as 1603 an Act of Common Council had ordered that Southwark landlords were to maintain their tenants.[65] Efforts to tax landlords increased in the 1630s and 1640s. In 1636 an attempt was made to assess the 'outlandlords' of Boroughside property for Ship Money.[66] Following the 1636 plague the need to tax the 'outlandlords' for the relief of the 'poor and visited' became imperative. The 1637 returns were intended to facilitate this action.[67] A certificate which accompanied the 1637 return illustrated the problems of collection:

some of the outlandlords having been rather under than over taxed towards the relief of the poor and visited by reason of remote dwelling cannot be met with and some others dwelling nearer do obstinately deny to pay the same and threaten to spend much money in law…so…such taxation cannot be levied on their tenants or out of their rents…much trouble and charge doth ensue to the parishioners wherefore we humbly beseech your worships…that some speedy redress may be had therein for the relief of the poor whose numbers and charge is so great that the abler parishioners are thereby much impoverished…the outlandlords taxations…being 5 or 6 years behind.[68]

The 1637 returns list both the landlords and the principal lessees of most of the alleys and yards in the Boroughside.[69]

Parliamentary taxation placed the rating of landlords on a sounder footing. A 1643 taxation assessment confirms much of the information on property ownership contained in the 1617 and 1637 surveys and also supplies interesting information on sub-letting. The 1643 tax was on 'the several inhabitants and occupiers of lands, tenements, rents and hereditaments within the parish of St Saviour's Southwark'.[70] In practice this meant

[63] C.L.R.O. Southwark Box 9.7; G.L.R.O. P92/SAV/207.
[64] C.L.R.O. Presentments of the jurors of the Great Liberty Manor 1622, Southwark Box 4; Kings Manor 1624, Southwark Box 2; Guildable Manor 1624, Southwark Box 2.
[65] Hibberd 1981: 223; P. Styles, 'The evolution of the law of settlement', *University of Birmingham Historical Journal* 9 (1963), 35–41.   [66] G.L.R.O. P92/SAV/1353.
[67] Barnes 1970: 1353–4.   [68] G.L.R.O. P92/SAV/1330.
[69] G.L.R.O. P92/SAV/1331.   [70] P.R.O. E179/257/22 dated 20 March 1643.

that the compilers assessed not only the tenant of each dwelling but also his 'landlord'. A typical entry for a High Street dwelling therefore reads, 'Mr Beacon 20s., Masters of the Hospital landlord 2s. 4d.'. In some districts landlord and tenants were sometimes separately assessed because the 'landlord' was assessed on all his property but only a few of his tenants were able to pay. Hence in Foul Lane in 1643 Mr John and Thomas Maddox were assessed 'for tenements £1 6s.', Richard Barnes 'for tenements 4s. 8d.' and seven inhabitants of the lane were assessed on their personal estates at amounts ranging from one to 3s.

Information drawn from the 1617, 1637 and 1643 listings, supplemented by information contained in the records of St Thomas's Hospital, can be used to reconstruct the pattern of property ownership in the Boroughside in the early seventeenth century.[71] Since the surveys were taken at different points in time the assumption is made that the way in which back street and High Street property was held did not alter significantly between the dates of the surveys. It should also be remembered that the only measure of the size of a property holding that can be recovered is the number of tenants inhabiting the property owned by each landlord. The number of inhabitants in each property is given in the sacramental token books. Such a measurement is useful since it not only indicates size but also puts a numerical value on the possible influence of each property owner. The last reservation that should be made about this reconstruction is that the 'multi-layered landlord–tenant relations' commonly found in sixteenth- and seventeenth-century London are notoriously difficult to disentangle. In particular from the sixteenth century many institutions (and some private property owners) increasingly let out their property on long-term leases to tenants, who sometimes sublet in their turn.[72] The 1643 assessment often named the intermediary leaseholder rather than the true chief landlord of property as 'landlord'. Hence the 1643 entry for Ship Yard assessed 'Mr George Hunt for his land £2 14s. 4d.' but is clarified by the following entry in the 1637 survey concerning that yard: 'John Thornhill gent. who now is or late was gentleman usher to the Countess of Salisbury is Chief landlord of the tenements in this yard and George Hunt, mercer, dwelling on London Bridge or Felix Hunt grocer of this parish who are now in suit of law thereabout is lessee thereof.' It is possible that, in a few cases, even the 1637 survey supplied the name of such a lessee rather than the true 'chief landlord' or freeholder. Thus the 1637 survey named Jane Evelyn of Drury Lane as landlady of tenements in Bell Yard. The 1643 taxation assessment listed her owing £2 12s. 3d. for this property and also listed six of her

[71] See the detailed property surveys, governor's minutes and fine book of the hospital, G.L.R.O. HI/ST/E105; HI/ST/A1; HI/ST/E26.
[72] Keene 1984: 16. For similarly complex patterns see, Langton 1977: 219.

sub-tenants there. However, a survey of the property owned by St Thomas's Hospital 1632 reveals that, in fact, Mrs Evelyn held the 'Bell' from the institution on a sixty-year lease.[73] Such qualifications do not diminish the value of the present exercise greatly since it is the *immediate* landlord–occupier relationship which is likely to have had most effect on social and economic behaviour. The identification of the 'true' owner of property who has abandoned any direct relationship with his or her tenants tells us more about private investment strategy. Social interaction between landlord and tenant, payment of rent and landlord control in the Boroughside would have been restricted normally to the two lowest levels of this complex tiered hierarchy both of which can be identified with confidence from the sources used.

As far as it is possible to judge most alleys and yards were held as single block properties by one landlord. This pattern fits in with what is known of their original conversion from single properties. Unfortunately a number of alleys and yards, notably Swan Alley, the Soap Yard and the College Churchyard, were omitted from both the 1617 and 1637 surveys but other evidence suggests that these, too, were held as single properties.[74] Fifteen chief landlords held most of the back street property listed in the 1617 and 1637 surveys. Three of these were members of the Surrey gentry and two came from elsewhere. Five London-based gentry or merchants held individual alleys or yards, one such being Thomas Collett, gentleman at London Wall, who held 3 Crane Yard in 1637 and another James Rudge, a salter in Friday Street, London, who owned Horsehead Alley.[75] Five local inhabitants held the rest of this back street property. Thomas Browker owned Angel Yard in 1637 and John Urrick, his brother-in-law, held it in 1617. Richard Yearwood, a High Street grocer, owned the freehold of Green Dragon Yard and the wealthy brewer John Watts owned Saints Alley. The Richardsons and the Marshalls shared in the ownership of Axe Yard. In the 1640 token book the Richardsons' tenants each had a capital 'R' entered against their names and those of the Marshalls' a capital 'M'.[76] Overall these fifteen landlords held property inhabited by 365 householders in 1618, a ratio of tenants to landlords of twenty-four to one.

The wealthier alleys and yards were owned in a far more piecemeal

[73] P.R.O. SP16/216/114.

[74] Two small alleys, Castle Alley and Browns Rents, were also omitted from the 1617 and 1637 surveys. Evidence from the vestry minutes suggests that the Corporation of the Wardens of St Saviour's owned the freehold of the Soap Yard, the College Churchyard and Browns Rents, see, G.L.R.O. P92/SAV/450, 24 September 1610, 3 December 1610, 8 July 1611, 15 November 1611, 26 November 1611, 20 January 1617, 9 April 1617. In 1643 Mr John Hayman, a local grocer, paid £1 3s. 4d. 'for his land' in Swan Alley but whether he was the lessee or chief landlord of the alley is not known.

[75] These persons are listed by name in Boulton 1983: 205, n. 106–7.

[76] G.L.R.O. P92/SAV/233.

fashion. The 1617 survey lists six different landlords for only nineteen tenants in the Chaingate Churchyard; four landlords had only eight tenants in Counter Alley and three landlords shared in Chequer Alley. High Street property was held in much smaller parcels than that in alleys and yards. By matching the 1617 survey to the 1618 token book it appears that the property occupied in 1618 by 164 tenants was held by fifty-one different landlords, a ratio of tenants to landlords of about three to one. Any social or economic control over High Street tenants must therefore have been extremely fragmented. Only 35 householders out of the 164 (21.3%) listed in areas covered by the 1617 survey inhabited single blocks containing six tenants or more. The largest single block of property was that occupied by thirteen tenants held in 1617 by Mrs Avis Beckingham. Local inhabitants made up eleven out of the fifty-one (21.6%) landlords identified. Thus for example the local Humble family owned five blocks of High Street property and George Payne, a High Street grocer, held two houses on the west side of that street.[77] John Urrick, a gentleman sharing a High Street house with a relation in 1622, had seventeen tenants living in five separate blocks of property on both sides of the High Street in 1617. The original conversion of alleys from High Street property explains how it was that such property was often part of a larger holding that included an adjacent alley. John Watts held both Saints Alley and adjoining High Street property. Local chief landlords held 34.8% of all High Street property included in the 1617 survey. Most of the property in the Close and Pepper Alley sub-district was held by one landlord. Montague House and the Close were held by the Montague family until 1625 when they passed to the local Bromfield family. By 1643 all the property held by Edward Bromfield and his brother Robert had passed to their brother-in-law, Thomas Overman, the local soapboiler. With the exception of a few tenants in Pepper Alley, most householders in the Close area therefore had the same local landlord. Information about the pattern of property-holding in Counter Lane is not often given in early seventeenth-century sources.

As noted above, property was held in two or three tiers in the Boroughside. The chief landlord usually, but not invariably, owned the freehold of the property but frequently this individual leased out his interest to others who often sublet in their turn. The 1643 taxation assessment when used in conjunction with the 1617 and 1637 surveys can supply some information about the extent to which landlords leased away their interest in Boroughside property. The overall effect of this pattern of letting and sub-letting seems to have been to greatly increase the importance of the local property owner. Many absentee 'chief' landlords in fact leased out

[77] These properties were disposed of in his will, P.C.C. Will Register 88 Clarke.

their block holdings of alleys and yards to wealthy local inhabitants. Hence in 1637 Nicholas King, a High Street grocer, was paying Daniel White of Winchelsea, Sussex, £40 per year for the lease of Boarshead Alley. As we have seen Ship Yard was on lease to the Hunts and in a similar fashion Thomas Collett let 3 Crane Yard and adjoining High Street property to Thomas Stone 'of this parish gent'. In the 1622 token book this yard was, in fact, known as 'Stones Rents'. Christopher Yard was owned by William Hurst who 'receiveth the rent as landlord of the same of Nicholas Newton...innkeeper Lessee thereof'. Newton, resident on the High Street, also leased out Goat Yard from a London lawyer. Thomas Browker leased out Angel Yard to a local bricklayer and Thomas Sturmey of Clements Inn let part of Counter Lane to 'John Creswell a smith dwelling in the New Rents'.[78]

However, not all absentee landlords leased away their interest in Boroughside property. Some of the gentry like Thomas Swingfield of Peckham and the Evelyns retained their back street properties intact. In particular much of the High Street property was held by absentee landlords in both 1617 and 1643. Thirteen of the fifty-one chief landlords listed in 1617 can be identified as holding the same property in 1643. Thus for example Alderman Christopher Woodward and his heirs maintained a direct interest in the King's Arms tavern.[79] A small number of absentee and small-scale landlords leased out their property to other absentees. Thus in the 1630s George Wilmore, absentee owner of Frying Pan Alley, leased it to William Butler, an apothecary in Cornhill. Presumably the decision to lease out such property depended on its value relative to the ease of rent collection, which was dependent on the geographical distance between owner and tenants and on the number and financial condition of the latter.

Particularly interesting in this respect is the retention by the Beckingham family of their block of property in the butchers' shambles. The Beckinghams had lived in Southwark in the early sixteenth century and seem to have maintained an active interest in, and family attachment to, their holding. Stephen Beckingham, husband of Avis, the owner in 1617, mentioned 'all my eleven houses or tenements now called Beckingham's tenements lying together in the parish of...St Saviour's...between Chaingate and Pepper Alley' in his will dated 1606, and had by the terms of this document, kept the property 'in male blood' via the offspring of his brother Thomas. The Stephen Beckingham who held the tenements in 1643 was this Stephen's nephew. This same testator was affecting the economic activity of one of his tenants in the early seventeenth century. In 1604 the vestry minute book noted that: 'weaver's wife being demanded for tithes said that she hath

[78] G.L.R.O. P92/SAV/1331.   [79] For Woodward see, Lang 1971: 2, 244.

every year sold Bacon and other things in the house for her landlord Stephen Beckingham's use, and that he and his servant do use the house themselves, whereby he is to pay the tithe'.[80]

Local chief landlords or lessees of large blocks of property sometimes sub-let part of their holdings to other local inhabitants. These 'undertenants' often held such property in addition to their own dwelling house. In fact such 'undertenants' or 'sub-lessees' often leased out property adjacent to, and probably originally part of, their own dwelling. Whether originating from sub-division or new building such sub-letting was an important method by which relatively humble residents of yards or alleys became the immediate landlords to a number of their neighbours; it also enabled them to enter the local property market. Such leasing produced distinctive entries in the 1643 returns (see Table 7.8). Isaac Beane for example was leasing four dwellings from Thomas Overman in 1643, dwelling in one and sub-letting the other three. Axe Yard was owned jointly by the feoffees of John Marshall and the Richardsons.[81] Both of these major landlords clearly preferred to hold most of their property direct but nevertheless two local residents, Isaac Joice and Thomas Quartermain, were sub-letting. It is possible to make a crude estimate of the number of householders who leased or held directly local property other than their own dwelling house. Combining the 1617, 1637, 1635 and 1643 listings it can be shown that about forty householders held some local property, about 3.7% of those resident in 1635. The effect of the leasing out of property by absentee landlords meant that the number of tenants per *local* landlord was slightly greater than that per chief landlord since some local inhabitants leased property from more than one absentee property owner. It is of particular significance that, through a combination of leasing and direct freeholding, in 1635 some 334 householders out of 619 or 54% of those resident in back alleys and yards must have been paying their rent to a local inhabitant.

The influence of many landlords must have been increased by their residence adjacent to their property. The immediate proximity of landlord and tenant is apparent when local landlords are identified on the schematic maps of the Boroughside. Thus John Watts dwelt in his main street brewery immediately adjacent to his Saints Alley property. Nicholas King, grocer, lived next to his Boarshead Alley tenants and Nicholas Newton, Richard Wright, William Batty and others all leased substantial amounts of property

[80] Jordan 1960: 221, 388; G.L.R.O. P92/SAV/450, 14 February 1604; P.C.C. Will Register 40 Wood; Carlin 1983: 144.

[81] The thirteen feoffees of John Marshall, one of whom was the Mr White listed in the 1643 tax, are listed in his will. The rents from this and other property were used to make several large charitable endowments. A special collector of rents was to be appointed, the feoffees being enjoined 'not to rack [the] rents over high'. The feoffees were also enjoined to 'finish and perfect the building and furnishing of the house in Axe Yard...wherein I now dwell'. P.C.C. Will Register 38 St John.

Table 7.8. *Transcript of 1643 taxation assessment showing entries for Axe Yard and the Close*

Axe Yard		
Isaac Joice	5s.	} 12s.7d.
For his tenements	7s.7d.	
John Prichard	1s.	
Francis Europe	1s.	
John Greene	3s.	
Henry Tucker	2s.6d.	
Edward Parker	2s.6d.	
Thomas Quartermain	2s.6d.	} 8s.11d.
his tenements	6s.5d.	
Mr Robert Christy	10s.	
John Prentice	2s.	
Mrs Grace Richardson	10s.	} £2 17s.10d.
for her tenements	£2 7s.10d.	
Mr White for his tenements	£1 11s.	
William Brian for his tenements	8s.9d.	
The Close		
Widow Goodgee	2s.6d.	} 8s.4d.
Landlord Mr Isaac Beane	5s.10d.	
Mr Isaac Beane	6s.8d.	} 16s.
Landlord Mr Thomas Overman	9s.4d.	
John Dyson	2s.	} 4s.8d.
Landlord Mr Isaac Beane	2s.8d.	

Source: P.R.O. E179/257/22.

in close proximity to their dwelling houses. The social intermingling observed in the residential patterns was also directly related to this feature of property ownership. Many gentry chose to live surrounded by their poorer tenants. Hence Robert Bromfield, gentleman and subsidy payer, lived in his Close property as did William Richardson, undermarshall, in Axe Yard in 1622. Similarly Thomas Stone resided in his leasehold property of 3 Crane Yard and John Marshall, junior, was dwelling amongst family property in Axe Yard at his death in 1631. This pattern, of wealthy inhabitants holding adjacent property, has also been found in sixteenth- and seventeenth-century Cheapside.[82] Such local landlords must have been in a better position to recover rent.[83] More importantly such a pattern of property holding could have reinforced the distribution of power and authority. Since most landlords were drawn from the wealthier inhabitants they often also held

[82] Keene 1984: 16.   [83] Boulton 1983: 212, n. 122.

local office. In fact all the individuals referred to in this paragraph were (or became) vestrymen or held manorial office. Their position and effectiveness in the local administration might well have been increased by their property ownership.

Local leaseholders and landlords played the major part in early seventeenth-century property development in the Boroughside. The absentee landlord had probably been responsible for the original construction of alleys and yards. Hence Henry Campion, the owner of Goat Yard in 1617, had been instrumental in its conversion from a brewhouse in the first decade of the seventeenth century. Those gentry who retained an interest in their property were also responsible for some of its later piecemeal development. The 1635 and 1637 surveys, however, reveal that most of the seventeenth-century building was initiated by local inhabitants. Robert Bromfield was responsible for the redevelopment of the Close. Much building work was undertaken by lessees whose chief landlord would be expected to take the costs undergone in new building into account when renewing the lease. This was common practice in the sixteenth and seventeenth centuries. St Thomas's Hospital excused lessees payment of part or all of their entry fines on renewal of the lease in return for repair work or new building of this sort. Of the 107 leasehold properties owned by the institution in St Saviour's and St Thomas's parishes in 1632, twenty-one or 20% had paid a reduced or no entry fine on these grounds. This suggests that something like one in five houses in Southwark was being substantially repaired or improved by their occupants in the early seventeenth century.[84] Thus, in Horsehead Alley, Thomas Raunce 'tenant to Mrs Bridgit Jones' built a barn and shed there. In Axe Yard Mrs Grace Richardson 'is landlady of two...tenements lately built by Gilbert Colman living there...who payeth £3 yearly rent for the same, and was at charge of building thereof'. A wealthy High Street cheesemonger, John Crowder, built two small brick tenements in Pepper Alley 'the inheritance whereof is one Sir John Portmans a west country knight'. Nicholas Newton, lessee of Goat Yard, built '8 stables and haylofts there'. Local bricklayers seem particularly likely to have initiated small-scale building, as they were in the city and eastern suburbs in the late sixteenth and early seventeenth century.[85] John Mathews, bricklayer, who leased Angel Yard and 'dwelling in the same yard...hath lately built there divers tenements with brick which were formerly stables'. Charles Dallyn, a bricklayer resident in Christopher Yard in 1622, built a block of five tenements in the New Rents and two houses in the Close.

[84] See, P.R.O. SP16/216/114, and also E. Kerridge, 'The movement of rent 1540–1640', *Economic History Review*, 2nd ser., 6 (1953), 16–34; Keene 1984: 19.
[85] See, Power 1978a: 30; Barnes 1970: 1338. For the ease with which housing could be erected in the eighteenth century see George 1966: 90.

It should be noted that institutional landlords holding property direct were unusual in the Boroughside and that consequently their influence on the social and economic life of the inhabitants there was minimal. This appears to have been a relatively new feature, perhaps produced by the property sales associated with the Reformation and dissolution of ecclesiastical institutions. In Medieval Southwark a high proportion of property had been owned by religious houses.[86] The Corporation of Wardens of St Saviour's owned the College Churchyard and the Soap Yard and occasionally attempted to control the behaviour of their tenants. Thus a vestry minute recorded that: 'Warning was given to Richard Prior's wife and John Cottrell's wife (who came instead of their husbands) that they shall avoid their houses by midsummer next in regard they slaughter in their houses, or else that they shall slaughter elsewhere'.[87] Unlike some London parishes, however, the amount of local property held by the parish was relatively small and much of what there was, was leased away.[88] In 1617 Christchurch Hospital was chief landlord to a small block of High Street properties and St Thomas's Hospital also owned property in the Boroughside. St Mary Magdalen College, Oxford, held Boarshead Alley in 1617. Although London companies did hold property in the Southwark Manors none of it was located in the Boroughside area.[89]

One other related aspect of the pattern of property ownership was that owner-occupation was extremely rare. In 1617 only two householders held the freehold to their dwelling house. Owner occupation seems to have been commoner in seventeenth-century Ipswich.[90] Most housing was held either by lease or 'at will'. The advantage of leasehold property was that it gave the tenant greater tenurial security than the individual who merely held a dwelling 'at will'. It was easier for a landlord to evict the latter. The vestry of St Saviour's was required to go to law to evict parish tenants occupying leasehold property but tenants-at-will were more vulnerable. In 1611 the vestry ordered that: 'the churchwardens shall warn all those that are tenants to the parish (which are but tenants-at-will and have no leases) to come in at the next vestry to the end it may be known which are fit tenants and which not and that the unfit tenants shall have warning to avoid'.[91]

The lengths of leases varied somewhat but evidence from the records of St Thomas's Hospital suggests that, for a dwelling house, twenty-one

[86] See, Carlin 1983: 121–5. [87] G.L.R.O. P92/SAV/450, 26 November 1611.

[88] For property held by London parishes, see, McCampbell 1976: 112–15.

[89] The Saddlers' company and the Fishmongers' company held property in the King's Manor in 1620 and 1624. The Drapers', Tallowchandlers' and Girdlers' held property in the Guildable Manor, C.L.R.O. Presentments of the jurors of the King's Manor 1620 and 1624, Southwark Box 2; Presentments of the jurors of the Guildable Manor 1624, Southwark Box 2.

[90] Reed 1981: 118.

[91] See, G.L.R.O. P92/SAV/450, 10 December 1616, 15 November 1611.

years was the normal period. In 1632 of the 107 properties owned by the Hospital 65% were held on a twenty-one year lease and 79% on leases of between nineteen and twenty-six years; 19% of leases were held on thirty or thirty-one-year terms.[92] Better quality housing, such as that owned on the High Street by St Thomas's Hospital, seems normally to have been held by lease. The 1643 taxation assessment can perhaps be used to make a rough distinction between leasehold property and that held 'at will'. This can be done by assuming that all properties allocated a specific landlord as well as a tenant were held by lease. Most of these properties were located on the High Street and in the Close which suggests that they were indeed the more substantial dwellings. The results of this exercise indicate that 254 householders in 1643 inhabited leasehold property, 24.0% of all the householders listed in the 1640 token book.[93]

The Boroughside therefore contained four residential sub-districts which exhibited different rates of growth, occupational composition and levels of wealth. The High Street was by far the wealthiest district but wealthy individuals were also found in poorer areas. In both alleys and on the High Street there was significant variation in the quality of housing stock. In part the residential location of such individuals was caused by their employment in manufacturing industry but it was also related to the pattern of property ownership. The absence of occupational segregation was less surprising given that there were no landlords, such as London companies, with a vested interest in maintaining occupational homogeneity in any particular street. The social influence of landlords would have been greater in back alleys and yards, which were commonly held as single block properties, than on the High Street where property holdings were fragmented. The overall effect of the way in which property was held may have worked to reinforce the pattern of power and authority in this society since local officials were often also the landlords and neighbours of the poorer sort. Furthermore since few individuals owned the freehold of their dwelling houses they may have displayed little sentimental attachment to such properties and may have been more vulnerable and responsive to forces influencing the local housing market. The pattern of property ownership might have facilitated residential mobility in the Boroughside.

[92] P.R.O. SP16/216/114.   [93] G.L.R.O. P92/SAV/233.

8

The Dynamics of a Local Community

A number of recent studies have suggested that considerable residential mobility was a feature of pre-industrial urban society.[1] The residential patterns reconstructed so labouriously in the previous chapter, therefore, may well give a misleading impression of stability. In fact many of the maps and diagrams produced by urban geographers should be interpreted not as unchanging and rigid patterns but as snapshots of a shifting population, constantly redistributing itself according to various social and economic imperatives. An analysis of such movement is crucial to an adequate understanding of pre-industrial urban society.

The degree of residential mobility and stability is particularly important for those interested in the existence or otherwise of urban 'communities'. Many authorities believe that the population turnover and sheer size of London produced 'anomie' in a manner similar to that described for nineteenth- and twentieth-century cities. Peter Burke has suggested recently that, at whatever date, 'it seems reasonable to suggest that it is the large city, the city of 100,000 inhabitants or more, which engenders privacy and anonymity'.[2] Lawrence Stone has described the population turnover in seventeenth-century London as resembling 'nothing so much as Los Angeles in the mid-twentieth century' and Christopher Hill sees London as a place of refuge, one of the 'vast anonymous cities and towns' in which masterless men escaped from the bonds of feudal lordship.[3] Clark and Slack recently suggested that, 'The rapid growth of London and its high turnover of population may have led to that impersonality which is said to have occurred in some great continental cities and which is usually associated

---

[1] See, Hibberd 1981: 398–442; Palliser 1979: 114; Langton 1977: 272; Beier 1981: 60; Reed 1981: 94; Phythian-Adams 1979: 191–2; Clark 1972: 125–6; T. B. James and N. A. Price, 'Measurement of change in populations through time: capture-recapture analysis of population for St Lawrence parish, Southampton, 1454–1610', *Journal of European Economic History* 5, 3(1976), 719–36.

[2] P. Burke, 'Some reflections on the pre-industrial city', *Urban History Yearbook* (1975),19.

[3] Stone 1966: 31; C. Hill, *The World Turned Upside Down*, Harmondsworth, 1975, pp. 40–2.

with the modern metropolis'.[4] Turnover on the scale described would have prevented the formation of self-conscious neighbourhoods by greatly restricting personal acquaintance. Gregory King (as quoted in Finlay 1981: 77) stated that one reason for defective returns from the 1695 Marriage Duty Act assessments was that, 'For the parishes in England, there is scarce an assessor but knows every man, woman, and child in the parish but it is much otherwise in London, where the parishes have one with another 800 houses and 4000 souls and where an assessor shall scarce know 5 families on each side of him.'

However there are those who take a different view of social relationships in London society. Roger Finlay has recently pointed out that, due to the very small size of many city parishes, 'it is difficult to argue that...people were less likely to know each other than in rural parishes, except of course in the case of some individuals in the population who were very mobile, for example the apprentices and servants'. Clark and Slack noted that 'face-to-face relationships may have been preserved...in separate streets and quarters of towns which were often dominated by a single occupational group'.[5]

There are reasons for supposing that the Boroughside district of St Saviour's, Southwark, might have contained a transient society. The Boroughside, with 958 householders in 1622, resembles Gregory King's hypothetical London parish. Furthermore, as we have seen, there was little concentration of occupations in particular streets or alleys which might have preserved social relationships. Moreover, with the main highway to the south of England bisecting it, the Boroughside could, like some other pre-industrial suburbs, have been acting as a staging post for immigrants to London.[6] This latter possibility is reinforced by the fact that with its High Street inns and large market, the district was an important communications centre for the whole of London south of the river. Lastly, as we have seen, considerable immigration was needed to maintain Southwark's population growth. It may be that, as some authorities have suggested, many newcomers to London were temporarily resident, staying for only a short period in the capital before returning home.[7] The extent and nature of population turnover therefore is of great importance to an understanding of local society in the Boroughside.

The turnover of householders in the Boroughside can be accurately measured using the sacramental token books. As we have seen, the latter

[4] Clark and Slack 1976: 142; Finlay 1981: 77.
[5] Finlay 1981: 77; Clark and Slack 1976: 142.
[6] Clark 1972: 141–2; Roy and Porter 1980: 203.
[7] Hibberd 1981: 442; D. Souden, 'Pre-industrial English local migration fields', Cambridge (1981), p. 146.

list each household street by street and, if used with some care, yield reliable information about turnover. The procedure by which the token books were compiled between 1597 and 1626 meant that each book lists both those householders present in the district at the time of compilation and also subsequent newcomers and householders who moved from one dwelling to another. To avoid the resultant problem of duplication the procedure adopted in studying turnover was to trace the persistence of those householders resident at the time of each book's compilation. Practically speaking this meant taking all householders written in neat Secretary Hand by the vestry clerk and ignoring the hastily scrawled names of newcomers. The problem of newcomers does not arise after 1626 due to changes in administrative procedure. The lists of householders followed the path that the churchwardens took as they delivered out the tokens. Fortunately from the late sixteenth century the churchwardens almost invariably took the same route and so the names on each book represent the relative position of each household to others in any given year. The rare occasions when the churchwardens slightly altered their route can be identified and allowed for.[8]

It is possible to trace persistence in the same dwelling from these unnumbered lists of householders. Households can be 'fixed' on the listings relative to each other and to the street names given in each token book. The known positions of large establishments, such as inns and breweries, also helped to establish the relative positions of households.[9] For this reason all streets and alleys must be clearly identifiable on a ground plan and the exact position of one street to another discernible. This topographical information has been set out in the preceding chapter. Tracing the per-sistence of every householder in the Boroughside at a number of different points in time over a ten-year period was not a practical proposition and consequently samples of householders were taken. The sampling procedure adopted was to measure the persistence of every householder resident on the east side of the Boroughside. The east side is particularly well defined on the Roque map (Fig. 7.1) and little major building had taken place there from the first decade of the seventeenth century. Moreover the distribution of wealth in the Boroughside was reflected since both the rich on the High Street and the poorer sort in the back alleys received reasonable representation. In 1622, 116 out of 329 householders (35.3%) living in this area contributed to the poor rate compared to a figure of 30.7% for the whole district. Despite the care taken the results will tend to overestimate

---

[8] For a full account of the administrative procedure which lay behind the token books of St Saviour's, Southwark, see Boulton 1983: 362–79.

[9] For this procedure see, Carter 1979: 19–20. For the methodological problems encountered in studies of mobility in nineteenth-century cities, see, Lawton 1979: 213–14.

the persistence of householders resident in back alleys because small residential movements in such districts cannot always be identified with certainty.

There is good reason to suppose that the coverage of householders supplied by the token books was almost universal. Even households outside the Anglican church were recorded and tokens were also delivered to paupers, to the sick, and to all parochial officials, including the two ministers responsible for administering the communion. Another indication of the comprehensive coverage given by the token books is that they invariably list householders known to have been attending the Dutch or French rather than the Anglican Church at this time.[10] In very exceptional circumstances mobility from one dwelling to another might lead to omission from the token books if the move occurred very close to the time of their compilation.

It is important to note that it is only the turnover of household heads that can be measured from these books. Although each communicant received a token, only the household head was normally named.[11] Consequently the more mobile elements of London's population, such as lodgers, inmates and servants, are excluded.[12] It might be argued, however, that the residential behaviour of the householder is of greater social significance than those other members of the population known to be in a transitory stage in the life-cycle.[13] The social and economic importance of the household head in running and disciplining the household and in participating in local government has been discussed above.[14] It is the residential behaviour of these individuals that will be one of the prime factors in the formation or otherwise of a local 'community'.

The dates of each sample were determined by methodological considerations. The 1618 and 1631 samples were chosen because taxation assessments survived for the same dates; the 1631 book also contained information on household size. Following the precedent set by studies of nineteenth-century mobility it was felt that persistence should be measured over a ten year period.[15] The token books for the late sixteenth century did not survive in sufficiently large numbers for persistence over time to

---

[10] 'Aliens' resident in the Boroughside are listed in Kirk 1900–7: 3, 218–19.

[11] The 1621 and 1622 token books gave the christian name of every servant of communicable age, G.L.R.O. P92/SAV/210, 211.

[12] For the floating population see above Chapter 2 and Finlay 1981: 77; Glass 1972: 281–2.

[13] S. R. Smith, 'The London apprentices as seventeenth-century adolescents', *Past and Present* 61(1973), 149–61.

[14] The participation of householders in the parish administration is further discussed in Chapter 10, below.

[15] See, Pooley 1979: 259–61. Lawton 1979: 221. To trace the 1618 and 1631 samples over a ten year period the following token books were consulted: 1618, 1619, 1622, 1624, 1626, 1628, 1631, 1632, 1633, 1634, 1635, 1637, 1640, 1641, see G.L.R.O. P92/SAV/207, 208, 211, 213, 215, 217, 219, 221, 223, 224, 227, 229, 233, 234 respectively.

be measured in such periods. The disruption caused by the 1593 and 1603 plague epidemics was responsible for some of this patchy survival. The 1608 and 1609 books were the earliest which could be used to measure turnover for a relatively uninterrupted ten year time span.[16]

Four samples of householders were taken and their persistence in the same dwelling measured over time (see Table 8.1). A householder was counted as persistent only if he or she remained resident in the same position relative to other householders in the original sample. In line with nineteenth-century studies widows remaining in the same dwelling or children continuing their parents' occupancy are not counted as persistent.[17] The survival of *families* in the same dwelling will therefore be a few percentage points higher than that of household heads alone.[18] After one year 79% of the aggregated sample were still persistent in the same dwelling, after four years about half were still resident and half had left, and after ten years about a quarter were still resident. If the 1618 sample, which included the 1625 plague crisis, is omitted persistence in the same dwelling was 27% over a ten-year period. Figures from nineteenth-century Liverpool suggest that persistence rates in that city were lower than those found in the Boroughside: 18% as opposed to 27%.[19]

A number of social and economic factors affected the levels of persistence in the same dwelling. A breakdown of the 1631 sample by sex of household head revealed that female householders were less persistent than their male counterparts. After one year 79% of all male householders were still persistent compared to 70% of female householders and after ten years 27% of male householders were persistent compared to 21% of females. This difference is more apparent than real, however, since widows who remarried and remained in the same dwelling under a different surname were not counted as persistent. Remarriage of widows often led to the new husband coming to live in the same dwelling. Hence for example this entry in the 1624 token book

Sara Goodwin
[John] Cooper

represents the remarriage of Sara to her new husband. Her first husband Nicholas Goodwin, a butcher, was buried on 22 January 1624 and Sara married John Cooper on 6 April 1624. Unfortunately the degree to which remarriage resulted in the new husband's settlement in the Boroughside

---

[16] To trace the 1608 and 1609 samples over a ten year period the following token books were consulted: 1608, 1609, 1610, 1612, 1614, 1616, 1618, 1619, see G.L.R.O. P92/SAV/198, 199, 200, 201, 203, 205, 207, 208 respectively.   [17] Pooley 1979: 265.

[18] If widows remaining in the same dwelling as deceased husbands are also counted as persistent the percentage persistence of the 1608 sample over a ten-year period rises from 25% to 28%.

[19] Pooley 1979: 265.

Table 8.1. Persistence of householders in the same dwelling 1608–1641

Number of years of persistence	1608 sample		1609 sample		1618 sample		1631 sample		Total sample of householders	
	N 257	%	N 258	%	N 313	%	N 330	%	N 1158	%
1	197	(77)	214	(83)	245	(78)	254	(77)	910	(79)
2	167	(65)	—		—		218	(66)		
3	—		156	(61)	—		199	(60)		
4	134	(52)	—		153	(49)	170	(52)		
5	—		121	(47)	—		—			
6	102	(40)	—		125	(40)	129	(39)		
7	—		100	(39)	—		—			
8	88	(34)	—		76	(24)	—			
9	—		—		—		99	(30)		
10	63	(25)	74	(29)	57	(18)	87	(26)	281	(24)

Note: Percentages expressed as a proportion of the original number of householders in each sample.
Source: See discussion in text, p. 210.

cannot be totally recovered, since only the spouses of widows who remarried in St Saviour's parish church can be identified. Of those Boroughside remarriages that took place between 1622 and 1630 and which were held in the local church, 23 out 52 (44%) resulted in the new husband moving into the dwelling previously occupied by the widow.[20] This social custom may have been a significant mechanism by which a family retained a connection with a particular dwelling.[21]

A breakdown of two of the samples by wealth reveals that the richer householders were more likely to remain in the same dwelling than their poorer neighbours (see Table 8.2). In the 1618 sample 91% of those householders paying the 1617 assessment for the Provost Marshall's wages were still resident in the same dwelling after one year, compared to only 74% of those not assessed.[22] After ten years 29% of those assessed were still resident, compared to only 14% of the non-contributors. Similarly poor-rate payers were more likely to persist than non-rate payers. In the 1631 sample 86% of all poor-rate payers were still resident after one year, compared to 72% of non-rate payers, and after ten years 32% persisted compared to 23%. The higher turnover among poorer householders has also been observed in fifteenth-century Cheapside, the shortest tenancies being recorded for those who inhabited the smallest and cheapest accommodation. Nineteenth-century studies have also found this phenomenon.[23]

The rate of mortality among household heads in the Boroughside played a significant but not a predominant part in turnover. The turnover in the 1609 sample caused by death of household heads was measured using information contained in the token books and the parish burial register (see Table 8.3). Of the original sample 29% were still resident in the same dwelling ten years later, whilst 25% had died and the remaining 46% had moved out of their dwelling. Of the total turnover (the number of householders no longer resident in the same dwelling) 35% had been caused by death. The observed difference in persistence between rich and poor does not seem to have been caused by selective mortality. Reworking the 1618 sample backwards in time to eliminate the effect of mortality confirmed that the wealthier and poorer sort exhibited different levels of residential stability. After ten years (between 1618 and 1608), 41 out of 228 (18%) of the householders not assessed for the Provost Marshall tax were resident in the same dwelling compared to 34 out of 85 (40%) of the householders who were assessed.

[20] For the methodology adopted to look at remarriage and residence see Boulton 1983: 229, n. 24.
[21] Changes in surname are thought to have concealed considerable dynastic continuity in a small district of pre-industrial Oxford, M. Prior, 'Fisher Row, The Oxford community of fishermen, bargemen and canal boatmen 1500–1800', Oxford (1977), pp. ii, 6, 11, 101, 259.
[22] The 1617 tax was based on the subsidy roll, G.L.R.O. P92/SAV/1340.
[23] Keene 1984: 17; Pooley 1979: 265–7; Lawton 1979: 220; Ward 1980: 155–8.

Table 8.2. *Persistence of householders in the same dwelling by wealth, 1618 and 1631*

Number of years of persistence	1618 Householders not assessed in 1617		1618 Householders assessed in 1617		1631 Non poor-rate payers		1631 Poor-rate payers	
	N 228	%	N 85	%	N 205	%	N 125	%
1	168	(74)	77	(91)	147	(72)	107	(86)
2	—	—	—	—	121	(59)	97	(78)
3	85	(37)	—	—	107	(52)	92	(74)
4	—	—	58	(68)	90	(44)	80	(64)
5	78	(34)	—	—	—	—	—	—
6	—	—	47	(55)	64	(31)	65	(52)
7	43	(19)	—	—	—	—	—	—
8	—	—	33	(39)	—	—	—	—
9	—	—	—	—	48	(23)	51	(41)
10	32	(14)	25	(29)	47	(23)	40	(32)

Note: Percentages expressed as a proportion of the original number of householders in each sample.
Source: See discussion in text, p. 212.

Table 8.3. *Role of mortality in turnover of householders 1609–19*

Number of years of persistence	Householders in 1609 sample		Total turnover of householders	Turnover caused by mortality	Mortality loss as a percentage of turnover
	N 258	%			
1	214	(83)	44	19	43
3	156	(61)	58	16	28
5	121	(47)	35	6	17
7	100	(39)	21	15	71
10	74	(29)	26	9	35
Total			184	65	35

Source: See discussion in text p. 212.

A number of social and economic factors might well explain the different residential behaviour of rich and poor. The age structure of the householders may have been one important determinant. Nineteenth-century studies indicate that the elderly were more likely to remain in the same dwelling than younger householders.[24] It is conceivable that wealth may have accumulated with age in the Boroughside so that the richer householders would have been, on average, older than the poorer sort. Housing tenure may have had an important influence over residential behaviour. As we have seen in the previous Chapter very few householders owned the freehold of their dwelling; the richer ones tended to live in leasehold property whilst the poorer sort occupied tenements held 'at-will'. A contemporary pamphleteer contrasted the security of the lease to the insecurity of the 'tenants-at-will' who, 'are men that will take short warning a quarter of a year...they are not unlike courtiers, for they often change places'.[25]

Measuring persistence in the same dwelling, however, has its limitations in part because there is little comparable material available before the nineteenth century. More seriously, as some historians of nineteenth-century cities have noted, it is overall persistence within a particular *area* rather than a particular dwelling that has important social consequences.[26] Studies of this latter sort might reveal something about the extent to which individuals identified themselves with the Boroughside district.

It is clear from the occasional memoranda on the token books that their compilers were conscious of movement from house to house and from alley to alley within the area. In 1612 for example Thomas Berry, listed in Ship Yard,

[24] Pooley 1979: 267; Lawton 1979: 220.   [25] Lupton 1632: 112–13.
[26] Lawton 1979: 220; Pooley 1979: 272; Dennes and Daniels 1981: 10.

was reported to be 'in the Close', Simon Fowler, resident on the High Street, was reported to have moved to 'Fowl Lane', and John Smith and Robert Clarke, both resident in Horsehead Alley in 1612, were noted to be 'in Bell Yard' and '3 Crane Yard' respectively. The compiler also noted intra-alley movement. Nicholas Rogerson in Horsehead Alley was reported to be resident on the 'south side' of the alley in 1612, a move confirmed by the token book itself.[27]

The baptism entries in the parish clerk's notebook supply a crude estimate of the amount of residential mobility within the Boroughside.[28] Since each entry supplied both the address and occupation of the father the residential behaviour of all individuals baptising two or more children in the period covered by the notebook can be measured. Between March 1619 and September 1625, 243 householders baptised two or more children apiece in the Boroughside area. Of these, 165 or 68% consistently supplied the same address. Hence for example all five children of William Stubbes, baker, were born in his dwelling on 'the High Street', and both those of Edward Tart, silkweaver, in his house in Saints Alley. However 77 or 32% clearly made one or more residential moves during the period. Thus Nicholas Wyburne, tailor, lived on the High Street at the baptism of his sons Nicholas and William in 1621 and 1623 but in Christopher Yard at the baptism of his daughter Elizabeth in 1625. In all cases the residential movement indicated by the baptism entries is confirmed by the addresses of the householders in the sacramental token books. In this way each source confirms the reliability of the other. However, the token books indicate that the baptism entries overestimate the number of 'stayers' since they do not detect residential changes within an alley or between particular dwellings on the High Street or in Counter Lane and the Close. In addition it might be suspected that householders baptising children are predominantly younger than other householders and therefore represent a sample biased towards the more mobile. Any detailed examination of residential mobility should be based on the token books, which are more sensitive to movement, and which represent both old and young householders.

Overall persistence within the Boroughside was traced by indexing complete token books at different dates and tracing householders from one book to another. Care was taken to overcome the problems of nominal linkage that inevitably arose, such as individuals of similar surnames or sons succeeding fathers in the same dwelling.[29] There might well be a small

---

[27] G.L.R.O. P92/SAV/201.   [28] G.L.R.O. P92/SAV/406.

[29] For a rehearsal of some of the problems of nominal linkage see, E. A. Wrigley, 'Family reconstitution', in E. A. Wrigley (ed.), *An Introduction to English Historical Demography*, London, 1966, pp. 108–9; I. Winchester, 'The linkage of historical records by man and computer: techniques and problems', *Journal of Interdisciplinary History* 1(1970), 110–13.

number of wrong linkages but these will have been more than compensated for by the underestimation in persistence caused by the difficulty of linking individuals with common surnames, such as Smith, Jones or Brown. Where possible moves were checked against the entries in the parish clerk's notebook. In order to save time many of the samples were selected to correspond to indexes compiled for other purposes. Hence, because indexes had been compiled for the 1622 and 1624 token books the overall persistence of householders living on the east side of the Boroughside in 1612 and 1614 was examined. In order to look in detail at the types of residential moves made it was necessary to obtain a large number of them. For this reason the persistence of *all* householders was looked at for two four-year periods, 1618–22 and 1631–35 and one nine-year period, 1622–1631, the particular periods being determined by the amount of other information available. It should be noted that the methodology can only distinguish between those householders who made no moves in a given period and those who made one or more. Between 1619 and 1625, eight of the 111 individuals (7.2%) baptising three or more children made two or more residential moves within the Boroughside area. To recover the number of moves made by each householder in any given period, however, would have required the indexing of every token book in each period, a task which was not thought to justify the probable return.

Short-range residential mobility was a means by which the Boroughside achieved a measure of stability, much in the manner of some parts of nineteenth-century cities.[30] Thus after nine years 30% of the original 1631 sample of householders were resident in the same dwelling (see Table 8.1) and 45% were still living in the Boroughside district. Similarly of the 559 householders resident in the Boroughside in 1612 and 1614, 238 or 43% were still to be found in the district ten years later. Between 1618 and 1622, 432 of the original 891 householders (49%) remained in the same dwelling and a further 141 (16%) made short residential moves within the Borough-side. In a similar fashion, between 1631 and 1635, 474 of the 966 householders resident in 1631 (49%) remained in the same dwelling and overall 616 (64%) remained within the district. The probability of moving house at least once within the Boroughside increased over time. Between 1622 and 1631, 169 of the 958 householders resident in 1622 (17.6%) remained in the same dwelling and a further 160 (16.7%) moved to a different residence within the area. The 1625 plague reduced the overall level of persistence of the 1622–31 generation.

The overall levels of persistence found in the Boroughside compare

---

[30] Ward 1980: 157; Pooley 1979: 274; Lawton 1979: 220; Anderson 1971: 41–2; Dennes and Daniels 1981: 9–13.

Table 8.4. *Overall persistence within districts of sixteenth- and seventeenth-century London*

District and dates of samples	Householders N	Number of householders persistent after ten years	
		N	%
St Christopher le Stocks, 1576–80[a]	227	64	(28)
St Bartholomew by the Exchange, 1626–40[a]	1004	337	(34)
St Margaret Lothbury, 1642–6[a]	406	112	(28)
Boroughside, 1612 and 1614[b]	559	238	(43)
Goldsmith's Row, Cheapside 1558[c]	61	30	(49)

Sources: [a] Figures calculated from those given in Finlay 1981: 46–7.
[b] See discussion in text, p. 216.
[c] Reddaway 1963: 192–206, for an eleven year period.

favourably with those found in some rural areas of pre-industrial England.[31] This suggests that the relative stability of that district was considerable and adds further weight to Finlay's conclusion that 'the stability of London's population has been underestimated'.[32] Some 52% of household heads were still resident in Cogenhoe after a ten-year period and 50% of householders in Clayworth after a twelve-year period, compared to the 43% of householders persisting within the Boroughside between 1612–14 and 1622–4.[33] It should be noted that the large geographical area of many rural parishes may also have produced internal short-range residential movement. The rural parish of Cardington experienced intra-parish mobility in the eighteenth century and it can be assumed that Clayworth and Cogenhoe experienced mobility of a similar type.[34]

Direct comparison with other areas of pre-industrial London suggests that overall persistence of household heads varied according to the size and social composition of the district in question (see Table 8.4). Overall persistence in the Boroughside was considerably higher than in the three small city

[31] For rural turnover see, P. Laslett, 'Clayworth and Cogenhoe', in P. Laslett (ed.), *Family Life and Illicit Love in Earlier Generations*, Cambridge, 1977, pp. 50–101; W. R. Prest, 'Stability and Change in Old and New England: Clayworth and Dedham', *Journal of Interdisciplinary History* 6, 3(1976), 359–74; Wrightson and Levine 1979: 80–1; A. Macfarlane, *The Origins of English Individualism*, Oxford, 1978, p. 69.
[32] Finlay 1981: 46.   [33] Laslett 1977a: 99.
[34] For intra-parish mobility in rural England see, Schofield 1970: 263; Souden 1981: 138.

parishes analysed by Finlay.[35] This difference is largely a product of size. Even short residential moves in the city parishes examined by Finlay would have taken individuals across parish boundaries and out of observation. Goldsmith's Row may have owed part of its high stability to its position as the premier centre of the London goldsmiths' trade. An analysis of the occupiers of housing in the Row listed by Reddaway reveals that this level of persistence followed a substantial amount of residential mobility within the Row.[36] Perhaps some Boroughside householders were consciously remaining within the district because it, too, was an important trading centre. Derek Keene's wide-ranging and sophisticated reconstruction of an adjacent area of Cheapside housing has recently confirmed the extensive short-range residential mobility within the district: 'moving house was…a common occurrence, and a large number of moves were over very short distances to other houses in the same street or parish'.[37]

To examine overall persistence in greater detail the 1631–5 population was broken down by wealth and household size (see Table 8.5). Overall persistence within the Boroughside area, in contrast to persistence in the same dwelling, was less affected by relative wealth than persistence within the same dwelling. Hence 67.2% of poor-rate payers remained within the district compared to 62.1% of non-rate payers. The poor moved house more often than the better-off but were nearly as likely to remain within the district. Households larger than six persons or more exhibited greater persistence within the area than their smaller neighbours, in both rated and non-rated groups.

The residential moves made by Boroughside householders between 1618 and 1635 have been classified according to type. We have already seen in the previous chapter how the Boroughside can be loosely divided into four residential sub-districts. All residential movements have been grouped according to the sub-district in which or between which moves took place (see Table 8.6). Thus the move of George Perrin, barber-surgeon, from his dwelling on the east side of the High Street to one on the west side in 1622, was classed as within the High Street. Since the table cannot take account of those individuals who moved more than once in any given period it is only an approximate guide to the actual amount of each type of residential behaviour. In particular, since the poorer sort were less likely to remain in the same dwelling than the better-off, multiple movements within and between alleys and yards, where most of the poorer sort lived, are likely to be undercounted.

The majority of residential movements within the four-year periods seem to have taken place within residential sub-districts. Movement between alleys and yards and within particular alleys and other sub-districts

---

[35] Finlay 1981: 45–7.   [36] Reddaway 1963: 181–206.   [37] Keene 1984: 17.

Table 8.5. *Overall persistence within the Boroughside by wealth and household size 1631–5*

Household size	Non poor-rate paying householders	Persistent		Poor-rate paying householders	Persistent	
	N	N	%	N	N	%
1–5	597	368	(61.6)	199	123	(61.8)
6+	55	37	(67.3)	115	88	(76.5)
Total	652	405	(62.1)	314	211	(67.2)

Source: See discussion in text, p. 218.

accounted for 98 out of 141 moves (69.5%) between 1618 and 1622, and 108 out of 142 (76.1%) between 1631 and 1635 (see Table 8.6). Nonetheless no sub-district was a self-contained segregated unit since the remaining moves took place between different areas. This interchange of personnel between districts increased over time. Between 1622 and 1631, 60 out of 160 residential moves (37.5%) took place between one sub-district and another.

The volume of residential mobility and its internal direction has important social and topographical implications. It is clear that patterns of the residential distribution of occupations at one point in time were partly an artificial creation of the methodology. The existence of residential mobility in fact goes some way towards explaining the absence of occupational groupings by street. As has been suggested above, only a single landlord with a vested interest could have preserved the occupational integrity of a street.[38] Furthermore the movement between sub-districts in the Boroughside must have increased the physical contact between rich and poor already promoted by a degree of residential intermingling.

The population turnover might seem to indicate that there was little possibility of street 'communities' developing or surviving in the Boroughside as they are thought to have done in some sixteenth-century English cities.[39] Persistence within a particular alley or yard was considerably lower than in the district as a whole. Between 1612 and 1622 fifteen out of fifty householders (30%) remained in Horsehead Alley. Only eight out of seventy-one householders (11.3%) living in that alley in 1620 were still resident in the same place in 1640. However, much lower rates of persistence

[38] Reddaway 1963: 189–90.
[39] See, Dyer 1973: 177; Phythian-Adams 1979: 166–8.

Table 8.6. *Types of residential move within the Boroughside, 1618–35*

Description of residential behaviour	Householders moving 1618–22		Householders moving 1631–5		Householders moving 1622–31	
	N	%	N	%	N	%
Alley – Alley	41	29.1	43	30.3	43	26.9
Within Alley	36	25.5	37	26.1	22	13.8
Alley – Counter Lane	12	8.5	14	9.9	24	15.0
Alley – High Street	11	7.8	13	9.2	22	13.8
Alley – Close	9	6.4	1	0.7	9	5.6
Within Counter Lane	5	3.6	12	8.5	9	5.6
Counter Lane – High Street	9	6.4	2	1.4	4	2.5
Counter Lane – Close	2	1.4	0	—	2	1.3
Within High Street	9	6.4	10	7.0	21	13.1
Within Close	7	5.0	8	5.6	4	2.5
Close – High Street	0		2	1.4	0	
Total	141		142		160	

Note: Percentages expressed as a proportion of the total number of householders in any given period.
Source: See discussion in text, p. 218.

than these are not thought to have undermined alley life in nineteenth-century Washington, and it is possible that similar social mechanisms operated to provide a measure of continuity in the Boroughside alleys and yards.[40] It may be that the long stayers in each yard acted as informal 'overseers' and introduced newcomers to the place. In this connection it is noticeable that it was often long-term residents who rented local property and who could have provided accommodation for new immigrants. Thus in May 1637 it was reported that, 'John Brown lately come with his wife and 3 children from Newington parish hath taken a house of Thomas Raunce [a long-term resident] in Horsehead Alley.'[41] Certainly a long period of residence in an alley or yard seems to have engendered a certain identity with the area. Hence Thomas Prior, a victualler long resident in the Close, described himself as 'of Montague Close' in his will; similarly Thomas Horne, resident in Axe Yard for thirty years, described himself as of 'Axeyard, St Saviour's, Southwark' in his will.[42]

It should be noted that the causes of residential mobility are too complex

[40] In nineteenth-century Washington only one third of the heads of household resident in six 'north-west' alleys were still resident in the same alleys *five years* later, Bourchet 1981: 621.
[41] G.L.R.O. P92/SAV/1335.
[42] G.L.R.O. Archdeaconry of Surrey Will Register, 151 Yeast; 23 Harding.

to be quantified easily. It is clear from other studies that personal whim, the births or deaths of children, life-cycle stage or the desire to alter business premises played some part.[43] In this connection we should see the heterogeneous housing stock of the Boroughside as one important precondition of short-range movement. In addition, the wide range in rental value between and within the various sub-districts gave inhabitants the opportunity to make significant adjustments to their life-style *within* the locality.

The poorer sort were vulnerable to parochial harassment: 'William Milwood his wife and 2 children being come to dwell in Horsehead Alley I made it known to the churchwardens, and afterwards warned them to put in sureties, and being not able for fear of further troubles they left this parish, and went to dwell in St George's parish, and so we were rid of them.'[44] The settlement strategy of the poor might have often involved some residential mobility designed to help them escape from the attention of such parish officials and thereby to fulfil whatever period of residence in the parish was required to establish a successful settlement. Dalton wrote in 1633 that a month was the minimum legal qualification. The 1662 Act of Settlement extended the residence qualification to forty days. A subsequent Amending Act of 1685 noted that, as a consequence, 'poor persons at their first coming to a Parish do commonly conceal themselves'.[45]

Occupation also influenced residential behaviour, as has been shown in a number of recent studies.[46] Hence one John Potfield, starchmaker, moved from Boarshead Alley to Parkside (in Counter Lane) in 1621 and thereby next door to John Dover, the only other recorded starchmaker in the Boroughside, and adjacent to the facilities of the Soap Yard. An examination of the effect of occupational label on the mobility of householders in the 1622–31 sample, however, could find few significant differences in residential behaviour between different occupations, perhaps due to the large variety of causes lying behind residential moves.

Mobility studies based on listings suffer the disadvantages that, at best, it is only possible to measure persistence within what might be an artificial administrative district. As Prest and others have pointed out, much movement from rural parishes was short-range to neighbouring parishes and often included an amount of circular movement.[47] The 'great majority of lifetime movements...took place within very circumscribed general limits'. Similar 'social areas' have been identified in nineteenth-century cities.[48]

---

[43] See, Pooley 1979: 272; Reddaway 1963: 186; Keene 1984: 17; M. Thale (ed.), *The Autobiography of Francis Place 1771–1854*, Cambridge, 1972, pp. 107–215, passim.

[44] G.L.R.O. P92/SAV/1423.   [45] Styles 1963: 47.

[46] Hibberd 1981: 424; Souden 1981: 241; Glass 1972: 281; Pooley 1979: 265.

[47] Prest 1976: 361; Schofield 1970: 264; Souden 1981: 26.

[48] Souden 1981: 137; Pooley 1979: 272; Dennes and Daniels 1981: 11.

It seems possible that much of the residential movement across the administrative boundaries of the Boroughside also took place within a relatively restricted area. A certain amount of residential movement took place between the Boroughside and the two outliberties of the Clink and Paris Garden. Of the 242 householders baptising two or more children and resident within the Boroughside at one point in time, thirteen (5.4%) had some experience of residence in one of the two liberties. Hence for example Richard Gooderidge, dyer, resident in the Close in 1622 had moved to the 'Moldstrand' by 1625.[49] Of all the householders resident in the Boroughside in 1618, sixteen (1.8%) were resident in the Clink liberty in 1622. In 1636, four out of twenty-eight newcomers to the Boroughside (14%) were explicitly recorded as having come from the Clink liberty. The previous residences of ten out of seventeen incoming male heads of families were given by the searcher for inmates in 1622. Seven of the ten had been previously resident in an adjacent parish and failure to achieve settlement in the Boroughside forced a number of them to return to those parishes as in the case of William Milwood quoted above.[50] Short-range movement took place among the ruling élite, resulting in vestry orders to readjust vestry representation. It was ordered in 1615, 'that although Mr Carter be gone to dwell on the Bankside, yet he shall be counted as a vestryman of the Boroughside, and when he die or remove out of the parish, one out of the Boroughside shall be chosen in his place'.[51] The internal residential mobility in the Boroughside and the short moves made between it and adjacent districts may indicate that many householders were pursuing their social and economic life within a relatively restricted locality.

As noted above, one influence over residential moves might well be the life-cycle stage reached by individuals. 'Life-cycle' changes are thought to have lain behind the exchange of houses by two Cheapside grocers in 1531.[52] Since there appears to be good reason to think that individual social and economic fortunes varied considerably with age as discussed in Chapter 6, a reconstruction of some individual careers might, therefore, furnish an appropriate context for the study of residential mobility.

Before considering individual careers, however, it might be useful if we look at the extent to which residential mobility was related to observed alterations in financial circumstances. This can be done by taking those householders resident in 1622 and 1631 who contributed to the poor rate in at least one of those years, and then grouping them according to their residential behaviour and the movement of their poor-rate assessments (see

---

[49] A move detected in the baptism entries in the parish clerk's notebook, 28 November 1622, 3 July 1625. Gooderidge's arrival is also recorded in the 1624 Clink token book, G.L.R.O. P92/SAV/272.

[50] See, G.L.R.O. P92/SAV/228, 1423.   [51] G.L.R.O. P92/SAV/450, 17 February 1615.

[52] Keene 1984: 17.

Table 8.7. *Residential behaviour and social mobility 1622–31*

Residential behaviour	Householders whose assessments were raised 1622–31[a]	Householders whose assessments were reduced or abolished 1622–31	Householders whose assessments were unaltered 1622–31	Total
Making one or more moves	41	16	5	62
Remaining in same dwelling	48	19	19	86
Total	89	35	24	148

Note: [a] Includes 43 householders present but not assessed in 1622 who were assessed in 1631.
Source: See discussion in text, p. 222.

Table 8.7). Changes in financial circumstances were clearly the rule rather than the exception. Of the 105 householders assessed for the poor rate in 1622 who were still resident in 1631 only twenty-four (22.9%) had unaltered assessments. As the disadvantageous social and economic position of females would lead us to expect, widowhood almost invariably led to a reduction in poor-rate assessment: of the twenty-three poor-rate paying householders whose widows were still resident in 1631 (who are *not* included in Table 8.7) twenty had their ratings reduced or abolished and only one had her rating increased.[53]

It is clear that changes in financial circumstances did not necessarily result in residential adjustments but a greater likelihood of residential mobility does seem to have been associated with financial change. Of the 124 householders whose assessments were altered fifty-seven (or 46%) made one or more moves, while of the twenty-four whose assessments were unaltered only five (or 21%) moved. On the other hand, continued residence was also sometimes compatible with changes in economic circumstances. A relatively long period of residence in the Boroughside was often associated with an improvement in financial circumstances. After nine years of residence forty-three out of 223 householders (19.3%), who were not rated in 1622, *were* rated in 1631. Interestingly, the parochial authorities seem to have linked a relatively long period of residence *explicitly* with ability to pay the poor rate. In 1613 they stated that widow Payne had

inhabited [the] parish for 12 years at the least by reason whereof at an assessment…for the poor made…the said complainment was assessed… at the sum of one half penny every week…the charge of the parish toward the relief of the poor being very great and the estate of the said complainant as these defendants are informed and do conceive to be true being well able to bear a greater proportion.[54]

A link between long residence and financial improvement was made in another parish of seventeenth-century London.[55] Downward social mobility also occurred in the other direction, however: eleven of the 105 male householders contributing to the poor rate in 1622 were no longer assessed by 1631.

It is occasionally possible to flesh out the changes that lay behind rises and falls in poor-rate assessments by reconstituting individual careers or life-cycles. Thus, Roger Cotten, victualler, married his wife Edith in 1594 and set up house in the New Rents. By 1609 he had moved to a High Street dwelling and was assessed at one penny in the 1622 assessment, but in that year he moved from the High Street into Goat Yard. Cotten was not rated in 1631. He twice petitioned the vestry for relief in the early 1630s and

[53] For similar cases see, Pearl 1981: 125; Smith 1981b: 607–8.
[54] P.R.O. STAC8/228/8.   [55] Dingle 1974: 105.

eventually died in a parish almshouse in 1636. Edith Cotten, twenty years his senior, died in 1634 and a year before her death had been a recipient of the charity of Henry Smith, when she was described as a 'poor aged woman [receiving] a petticoat and a waistcoat with a badge of HS on the breast of the waistcoat'. Roger Cotten's petitions confirm his financial decline showing

that your petitioner having been a parishioner these 50 years and upwards and a man of good demeanour in times past and one whose behaviour hath been lawful and honest in his demeans and carriage and one which hath paid scot and lot in the parish all the time of their abode here in the parish. But now so it is…that your poor petitioner with his aged wife is grown into years whereby their labours are both past that they cannot take pains whereby to relieve themselves by reason of their decrepit old age but are in election to come to great misery and want.[56]

Michael Mossendue was a £3 subsidy man in 1622 and assessed at 2*d.* for the poor rate. He had arrived in the parish by virtue of a second marriage to a Boroughside widow, Alice Greene, in 1614 and lived on the High Street. Mossendue's troubles may well have begun with the death of Alice in 1623. In 1626 the vestry authorities purchased the freehold of his house, 'the dagger', for £110 and at the end of December 1627 Mossendue was bound for £30 to pay £14 arrears of rent. In March 1628 the churchwardens decided to sue him for the rent and by May 1628 Mossendue had given up his main street dwelling and removed to poorer housing in Axe Yard. He was not rated in 1631. By 1635 he had moved into Goat Yard (in the dwelling there with Roger Cotten).[57]

Another subsidy payer who ended up on parish relief was one John Mee, described as a tallowchandler at his burial on 3 February 1655. Mee was born in 1583, the son of William Mee, a wealthy vestryman, citizen and tallowchandler. John continued his father's occupancy of a main street house and in 1622 was rated at 3*d.* in the poor rate and at £4 in the subsidy books. By 1631 however John Mee was not rated for the poor rate though still living on the High Street. Between 1631 and 1635 he moved into poorer accommodation in Goat Yard and in 1640 was dwelling in the New Rents. In 1638 he became a recipient of the charity of Henry Smith receiving a badged coat.[58] Although, as we have seen, alterations in poor-rate assessments were not invariably linked to residential mobility, long-term

[56] See charity accounts and petitions, G.L.R.O. P92/SAV/1762, 768, 769. Information for the following biographies has been taken from the parish register, appropriate token books and the Overseer's accounts, all of which are listed in the manuscript bibliography. Other sources used are specified. Specific references can be found in Boulton 1983: 257–61.

[57] See the vestry minute book, G.L.R.O. P92/SAV/450, 31 December 1627, 3 March 1628 and appropriate token books.

[58] Information from Overseers' accounts, token books, William Mee's will, P.C.C. Will Register, 5 Wood, and charity account G.L.R.O. P92/SAV/1780.

financial decline often involved one or more moves to cheaper accommodation.

It is clear, too, that improvements in financial position could lead to residential changes. For those householders involved in occupations that required a retailing outlet or a particular site, moves may have been an integral part of financial advancement. Hence David Soane, butcher, arrived in the Boroughside in 1613 taking up residence in Axe Yard. In 1617 he moved to Boarshead Alley and in 1622 moved from there to the High Street butchers' shambles. Between 1622 and 1631 his poor rate assessment increased from $\frac{1}{2}d$. to $1\frac{1}{2}d$. In 1635 Soane was renting a stable in Goat Yard from a local innkeeper.[59]

For the poorer householder, involved in small-scale domestic manufacturing such as tailoring or shoemaking, long-term residence within a particular alley or yard may have promoted the gradual accumulation of wealth. Familiarity with the immediate locality may have enabled such individuals to invest in local property when the opportunity arose. Financial improvement of this sort may have required diversification into property, and perhaps the keeping of livestock, in order to offset the loss of earning power that would have come with age. Thus Walter Leech, tailor, married in 1608 and from that date until our residential information ends in 1643 he lived in Horsehead Alley. In 1618 Leech was listed as poor, along with a wife and two children. He was not listed as receiving any charitable payments between 1621 and 1622 nor was he assessed for the poor rate. His subsequent taxation history reveals a substantial increase in his personal estate. In 1631 he was rated at 2*d*. in the poor rate and in 1635 contributed 4*s*. 6*d*. to the Ship Money assessment. The 1643 tax rated him at 3*s*. 'for his estate' and 13*s*. 'for his tenements'. Leech, as the 1643 tax indicated, had invested in local property: 'In Nag's Head Yard [i.e. Horsehead Alley] 3 small tenements and a barn built with brick by Walter Leech dwelling there upon old foundations about nine years since for which he payeth £5 yearly rent to Mrs Bridget Jones landlady thereof'. Like some other inhabitants of Horsehead Alley, Leech supplemented his earnings by keeping hogs and at his burial on 12 September 1658 he was described as a 'cowkeeper'.[60] If it is assumed that Leech was 25 years of age at his marriage he would have been 60 in 1643 and 75 at his death.[61] By financial

---

[59] See G.L.R.O. P92/SAV/1336, and Overseers' accounts and relevant token books. Soane's 1622 move can be confirmed from the parish clerk's notebook, see the baptism entries 26 November 1620 and 6 February 1623 G.L.R.O. P92/SAV/406.

[60] See, Survey of Poor 1618, G.L.R.O. P92/SAV/1465; survey of divided tenements G.L.R.O. P92/SAV/1336; 1643 assessment P.R.O. E179/257/22 and G.L.R.O. Presentments of the jurors of Great Liberty Manor 1634, 1637–9, Southwark Box 4.

[61] For age at marriage in London see, Finlay 1981: 139.

diversification and (possibly) residential stability, Leech had avoided the economic decline often associated with the aging process.

Overall, therefore, a significant number of householders spent a large proportion of their lives within a restricted urban area. Changes in financial circumstances, sometimes prompted (as in the case of Roger Cotten) by the onset of old age, may have led to some of the short residential moves made within the Boroughside area. Their residential behaviour also implies that many Boroughside householders possessed considerable local knowledge of the housing stock and relatively restricted social horizons. In many respects, therefore, the pattern of moves resembled that of nineteenth-century cities, and, as in the latter case, the predominance of short-range movements may testify to a sense of familiarity with, and possibly attachment to, an urban neighbourhood. How far this amounted to a sense of neighbourhood and community and what the geographical and social limits of such entities were, are questions to which the material discussed in this chapter can provide only partial answers.[62]

---

[62] For similar sentiments see Pooley 1979: 274; Keene 1984: 17 and J. Boulton, 'Residential mobility in seventeenth-century Southwark', *Urban History Yearbook* (1986 forthcoming).

9

Social relationships in the urban neighbourhood

9.1 Community and neighbourhood in pre-industrial cities

Studies of sixteenth-century provincial cities tend to use the term 'community' to describe either the whole city or an urban 'sub-community' within it.[1] Dyer thought the urban parish 'a very distinct community to those living in it' but also went on to make the unsupported claim that 'parishes in their turn must have been broken down into street communities'. Phythian-Adams also noted the 'informal grouping of people into...the neighbourhood' in early sixteenth-century Coventry and pointed to the evidence for street parties and maypoles as indication of neighbourhood solidarity.[2] The neighbourhood and street communities sometimes identified in pre-industrial cities are thought to be bolstered and maintained by a number of formal and informal institutions. As we shall see in Chapter 10 participation in, and the scope and effectiveness of, local government and church life are often thought to represent the formal foundations of neighbourhood life. Less formally, residential patterns are thought to provide another basis for social cohesion. The 'degree of contact and intimate intermingling between the various social groups' is stressed in York, Worcester and Coventry.[3] The existence of the 'sub-community' in Worcester was demonstrated by the frequency with which 'friends and relations all lived in the same small area'; while Phythian-Adams produced some evidence intended to show that kinship 'lent some reality to the concept of neighbourhood at the street level'. More recently Peter Clark has written of the Canterbury suburbs that social 'coherence was given to these poorer areas of the city by a network of neighbourhood ties and connections'.[4]

[1] For towns and cities as single communities see Dyer 1973: 176; Palliser 1979: 288; Phythian-Adams 1979: 170–9; Clark and Slack 1976: 4–10, 32.

[2] Dyer 1973: 177; Phythian-Adams 1979: 158–69. See also P. Burke, 'The early modern town, its history and historians: a review article', *Urban History Yearbook* (1981), 57.

[3] Phythian-Adams 1979: 166; Dyer 1973: 179; Palliser 1979: 294.

[4] Palliser 1979: 78; Phythian-Adams 1979: 157; Clark 1983b: 80.

Such urban neighbourhoods existed despite possible dislocating influences. Clark has alleged that a substantial number of poor immigrants might erode neighbourhood consciousness.[5] Worcester, York and Coventry all experienced extensive immigration and both Palliser and Phythian-Adams noted the extent of residential mobility across city parish boundaries. The geographical area of the 'neighbourhood' found in the suburbs of Canterbury is thought to have actually criss-crossed parish boundaries seemingly overriding and ignoring questions of parochial loyalty.[6] The extent to which the population of urban parishes actually participated in church life is also open to question. The possibility of finding details about the urban neighbourhoods of sixteenth-century provincial cities in seventeenth-century London would seem to be lessened both by London's exceptional size and growth and also by the changes in civic and church ceremonial which followed the Reformation.[7]

Nonetheless some studies of London society in the later sixteenth and seventeenth centuries do find evidence of urban 'communities' and neighbourhoods in the capital. Reddaway described Goldsmith's Row in the mid sixteenth century as 'a community in an area in which houses and shops were at a premium...the community in the Row was flourishing, close-linked and prosperous'. Michael Power unequivocally described Shadwell in 1650 as a 'sub-community', 'a society "writ small" in which people lived and worked in the same small area where they bought their food and met to drink'. This despite Shadwell's admitted lack of 'unity or identity'; the area had no church, market, physical centre or even adequate government.[8] The wards and precincts of the wealthy inner city areas have been described recently as 'tight communities, intimate in size...where everyone knew everyone else'. Conversely, however, Burke has pointed to the 'relative weakness of cultural activity based on parish or wards', which may indicate the diminution of the importance of the areas as neighbourhood units. Moreover, borrowing from sociological writing like Peter Clark, Burke has pointed to the possible strains of heavy immigration.[9] Such sociological writings in fact provide more systematic ways in which to look at the society of pre-industrial cities.

Urban sociologists have recently highlighted the semantic, methodological and ideological problems associated with attempts to establish the existence of urban 'communities' in nineteenth- and twentieth-century

[5] Clark 1972: 153.
[6] Phythian-Adams 1979: 158–303; Dyer 1973: 26–7, 48; Palliser 1979: 112, 127; Clark 1983b: 81.
[7] C. Phythian-Adams, 'Ceremony and the citizen: the communal year at Coventry 1450–1550', in P. Clark (ed.), *The Early Modern Town*, London, 1976, pp. 122–4; Clark and Slack 1976: 26–7; P. Burke, 'Popular culture in seventeenth-century London', *London Journal* 3 (1977), 143–62.
[8] Reddaway 1963: 188; Power 1978a: 40.
[9] Pearl 1979: 19; Burke 1977: 158–9.

towns and cities.[10] The methods and arguments they employ hold valuable lessons for historians of pre-industrial urban society. 'Community' as a concept has been subjected to intensive study (one author counted ninety-seven definitions) and the confusion surrounding its meaning has led a number of authorities to abandon it altogether.[11] Two basic definitions have recently been put forward: 'community' can indicate 'a particular social group living in a certain area', or it can be used as an evaluative term meaning 'a positive neighbourly quality of social relationships'.[12] Further problems derive from the difficulty of establishing the actual geographical boundaries to any particular area.[13] Stacey and others concentrate on the idea of the 'local social system...the residents of which are related by bonds of kinship, occupation, class, religion and politics...a set of inter-relations' existing in a 'geographically defined locality'.[14] The concept of the local social system has been employed recently as a valuable methodological tool with which to look in fresh and revealing ways at pre-industrial English rural society.[15]

Urban sociologists have applied the concept of the local social system to towns and cities. The 'urban village' has proved to be a powerful concept among many authors and can be defined as 'the existence of a local social system within an urban area'.[16] Unfortunately, as several authorities have pointed out, an ideological bias often colours much research in the urban field. Lee has pointed out that 'perceptions about the actual local basis of social activity have become...intertwined with the desire to promote such a basis'.[17] The 'ideology of community' which this represents grew up in response to the industrialisation of the nineteenth century and the contrasts drawn at the time between 'face-to-face' rural life and urban anonymity.[18] The key question in establishing the existence or otherwise of an urban local social system is to gauge and, if possible, *measure* the extent to which the social and economic life of individuals took place *within* the locality. Dennes

[10] See, Dennes and Daniels 1981: 7–23; C. Bell and H. Newby, 'Community, communion, class and community action', in D. T. Herbert and R. J. Johnston (eds.), *Social Areas in Cities*, Chichester, 1978, pp. 283–301; J. C. Mitchell (ed.), *Social Networks in Urban Situations*. Manchester, 1979, pp. 1–50; J. Connell, 'Social networks in urban society', in B. D. Clark and M. B. Gleave (eds.), *Social Patterns in Cities*, London, 1973, pp. 41–52; C. Bell and H. Newby, *Community Studies*, London, 1971; Macfarlane 1977.
[11] Dennes and Daniels 1981: 7; Macfarlane 1977: 2; Bell and Newby 1971: 27–53.
[12] Dennes and Daniels 1981: 7.   [13] Ibid.; Macfarlane 1977: 9–15.
[14] M. Stacey, 'The myth of community studies', *British Journal of Sociology* 20 (1969), 134–47; Dennes and Daniels 1981: 8.
[15] Wrightson and Levine 1979: 73–109.
[16] See, Connell 1973: 44; Wrightson 1982: 56. For the classic urban village see, Young and Willmott 1957: 81–92.
[17] T. R. Lee, 'Cities in the mind', in D. T. Herbert and R. J. Johnston (eds.), *Social Areas in Cities*, Chichester, 1978, p. 258.
[18] Bell and Newby 1978: 286; Bell and Newby 1971: 22–5.

and Daniels have suggested that persistence within a particular area, kinship density, employment patterns and social and religious behaviour are important measures of community structure.[19]

9.2 The foundations of an urban local social system?

Evidence drawn from the preceding chapters can be used to provide some information about a local social system. Firstly, as was demonstrated in chapter 8, the persistence of householders in the Boroughside area was relatively high and the short moves made by many householders could be taken as a sign of local attachment. However, persistence within an area is only a 'useful index' of community since extensive short-range mobility may only reflect a lack of alternatives, the 'heterogenous nature of the local housing stock and the inefficient flow of information about housing vacancies over long distances'.[20] At the least, such persistence emphasises the inherent tendency towards localism within metropolitan society.

There is certainly evidence which suggests that local social horizons may have been restricted considerably by poor intra-metropolitan communications in the seventeenth century. The capital's newsbooks did not carry advertisements regularly until the middle of that century and the first advertising sheet, too, dates from 1657. Despite the rapid expansion of advertising in the late seventeenth century information concerning travel remained poor and mostly centred on inns.[21] Access to printed advertisements and newsheets was denied to the illiterate. Although London had overall relatively low rates of illiteracy by 1640 compared to the rest of England, illiteracy rates amongst some of the poorer tradesmen and craftsmen in the captial remained high. Furthermore no really useful street map of the capital was available before 1676.[22] Travellers remarked on the sociological effects of all this. As late as 1690 a Scottish visitor noted that,

The city is a great vast wilderness. Few in it know the fourth part of its streets, far less can they get intelligence of the hundredth part of the special affairs and remarkable passages in it, unless by public printed papers, which come not to every man's notice. The most attend their business, and an inquisitive stranger will know more of the varieties of the city than a hundred inhabitants.[23]

Current sociological theory identifies local work-places as particularly important in maintaining a local social system since they reduce 'the need

---

[19] Dennes and Daniels 1981: 16.   [20] Dennes and Daniels 1981: 10.
[21] See, R. B. Walker, 'Advertising in London newspapers, 1650–1750', *Business History* 15 (1973), 112–30.
[22] See, Cressy 1980: 72–5, 132–5; Ida Darlington and J. Howgego, *Printed Maps of London c. 1553 and 1850*, London, 1964, pp. 1–25.
[23] See, D. Maclean, 'London in 1689–90 by the Revd R. Kirk', *Transactions of the London and Middlesex Archaeological Society*, n.s., 6 (1929–33), 333.

for residents to move outside their spatial environs'.[24] As we have seen in Chapter 3 many Boroughside householders were employed in the immediate neighbourhood. A number of retailers were supplied by local manufacturers, and many of the latter were tied to specific sites. Furthermore, many retailers were dependent on the maintenance of a local reputation and specific customer ties. In 1662 one Stephen Harris, responsible for the capture of the radical Hugh Peters and the detection of a number of conventicles, sent in a petition to the privy council complaining that,

for which service done to your Majesties your petitioner hath quite lost his trade, living in the Borough of Southwark amongst the most numerous factious people...and consequently ruined himself by being marked out by them as a Saul or persecutor of the people as they term him.[25]

The importance of local customer ties has been noted in other urban areas.[26] For the employee as well as the retailer a move to a new neighbourhood might result in serious economic dislocation. Following a Star Chamber case a Southwark tailor complained that he had been

enforced to...depart from his said house and liberty albeit to his utter undoing in driving your said subject from amongst all his acquaintance and custom of trade into a strange unknown place where he was and yet is lost of all acquaintance and friends, and hath thereby lost all his custom of work to his utter overthrow and decay of his trade and maintenance.[27]

The structure of much of the local economy rested, to a significant extent, on a local foundation. Perhaps in the Boroughside as in late seventeenth-century Newcastle,

living in the same neighbourhood as your employer might have strengthened feelings of economic interdependence, if not community of interest, and certainly reduced the anonymity that could be associated with urban life.[28]

However, other factors could have been working against the maintenance and development of a local social system. Despite the strong local element in the economy, a number of occupations took their practitioners out of the Boroughside for certain periods of time. Some occupations involved regular contact with other parts of London and this was sometimes reflected in the tradesmen's wills. Thus, watermen were often involved in credit networks that stretched across the River Thames.[29] Similarly the large-scale

---

[24] Stacey 1969: 143; Lawton 1979: 216.   [25] Hart 1865: 195.
[26] See, Dingle 1974: 34; Palliser 1979: 180; Anderson 1971: 104.
[27] P.R.O. STAC8/125/7.
[28] Joyce Ellis, 'A dynamic society: social relations in Newcastle-upon-Tyne 1660–1760', in P. Clark (ed.), *The Transformation of English Provincial Towns*, London, 1984, p. 199.
[29] Thus Robert Hautes bequeathed 'all the monies that is due to me on the Queen's side whensoever it shall be paid' and Anthony Man also left 'all the monies that is due unto me of the King's side and of the Queen's', G.L.R.O. Archdeaconry of Surrey Wills Register 530 Yeast, 521 Yeast.

manufacturer, dealer, or retailer must have had extensive contacts with city merchants to obtain raw materials, with customs authorities and with shipping concerns. Membership of city companies, which was widespread among the wealthier householders, involved movement outside the Boroughside area and may also have been an alternative source of office-holding, and consequently a rival to the local neighbourhood. The use of company titles in wills and on funeral monuments also indicates that company membership may have rivalled, or provided another social dimension to, those bonds of neighbourhood and overcome some of the inherent tendencies towards localism discussed earlier. In this connection it is also worth noting that one effect of substantial immigration must have been that many, perhaps most, Boroughside householders possessed 'extra local' ties of birthplace and kinship to other areas of England.[30]

Whether residential intermingling of social groups by itself is a force for social cohesion is also something of an open question. The residential environment of the Boroughside exhibiting as it did significant residential mixing would suggest to many a source of social stability of this sort. But, as Wrightson has noted, one-class communities might well have formed in some pre-industrial towns.[31] It has also been pointed out that the 'ideology of community' can colour the interpretation of residential patterns:

some contemporaries [in the nineteenth century] assumed that "community" required social mixing and therefore declined as segregation intensified, whereas modern writers assume that "community" is based on class and therefore more likely to develop as segregation increases.[32]

In addition the presence of a large number of foreign householders with a different language, church and cultural background might also have been a dislocating influence. The wills of a number of aliens in the Boroughside do indicate a certain social isolation from their neighbours, but, as has been pointed out in Chapter 3, by the early seventeenth century alien householders formed an insignificant minority in the Boroughside.[33] The alien 'ghetto' could, however, have been a more significant social force in eastern Southwark.

To examine the nature of pre-industrial urban society adequately we must seek to examine some of the topics put forward by urban sociologists, many of which are rarely looked at systematically by urban historians of pre-industrial towns and cities. To what extent did bonds of kinship and

---

[30] Wrigley 1967: 50.   [31] Wrightson 1982: 56.
[32] Dennes and Daniels 1981: 8. See also Ellis 1984: 198–9.
[33] The will of Croft Castell, a dutch silkweaver resident in Pepper Alley for forty years until his death in 1627, shows that he retained close links with the dutch community. Castell left 40s. to the poor of the Dutch Church and nominated two non-resident aliens as overseers of his will, P.C.C. Will Register, 32 Skynner; Kirk 1900–7: 3, 219.

neighbourliness exist in the Boroughside area? When social or economic support was sought by a Boroughside householder to what extent were neighbours chosen to the exclusion of distant kin, non-local company contacts or business partners? What was the geographical shape and extent of the social area of Boroughside inhabitants?

9.3 Social relations: marriage partners

The origins of marriage partners have been used to examine the extent of the 'social area' of pre-industrial rural villagers.[34] After 1653, following the Commonwealth Marriage Act, the parish register of St Saviour's regularly supplies the places of residence of bride and groom.[35] If a number of reservations are borne in mind such a source can be used to delineate the social area of the inhabitants. The first of these is that marriage data deals predominantly with the younger, more mobile, section of the population rather than with established householders. Furthermore, place of residence does not tell us anything about period of residence and it is possible therefore that many brides and grooms may have been inhabiting the parish for only a short time, as servants, apprentices or lodgers before their marriage. Choice of marriage partners will also be affected by criteria other than geographical proximity, such as the social status of the bride and groom's parents, previous residence in other areas, ties to place of origin and employment prospects.[36] It is also possible that the Commonwealth period might have produced an atypical marriage pattern. The other disadvantage of using the parish register as a source is that the marriage entries do not distinguish between the three administrative units of the parish and consequently we are forced to analyse the marriage pattern of the whole parish rather than the Boroughside district. The marriage register does, however, have the advantage that it covers all social groups, supplies detailed addresses and contains a very large number of suitable entries every year. Table 9.1 sets out the places of residence of all partners who married individuals stated to be resident in St Saviour's over an eleven year period. In the original exercise brides and grooms were tabulated separately but since there proved to be little significant difference between the marriage horizons of each sex the results were aggregated. Marriages where both

---

[34] See, J. Patten, 'Rural-urban migration in pre-industrial England', *University of Oxford School of Geography Research Papers* 6 (1973), 18; R. F. Peel, 'Local intermarriage and the stability of rural population in the English Midlands', *Geography* 27, 1 (1942), 22–30; B. Maltby, 'Easingwold marriage horizons', *Local Population Studies* 2 (1969), 36–9; E. Underwood and J. H. Farrant, 'Marriage mobility in Brighton's rural hinterland', *Sussex Family Historian* 3, 2 (1977), 32–7.

[35] See, D. Mclaren, 'The Marriage Act of 1653; its influence on the parish registers', *Population Studies* 28, 2 (1974), 319–27; Woodward.1975: 15–31.

[36] See, Peel 1942: 28; Elliott 1978: 343–67; Elliott 1981: 84–9.

Table 9.1 *Residence of marriage partners of St Saviour's inhabitants 1655–65*

Place of residence of partner	Number of partners	
From within St Saviour's	1514	83.1%
London	159	8.7%
Neighbouring parishes	94	5.2%
Surrey	23	1.3%
Middlesex	12	0.7%
Kent	7	0.4%
Essex	6	0.3%
Miscellaneous	7	0.4%
Total	1822	

Note: Percentages based on the total number of partners. Twenty-three marriages were excluded since residence of both partners was not given.
Source: See discussion in text, pp. 234–5.

partners were non-resident were excluded.[37] The entries between October and December 1665 have also been excluded since the quality of registration declined after the plague outbreak in that year.

The most striking feature of Table 9.1 is that the overwhelming majority of inhabitants chose their marriage partners from within the parish. Overall 83.1% of all those marrying chose fellow parishioners, a finding similar to that found in East London in the seventeenth century.[38] A further 5.2% chose partners from adjoining parishes, notably St Olave's and St George's.[39]

[37] During the Commonwealth period St Saviour's became a centre of clandestine marriages and large numbers of non-resident couples were entered in the marriage register. Most of these couples did not settle in the parish after their marriage; this can be deduced from the fact that very few can be traced subsequently in the baptism register of St Saviour's. The proportions of non-resident couples marrying in St Saviour's was as follows: 1655 – 5% of all marriages; 1656 – 11%; 1657 – 17%; 1658 – 38%, 1659 – 60%; 1660 – 67%; 1661 – 59%; 1662 – 37%; 1663 – 29%; 1664 – 35%; 1665 – 47%. See, Mclaren 1974:323–7; R. L. Brown, 'The rise and fall of the Fleet marriages', in R. B. Outhwaite (ed.), *Marriage and Society. Studies in the Social History of Marriage*, London, 1981, pp. 117–36; R. Houlbrooke, *The English Family 1450–1750*, Harlow, 1984, pp. 43–53; E. A. Wrigley, 'Clandestine marriage in Tetbury in the late seventeenth century', *Local Population Studies* 10 (1973), 15–21.

[38] See M. Power, 'The urban development of East London 1550–1700', London (1971), p. 78; East London History Group 1968: 48; Wrightson 1982: 56.

[39] The total number of partners from each place of residence breaks down as follows: *Neighbouring parishes* St Olave's, Southwark – 36; St George's, Southwark – 20; St Thomas's, Southwark – 10; St Mary Magdalen, Bermondsey – 15; St Mary, Lambeth – 13; *Surrey*, Rotherhithe – 7; Newington – 6; Egham – 1; Battersea – 2; Martin Abby – 1; Streatham – 1; Okeley – 1; Croydon – 1; Wandsworth – 2; Clapham – 1; *Kent*, Goudhurst – 1; Chiselhurst – 1; Wickham – 1; Milton – 1; Westram – 1; Greenwich – 2; *London* (districts as defined in, Finlay 1981: 168–7), City within the Walls – 88; Liberties – 32; Outparishes – 23; Distant parishes – 16; *Middlesex*, Barnet – 1; Chelsea – 1; Chiswick – 1; Finchley – 1; Uxbridge – 1; Twickenham – 2; Hendon – 1; Fulham – 1; Hammersmith – 2; Acton – 1; *Essex*, Low Layton – 1: Blackwall – 1; Stratford Bow – 1;

Another striking feature is that links with the surrounding countryside in Surrey and Kent which might have been expected to form a significant catchment area, were of little numerical significance. In fact St Saviour's parishioners preferred to seek their partners from north of the river, notably in the City and its liberties. The London area may have been more important than adjoining parishes in the social area of such individuals – 8.7% of all marriage partners were drawn from there compared to 5.2% from neighbouring parishes. This is a small pointer to the economic and social links that joined Southwark to London and serves as a warning to those who would class Southwark as a separate town. It is also notable that within the City the most accessible parishes to Southwark provided the most marriage partners. Nearly a third of all partners chosen from the 97 parishes within the walls were drawn from six clustered around London Bridge.[40] The choice of marriage partners, like some of the evidence presented earlier, also suggests that the social horizons of the parishioners of St Saviour's were fairly restricted.

9.4 Social relations: neighbours

In January 1622 Henry Cawdery, 'citizen and plumber of London', resident in Counter Alley, died. In his will he nominated his wife Elizabeth as executrix.[41] For overseers (individuals whose duty it was to supervise the execution of the terms of the will), Cawdery chose a close neighbour, John Wright, brewer, then living on the High Street immediately opposite Counter Alley and one William Gray, citizen and plumber, who was not resident in the Boroughside. The two witnesses to Cawdery's will were the Bailiff, Thomas Foster, who lived a few doors away at the Borough Compter and George Garrard, apothecary and grocer, who lived on the east side of the Borough High Street. This example serves to introduce a method by which to estimate the importance of the immediate neighbourhood as a source of social and economic support. The choice of overseers and witnesses has been used by Wrightson to examine bonds of neighbourliness and reciprocal obligations in the Essex village of Terling. Similar material has been used recently in a study of social relations in a Canterbury suburb.[42] This source, with a number of modifications, can be adapted to study social relationships in seventeenth-century Southwark.

Lee – 1; Raynam – 1; Stratford Lancton – 1; *Miscellaneous*, Chalgrave, Oxfordshire – 1; Saccam, Hertfordshire – 1; Tunwell, Rutland – 1; Washington, Sussex – 1; Chard, Somerset – 1; Bridlington, Yorkshire – 1; 'Wiltshire' – 1.

[40] Namely St Magnus the Martyr (6 partners); St Martin Vintry (6); Allhallows the Great (5); St Margaret New Fish Street (4); St Lawrence Pountney (3); St Michael Queenhithe (3).

[41] G.L.R.O. Archdeaconry of Surrey Wills Register, 163 Stoughton.

[42] Wrightson and Levine 1979: 101–2; Clark 1983b: 80.

Since one of the most important objectives must be to estimate the degree to which Boroughside householders chose *local* individuals as overseers or witnesses to their wills it is necessary to know both the residential location and identity of all householders in the area at the time the will was made. Only if this information is available can the influence of residential propinquity be accurately assessed, and the recently arrived householders identified. This line of thought means that only a very limited period of time can be studied since to keep the population in view for a lengthy period would be impractical. However, if only a short period of time is examined then the number of householders dying and making wills will be very small and the results consequently inconclusive. To meet such objections the wills made by householders between 1620 and 1626 were analysed. The short time interval kept the task of holding the population under observation relatively manageable, and the large numbers of deaths that occurred during the 1625 plague greatly increased the number of will-makers. Although the inclusion of plague victims may have distorted the results slightly, it was thought preferable to include them in order to increase the sample size and also to gain a more comprehensive cross-section of the population.[43] The other distortion in using wills is that of the wealth bias referred to elsewhere. Unless otherwise stated therefore, this study concentrates on the choice of witnesses and overseers of the wealthier social groups. A further distinction was made between householders resident in 1622 and those few will-makers who came into the Boroughside after that date, in order to distinguish between the social relationships of such newcomers and the more established householders. The token books for the Boroughside for the years 1620, 1622, 1624 and 1626 were indexed, and individuals named as overseers or witnesses in the wills of the period were identified.[44] In the case of overseers linkage was normally based on name and occupation and that of witnesses by name only (see Table 9.2). It is probable that very few wrong linkages were made. Some links could be cross-checked against other sources; in some wills, the addresses of overseers were also supplied and in a number of cases the same individual was chosen by more than one testator.

The fifty male householders making wills between 1620 and 1626 chose seventy-three overseers.[45] Twelve will-makers did not nominate overseers, a far smaller proportion than that in Terling and an indication that overseers were more commonly chosen in London than in rural Essex where the

[43] It is possible that younger men may have been more vulnerable to plague than the elderly and that consequently plague victims may, on average, have been younger than householders dying in normal years. Beier has noted, however, that even in the latter periods high London death rates lessened the possibility that burials of adult males were biased strongly in favour of the elderly; Hollingsworth 1971: 143–4; Finlay 1981: 127–9; Beier 1978: 211, n. 19.

[44] G.L.R.O. P92/SAV/209, 211, 214, 215.

[45] For names of the fifty male will-makers see Boulton 1983: 285–6.

Table 9.2. *Choice of overseers of fifty male will-makers in the Boroughside 1620–6*

Period of residence in Boroughside of will-maker at death in years	Total number of overseers nominated	Per cent 'local' overseers nominated	Per cent 'outsiders' chosen as overseers
10+	39	56	44
3–10	28	64	36
0–3	6	17	83
Total	73	56	44

Source: See discussion in text, pp. 237–8

custom was declining.[46] The testator normally designated his overseers as his 'loving friends', 'good friends' or where locals were chosen 'my loving neighbours and friends'.

It is clear that the Boroughside district was the biggest single source of overseers. Of seventy-three overseers chosen, forty-one (56.2%) were living in the Boroughside at the time of the testator's death. Of the six overseers chosen by three recently arrived householders only one was a local man. Overall 79% of all householders choosing overseers nominated at least one from the Boroughside, 32% nominated only locals and 21% only outsiders. Although the influence of the neighbourhood was paramount it is clear that, as was expected, other criteria played a part in determining the choice of overseer. A number of non-resident overseers were members of the same city company as the testator. Hence John Elliottson, citizen and cooper, a recent arrival, chose three members of that company as overseers. Similarly Robert Loward, citizen and basketmaker, chose two non-local members of his company as overseers. As expected nomination of non-resident kin proved to be a further 'extra-local' factor. George Garrard, the grocer, nominated a local stationer but also his non-resident brother Henry; similarly George Payne chose Richard Yearwood, a local kinsman, but also his brother-in-law resident in 'Twyneham', Sussex. Ties to place of origin also promoted the choice of non-resident overseers. Hence Anthony Alfray, grocer, chose an overseer living in East Grinstead and Stephen Brightling, tailor, chose two overseers from Tunbridge Wells. Both testators owned land in the same places. It is worth noting that the 'social area' of some testators extended into adjacent districts. A number of 'non-local' overseers therefore lived in the Clink liberty and in the adjacent parish of St George's.

[46] Wrightson and Levine 1979: 100.

Locally resident overseers were almost invariably of similar social standing to that of the testator, and occasionally followed the identical occupation. Robert Pemell, grocer, chose a local man, Drew Stapely, grocer, as one overseer. Occupational solidarity, however, was unusual. A far more powerful determinant, influencing choice of overseer, appears to have been close residential proximity. A number of testators chose overseers living in their very immediate neighbourhood. Andrew Baxter, victualler, living in Pepper Alley, nominated John Crowder, cheesemonger, and Robert Burbage, linendraper, both then resident close to Baxter on the west side of the High Street. Similarly Robert Hawfield, sawyer, dwelling in Axe Yard chose John Williamson, a wealthy baker, living in the same yard and one Abraham Dickerman resident on the High Street adjacent to that yard. Other examples of the influence of residential propinquity could be quoted. The dynamics of residential mobility seem to have exercised an influence over choice of overseers since testators occasionally nominated previously close neighbours. Hence Thomas Fearman resident in Bell Yard at his death chose as one overseer William Cumber, resident on the High Street adjacent to that yard but also William Harper, a shoemaker living diagonally opposite on the east side of the High Street close to Christopher Yard. Until 1618 Fearman himself had lived in Christopher Yard. However, close residential proximity was by no means the sole criterion of choice. Choice of overseers linked householders in different 'sub-districts'. Such bonds of friendship and mutual support formed perhaps during a period of shared local office-holding or following a marriage alliance, may have been an important 'social cement' in the Boroughside.

The choice of witnesses to wills can also be used to gauge the extent of neighbourly interaction. A number of factors, however, need to be borne in mind. The use of personal servants and nurses will tend to inflate artificially the number of outsiders since such individuals cannot usually be linked to a Boroughside householder unless they are also referred to in the text of the will. Furthermore the high proportion of plague victims among the testators could have restricted the choice of witnesses. In practice, however, it was found that plague victims were only marginally more likely to have chosen local witnesses.[47] Encouragingly for our purposes the choice of signing witnesses was clearly not random. Most local witnesses proved to be of similar status to the testator, and few women or servants were in fact used. Although a large number of neighbours were often drawn to the deathbed, care was exercised over selection of the actual signatories, presumably because signing might entail further legal obligations. Witnesses to the will of one Margaret Dansir of the Clink liberty had been 'especially

[47] Of those witnesses used by plague victims 72% were local householders compared to an overall figure of 67%.

Table 9.3 *Choice of witnesses of fifty male will-makers in the Boroughside 1620–6*

Period of residence in Boroughside of will-maker at death in years	Total number of witnesses used	Per cent 'local'	Per cent 'outsiders'
10+	55	69	31
3–10	45	64	36
0–3	15	67	33
Total	115	67	33

Source: See discussion in text, pp. 239–40.

called thereunto'.[48] In Table 9.3 local scriveners acting as witnesses were excluded since their role as witnesses reflected a professional service rather than a fulfilment of a neighbourly function.

The overall pattern of choice reveals that the majority of householders used witnesses drawn from the Boroughside area. Of the 115 witnesses chosen, seventy-seven (67.0%) were resident there. Choice of witnesses was not affected by the length of residence of the testator since newcomers were just as likely to use local witnesses as long-term residents. This probably indicates that the choice of overseers represented a deeper neighbourly bond, and that such burdens were not imposed as lightly as the less onerous function of witnessing. Of the forty-eight wills that employed witnesses (other than scriveners) twenty-one (43.8%) used only local men and only eight (16.7%) wills were signed solely by outsiders. All in all 83% of will-makers chose at least one witness from the Boroughside area. Local witnesses were, like overseers, of similar social status to the testator but tended to be drawn to an even greater degree from neighbours. Such witnessing functions linked households in different sub-districts but witnesses were more likely to be drawn from households located very close by, in the same street or a few dwellings away.

There was often little correspondence between those will-makers who chose non-local overseers and those who chose non-local witnesses. Hence the will of Peter Senthill, glassmaker, who chose two non-resident London citizens as overseers, was witnessed by both his next-door neighbour and a neighbour only a few dwellings away. This lack of correspondence was partly a reflection of the greater burden of the overseership but may also

[48] P.C.C. Will Register 78 Russell.

have been related to the observable pattern that even when local overseers were nominated such individuals did not necessarily act as witnesses. Thus a local grocer acted as overseer for Robert Pemell but a more immediate neighbour, one George Perryn, who lived only a few doors away, witnessed the will. Such anomalies could presumably have been caused by simple availability but also perhaps were designed to spread the legal responsibility among neighbours. It would have been unwise, given the high mortality rates and ever-present possibility of epidemic disease, to concentrate all legal responsibility in one or two individuals. In a few cases overseers were of observably higher social status than the witnesses, which might also reflect the different responsibility that each function entailed.

The executors of wills were in all but a few cases close kin, normally wives if available, a situation also found in Terling.[49] Of the fifty male householders who made wills, forty-two chose wives, and of the remaining eight all but three nominated close kin as executors. Only two householders nominated neighbours and John Gloster, goldsmith, nominated the churchwardens of St Saviour's, a practice observed elsewhere in London.[50]

The bequests made by Boroughside residents demonstrate that their main concern was to provide for their immediate family. Such bequests therefore are not a reliable guide to the degree of neighbourly contact, the more so because their number must have been dependent to some extent on the size of the testator's estate and the number of his dependents. Apart from bequests to kin, the nuclear family and to servants, only nine (18%) will-makers made token bequests to members of identifiable neighbouring households. This figure excludes the overseers who normally received bequests of rings or money 'for their pains therein'. Bequests were also made to neighbours' children. Hence Walter Ricroft made a bequest of ten shillings to Isaac Fawcett the five-year-old son of Christopher, resident like Ricroft on the east side of the High Street. Similarly George Payne left twenty shillings 'for a ring' to Katherine Underwood, the thirteen-year-old daughter of a scrivener then resident in the New Rents.[51] The degree to which children left home to go into service in the immediate neighbourhood is not recoverable, but the practice may explain bequests to the older children of close neighbours.

Only where the need to provide for wife and children was reduced or removed did testators make wills that often reflected explicit neighbourhood recognition and contact. The tendency for women to make frequent bequests to kin and friends has been found also in pre-industrial Banbury.[52]

[49] Wrightson and Levine 1979: 100.
[50] McCampbell 1976: 114.
[51] P.C.C. Will Register 27 Hele; 88 Clarke.
[52] Vann 1979: 366.

Between 1620 and 1626 eight females and one young bachelor made wills.[53]
Of the eight females, four were only recently widowed and their wills were
similar to those of their husbands with minor variations. Joan Bosse, a widow
resident in Angel Yard chose two local householders as overseers and 'my
neighbour and good friend' Robert Buckland, resident close by, as her
executor. Her bequests included two to neighbouring households, for whose
children she had acted as godmother, and also recognised her links to other
Boroughside households deriving from kinship and past domestic service.
Tomasin Cossey, widow and sometime nurse, made a general bequest to
'her very loving neighbours' in 1626. John Simonds, son of Samuel the
baker, displayed a more intimate local awareness. Simonds chose only one
local overseer and witness but went on to make ten specific charitable
bequests to named 'poor widows' living in Horsehead Alley where he also
lived. Simonds made the distinction between the widow Brown 'in the lower
yard' and 'the other widow Brown'. All ten widows can be identified in
Horsehead Alley in the 1624 token book and one of these was still resident
in that yard in 1635 when she received a further bequest from John's father.
The Simonds's bequests are interesting because they indicate that residential
intermingling between rich and poor may well have promoted an awareness
of local social conditions among the better off.[54] Personal acquaintance
based on residential proximity may have been at work in the case of one
Timothy Oateley, leatherdresser, who petitioned the vestry for relief in the
1630s. At that time Nicholas Morton, minister of St Saviour's, lived in Axe
Yard only a few dwellings away from Oateley. This may explain the note
scrawled on Oateley's petition to the effect that 'Nicholas Morton desire's
your compassion on this distressed petitioner'.[55]

Another method of examining the extent and pattern of neighbourly
contacts is to examine the choice and residential location of bondsmen.
Recognisances, by which individuals pledged sums of money to the
authorities to ensure a person's good behaviour or appearance at a court
of law, were used by Wrightson and Levine to analyse social and
geographical patterns of neighbourly obligation in Terling.[56] Unfortunately
recognisances taken at the Surrey quarter sessions in the early seventeenth
century have not survived and those few that survive in the assize files are
few and scattered over a long period of time. However, those recognisances
undertaken to enforce the prohibition on consumption of meat during Lent

---

[53] See, Tomasin Cossey – Archdeaconry of Surrey Will Register 374 Yeast; Elizabeth Hughes – 203
    Yeast; Agnes Vickars – 152 Yeast; John Simonds – 278 Yeast; Joan Bosse – 278 Peter. P.C.C. Will
    Registers, Joan Angell – 10 Hele; Agnes Faireman – 2 Hele; Jane Mayhew – 56 Swann; Margaret
    Payne – 88 Clarke.
[54] For the corresponding point that growing social segregation reduced middle-class awareness of
    the social conditions of the poor, seee Ward 1980: 134.
[55] G.L.R.O. P92/SAV/777.   [56] Wrightson and Levine 1979: 101–2.

can be used to measure the neighbourly support received by butchers and victuallers.

The prohibition on eating meat during Lent was actively enforced in early Stuart London. Orders from the Privy Council and royal proclamations reinforced the efforts of the ecclesiastical authorities.[57] In St Saviour's a number of the wealthier individuals were recorded as receiving special licences of dispensation and the Privy Council licensed a poor butcher in the Close to sell meat during Lent.[58] The problem of controlling the consumption of meat extended from the butchers, who both prepared and sold meat, to victuallers, innholders, cooks and vintners whose establishments acted as outlets. Since the reign of Henry VII victuallers and others had been subject to a licensing system to control their behaviour. By 1618 a system of control had developed based on 'elaborate recognisances, in which were inserted many specific conditions imposed by the justices, and prescribed by the royal proclamations of that year'.[59] The form of the recognisances for the observation of Lent was laid down in proclamations and taken for one year at a time.[60]

An examination of the victuallers' and butchers' recognisances that survive for the year 1620 was made to consider neighbourly relations. These recognisances were taken following a royal proclamation of 1619. Butchers were to provide sureties of £10 and two bondsmen who would be prepared to put up five pounds each to ensure that the subject of the recognisance 'shall not kill flesh during Lent'. Victuallers, innholders, vintners and cooks were to provide sureties of one hundred pounds each and to find two bondsmen prepared to provide additional sureties of £30 apiece that 'they shall not dress any flesh in their several houses in the Lent time'. Londoners were bonded for greater sums of money than were their rural colleagues.[61] By matching those entering recognisances and their bondsmen to the householders listed in the 1620 token book it is possible to look at the degree to which neighbours provided such financial support. It should be noted, however, that butchers and victuallers were in some respects not typical occupational groups. Butchers were residentially concentrated and recognisances were taken from the wealthier elements of each occupational group.

[57] See, Jones 1976: 123–9; W.H. and H. C. Overall (eds.), *Analytical index to the series of records known as the Remembrancia preserved among the Archives of the City of London A.D. 1579–1664*, London, 1878, pp. 392–403; Steele 1910: 1, 1055, 1137, 1236, 1265, 1347, 1501. For a detailed account of the taking of the 1620 Lenten certificates see also, N. J. Williams (ed.), *Tradesmen in Early Stuart Wiltshire*, Devizes, 1960, pp. xi–xv.

[58] Rendle and Norman 1888: 45; Jones 1976: 125; *C.S.P.D. 1611–18*, 96.43.

[59] See, S. and B. Webb, *The History of Liquor Licensing*, London, 1963, p. 11; Clark 1983a: 172–6.

[60] Webb 1963: 14; Steele 1910: 1, 1055, 1265.

[61] See, Steele 1910: 1, 1265; P.R.O. E180/140. For a transcription of a 1620 recognisance, and some Wiltshire examples see Williams 1960a: xii, 11–51.

Of the twenty-two butchers taking out recognisances and resident in 1620 and 1622, all but one were poor-rate payers; poorer back street butchers who would rarely have operated slaughterhouses were excluded. Similarly all but four of thirty-nine victuallers and innholders resident in 1620 and 1622 contributed to the poor rate.

The pattern of neighbourly support is broadly similar to that revealed by the evidence from wills. Overall eighty butchers and victuallers chose 160 bondsmen of whom 110 (68.8%) were clearly identifiable as Boroughside householders in the 1620 token book (see Table 9.4). Butchers were more likely to choose local householders than victuallers were: 85% of all bondsmen acting for butchers were local householders compared with 61% of all those putting sureties for victuallers. This discrepancy is partly caused by the tendency of innkeepers to choose as bondsmen 'on site' servants, such as tapsters, who cannot be linked to the token book. The choice of such individuals may have been caused by a clause in the royal proclamations which laid down that 'servants at ordinaries Inns etc. to be examined by the Lord Mayor and Justices as to flesh cooked in Lent'.[62] Hence Ellen Salter, widow and keeper of the White Hart, chose as one bondsman a certain William Newell 'yeoman', known to be a personal servant.[63] Since only household heads who acted as bondsmen could be identified Table 9.4 provides only a minimum estimate of the number of locals chosen.

As with overseers and witnesses the Boroughside was the single most important source of financial support. Some 44% of all victuallers and 77% of all butchers chose both bondsmen from the area compared to only 22% of victuallers and 8% of butchers who nominated only outsiders. The pattern of choice was not greatly affected by the period of residence spent in the Boroughside, although it does seem that the probability of victuallers choosing local bondsmen was somewhat higher if they had spent more than two years in the district.

The residential concentration of the butchers clearly affected their choice of bondsmen. Coincidence of residential proximity and occupational similarity meant that butchers were particularly likely to choose close neighbours to act as sureties. All in all 65.4% of all bondsmen chosen by butchers were other butchers, resident in the High Street shambles. The agreements often took the form of 'tri-partite bonds' where three butchers each went bond for the other two. The 'tri-partite' bond occasionally involved those entering victuallers' recognisances and also reflected both close residential proximity and occupational similarity. Hence John Heath-

---

[62] Steele 1910: 1, 1265.
[63] Newell was probably the 'William the tapster' listed as resident in Salter's household in 1622. In 1626 Newell received a small bequest from Salter's son-in-law, Anthony Alfray, P.C.C. Will Register 92 Hele.

Table 9.4. *Choice of bondsmen by Boroughside victuallers and butchers 1620*

Period of residence of individual entering recognisance in years	Chosen by butchers		Chosen by victuallers	
	Number of bondsmen	Per cent 'local'	Number of bondsmen	Per cent 'local'
10+	24	83	42	67
2–10	26	88	48	58
0–2	2	50	18	56
Total	52	85	108	61

Source: See discussion in text, pp. 242–4.

erly, Ralph Roper and John Allom, victuallers living on the west side of the High Street, acted as bondsmen for each other, and similarly two vintners and an innkeeper on the east side of the High Street took part in a similar arrangement; two of these latter individuals were next-door-neighbours. However, victuallers, unlike butchers, chose bondsmen from a large variety of occupations and occupational solidarity was relatively unusual. Apart from thirty-two 'yeomen' (an ill-defined status term) and twelve members of victualling trades, sixty-four bondsmen followed twenty-nine different occupations from shoemaker and tailor to cutler and smith.[64]

Wealth alone was not the predominant criterion by which victuallers' bondsmen were chosen. Only half the local bondsmen still resident in the Boroughside in 1622 contributed to the poor rate and consequently many poor-rate paying victuallers were linked to non-rated households. This could indicate that the financial responsibility was by no means equivalent to the duties required of an overseer, and that the possibility of an individual surrendering a bond was slight. As we have seen, innholders chose dependent servants and occasionally their choice of bondsmen highlights the networks of dependent householders described in Chapter 3. Hence John Leigh, innkeeper at the Talbot, chose Robert Frith, an ostler then resident in Fishmonger Alley and Frith's close neighbour Henry Brooks in the same

[64] For the vaguely defined 'yeoman' in the urban context see, Goose 1980: 36; Elliott 1978: 38. The occupational breakdown of bondsmen chosen by Boroughside butchers and victuallers was as follows: butchers chose, 43 butchers; 1 feltmaker; 1 tailor; 2 victuallers; 1 'yeoman'; 1 shipwright; 1 waterman; 1 glover; 1 cooper. Victuallers chose, 32 'yeomen'; 3 silkweavers; 4 clothworkers; 6 vintners; 4 smiths; 1 chandler; 2 turners; 6 tailors; 8 shoemakers; 2 coopers; 4 haberdashers; 1 skinner; 1 farrier; 1 barber; 2 'husbandmen'; 1 gunfounder; 1 widow; 4 victuallers; 1 shipwright; 1 joiner; 6 cutlers; 2 butchers; 2 leatherworkers; 2 innholders; 1 winecooper; 3 barber-surgeons; 1 brassmaker; 1 glover; 1 goldsmith; 1 brasier; 1 poulterer; 1 gentleman; 1 gunner.

alley as bondsmen. Similarly, John Bryan, brewer at the 'Maidenhead' in Fishmonger Alley, chose Richard Belldam, a multi-occupationed 'serving-man' and George Eden, silkweaver, both of whom also lived in that alley.

Residential propinquity was, in fact, the most striking criterion by which bondsmen were chosen by victuallers. Over half the local householders acting as victuallers' sureties lived in the immediate vicinity of that household.[65] Hence Ralph Rowley, a victualler resident in Ship Yard, chose Edward Adnett, shoemaker, and James Leigh, tailor, both living nearby in the same yard. James Barlow, innkeeper at the Boarshead, used a next-door neighbour David Soane, butcher, and a shoemaker living close by on the High Street. Similarly William Batty, innkeeper, chose two close neighbours, a smith and a chandler living adjacent to the Green Dragon Inn on Foul Lane. Residential proximity therefore did result in a significant level of neighbourhood contact and suggests strongly that such contact broke down barriers between different occupational and social groups. It is noteworthy too that households located on the High Street adjacent to alleys can be linked to bondsmen in those alleys. Thus Richard Rie, a victualler resident on the High Street adjacent to Horsehead Alley in 1620, chose as one bondsman Humphry Baker, innkeeper at the nearby Spur Inn, but for the other chose one Nicholas Burton a humble shoemaker dwelling in that alley. It is also interesting that neighbourly links can be shown to have survived the effect of short-range mobility. Hence Ellen Salter the keeper of the White Hart, used as one bondsman James Jackson a cutler resident in the New Rents in 1620; this contact probably derived from previous residential propinquity: Jackson until 1618–19 had been Salter's next-door neighbour. Similarly Giles Foster, a High Street butcher, chose a butcher in the New Rents as one bondsman, a contact presumably made during his previous residence in the area. However, households were linked by similar bonds of obligation without a history of residential proximity. Hence William Wright, a victualler in Pepper Alley, chose Edward Sewell, a High Street cutler and Walter Leech, the self-made tailor dwelling in Horsehead Alley, as his two bondsmen in 1620. Victualling houses, which, as we shall see, may have acted as informal neighbourhood meeting places, may have been able to draw on local 'regulars' to act as bondsmen.[66]

Boroughside households were linked, in effect, by a network of neigh-bourly obligations and interactions.[67] If it can be assumed that providing such a service or performing such a function for another household at any time between 1620 and 1626 is an accurate guide to the existence of a

---

[65] In this case 'immediate vicinity' is defined as within ten dwellings or in the same alley or yard.

[66] For victualling houses as the 'hub' of neighbourhood activity in the suburbs of Canterbury, see Clark 1983b: 82.

[67] For a 'high incidence of neighbourhood contacts' in Canterbury suburbs see, Clark 1983b: 82.

special relationship with that household in 1622, then 167 households were so linked at that date. In 1622 therefore 17.4% of all householders provided a surety, acted as witness or were nominated as overseers for another household in the Boroughside. Since many of these householders were poor-rate payers it is possible to estimate that one in three poor-rate payers were linked to another in this way in 1622. Such numerical calculations can only be minimum estimates since this study has only touched a small proportion of the total number of possible neighbourly functions. Many sources which would have undoubtedly revealed many more neighbourly relationships such as church court material, apprenticeship records and quarter sessions are not available. Nonetheless the available evidence suggests that, for Boroughside householders, their neighbours, rather than outsiders, were the single most important source of such financial and social support.

It may well be the case that the distancing of kin by migration led to a corresponding increase in dependence on immediate neighbours as a source of aid. Although non-local (and local) kin were occasionally chosen in preference to neighbours as overseers of wills, *overall* in the Boroughside only some 20% of overseers nominated were kin compared to some 45% in Terling. A substitution of neighbourly for kin support is now thought to have been a feature of suburban society in sixteenth-century Canterbury.[68] How extensive and important was kinship in Boroughside society?

9.5 Social relations: kinship

Kinship has been the subject of a number of recent historical studies.[69] Recent research has established that the nuclear family was the norm in pre-industrial England and that the presence of kin within the household was relatively unusual. In England listings of 46 pre-industrial communities suggest that only 10.1% of households contained resident kin. The proportion varied from region to region and according to socio-economic group. In 1700 5.5% of households in Kent contained kin compared to 7.9% in Wiltshire. Yeomen households were twice as likely to contain kin as those headed by labourers.[70] Figures recently published for London in 1695 suggest

---

[68] Clark 1983b: 83.
[69] Wrightson and Levine 1979: 82–103; A. Macfarlane, *The Family Life of Ralph Josselin, a Seventeenth-Century Clergyman: an Essay in Historical Anthropology*, Cambridge, 1970, pp. 126–60; Miranda Chaytor, 'Household and kinship: Ryton in the late 16th and early 17th centuries', *History Workshop Journal* 10 (1980), 25–60; K. Wrightson, 'Household and kinship in sixteenth-century England', *History Workshop Journal* 12 (1981); R. Houston and R. Smith, 'A new approach to family history', *History Workshop Journal* 14 (1982), 120–31.
[70] See, P. Laslett, 'Characteristics of the western family considered over time', *Journal of Family History* 2,2 (1977), 101; Goose 1980: 376; Wall 1979: 103; Houlbrooke 1984: 43–53.

that in a sample of seven parishes 8.3% of all households contained resident kin. Wealthy areas of the capital containing a small number of large households were more likely to contain kin: Glass found that 23.9% of all the households in St Matthew, Friday Street, contained resident kin in 1695.[71] In the absence of detailed listings, such as are available under the 1695 Marriage Duty Act returns, it is not possible to say a great deal about kinship within the household in the Boroughside. The nearest document to a listing is the 1622 token book which, since it names each communicant, can be used to supply a minimum estimate of the number of households containing kin over the age of communion. In this case kin could only be identified if they possessed the same surname as that of a male household head or the maiden name of his wife or were referred to in a will.[72] From such a survey no more than thirty households (3.1%) seem to have contained resident kin in 1622. This low figure may partly reflect the inadequacies of the source material. The first of these is that the maiden names of wives were only recovered for just under a third of all householders. Furthermore many of the inmates, lodgers and servants (present in over one third of the households in 1622) could have been related to other members of the household but such relationships are not specified and the surnames of servants rarely given.[73] Nonetheless the small number of co-resident kin is strikingly similar to the proportion found in poor areas of other pre-industrial towns and cities. In the Canterbury suburbs only 2.3% of households contained resident kin, in the poorer parts of early seventeenth-century Cambridge only 3.1%. The low proportion of kin found in Boroughside households as compared to the rest of the capital may reflect the former's relative poverty.[74]

The seeming absence of kin resident in the household does not mean that they were not present in the locality. As a nineteenth-century study pointed out recently, kinship 'does not stop at the front door'. There is evidence that in nineteenth-century Preston the presence of kin living nearby was an important source of social and financial support for some households.[75]

Pre-industrial historians, lacking census data of the sort found in the nineteenth century, are faced with particularly severe methodological problems when examining kinship beyond the household. Wrightson and Levine linked entries in a parish register and other source material to a listing of inhabitants at one point in time in order to recover blood and marriage links between households on the list.[76] Unfortunately this procedure cannot

---

[71] Wall 1979: 103; Glass 1966: xxxiii.

[72] Will evidence alone supplied only three resident kin, Boulton 1983: 309, n. 88.

[73] It was rare, but not unknown, for kin to act as servants in a relation's household, Macfarlane 1970: 148; Houlbrooke 1984: 46.

[74] Clark 1983b: 73; Goose 1980: 376.   [75] Anderson 1971: 43–67.

[76] Wrightson and Levine 1979: 84–5.

be followed for a large urban area partly because the size of the task is prohibitive but especially because a household is rarely traceable beyond one generation. The results obtained by this method will be biased towards the most easily recoverable links and towards the long-stayers in the area. In particular 'first order' kin links (those established through parents and children or through siblings) could be overrepresented. At their worst studies of pre-industrial kinship links become entangled in dense thickets of genealogy.[77]

One, less arduous, means by which to assess the importance of kinship links between households is to look at surname sets.[78] Historians have used similarity of surname to make estimates of kinship in pre-industrial towns. Laslett has noted that residential propinquity to relatives was 'common enough in Lichfield, ... in a street of some sixty-five households, only fifty-two surnames were counted in the survey of 1696'. Phythian-Adams based his estimate of kinship in sixteenth-century Coventry on an analysis of shared surnames, finding that 18.6% of households 'were headed by people with similar surnames to at least one other household head in the same ward'.[79] Such an approach has the disadvantage that only a certain type of kin link can be recovered and that the 'order' of kinship is difficult to establish. The effect of heavy immigration might also be expected to duplicate unrelated surnames to an unacceptable degree.[80] Nonetheless comparison of surnames is one way to exploit nominal listings and accordingly this was done for all the householders listed in the 1622 token book. Overall there proved to be an extremely large surname set: 958 householders possessed 672 different surnames. If the twenty-two commonest surnames are excluded then 827 householders possessed 650 surnames.[81] More than half (524 or 54.7%) of the householders had unique surnames, 170 (17.8%) were similar to only one other, 81 (8.5%) were similar to two others and 56 (5.9%) matched three or four. This procedure can be refined by matching the known maiden name of wives, recovered from the parish register, to the surname set of 1622. A relatively large number of marriages made by householders in 1622 took place in the local parish church and an analysis of them might reveal more possible links between Boroughside householders. Of the 295 maiden names recovered 143 (48.5%) could not be matched to another household in 1622, 58 (19.7%)

---

[77] Prior 1977: 101–239; Chaytor 1980: 35, 45–9.

[78] See, Wrightson and Levine 1979: 84; Macfarlane 1978: 75; R. Watson, 'A study of surname distribution in a group of Cambridge Parishes 1538–1840', *Local Population Studies* 15 (1975), 23–32.

[79] Laslett 1971: 117; Phythian-Adams 1979: 154.

[80] Macfarlane 1978: 76.

[81] The most popular surnames of household heads in 1622 were as follows: Smith – 13; Tailor – 8; Brown, Johnson, Williams, Wright – 7; Harrison, Lee – 6; Berry, Clark, Fisher, Fletcher, Ford, Foster, Griffin, Hunt, Jackson, Jones, Marshall, Martin, More, Wood – 5.

were only linked to one, 32 (10.9%) to two and 62 (21.0%) to three or four. By itself such a study cannot be used to estimate the number of kinship links since no account has been taken of the large numbers of unrelated households possessing commonly held surnames.

A method by which to estimate minimum levels of kin linkage by surname would be to exclude all surnames that were known to be relatively common in early seventeenth-century London and thereby to reduce the possibility of linking unrelated households, even at the cost of also excluding an unknown number of related households. This can be done by matching the Boroughside surname set to those listed in the index to Dale's *The inhabitants of London in 1638* and excluding from consideration all surnames that appear more than five times in the whole of the City. The 1638 listing gave the surnames of some 16,900 household heads inhabiting 87 of the 97 parishes within the walls and seven parishes in the liberties.[82] By these means it is hoped to identify local concentrations of unusual surnames in the Boroughside, which can best be explained by kinship ties. For example, two householders in 1622 shared the surname Bowers: Peter, a butcher in Fishmonger Alley and John, a merchant-tailor in the Close. According to Dale the surname Bowers occurred only three times elsewhere in London in 1638 and consequently a kin link of some type seems likely, the more so since, because the 1638 listing was made sixteen years after that of 1622, it may duplicate individuals who moved from the Boroughside to the City during the period. Similarly there were two Charslye's resident in 1622: Thomas, a silkweaver in the Churchyard, and John, a joiner in the Close. A kin link is likely for the surname Charslye only occurred once in London in 1638. Conversely, although there were only two households surnamed Evans in 1622, Jane, a widow in Goat Yard, and John, a grinder in Saints Alley, there were twenty-four other Evans's in London in 1638 and consequently no link can be made between the two Boroughside households with any confidence. The same procedure was adopted for the matching of wives' maiden names to established householders. Hence for example George North married one Elizabeth Meeke and can consequently be linked to the household headed by one John Meeke, whose surname was unique in both the Boroughside and the city of London. Similarly the maiden name of the wife of Thomas Swinbourne, Sheldrake, can be linked with confidence to Richard Sheldrake whose surname was unique in the Boroughside and only appears once in London in 1638.

Overall eighty-eight households (9.2%) can be linked by virtue of shared unusual surname and eighty-one (8.5%) via maiden names of wives. If these are aggregated, and duplicate households removed, then some 140

---

[82] Finlay 1981: 71, 168–72; Dale 1931: iv, passim.

households (14.6% of the total in 1622) were linked to one or more of their neighbours. That maiden names provided almost as many linkages as matching surnames is striking since only one third of all maiden names were available for analysis. This suggests that marriage, and subsequent settlement in the locality of the bride's parents, may have been a significant method by which urban kin networks were created. That the methodology outlined above has a certain accuracy is indicated by a repetition of the same exercise on unusual surnames in the Clink Liberty in 1622.[83] A number of unusual surnames (forty-one) linked ninety-one households in that district. What is particularly striking is that none of these were duplicated by a similar concentration of surnames in the adjacent Boroughside district and this reinforces the impression that the method adopted successfully identifies idiosyncratic surnames.

The wills made by those householders resident in 1622 help to supplement the evidence for kin linkage derived from a comparison of unusual surnames.[84] Unfortunately the use of wills for the study of kinship is limited by the observable wealth bias and also by other factors. The spread of wills over time (between 1622 and 1660) means that care must be taken to eliminate kinship links between households formed after 1622. More seriously it is clear that, as other studies of kinship have noted, will-makers only recognised a limited range of kin when disposing of property.[85] It is known for example that a number of will-makers ignored the presence of kin known to be living nearby, possibly reflecting the central concern that most wills displayed for providing for members of their nuclear family. Widows and younger sons tended to be more likely to recognise kin than the male householder. Hence Katherine Gilding (née Whittingslow) made small bequests to her 'sister Whittingslow', resident in Windmill Alley, and to one William Gilding, a kinsman resident in Christopher Yard. Both these latter individuals although present, had not been recognised in the will of Katherine's husband Francis, made two years earlier.[86] The wealth bias in wills affects recognition of kin in other ways, it may be that the greater the size of the estate the greater the possibility of making bequests. In addition individuals higher in the social hierarchy may often have been more conscious of their kin ties for reasons of social prestige or because of the legal dictates of property inheritance.[87]

As expected, the evidence from wills shows that surnames are an

[83] See the 1622 Clink token book, G.L.R.O. P92/SAV/270.
[84] Apart from the wills made by householders a small number of wills made by the widows of those resident in 1622, their adult offspring, servants and co-resident kin were used to recover kinship links. For the wills consulted, see Boulton 1983: 285–6, 293, 315–16.
[85] Wrightson and Levine 1979: 92–3; Macfarlane 1970: 158, 211–13.
[86] G.L.R.O. Archdeaconry of Surrey Wills Register, 399 Yeast, 242 Yeast.
[87] Wrightson 1982: 47; Houlbrooke 1984: 39–42.

uncertain guide to the *type* of kin link. Thus the two Harvards, Robert and Thomas, butchers resident in the Shambles, were not father and son, nor brothers, but were cousins.[88] Will evidence also enables links to be made between households sharing commonly held surnames, such as Russell or Marshall, and between wives and parents whose marriages took place outside St Saviour's. Wills also supply more distant kin links that cannot be identified from unusual surnames such as 'niece's husband', 'nephew' or the ill-defined 'kinsman'.[89] Furthermore, links made by virtue of marriage alliances are also discovered; such relationships can rarely be deduced from surname evidence alone. Hence for example Richard Yearwood and George Payne, grocers, were related following the marriage of Hannah Yearwood to Edward Payne. It seems likely therefore that the evidence from surnames under-estimates the degree to which households were related by blood or marriage to others in the Boroughside.

The possibility that our source material does not reveal more distant kin relationships that existed between households can be illustrated with a little historical detective work. On the face of it there is no reason to infer any kin relationship between Anthony Alfray, High Street grocer, and George Payne, grocer and vestryman, who also lived on the High Street. Neither mentioned the other in his will, the St Saviour's parish register reveals no link by marriage. The only possible link would seem to be geographical – both men came from the same part of Sussex. Alfray noted in his will that his birthplace had been Withiham, Sussex and George Payne owned property and possessed a brother-in-law in the same county. The Payne family possessed an idiosyncratic practice of naming daughters 'Timothye' as George's son Edward did in 1624, thus confusing the parish clerk of St Saviour's who then corrected his mistake:

16 September 1624 Timothye Payne $ d of Edward a gent

In fact the published parish register of East Grinstead in Sussex demonstrated some sort of kin link between the Payne and Alfray families. On 4 May 1601 a certain William Alfray 'of Withiham' had married Timothye Payne of East Grinstead. George Payne's two sisters alive in 1624 had also married into East Grinstead families.[90] It seems more than a coincidence that two, albeit distantly, related householders should find themselves living on Southwark High Street in 1622. Perhaps Alfray had been introduced into the district as George Payne's servant or apprentice, a needed contact to

---

[88] P.C.C. Will Register, 111 Clarke. For an assumption that individuals of similar surname *were* father and son, see, Phythian-Adams 1979: 155.

[89] It has been pointed out that the use of vague terminology may, *in itself* indicate a lack of awareness of wider kin links, Wrightson 1982: 41.

[90] See, R. P. Crawford (ed.), *The Parish Register of East Grinstead, Sussex, 1558–1661*, Sussex Record Society 24, 1917, p. 10.

get him started in the metropolis. This case study, however, could not be realistically duplicated for more than a tiny fraction of the Boroughside householders. Our study of kinship must restrict itself to the evidence of wills and surnames.

Combining the evidence of both wills and surnames suggests that a significant number of households had kin living nearby. Of the fifty male householders making wills between 1620 and 1626, twelve (24.0%) referred to kin living in the Boroughside.[91] If individual households linked on the basis of unusual surname, will evidence and miscellaneous sources are aggregated, some 172 households (18.0%) were related to at least one other in the Boroughside. This figure is relatively large compared to what we learn from the meagre data available for other modern and pre-modern cities. In nineteenth-century Preston only eighty out of 1700 households (4.7%) were found to be so related. In the suburbs of sixteenth-century Canterbury the maximum figure that could be obtained was only 9.2% of households. Only sixteenth-century Coventry approached the Boroughside figure, using, however, the evidence of similar surnames only.[92] The evidence presented here suggests strongly that kin ties beyond the household may have been an important component of social contacts and a significant social force in the Boroughside. What form did these relatively extensive kin ties take and what function did they perform?

In line with evidence from Terling and Coventry, kin networks involving more than three households were rare. Only six out of seventy networks (8.6%) contained more than three households and the majority (74.3%) involved only two.[93] Although, due to the great difficulty encountered in identifying the type of kin link, the precise percentage of each sort of kin link is not known, a tentative impression is that a significant number of kin links were based on a marriage connection rather than a blood relationship (that is they were often affinal rather than consanguineal). Of the former, as noted above, the settlement of a couple in the same area as the wife's parents (or parent) may have been of particular importance.

Fairly extensive local kinship networks can be reconstructed for the wealthier householders, especially where wills and other sources exist. One of these networks was that centred on the household of John Marshall, senior, the wealthy baker. A case study of this network reveals a number of ways in which urban kin links could influence the social, occupational and residential structures in the Boroughside. Marshall, assessed at 40s. in

---

[91] Two will-makers, Walter Ricroft, pewterer, and Edward Ashton, victualler, had kin links to households in the Clink liberty. P.C.C. Will Register, 27 Hele, G.L.R.O. Archdeaconry of Surrey Wills Register, 246 Herringman.

[92] Anderson 1971: 57; Clark 1983b: 74; Phythian-Adams 1979: 155.

[93] Wrightson and Levine 1979: 87; Phythian-Adams 1979: 155.

the 1622 poor rate and £10 in the 1622 subsidy was elected to the vestry in January 1601. He belonged to two London companies and was a baker by profession. In 1611 he was granted a coat of arms.[94] Originally from Mallows, in Stamford, Lincolnshire, John married Elizabeth Heycock of Clifton, Chester, in 1585 in St Saviour's, Southwark. Elizabeth broke all records by producing nineteen children between 1585 and 1609, fifteen of whom were baptised in the parish church. Marshall's brother Henry also baptised a child in the parish. By 1622 only six of John's children were still alive. The eldest son Thomas (aged 30 in 1622) was not resident in the Boroughside but settled in family property in Axe Yard in 1624. The second son John, an attorney, headed a household on the west side of the High Street, opposite his father, and contributed three pence to the poor rate in 1622. Marshall's eldest daughter Mary married one William Maddox in 1610 on her seventeenth birthday. Maddox, a goldsmith, lived next door but one to John Marshall, junior, in 1622 and paid four pence to the poor rate. Marshall's second daughter Susan married Richard Thickens, baker, in 1617. Thickens lived on the east side of the High Street near the Talbot Inn, and paid 3*d.* to the poor rate in 1622. In his will John Marshall, senior, also recognised William Marshall, son of his deceased brother Henry, as 'nephew'; William, a humble tailor, lived in a small back alley in 1622. John also left a bequest to his 'kinsman' Henry Vero, who had married his brother's daughter Jane. Vero, a labourer, lived in a back alley in the New Rents having immigrated from Newington parish in 1618.[95] Apart from these locally resident kin Marshall only recognised two other relations 'cousin Wright of Grantham' and a London scrivener, Charles Yeomans, who wrote his will. The extensive network centred around John Marshall was a product of his wealth, long period of residence in the parish and the high fertility of his wife. This network was peculiarly visible, in both his will and in the genealogical survey carried out by the College of Heralds. Nevertheless the existence of such an urban kin network raises a number of interesting possibilities. Five household heads must have made a definite decision to reside in close proximity to their father, father-in-law, or uncle. The Marshall kin network ranged over the social scale. His brother's side of the family were clearly poor relations. Henry Vero was described as poor in 1618 and appeared twice for theft at the Surrey Assizes, once for stealing a bed from his next-door neighbour.[96] Neither Vero nor William Marshall

---

[94] As well as Overseer's accounts, token books, parish register material and the vestry minute book of St Saviour's, for this biographical information see also, P.C.C. Will Register, 83 Clarke; W. B. Bannerman (ed.), *The Visitations of the County of Surrey Made and Taken in the Years 1530,…1572 and 1623*, Harleian Society Publications 43, 1899, p. 132.

[95] G.L.R.O. P92/SAV/1465.

[96] J. S. Cockburn (ed.), *Calendar of Assize Records Surrey Indictments James I*, London, 1982, p. 252.

contributed to the poor rate in 1622 and William took in a lodger in 1637.[97] It seems likely that such poor relations could have been attracted to the area in the hope of benefiting from their kin link. William Marshall subsequently moved to Axe Yard into the Marshall's property there and by the terms of the will of John Marshall, junior, was granted his house rent free for life.[98] Both Henry Vero and William received substantial bequests in John Marshall senior's will. Marshall's local reputation and established business ties might have been a factor in the decision of his son and sons-in-law to live close by. Thickens is known to have come from a London baking family and, following Marshall's death, a relation of Thickens took over the family bakery. Perhaps here we have an urban expression of the importance of affinal connections noted by Houlbrooke recently; men being seen often by their daughter's husbands 'as the chief means of their advancement'.[99]

From an analysis of the seventy recovered networks it seems that, as with the Marshalls, larger kin networks sometimes included a certain spread of wealth. Such networks were often centred on a wealthy household, frequently on a large manufacturing establishment, and included poorer 'satellite' households. Poorer kin sometimes received bequests in wills although the kin ties were not invariably specified.[100] Among small networks 'social mixing' occurred in one third (29.7%) of all cases although this may be distorted by the failure to recover more distant kin linkages. There were clearly kin networks restricted to members of a similar social group. Where a spread of wealth did occur it was sometimes a result of the financial rhythm of the life-cycle referred to above. Thus although Elizabeth Grubb (resident with her son-in-law William Bromley) paid 4d. to the poor rate, her recently married son Moses, who lived nearby, made no contribution at all. As far as it is possible to judge from the limited number of known types of kin relationship the most striking contrasts in social status were between blood relations, while links resulting from marriage alliances, as Elliott's work suggests, tended to be between households of similar social rank.[101] A number of kin links by marriage seem to have been based on similar wealthy occupations such as soapboiling, baking or grocery. Among the more extensive networks, however, kinship transcended occupational divisions. As we have seen, the Marshall network involved two bakers, one goldsmith, an attorney, a labourer and a tailor. Fathers and sons frequently followed similar occupations, notably among the wealthier trades and crafts. A number of such householders formed occupational dynasties in the

[97] G.L.R.O. P92/SAV/1335.   [98] P.C.C. Will Register 38 St John.
[99] William Powell, who had married one Jane Thickens in 1618, shared a dwelling with John Marshall senior's widow in 1635, see G.L.R.O. P92/SAV/227.
[100] For a case of this see, Boulton 1983: 322, n. 124.   [101] Elliott 1978: 362.

Boroughside, members of which can be identified in the same area forty years later. Overall at least fifty Boroughside householders produced sons who subsequently married and set up house in the district. It may be that this represents an example of the way, noted by Houlbrooke, in which economic opportunities in London encouraged the formation of local kin networks. Lack of openings might otherwise have 'pushed' offspring away from the parental home.[102]

This possibility must remain tentative, however, both because this practice was by no means an invariable rule and because since only local networks can be identified it takes no account of offspring setting up in trade outside the Boroughside. Among lower status occupations such endogamy seems to have been relatively unusual.[103] The overall effect of kinship in the Boroughside might well have been to bind households together despite differences of occupation and social standing.

Another way of looking at the importance of kin ties to Boroughside householders is to see if kin preferred to live close to each other. To examine the effect of kinship links on the residential patterns described in Chapter 7, households linked by shared unusual surname, references in wills and other sources were broken down according to residence (see Table 9.5). Such an analysis will be subject to the distortion of incorrectly linked households and the proportion of kin links not recovered. Residential propinquity has not been used as a criterion of kin linkage to avoid predetermining the issue. This means that the few examples of closely resident households with similar but 'common' surnames are excluded. On occasion this methodology excluded very strongly suspected links. Hence, for example, John Bland, married one Elizabeth Woodroffe in 1617 and lived next door to one Roger Woodroffe in 1622 in Green Dragon Yard, but since the surname Woodroffe just fails to qualify as an unusual surname the link was not made. In practice therefore the figures in Table 9.5 may well underestimate the tendency of related households to live in close proximity. A further limiting factor to bear in mind is that it is not always possible to assume that kinship was the dominant motive for any residential propinquity. Related householders living close together on, say, the High Street might have been following the dictates of their occupation or social standing rather than that of their local kin ties. Furthermore if householders did have restricted social horizons (a limited 'social area'), then this might in itself explain their clustering around the parental home.[104]

Kinship links seem to have had an influence over the residential location

[102] For occupational dynasties and kin networks operating family businesses, see, Rappaport 1981: 19; Grassby 1978: 358–68; Prior 1977: iv; T. K. Hareven (ed.), *Family and Kin in Urban Communities 1700–1930*, London, 1977, p. 9; Houlbrooke 1984: 52.
[103] Elliott 1978: 66.   [104] Drake and Hammerton 1974: 82–3.

Table 9.5. *Residential proximity of households to suspected kin*

Residential proximity to kin	Number of households	%
Within five dwellings	35	20.4
Within ten dwellings	9	5.2
Same alley or yard	6	3.5
Adjacent alley or yard	18	10.5
Elsewhere	104	60.5
Total	172	

Note: This table cannot take account of related kin living opposite one another on thoroughfares.
Source: See discussion in text, pp. 253–6.

of a significant number of households. As Table 9.5 makes clear just under one third of all households thought to be linked to others by kin ties were living in the immediate vicinity of their relatives, often in fact next door. Hence Richard Yearwood, grocer, lived next door to his cousin Nicholas King, another grocer, and John Godley, tailor, chose to live next door to his brother-in-law in the Chaingate Churchyard. Settlement in an adjacent alley or yard also seems to have occurred. Oliver Dorrington, weaver, resident in the Close in 1622 was related by marriage to one Stephen Stretch living in the adjacent Churchyard. Joan Bosse, resident in Angel Yard, left a small bequest to her 'sister's son' John Britten, a tailor who lived nearby in the Churchyard.[105] Residential propinquity between kin has been noted in early sixteenth-century Coventry and pre-industrial Oxford. The presence of kin living in close residential proximity to each other has also been discovered in some nineteenth- and twentieth-century towns and cities.[106] There is evidence, too, that it occurred elsewhere in seventeenth-century London. Nehemiah Wallington, the Eastcheap turner, lived on the same street as his father in the early seventeenth century.[107]

It is clear, however, that many local kin (60.5%) felt no overwhelming urge to live in very close proximity to their relations. Issac Roffe a victualler resident in Goat Yard was some distance away from his brother Mark, dwelling in an alley in the New Rents. Similarly Richard Prior, butcher, lived near the Soap Yard whilst his kinsman Thomas Prior, victualler, dwelt in the Close on the other side of the Boroughside. Much the same pattern was

[105] G.L.R.O. Archdeaconry of Surrey Wills Register, 268 Peter.
[106] See Prior 1977: 8; Phythian-Adams 1979: 155; Anderson 1971: 57–61; Hareven 1977: 10; Young and Willmott 1957: 20–2; Bourchet 1981: 620. [107] Wallington 1869: I, xv.

found in nineteenth-century Preston. Anderson found that out of fifty-two pairs of related households 62% were separated by distances of one hundred yards or more.[108] Kinship ties could serve to link households together in different residential sub-districts as well as within the same street or alley. In this connection it should be noted that even kin living in different sub-districts from their relatives would have only been a few minutes walk away.

It also seems likely that close proximity to kin whether by co-residence or residence in the very immediate vicinity, was often only a transient phenomenon. The high mortality rates in London must have meant that, where parents and adult children both survived, close residence was perforce only temporary.[109] Residential mobility can occasionally be observed as a response to the decline in parents' fortunes with old age. A number of householders made moves in order to be near to kin undergoing a period of hardship. Hence for example Richard Ashton, shoemaker and parish pensioner, lived in Counter Alley in 1619 and one Henry Ashton, shoemaker, in Goat Yard. In 1622 both men were co-residing in Counter Alley. Interestingly Richard was not receiving a pension at this time, perhaps because of this kin support. In 1623 Richard was elected to the College of the Poor and left Counter Alley for that place, where he died in 1625. Henry Ashton remained in Counter Alley after Richard's removal and death, but by 1631 had moved to an alley off the east side of the High Street. Residential proximity could also have been restricted by the availability of suitable accommodation in the immediate vicinity of kin. Thus in 1613 Anthony Alfray, the grocer, married the daughter of Richard Salter, keeper of the White Hart Inn, but continued to live on the east side of the High Street some twenty dwellings away. In 1619 James Jackson, cutler, Salter's (actually his widow's) next-door neighbour removed to Counter Lane in the New Rents. Shortly after this Alfray moved into the dwelling vacated by Jackson and therefore next door to his mother-in-law, seven years after marrying her daughter.[110]

Information as to the degree to which numbers of kin in the Boroughside actually provided meaningful social and financial support for each other is not recoverable. As in some village communities, it can be shown that a few Boroughside householders preferred neighbours over local kinsmen in their choices of overseer or bondsman.[111] It also seems probable that householders, in the absence of local kin, tended to rely more on neighbours for overseers than their counterparts did in rural areas.

[108] Anderson 1971: 59.
[109] Similar points are noted in Anderson 1971: 59; Phythian-Adams 1979: 155–6; Laslett 1977b: 106.
[110] See the similar examples in Anderson 1971: 59.
[111] Wrightson and Levine 1979: 102.

It may not be possible, however, to draw a simple correlation between numbers of kin present and the strength and importance of urban kinship ties. It may be that the need for support in the metropolitan environment increased the importance of the fewer available kin, particularly for the recently arrived immigrant. Local kin ties may have been less common but more useful to a newcomer, at least initially, before neighbourly contacts could be established. Certainly recent studies have indicated that kin could be of considerable importance and value to urban immigrants as a means of help and assimilation, providing lodgings or financial aid. In seventeenth-century London kin are thought to have played a significant role in the marriage market. Anthropological work on early modern Italian cities also suggests that kin played a significant part in the assimilation of immigrants. The case study of the Marshall network suggests positive ways in which kin links might have provided support of considerable social and economic value.[112]

The 1601 Poor Law Act had placed an obligation to support 'impotent' poor on their grandparents, parents and children. Old persons therefore were to be supported where possible by their children. Young children were to be supported by parents and grandparents. Two case studies that by chance can be reconstructed show, together with the case of Richard Ashton noted above, that local kin could play an integral part in the system of parish poor relief.[113] In 1622 James Clough, the individual noted as following five related occupations in Chapter 3, lived in Ship Yard next door to his son-in-law, James Davies, a tailor. In 1624 both households moved from Ship Yard to the New Rents; although no longer in adjacent dwellings Davies and Clough remained in close proximity. James Clough died in 1626, but his widow, Rose, and James Davies were still in their respective dwellings in 1631. Davies baptised seven children in the parish church, one a son, Miles, in 1623. That Davies received some support from his kinship link with his mother-in-law is shown by a petition sent in to the churchwardens by Rose Clough in the 1630s:

that whereas...your worships were favourably pleased to allow her a pension of 12*d*. a week towards keeping her grandchild Miles Davies a miserable and Bursten child, the which (it is well known) was not without need such being her poverty and the said Miles his parents also. But now so it is may it please your worships the collectors of the poor...have not this month allowed her any pension, as formerly she had of 12*d*. the week towards keeping the said Miles, pretending that

---

[112] See Clark 1972: 135–9; Elliott 1981: 90–5; Burke 1983: 71–3; Patten 1973: 6–7; Anderson 1971: 62. Analysis of Pepys' diary suggests that 'certain features of life in the metropolis favoured the maintenance of ties of kinship', Houlbrooke 1984: 58.

[113] For the legal situation under the 1601 Act, see Smith 1981b: 607; Houlbrooke 1984: 48; W. Newman Brown, 'The receipt of poor relief and family situation: Aldenham, Hertfordshire 1630–90', in R. M. Smith (ed.), *Family, Kinship and Life-Cycle*, Cambridge, 1984, pp. 406–7.

the said Miles his father is of ability to relieve him, which is otherwise God knows insomuch that the petitioner is not able any longer to relieve herself and child but unless your worships be favourable to her they are both like utterly to perish. Her humble request is your worships would comiserate her poor estate and her aged years with the long time of sickness and lameness she hath had, so that little means a pension being all she hath to relieve them may not be withheld from them any longer.[114]

The second case concerns support for the aged. In 1618 Roger Cotton, victualler, lived on the west side of the High Street and his son-in-law, Nicholas Willis, shoemaker, in Pepper Alley. As we saw in Chapter 8, Cotten was in the process of social decline from Elizabethan subsidy payer to Caroline pauper. Perhaps it was this decline that prompted Willis to reside next door to Cotten in 1622, possibly in part of Cotten's house divided for that purpose.[115] Following Cotten's departure to poorer housing in Goat Yard, Willis seems to have left the Boroughside. However, Willis and his wife were certainly close enough to provide financial support to Cotten in his last illness, as a petition sent in by his daughter to the churchwardens makes clear:

whereas Roger Cotten your petitioners late father lived in one of the almshouses of your parish and now by the will of god is deceased. And whereas your petitioner hath been at great charges and expenses with him, by reason of providing things necessary for him, in time of his sickness and likewise for the burying of him, which he desired might be by her mother in the churchyard…which was accordingly performed. Therefore your petitioner in consideration of her great expenses and charges desires your worships favour to grant unto her such small things of household stuff which are remaining in the said almshouse as her said late father left behind him.[116]

It seems possible therefore that a substantial minority of Boroughside householders were involved in locally based kin networks. A comparison with the Essex village of Terling is instructive for what seems to be particularly striking is that differences in kinship ties are more of degree than of kind. This may well be because mobility and population turnover was common to both rural and urban situations. As with the Boroughside, the majority of the adult population of Terling, 'had experience of living in other communities'. Terling's population was 'highly geographically mobile', a society 'very far from being bounded by the bounds of the parish'. The kinship network in Terling was, as far as it is possible to judge, more dense than that of the Boroughside; between 37.3% and 52.5% of all its households were linked to at least one other in 1670 compared to perhaps

---

[114] G.L.R.O. P92/SAV/765. See a similar case in Laslett 1976: 109–113.
[115] The 1622 token book indicates that Cotten and Willis were living in a divided house since it places both householders in open-ended brackets. G.L.R.O. P92/SAV/211, see above Chapter 7.
[116] G.L.R.O. P92/SAV/785.

18% of those in the Boroughside.[117] However, as in the Boroughside such kin networks were loose: 'even those households who had kin among other households usually had only one such link', and extensive kin networks were untypical. Although turnover and population increase was greater in the Boroughside than in Terling and, consequently, kin networks were less frequent, it seems possible that kinship did operate as a significant social force in the neighbourhood.

There is considerable evidence to suggest then that social relationships in Boroughside society possessed many features often attributed by sociologists to local social systems. Much of the economy rested on a local foundation; neighbourly relationships were the most important source of support. Kin, although less commonly found than in rural areas, were present in significant numbers, enough to suggest that such relationships also played an important part in social life. Marriage partners were sought within a relatively small geographical area. Persistence within the Boroughside was high demonstrating a recognition of the various social and economic ties and attachments within the neighbourhood as well as what may have been an inherent tendency for much social and economic activity to be based locally in the capital. Thus far however, only the informal social and economic bonds of neighbourhood have been examined. To what extent did membership of formal institutions such as the various organs of local government or participation in the rites and ceremonies of the parish church bind local people together?

[117] Wrightson and Levine 1979: 79–85, 102.

10

The institutional structure of the neighbourhood

10.1 Local government: the framework and supervision of the neighbourhood

The previous chapter described the local basis of many social relationships in the Boroughside district. It was also noted, however, that urban communities are often thought to have been reinforced and bonded together by participation in and by the action and pervasiveness of formal institutions of government – bodies holding political, administrative or economic power. The extent and importance of office-holding and membership of craft fellowships has been described recently in sixteenth-century York and Coventry.[1] In sociological terms too, local social systems are thought more likely to develop (and be preserved in times of social stress) in the presence of enduring political, legal and economic organisations.[2]

Office-holding and the pervasiveness of local government has also become a central feature in an interpretation of seventeenth-century London which chooses to emphasise social stability and communal obligation in the capital. Valerie Pearl has suggested that the key institutions of the wardmote and the vestry, which made up the local government of the capital, may have been responsible for its social stability in the early seventeenth century. There was, notably in the wealthier wards, a high proportion of local officials to rate-paying householders. In Cornhill in the 1640s there were 118 officers to serve 276 householders. In the poorer ward of Farringdon Without (the largest in the City) there was one official for every eighteen householders. These relatively high ratios demonstrated 'a high degree of citizen participation in local matters and of communal obligation which has rarely if ever existed since'. Effective government was facilitated by the division of much of the City into small administrative units. The twenty-five City wards were divided into 242 precincts, each one on average under three

[1] Palliser 1979: 78; Phythian-Adams 1979: 116–17, 125–7.
[2] Stacey 1969: 142–3.

262

acres in size. Many of the parishes within the walls were also small and administratively convenient. Within the City this permitted an 'intense self-imposed registration and watch on inhabitants', a notable feature of its 'strict and punctual government'.[3] However, to date, it is the *wealthier* areas of London that have provided evidence for effective local government and extensive local participation. In the poorer suburbs,'more subject to social stress, we would almost certainly find stronger evidence for resentment and revolt'.[4]

Parochial administration had been slow to respond to the needs of population expansion in the suburbs so that the parishes in Southwark and the East End were on an unwieldy scale. Manorial courts rather than the ward and precinct system continued to serve as organs of local government in Southwark, East London and elsewhere.[5] John Graunt commented on the poor government in the 'greater out parishes' claiming that 'many of the poorer parishioners through neglect do perish and many vicious persons get liberty to live as they please, for want of some heedful eye to overlook them'. Clark and Slack have described London's suburban government at this time as 'an impotent alliance of parish, manorial and county author-ities...the government of outer London steadily disintegrated'.[6] How effective and comprehensive was the system of local government in the Boroughside, and how extensive was participation in local office? Did local government provide any sort of adequate framework for neighbourhood life in this part of suburban London?

The manorial and parish jurisdictions at work within the Boroughside and the ways in which holding associated local offices reinforced and complemented individual power deriving from the possession of wealth and property have been described in previous chapters.[7] The evidence from the Boroughside district suggests that, contrary to what might be expected, local government remained an important ubiquitous force in the social and economic lives of most of that district's inhabitants; a significant institution in neighbourhood life which lent structure and coherence to the society. Participation in local office was fairly common but, perhaps of more significance, was the extensiveness and number of contacts that householders had with local institutions of manor and parish. In particular the evidence suggests that the absence of the city administrative system of ward and

[3] Pearl 1979: 15–17. For local government in London see also, McCampbell 1976: 107–24; Finlay 1981: 77; W. G. Bell 'Wardmote inquest registers of St Dunstans-in-the-West', *Transactions of the London and Middlesex Archaeological Society*, n.s., 3 (1917), 56–70.

[4] Pearl 1979: 18.

[5] McCampbell 1976: 108; Finlay 1981: 171; Pearl 1979: 27; Johnson 1969: 292–329; Pearl 1961: 17. For a description of manorial government in Stepney see, H. Llewellyn-Smith, *The History of East London*, London, 1939, pp. 35–72.

[6] Graunt 1973: 58; Clark and Slack 1976: 71.   [7] See above Chapters 1 and 6.

precinct in an area of rapid population growth produced not 'impotence' and 'chaos' but the development of an increasingly complex and bureaucratised administration with considerable powers of social coercion at its disposal.

As noted above, there was no wardmote inquest for Bridge Ward Without and this goes some way to explain why the manorial courts of Southwark 'enjoyed...a long and unusually vigorous history', rather than atrophying as they did in some rural areas by the late sixteenth century.[8] The need to provide efficient trade and market regulation also explains the continued functioning of the manorial courts. It has been suggested that manorial government in Stepney may have been similarly active.[9] The ordinances and officials of the three Southwark manorial courts gave expression to and were appointed under civic jurisdiction. The ordinances were based on orders of the Court of Common Council of the City of London and approved by a special committee. The inhabitants of Southwark manors could petition the city authorities for changes in this local legislative framework.[10] Manorial jurors were empanelled by the bailiff and in turn chose a variety of manorial officials. The jurors made presentments based on their own initiative and on the complaints of the constables. In the early seventeenth century the Southwark manorial courts were dealing with maintenance of streets and paving, fire and pollution and the local water supply. The courts enforced the assize of bread and ale and regulated commerce and trade. As we have seen, the borough market was regulated by the manorial courts, in particular the Guildable Manor, and forestallers and engrossers were presented regularly.[11] Occasional 'bloodsheds' (minor assaults) were still being presented by the constables in the early seventeenth century although the vast bulk must have been going to the quarter sessions. Those presented in the courts were fined (the amount of which was determined by the 'assirors') and the fines collected by the bailiff to his own use. The courts were presided over by the steward who, together with the bailiff, was directly responsible to the City authorities. The bailiff was an important official whose duties extended beyond the manorial courts to include running the local gaol (the Borough Compter) and summoning juries to the borough court and the coroner's inquest.[12]

The most important manorial officer was the constable. Apart from setting the watch and presenting offenders to the manorial courts the constable was responsible for serving warrants and attended the assize

[8] Johnson 1969: 235–7; 151; Wrightson and Levine 1979: 42.
[9] Power 1971:252.   [10] Johnson 1969: 309; C.L.R.O. Rep. 30, f. 23.
[11] See above Chapter 3 and Johnson 1969: 304–11.
[12] The city authorities had returned to the practice of farming the bailiwick of Southwark in 1618, see, Johnson 1969: 180–220, 274–337.

sessions. The constable was also called upon to aid parish officials in the execution of their duties. The constable was a formal link between the manorial and parochial administrations and was sometimes present at vestry meetings; the vestry was also responsible for paying the constables to press soldiers. As in some city parishes, serving as constable was an essential qualification for vestry membership.[13] By the 1630s the importance of the parish as an administrative unit was increasing at the expense of the manor. Symptomatic of this was the growing tendency for constables to be allocated on a parish rather than on a manorial basis.[14]

Since the middle of the sixteenth century the vestry had controlled parochial administration in St Saviour's. From 1557 the vestry had been a 'select' vestry of thirty. Membership was for life or until the individual concerned left the parish. New vestrymen were chosen by the vestry which operated on a quorum of sixteen. Apart from serving as constable, vestrymen, as noted in Chapter 6, were to be £5 subsidy men and to have lived for at least eight years in the parish. The vestry was responsible for appointing a large number of minor parish officials as well as the two ministers.[15] The main burden of parochial administration fell on the churchwardens. Six were chosen by the vestry every year, three from the wardens of the previous year. The churchwardens held specific posts that covered the administration of poor relief, the college almshouse, parish property and the general accounts. The churchwardens were a legal corporation and since 1614 had owned the freehold of the Rectory and were hence responsible for collecting tithes in the parish.[16] The duties of the vestry and the churchwardens were summarised in 1606 in response to an attack on the select vestry and were clearly time-consuming and extensive.

1. In some years 20 vestries [are held] for that the churchwardens may not do anything extraordinary or lay out above 40s extraordinarily without the consent of a vestry. 2. In casting tokens and taking the number of communicants 4 or 5 days yearly are spent. 3. In gathering the tithes and delivering of tokens to 1442 households not less than 40 days. 4. In receiving the quarterly rents many days. 5. In overseeing the buildings and reparations of the Church, schoolhouse, almshouses and tenements very many days as occasion is offered. 6. In ending of controversy among poor people many days. 7. In inquiring after defaults and abuses

---

[13] For the overlap between wardmote and parish administration in London see, McCampbell 1976: 110–19; F. F. Foster, *The politics of stability: a portrait of the rulers in Elizabethan London,* London, 1977, p. 32. For the pressing of soldiers in St Saviour's see, G.L.R.O. P92/SAV/450, 8 December 1624.   [14] Johnson 1969: 303.

[15] See Johnson 1969: 320; Darlington 1955b: 69–76; Malden 1967: 4, 153–4. Officials appointed by the vestry included the parish clerk, sexton, gravedigger, bearers, conductor, searchers, sidesmen and surveyors of highways. The vestry also nominated persons to be Overseers of the Poor to local J.P.s, see, G.L.R.O. P92/SAV/450, 27 March 1607.

[16] See Malden 1967: 4, 154; Darlington 1955b: 75. For the efforts to collect tithes see the two surveys of tithes in arrears G.L.R.O. P92/SAV/664, 490 and the vestry minute book, G.L.R.O. P92/SAV/450, 24 September 1610, 19 February 1612, 23 May 1614, 3 March 1617, 11 November 1617.

making presentments providing for the poor putting out to keep and prentice poor children, avoiding inmates and vagrants above 20 days. 8. The churchwardens do make at the least 2000 receipts and payments yearly. 9. In following of suits and other extraordinary business very much time as occasion is offered.[17]

In addition to parochial administration members of the vestry were also made responsible for collecting and assessing the subsidy contribution for the parish, a task that fell to the wardmote in the City.[18] The churchwardens and the vestry shared some authority with the manorial courts. The vestry was responsible for keeping the market place clear and for whipping beggars from the parish.[19] Via presentments to the church courts the churchwardens enforced not only church attendance and various ecclesiastical canons but were also able to present offenders for misdemeanours similar to those presented in the manorial courts. Hence, for example, the proximity of the butchers' shambles to the Chaingate Churchyard caused many butchers to be presented for 'annoyances'. John Hands, therefore, was presented for, 'from April, May, June, July and ever more for using a slaughter house in Chaingate being forewarned because of the annoyance of the Church Way'. In the same way the church courts were used by the churchwardens to reinforce the authority of the manorial officials.[20] How pervasive was this combination of manorial and parish administration in neighbourhood life?

Although there may have been some parts of Southwark where local government was ineffective and social discipline weak there are good reasons for supposing that the Boroughside district may have been regulated closely. True, the inhabitants of the 'sub-district' of Montague Close in the Boroughside claimed some special privileges and exemptions. In the mid-sixteenth century a baker living in the area had been fined heavily for refusing to serve as constable, by the manorial jurors who thought it 'not well to lose any part of the liberty'. In the early seventeenth century the area still exhibited a tendency to resist some ecclesiastical jurisdiction. A small Catholic population lived there, perhaps under the protection of the local Catholic Montague family. Other inhabitants broke the prohibition on the consumption of meat during Lent and attempted, with some success, to resist the payment of tithes. By this period, however, the Close had become integrated fully into the local administration, some of its inhabitants paying the local poor rate and subsidy, all being listed in the sacramental token books and a number serving as parish officials, including vestrymen (who would also have served previously in the manorial administration as constables).[21]

[17] G.L.R.O. P92/SAV/794.   [18] Pearl 1979: 15.
[19] G.L.R.O. P92/SAV/450, 4 October 1624, 7 January 1623, 23 December 1623.
[20] G.L.R.O. P92/SAV/543, 541.
[21] See, G.L.R.O. P92/SAV/450, 4 January 1620; Rendle 1878: 237–8; Johnson 1969: 332; *Acts of the Privy Council of England 1630 June–1631 June*, London, 1964, ff. 744 and 760; C.L.R.O. Ms 39C, f. 268b.

Before 1640 the real trouble spot in the area of Southwark within the city's jurisdiction was the parish of St George's, Southwark (see Fig. 1.1). St George's contained a number of prisons that were sometimes the focal point for riots. There were riots at the King's Bench Prison in 1620 and 1640 and at the Marshalsea in 1639. St George's also contained two contiguous areas claiming special exemption from the jurisdiction of the City, Suffolk Place, otherwise known as the Mint and the 'Rules of the King's Bench Prison'. This latter district covered about two-thirds of St George's parish and was said to be inhabited by debtors and others claiming exemption from civil jurisdictions. Extortion and drunkenness were said to be rife in the area in the seventeenth century.[22] The institutions of local government were more effective in the Boroughside.

The commercial and economic importance of the district may have been responsible for this attention. Certainly that part of it which contained the market had long been under the jurisdiction of the City authorities and in the early seventeenth century the Bailiff resided in the area.[23] It may also be significant that the Boroughside was over-represented on some administrative bodies. Despite its size relative to the rest of Southwark it can be calculated that the area supplied three quarters of all the assize grand jurors for Southwark between 1618 and 1625.[24] Within the parish of St Saviour's the administrative predominance of the Boroughside was particularly marked. Twenty-two of the thirty vestrymen were chosen from it, although the Boroughside contained fewer inhabitants than the liberties of the Clink and Paris Garden. All the minor parish offices were taken by Boroughside dwellers and the two ministers resided there, a bias which reflected the concentration of parochial buildings in the area, namely the parish church and churchyards, the local almshouse and the grammar school.

Participation in these parochial and manorial offices was fairly widespread in the Boroughside. Within the Boroughside at any one point in time there were about forty-five manorial officials, twenty-two vestrymen, ten watchmen (identity unknown) and fourteen parish officials. There were therefore ninety-one office-holders out of 958 householders in the Boroughside in 1622 or about one office for every eleven householders. This ratio of officials to householders compares well with Pearl's estimate for Farringdon Without but poorly with the wealthy Cornhill Ward.[25] The ratio of office-holders to *eligible* householders would have been more favourable. Excluding the 135 ineligible female household heads then in 1622 there

[22] Johnson 1969: 334–6; Malden 1967: 4, 143–5; George 1966: 266; Rendle 1878: 91–110; Pearl 1961: 29; Lindley 1983: 115. For a fascinating account of life in the King's Bench Prison in the late eighteenth century see, Joanna Innes, 'The King's Bench Prison in the later eighteenth century', in J. Brewer and J. Styles (eds.), *An Ungovernable People*, London, paperback edn, 1983, pp. 250–98.
[23] Johnson 1969: 26–92, 130.   [24] See, Cockburn 1982: 158–300.
[25] Pearl 1979: 16.

would have been about one official for every nine male household heads. It should also be noted that the true ratio of office holders to householders must have been lower than that presented here because the figures are drawn from incomplete manorial records. Furthermore trial jurors at the assizes and quarter sessions have been excluded.[26] Over time of course an individual's chances of holding local office must have been greater. As we have seen in Chapter 6 this participation was particularly common amongst the wealthier householders: something like one in four poor-rate payers held office at some time between 1620 and 1624 and one in three subsidy payers. Amongst these wealthier groups the holding of unpaid, often arduous, time-consuming offices represents a genuine voluntary participation in neighbourhood institutions.

If a substantial minority of households participated actively in the local administration, *all* householders were caught up in some way or other with the local courts, local officialdom or local bureaucracy.

The impact of the manorial courts could well have been considerable. A large number of Boroughside inhabitants were presented to the manorial courts in the early seventeenth century (see Table 10.1). Judging from the social standing of offenders it is clear that the attention of the manorial courts was focused, as one would expect, on the 'economically effective' inhabitants; of those presented between 1620 and 1624, 117 of the 154 offenders (76.0%) were poor-rate payers. During the period 1620–4 some 16%, or one in six of the householders known to be resident in the Boroughside in 1622, infringed one or more of the manorial ordinances and found themselves presented to the manorial court. For poor-rate payers contact was more frequent: 117 out of 294 or 39.8%, more than one in three. This should be seen as a minimum estimate since the figures are derived from incomplete sources. Large numbers of individuals were presented for more than one offence. Butchers felt the burden of manorial ordinances especially heavily. For example, 60.6% of those individuals presented for forestalling were butchers, as were 25.6% of those presented for 'annoyances' and 53.5% for defective scales. For those living on the boundaries of two manors such harassment could intensify. Giles Foster, butcher, was presented by the Guildable jurors 'for sweeping down blood and soil in the way leading to the Church to the annoyance of passengers', for defective scales and forestalling the market in 1620, but also found himself presented by the jurors of the King's Manor for 'carrying offal in the day time' in 1624.[27] However, as has been mentioned in Chapter 3,

---

[26] Between 1620 and 1624, 28 Boroughside householders can be identified as trial jurors at the Assizes, Cockburn 1982: 188–286.

[27] C.L.R.O. Presentments of the jurors of Guildable Manor 1620 Southwark Box 2; C.L.R.O. Presentments of the jurors of King's Manor 1624 Southwark Box 2.

Table 10.1. *The poor rate assessments of those Boroughside inhabitants presented to the manorial courts 1620–4*

Poor rate assessment of householder presented	Category of presentment		
	Forestalling	Annoyances	Defective scales
+5d.	1	6	3
2d.–4d.	9	26	18
½d.–1d.	13	26[a]	15
Not rated	10	20	7
Total	33	78	43

Note: [a] Includes two individuals who were assessed for the poor rate but whose level of assessment is not known.
Sources: Presentments of jurors of Guildable Manor 1620 and 1624, C.L.R.O. Southwark Box 2; Presentments of jurors of King's Manor 1620 and 1624, C.L.R.O. Southwark Box 2; Presentments of jurors of Great Liberty 1622, C.L.R.O. Southwark Box 4.

enforcement of manorial presentments was less than total. It is particularly unfortunate in this connection that it is not possible to examine either the part played by quarter sessions in reinforcing the manorial courts or the number of Boroughside householders who appeared at them.[28] The manorial courts probably went into a decline in the 1630s as the influence of the Surrey justices and the part played in local government regulation by quarter sessions increased.

Victuallers and alehousekeepers were also involved frequently with local officialdom. Victualling houses were important popular alternatives to the church as centres of neighbourhood social life and activity in Stuart England.[29] Such establishments acted, in their own way, as informal binding institutions by providing meeting places for neighbours. Neighbours often seem to have met to drink in establishments in the very immediate locality, and in the same sub-districts from which they often chose bondsmen and overseers. In 1637, for example, Thomas Wilson at the Boarshead tavern was presented for having company in divine service.[30] The three men named as being present there, all of whom can be detected in the 1635 token book, were John Jones from Boarshead Alley and Clement Potts and John Davis, both of whom lived in the nearby Ship Yard. Edward Alleyn's diary contains

[28] For examples of this from the Restoration period and for the overlap between quarter sessions and manorial courts, see, Johnson 1969: 298–9.
[29] Wrightson 1982: 167–70; Clark 1978: 57–72; Clark 1983a: 145–65. Liquor houses performed a similar function in nineteenth-century Washington, Bourchet 1981: 624.
[30] G.L.R.O. P92/SAV/554.

similar references to his arbitrations of disputes between neighbours as well as other social activity which often took place in local inns, victualling houses or taverns.[31] Their importance as meeting places is reinforced by their ubiquitousness – in 1622 there was one such establishment for every fourteen householders in the Boroughside district.

In Southwark, as elsewhere, such establishments were associated by those in authority with criminal and moral disorder which consequently brought their owners into frequent contact with manorial and parish officials.[32] The Southwark constables reported in 1605 that 'In Southwark there are 350 alehouses, in which there is much disorder' and it was subsequently left to the Lord Mayor to deal with their regulation.[33] The occasional Southwark inhabitant was, in fact, presented at the assizes for keeping a disorderly alehouse, but their regulation did indeed fall mainly on the city authorities and on local government. Boroughside victuallers were licenced by the Lord Mayor in 1633, as were victuallers in other areas of the city throughout the early seventeenth century.[34] The manorial courts regulated their economic functions; as was noted in Chapter 3 virtually *all* the Boroughside victuallers were presented to the manorial courts between 1620 and 1624. Furthermore, also as we have seen, recognisances were imposed to enforce ecclesiastical prohibitions. By the 1620s victualling houses seem to have been fairly closely controlled in the Boroughside and their keepers often relatively wealthy. Their rivalry with the church was recognised by the city authorities as early as 1607 when searches were carried out to detect illegal drinking in time of divine service.[35] In the Boroughside in the 1630s we know that the churchwardens and sidesmen were making similar searches during Sunday services, noting down offenders who were subsequently presented at the bi-annual visitation of the Bishop of Winchester.[36]

Involvement of the Boroughside victuallers with these latter church courts was widespread. Between 1632 and 1640 at least 88 victuallers, vintners and innkeepers were presented for 209 offences connected with receiving company in divine service. Such presentments were normally couched in

---

[31] Note for example '14 September 1621 spent at the Bull Head at the arbitration with Jacob 5s', Young 1889: 2,218. For this and other disputes see also 135, 154, 230. For Alleyn's extensive social activity see ibid., p. 51 and passim..

[32] Clark 1983a: 166–76; Wrightson 1982: 167–70; K. Wrightson, 'Alehouses, order and reformation in rural England 1590–1660', in Eileen and S. Yeo (eds.), *Popular Culture and Class Conflict 1590–1914*, Hassocks, 1981, pp. 1–27.

[33] Cockburn 1982: 16.

[34] G.L.R.O. P92/SAV/1320. See, Johnson 1969; 256; Dingle 1974: 64; Ashton 1983: 10–13.

[35] Dingle 1974: 63–4; Ashton 1983: 11; Webb 1963: 7–23; D. A. Williams, 'Puritanism in the city government 1610–1640', *Guildhall Miscellany* 1,4 (1955), 8–9.

[36] Each liberty of the parish of St Saviour's sent in its own presentments. Visitations did not always take place; in 1639 the presentments were 'made and delivered...the parish not being *visitat*'. G.L.R.O. P92/SAV/563. Draft presentments survive for the 1630s, G.L.R.O. P92/SAV/514–90.

a standard form: 'we present Thomas Prior in the Close for having 2 men drinking in his house the 10 day of June being Sunday in the time of divine service'.[37] The large numbers involved, representing perhaps a third of all victuallers at one point in time emphasises the frequency of contact with these local officials. It is significant therefore that reaction to the activities of the churchwardens often took a standard, institutionalized form. It was common for victuallers to be presented for refusal to admit the church-wardens into their establishments or to refuse to answer verbal enquiries. Hence Nicholas Jarvis at the Peters Head in Pepper Alley was 'suspected because he stood at the door within and would not speak nor open his door'.[38] Like the manorial jurors the churchwardens met with open hostility. 'Mr Blunden' at the George Inn was presented for 'denying to open his gate and making a scoff at the churchwardens' and Richard Smith in Horsehead Alley for 'bidding the churchwardens to do their worst'.[39] As the figures imply victuallers were presented regularly. John Jennings keeper of the King's Arms tavern was presented ten times between 1633 and 1635 'having been divers times formerly presented'.[40] Victuallers were consequently more likely to be presented for non-attendance at church. Edward Bulmer, victualler, was presented in 1636 'being at home and usually selling drink in divine service and several times out of his doors being demanded of the churchwardens why he was not at church answered what had they to do with the same and other churlish speeches'.[41] However, it is clear that church-going and victualling were not necessarily incompatible. Thomas Pocock at the Wilderness was presented for having men drinking in time of divine service but, the churchwardens noted, 'the master and mistress were at church so that the door could not be opened'.[42]

If involvement with local courts was often widespread then a number of features of the parochial administration in the Boroughside suggest that that branch of local government may also have been particularly comprehensive and pervasive. The parish authorities were able to maintain what was, in effect, a system of registration on a par with that kept by some city wardmote officials.[43] In order to enforce the payment of communion dues a book was kept for each liberty of St Saviour's that listed each household head and the number of communicants in each household street by street. A new book was compiled each year and updated twice within each year and an index of street names was included in every book. Changes in residence, newcomers, and the delivery of sacramental tokens (to be returned at communion) were thereby recorded annually. This registration

[37] G.L.R.O. P92/SAV/524.
[38] G.L.R.O. P92/SAV/536.
[39] G.L.R.O. P92/SAV/523, 525.
[40] G.L.R.O. P92/SAV/542.
[41] G.L.R.O. P92/SAV/543.
[42] G.L.R.O. P92/SAV/522.
[43] Dingle 1974: 45–6; Pearl 1979: 17.

system reached its peak in 1622 when each communicant was named and numbered. The churchwarden responsible often put memoranda against certain names to record death, departure or religious recalcitrance. The system seems to have been particularly effectively compiled in the Boroughside.[44] The token books which are discussed in more detail in the following section, were in use from the late sixteenth century until the Civil War. The administrative achievement represented by the compilation of the token books is particularly impressive given the large numbers of households involved and the extensive residential mobility within the parish.[45]

The token books were only part of the system of registration operated by the Boroughside authorities. In common with some London parishes and provincial towns and cities the vestry appointed searchers to detect inmates.[46] Since the late sixteenth century these officials had had considerable success in the apprehension and ejection of such newcomers. In 1595 the searchers reported that, as a result of their activities 'In all this year the parish hath not been charged with child, newcomer, nor aged person, more than they were before'.[47] The vestry minute book reveals that these officials are known to have been appointed from 1597 to 1606.[48] It is possible that following the appointment of a provost marshall by the city authorities in 1616 as a stringent police measure to combat vagrancy and criminal activity in the city and its suburbs, and three months after the survey of the poor, this system was tightened up.[49] In July 1618 the vestry granted £3 to Christofer Fawcett and £2 to Lambert Daggert 'for their pains in searching out inmates, and to the end they shall prevent newcomers that may be chargeable by reason of their children'. Fawcett and Daggert were to submit monthly bills 'to show what they do therein'.[50] In December 1618 Fawcett was awarded Daggert's share of the money as a reward for his 'very diligent and careful' work therein. A typical entry from one of these reports reads

---

[44] The books for the Boroughside are consistently better kept and often include more detail than those of the other two liberties.

[45] For the use of token books in discussions of household structure, residential location and residential mobility see above Chapters 5, 7 and 8. A detailed account of the token book system can also be found in Boulton 1983: 362–79. For an updated discussion of the system in London see, J. Boulton, 'The limits of formal religion. The administration of Holy Communion in late Elizabethan and early Stuart London', *London Journal* 10, 2 (1984).

[46] See Dingle 1974: 45; Herlan 1977a: 27–8; Beier 1981: 61; Styles 1963: 35–45; Raine 1969: 79–85.

[47] G.L.R.O. P92/SAV/1315.

[48] G.L.R.O. P92/SAV/450, 2 March 1597, 11 August 1601, 17 September 1606.

[49] A Provost Marshall had been appointed by the City in 1589 but the experiment was discontinued in 1596. The 1616 reappointment, ordered by the Privy Council, followed complaints of vagrancy in and about Westminster and Southwark. See, Johnson 1969: 324–6; Steele 1910: 1, no. 1188; *Acts of the Privy Council of England 1615–1616*, London, 1925, fols 210, 693–4; *Acts of the Privy Council of England 1616–17*, London, 1927, fol. 5; Beier 1978: 204; L. Boynton, 'The Tudor Provost Marshall', *English Historical Review* 77 (1962), 454–5.

[50] G.L.R.O. P92/SAV/450, 6 July 1618.

'Annis Browne having 5 children newcome to lodge with widow Gray at Christopher Yard: I took a constable and warned widow Gray to put her away: which she did and sent her to Saint George's from whence she came.'[51] Newcomers to the Boroughside were, as in other parishes in Stuart England, required to enter a customary bond to discharge the parish from responsibility for providing poor relief, 'to save the parish harmless'. Fawcett's reports make it clear that newcomers unable to enter such a bond were ejected from the Boroughside. Hence

30. William Price with his wife and 2 children being come from St George to dwell in Fishmonger Alley: I took a constable with me: and went to them, and told them that either they must put in sureties to discharge the parish, or be gone again: when being unable to put in sureties: went again out of the parish, and so we were rid of them.[52]

The sixty-six cases from Fawcett's two incomplete reports are testimony to the degree of control that the parochial authorities were exercising in the Boroughside. In common with a number of other local authorities the vestry also passed vagrants out of the Boroughside.[53] The aim of the aforementioned police measures was, of course, to reduce the financial burden of non-native poor.

The three-tiered poor relief system itself represented an important means by which the poorer householder would have come into contact with formal neighbourhood institutions. The pensioners and those receiving extraordinary payments were paid *weekly* by whichever of their wealthier neighbours happened to be holding the appropriate local office: a regular face-to-face transaction. Poor rates too were collected from householders following a house-to-house assessment by local officials. The administration of poor relief also added significantly to the bureaucratic apparatus of the parochial administration.

One effect of population growth and increased pressure on local government seems to have been the creation of a heavily bureaucratic 'super parish' able to maintain an effective social disciplining of its parishioners. The heavy workload placed on parochial administration and the extensive far-reaching tools that it employed naturally generated extensive records

[51] G.L.R.O. P92/SAV/1423. Only two reports have survived. These two were incomplete; Fawcett noted in 1619 that he had omitted 'many other things which I should write [but] the time would be too short', G.L.R.O. P92/SAV/1422. See also Raine 1969: 79–85.

[52] G.L.R.O. P92/SAV/1423. For the entering of bonds elsewhere see Styles 1963: 39–45. The orders of the Southwark Guildable Manor also demanded that newcomers and their landlords should enter such bonds, C.L.R.O. Presentments of the jurors of Guildable Manor 1624, Southwark Box 2.

[53] In 1622, 300 vagrants were said to have been passed out of the Boroughside in only three months. This may have been an exaggeration; in eight months in 1627 passes were only issued to 68 and in a twelve month period ending in April 1631, 229 were passed on, Rendle 1878: 34; G.L.R.O. P92/SAV/673, 675, 1467.

and professional record keepers. In contrast to the small rural parish where the parish clerk might well be an amateur part-timer, the St Saviour's vestry employed not one but *two* salaried professionals, a vestry and a parish clerk.[54] Both these individuals one of which (the vestry clerk) was normally a professional local scrivener, produced fair copies of the originals of most of the documents required by the parochial administration. The responsibility of the parish clerk for handling church fees meant that he was required to put in security for £40 to be forfeited if he performed his duties dishonestly.[55] Such officials produced impressive quantities of paper annually. In the second decade of the seventeenth century the following parish records were being produced every year: the vestry minutes; the churchwardens' general accounts; the accounts of the overseers of the poor (for the Boroughside only) and those of the general poor[56]; three tithe books (one for each liberty of the parish); three sacramental token books; a book of pew placings; a book of parish leases; monthly bills of marriages, baptisms and burials (later copied into the parish register) recording names of parishoners and fees owing or paid; a book of statute extracts. In addition to this were the results of 'one off' surveys (like that of the poor in 1618), tradesmens' bills and receipts, bonds, searchers' reports, draft presentments, petitions and legal papers, correspondence and so on. Some of these records were fair copies compiled from rougher drafts or (like the parish clerk's notebook) detailed private memoranda.[57]

This extensive bureaucratic apparatus meant that all Boroughside householders were in regular contact with the local administration. All householders would have been contacted in the listing of communicants that took place in the parish two or three times a year. Furthermore, in 1621–2, while another 109 of the poorest received sums of money from the overseers of the poor, 294 different householders would have paid their poor rate to the same officials. Ninety-one householders would have been serving in the manorial or the parish administration at any one point in time. Presentment to manorial or ecclesiastical courts was another frequent (and often unwelcome) point of contact with local government. Parish officials were involved actively in the ejection of inmates and other officials patrolled the streets on Sundays. Local government was an ubiquitous social force

[54] For the poor quality of rural parish clerks see D. Hey, *An English Rural Community. Myddle Under the Tudors and Stuarts*, Leicester, 1974, pp. 222–3.

[55] G.L.R.O. P92/SAV/450, 15 September 1603.

[56] The administration of poor relief and some of the local government of the two outliberties was administered by separate administrative bodies whose records were not deposited with the Corporation of Wardens of St Saviour's, see Norman 1901: 54–123; Young 1889: 2, 29–31; Malden 1967: 4, 146–51.

[57] For a detailed list of much of the surviving documentation see the bibliography. The vestry minutes listed the documents in the possession of the parish every year in March, see, G.L.R.O. P92/SAV/450, 2 March 1596 and *passim*. The parish paid the vestry clerk £3 4s. for his work in 1627, for an itemised bill see, P92/SAV/685.

in the Boroughside. Comprehensive parochial administration was one reason why the rites and ceremonies of the Anglican Church continued to play a significant part in neighbourhood life.

10.2 Church and neighbourhood: participation and consensus

Both sociologists and historians see the local parish church as a further means by which the urban neighbourhood might be bonded together. Such an institution by fulfilling its role as 'a gathering of neighbours' may have counteracted the dislocating influences of heavy immigration by acting as a 'home-from-home for first generation immigrants'.[58] Common belief systems are thought to be an important component of a true local social system.[59] Historians of sixteenth-century English cities have also emphasised the social role of the parish church in the urban community. Religious ceremonial is thought to have acted as a form of 'social cement' in York, Worcester and Coventry.[60] If the church fulfilled the twin functions of communal meeting place and focus of a common belief system then this presupposes that popular participation in religious worship was widespread, something that cannot be taken for granted.

Urban sociologists would point to the assumed links between urbanisation and secularisaion and the general rule 'the country is more religious than the town'.[61] Moreover, despite the importance laid on the parish church by some historians the actual *level* of popular participation in formal religion is a matter for speculation. Palliser, although stating that, even in the later sixteenth century, 'the almost universal attendance at church gave each parish a focus for a sense of community' had earlier noted that after the Reformation 'the church ceased to be a centre of worship for the whole community, if indeed it had ever been so'. Phythian-Adams has also referred to the 'unknown proportion of the population who bothered to attend' the churches of early sixteenth-century Coventry.[62]

There are certainly grounds for supposing that the church was *not* a significant social force in St Saviour's in the early seventeenth-century. The radical religious reputation of Southwark would seem to imply that, rather than any 'common belief system', there must have been a strong, socially divisive, element of religious dissent and popular resistance to Anglican ceremony even before 1640.[63] Furthermore, as noted in the previous

---

[58] Wrightson 1982: 213; Thomas 1978: 182.   [59] Stacey 1969: 143.

[60] Palliser 1979: 228, 291–4; Dyer 1973: 177; Phythian-Adams 1979: 168–9.

[61] H. Mcleod, 'Religion in the city', *Urban History Yearbook* (1978), 10; C. Hill, *Society and Puritanism in Pre-Revolutionary England*, London, 1964, p. 486; Laslett 1971: 75.

[62] Palliser 1979: 258–9; 294; Phythian-Adams 1976: 123.

[63] Clark and Slack 1976: 72; B. Manning, *The English People and the English Revolution*, Harmondsworth, 1978, p. 176; Houlbrooke 1979: 256.

section, the very large size and rapid growth of St Saviour's parish might be expected to have greatly weakened ecclesiastical discipline, and thereby lessened the probability of extensive popular participation in the Anglican Church.[64] As we have seen, however, the parish possessed greater powers of social control than would have been predicted. How effective was this administration in practice and is it possible to make any meaningful measures of the extent of popular participation in church life?

It is probable that registration of baptisms, burials and marriages was evaded by few individuals before the Civil War. Under-registration of baptisms, 'a sign of mass alienation from the church' does not seem to have taken place on a significant scale in St Saviour's until the 1640s, following the demotion of the ceremony by the Commons in 1644 and the growth of separatism.[65] Such a measure is not a particularly convincing method of assessing the degree of voluntary popular participation in the ritual of the Anglican Church however, since registration of baptisms, burials and marriages was enforced by Act of Parliament.[66] A more effective measure of popular participation therefore would be a ceremony *outside* those normally recorded in the parish register and one whose observance can be measured quantitatively.

A particularly useful measure of popular religious observance might well be that of the degree to which women were churched following childbirth. Prior to the Reformation churching was an 'ecclesiastical ritual with a strong social significance' and represented the purification of women after childbirth. Associated with the element of purification ran a strong popular belief that women who died in childbed before being churched could not be given Christian burial.[67] The ceremony survived the Reformation although the Anglican Church treated it as a service of thanksgiving: 'religion requires a woman should return thanks to God in a public manner for so great a deliverance'. In the reign of James I the traditional wearing of the white veil during the ceremony was upheld in a legal judgement.[68] Observance of the ceremony is particularly significant because it was vigorously attacked by radical protestants who saw it, especially the wearing of the veil, as a popish survival. Henry Barrow satirised churching thus:

After they have been safely delivered of childbirth, and have lain in, and been shut up, their month of days accomplished; then are they to repair to church and to

---

[64] Hill 1964: 484; Clark 1972: 153–4; Clark and Slack 1976: 71. For a treatment of popular religion in London see also Boulton 1984.

[65] Wrightson 1982: 218; Thomas 1978: 180; Burke 1977: 149–51; M. Tolmie, *The Triumph of the Saints, the Separate Churches of London 1616–1649*, Cambridge, 1977; C. Burrage, *Early English Dissenters*, Cambridge, 1912, 2 vols; Finlay 1981: 22–3.

[66] J. C. Cox, *The Parish Registers of England*, London, 1910, pp. 2–8; W. E. Tate, *The Parish Chest*, 3rd edn, Cambridge, 1969, pp. 44–8.   [67] Thomas 1978: 42.

[68] R. Burn, *The Ecclesiastical Law*, 8th edn, London, 1824, 1, pp. 318–19.

kneel down in some place nigh the communion table…unto whom…cometh Sir Priest; straight ways standeth by her, and rendeth over her a certain psalm, viz 121 and assureth her that the sun shall not burn her by day, nor the moon by night…(after which ceremony) God speed her well, she is a woman on foot again, as holy as ever she was; she may now put off her veiling kerchief, and look her husband and neighbours in the face again.[69]

Consequently 'resistance to churching or to wearing the veil became one of the surest signs of puritan feeling among clergy or laity in the century before the Civil War'.[70] The ceremony appears to have been widespread in London before the Civil War and elsewhere in pre-industrial England.[71] Since the ceremony carried with it a fee, records of churchings in St Saviour's are recorded in the parish clerk's notebook and its incidence can thereby be measured. To examine the incidence of churching all baptisms from households resident in 1622 were matched, where possible, to the appropriate churching entry in the parish clerk's notebook. In this way it was possible to measure the extent to which churching followed known childbirths. Between 1619 and 1625 the fee for churching was 4*d*. if the child lived, and 1*d*. if it died. Non-parishioners paid 10*d*.[72] The ceremony was normally carried out by one of the two ministers but very occasionally the schoolmaster of the Free Grammar School officiated, presumably in their absence. Between 1619 and 1625, 732 baptisms were followed by 671 churchings, that is 91.7% of those women who gave birth and had their child baptised underwent the ceremony of churching. If the seven women who are known to have died in childbirth are excluded then the overall figure is 92.6%. The interval that elapsed between birth and baptism meant that a number of infants died unbaptised.[73] A small number of these can be recovered from the burial register and linked to an appropriate household. Of those women whose children died before baptism twenty-three were churched (69.76%) which, if those who died in childbed are excluded, gives an overall figure of 76.6%. Churching therefore was a ceremony linked to childbirth not merely to baptism. Although, as we shall see, there is a little evidence that the ceremony of churching fell into disuse during the Civil War, in the 1620s childbirth was almost invariably followed by this ritual in the Boroughside. Neglect of the ceremony, either from religious dissent or simple indifference, appears to have been insignificant.

The interval that elapsed between baptism and churching (Table 10.2

---

[69] Thomas 1978: 48–9.   [70] Thomas 1978: 69; Macfarlane 1970: 88.

[71] For references to churching see, Dale 1931: 18, 21, 26, 29, 48, *et passim*; Cox 1910: 71; Forbes 1971: 29. See also, Wright 1982: 153–6.

[72] For fees for churching see Hill 1971: 168.

[73] Finlay 1981: 23–4; Berry and Schofield 1971: 453–63.

Table 10.2. *Interval in days between baptism and churching and between burial of unbaptised children and churching*

Interval in days between baptism or burial and churching	Number of baptisms followed by churching	Number of burials of unbaptised children followed by churching
0–6	3	0
7–13	20	0
14–20	306	0
21–7	295	16
28–34	29	5
+35	18	2
Total Churched	671	23
Not churched	61	10
Grand total	732	33

Source: See discussion in text, pp. 277–8.

below) suggests that most households may have been observing the ritual period of seclusion between childbirth and the ceremony. The majority of women (89.6%) were churched between fourteen and twenty-seven days after the baptism of their child. If, using Finlay's figures, we assume that the interval between birth and baptism was four to eleven days then the figures suggest that most women were churched about a month after the birth of their child, the lapse of time suggested in ecclesiastical law.[74] This interpretation is reinforced by the fact that those women whose children died before baptism, in which case burial would follow very shortly after childbirth, recorded longer intervals between burial and churching. It can only be assumed that a period of isolation at home was actually observed. Pepys recorded that his friend Mrs Martin observed a 25 day period of such confinement following childbirth in 1666.[75]

Acceptance of churching was widespread right across the social structure. The poorer sort were no more likely to fail to undergo the ceremony than the better off. Two aliens and a Catholic did not have their wives churched but only two other households showed any signs of consistent rejection of the ceremony.[76] In itself the almost universal practice of churching must have multiplied the attendance at church dictated by vital events. London's

[74] Burn 1824: 1, 319; Finlay 1981: 24.
[75] Latham and Mathews 1970–83: 7, 383 and 413.
[76] A glover resident in Goat Yard failed to have his wife churched following the baptisms of his three children and the wife of a High Street shoemaker twice neglected the ceremony.

demographic regime of high fertility and mortality could therefore have underlined the role of the local church as a provider of ceremonies associated with important events in the individual life cycle in the neighbourhood. The widespread acceptance of churching also suggests that persons were observing the formal ceremonies of the Anglican Church in the Boroughside. The very high rate of observance may also stem from the efficiency of parochial administration. It is conceivable that one motive for the consistent supplying of addresses for all baptisms in the parish clerk's notebook may have been to check up on subsequent churching. Efficient parochial administration also played an important part in enforcement of attendance at Holy Communion.

Attendance at Holy Communion is held widely to be a useful method of measuring popular religious practice. Presentments for failure to receive communion 'command more respect' than the evidence of contemporary writings or will preambles of levels of popular religion although 'it is far from clear that they provide a reliable indication of that percentage of the adult population which performed this elementary christian duty'.[77] Communion attendance figures have been used in sociological studies of church membership in France and similar measurements have been used in studies of eighteenth- and nineteenth-century English and American churches.[78] Examination of communion attendance therefore might be a convincing way of assessing popular adherence to the Anglican Church in St Saviour's, Southwark.

According to the 1604 canons the Anglican Church required attendance at communion by the eligible laity three times a year but in practice annual attendance seems to have been regarded as sufficient.[79] The most important time for communion was at Easter, the others being at Whitsuntide and at Christmas. Communion was not to be administered to non-parishioners without licence, nor to 'notorious offenders' and 'schismatics'.[80] To what extent, however, did communicants in the Boroughside attend the service in practice?

Evidence for the level of attendance at Holy Communion in pre-industrial England is hard to come by. Palliser thought that in York in 1570

[77] P. Collinson, *The Religion of Protestants*, Oxford, 1982, p. 210.
[78] See Thomas 1978: 189; P. Bonomi and P. Eisenstadt, 'Church adherence in the eighteenth-century British American colonies', *William and Mary Quarterly* 39, 2 (1982), 260–2; R. Currie, A. Gilbert and L. Horsley, *Churches and Churchgoers: Patterns of Church Growth in the British Isles Since 1700*, Oxford, 1977, pp. 14, 17, 22–3; J. Sperber, 'Roman Catholic religious identity in Rhineland-Westphalia', *Social History* 7, 3 (1982), 305; N. Yates, 'Urban church attendance and the use of statistical evidence, 1850–1900', in D. Baker (ed.), *The Church in Town and Countryside*, Studies in Church History 16, 1979, pp. 396–8; R. B. Walker, 'Religious changes in Cheshire 1750–1850', *Journal of Ecclesiastical History* 17 (1966), 77–94.
[79] Wilson 1923: 21; Houlbrooke 1979: 247; Burn 1824: 2, 423–32; Wrightson and Levine 1979: 157; Boulton 1984.   [80] Wilson 1923: 21, 26–8; Burn 1824: 2, 430.

communion was an 'infrequent service attended only by the more prosperous'; at Great Yarmouth in 1633 there were reported to be 1200 absentees from Easter communion and at Cogenhoe in 1612 only half those eligible attended communion on Easter day.[81] Such low attendance figures in part derive from a failure to appreciate that communicants often attended communion over a period of time. Both rural and urban parishes deliberately staggered communion attendance for administrative reasons and to cater for different social groups, and consequently absence from communion during one festival may have been remedied at another.[82] Certainly figures of low attendance are countered by evidence of extensive participation; at Clayworth in the later seventeenth century 85% of communicants took communion, as did 88.9% at Godenstone 'at some time during the festival'.[83] It is possible, using the sacramental token books of St Saviour's, the 1603 communicant returns and some churchwardens' presentments to build up a picture of the level and pattern of communion attendance in the parish.

The sophisticated machinery of parochial administration, using communion tokens and books, designed to enforce the payment of communion dues and thereby to enforce attendance at Holy Communion has been described elsewhere.[84] The use of sacramental tokens and communicant listings was widespread in London in the first half of the seventeenth century, although the mechanics of administration varied from place to place.[85] The salient features of the system used in St Saviour's in the early seventeenth century can be summarised as follows: in March in any given year the churchwardens took the number of communicants in each household and entered the information in the sacramental token books. At this time too an initial partial delivery of tokens was made, primarily to the wealthier households. Households were meant to receive communion shortly after receipt of these tokens. Each household, unless officially excused on the ground of poverty, paid three pence for each token received. After delivery and payment, strokes were entered against a household's

---

[81] Laslett 1971: 76; Thomas 1978: 191; Palliser 1979: 258. Palliser's source was incomplete, Cox 1910: 226.

[82] See, W. Longstaffe (ed.), *The Acts of the High Commission Court Within the Diocese of Durham*, Surtees Society 2, 1857, p. 96; J. Baily, 'Book of Easter offerings, small tithes and "outen tithes" of the parish of Ryton', *Archaeologia Aeliana*, n.s., 19 (1898), 44; P. Collinson, 'Cranbrooke and the Fletchers: popular and unpopular religion in the Kentish Weald', in P. N. Brooke (ed.), *Reformation Principle and Practice: Essays in Honour of A. G. Dickens*, London, 1980, p. 174; Collinson 1982: 211; Houlbrooke 1979: 244.

[83] Wrightson 1982: 220; Laslett 1971: 74.   [84] Boulton 1983: 362–79.

[85] See Boulton 1984; Dale 1931: 2, 12, 13, 16, 18 *et passim*; Power 1971: 251; Kirby 1970: 98–119; M. Mahony, 'Presbyterianism in the City of London', *Historical Journal* 22, 1 (1979), 93–114; J. McMaster, *A short history of the Royal Parish of St Martin-in-the-Fields London W.C.*, London, 1916, p. 49.

name in the token books. Delivery of tokens took place at regular intervals between Easter and Whitsuntide and sporadically thereafter. In September or thereabouts a second visitation was made by the churchwardens responsible in order to deliver tokens to those households who had not yet received them and to make a verbal check on attendance at communion. To deal with the administrative problems involved in giving communion to between four and five thousand communicants admission to the sacrament was deliberately staggered over time. This was done by the delivery of tokens in batches, prior to each communion service, such delivery probably implying that it was a household's turn to attend.[86] The wealthier households were more likely than the less well off to receive tokens first, in the Easter period.[87] Tokens were delivered for every communicant in the parish, including the poor, the sick and foreign nationals. In 1622, 824 households out of 958 (86.0%) were delivered tokens or 2178 tokens to 2460 potential communicants (88.5%). In 1635 out of 1090 households 954 (87.5%) received and paid for tokens representing the delivery of 2401 tokens to 2623 (91.5%) communicants. These latter two figures should be revised upwards slightly to take account of the small numbers of communicants who received tokens free of charge. Non acceptance or delivery of tokens to a household, as memoranda in the books make clear, was caused by death or departure of potential communicants rather than any outright religious recalcitrance, which was rare. Given the turnover, residential mobility and mortality within the parish that occurred between the time of the initial listing of communicants and delivery of tokens a delivery rate of between 86% and 92% reinforces our earlier impression of the administrative efficiency and comprehensiveness of this parish government. How many individuals who received tokens actually attended communion subsequently?

The following calculation, written on the 1636 Boroughside token book, suggests that acceptance of a token was in fact almost invariably followed by attendance at communion.

Total in this book is	2471
Clink liberty is	1879
Old Paris Garden	1029
Total of all	5379
received back	5296
which received not	83

Only eighty-three out of 5379 tokens delivered in 1636 were not eventually 'received back'.[88] If, as this memorandum suggests, 98.5% of those who

---

[86] For similar practices see, Houlbrooke 1979: 244, McMaster 1916: 49.
[87] Boulton 1983: 370–1.   [88] G.L.R.O. P92/SAV/228.

received a token attended Holy Communion subsequently, then the evidence of the numbers *delivered* (88.5% to 91.5%) would suggest that between 87% and 90% represent the real level of attendance for the Boroughside, *including* all the potential communicants who died or departed in any one year. In reality, however, only those who *received* tokens should be considered if the numbers of tokens returned is to be the criterion of attendance.

Five memoranda which record explicitly the 'number of tokens returned at the communion table' are further important evidence of the large numbers of people attending Holy Communion in the parish. Table 10.3 presents the figures taken from these lists. To make comparison easier they have been adjusted to a standard scale based on the date of return relative to Easter Sunday. In the period of the year covered by these lists more than 4000 communicants attended Holy Communion annually. The lists do not record the return of tokens that may have been received back in the Christmas and early New Year period. There is therefore a significant difference between the number of tokens delivered out and the number of tokens recorded as being received back in the lists. Between 3 April and 7 August 1636, 4305 communion tokens were returned at the communion table, 80% of the 5379 delivered that year. The remaining tokens, which from the 1636 memoranda we know to have been returned ultimately, must have been given back after this period, possibly following the second September visitation which the churchwardens made to check up on communion attendance. Eighty per cent attendance therefore is the *minimum* figure for attendance at communion. The evidence of the 1636 memorandum suggests that the true figure was very much higher: 98.5% of all those who were able to receive tokens, 88.5% to 90.0% of all communicants resident in the parish at the beginning of the Easter festival. Such attendance could hardly have been higher, given the problems of administration and the number of communicants who died or departed in any one year.

The pattern of attendance revealed in Table 10.3 owes a great deal to the regulation on admission to the sacrament imposed by the authorities, but an element of popular observance might have played some part. Whit Sunday and Trinity Sunday were consistently the best attended communion services, followed by Easter Day and Low Sunday. Very small numbers of communicants attended communion services held on weekdays, namely Easter Thursday and Good Friday and on Ascension Thursday. It may be that these were socially exclusive services held for the households of the wealthier élite.

The high communion attendance rates in St Saviour's, Southwark, resulted in large-scale purchases of wine by the churchwardens. In 1594 between 30 March and 5 July an extant bill shows that the communicants

Table 10.3. *Tokens received back at the communion table, 1629–41*

Day of return relative to Easter Sunday	1629	1635	1636	1637	1641
2nd Sunday before Easter	105	82	93	99	96
1st Sunday before Easter	222	197	209	255	222
Thursday before Easter	60	49	45	67	24
Good Friday	68	80	88	96	90
Easter Sunday	536	413	481	480	397
Low Sunday 1st after Easter	448	397	400	405	316
2nd Sunday	300	335	343	337	250
3rd Saturday	—	—	278	245	—
3rd Sunday	250	250	—	—	242
4th Sunday	217	191	266	219	186
5th Sunday	153	198	224	260	—
6th Wednesday	—	—	—	18	—
Ascension Thursday	—	21	41	—	42
6th Saturday	—	—	333	—	—
6th Sunday	269	—	—	288	355
7th Monday	—	333	—	—	—
Whit Sunday	868	752	773	761	748
Trinity Sunday	—	516	559	590	612
9th Sunday	596	—	—	—	—
10th Sunday	—	244	—	—	116
11th Sunday	—	—	145	—	—
12th Sunday	—	—	—	100	—
13th Sunday	166	—	—	—	—
After 13th Sunday	47	54	27	—	—
Total	4305	4112	4305	4220	3696

Source: G.L.R.O. 1629 – P92/SAV/275; 1635 – P92/SAV/227; 1636 – P92/SAV/228; 1637 – P92/SAV/229, 1641 – P92/SAV/234.

were expected to gulp down 67 gallons of wine at a total cost to the parish of £9 19s. 8d. In 1613 (when wine was more expensive) another bill indicates that between 20 March and 4 July communicants were expected to consume 70 gallons of wine at a cost of £12 14s. 11d.[89]

The evidence from the 1603 communicant returns supplements that of the token books. According to these returns there were 4232 persons of communicable age in the parish of St Saviour's in that year.[90] Of these, 'non-communicants' numbered 500 and recusants 32. Consequently 3700

[89] The communion wine used in St Saviour's, cost 3s. per gallon in 1594 and 3s. 8d. per gallon in 1613, G.L.R.O. P92/SAV/174, 175.
[90] British Library Harleian Ms 595, 250.

out of 4232 (87.4%) of those eligible attended communion in 1603, a very
similar figure to that calculated from the token books. The figure of 4232
is close to the figure of 4089 communicants which can be derived from a
summation of the number of tokens delivered in the 1601 token books for
the parish.[91] This suggests, as one would expect, that the token books were
used as a basis for the 1603 returns. The churchwardens are known to have
used the token books for this purpose in 1631 and 1634.[92] It should be noted
therefore that the 12.6% of communicants who were classed as non-
communicants in 1603 probably represents those who failed to receive
tokens due to their death or departure rather than those exhibiting any
recalcitrance.[93] The evidence from both token books and churchwardens'
presentments indicates that open dissent from this apparent consensus was
unusual.

The parish of St Saviour's reputation for religious radicalism may have
derived in part from the early establishment of an endowed lectureship
which, before 1625, invariably went to protestant radicals.[94] One lecturer,
Thomas Sutton, to judge from his published 1622 sermon, was an early
hell-fire preacher.[95] However, before 1641 most of this religious radicalism
was contained within the framework of the Anglican Church. Both
separatists and Catholic recusants were 'an insignificant minority', as they
were elsewhere.[96] As we have seen, Roman Catholics made up less than
one per cent of communicants in 1603. These few were mainly concentrated
in Montague Close, owned until 1625 by the Catholic aristocracy. Only
nine householders can be identified positively as Catholics between 1618
and 1624. Many of them were presented regularly at the Surrey Assizes.[97]

Separatism, despite the impression given by at least one recent work, was
also numerically insignificant.[98] An Anabaptist sect was said to have met
'near St Mary Overy's church' in 1621, probably in the Clink liberty – and
three Anabaptist householders were detected in the Boroughside in 1618.[99]
However, even in terms of pre-1640 separatism this group was very small,
frequently leaderless and often forced to live abroad, notably in the 1630s
when they were 'forced to meet together in fields and woods' and were

[91] G.L.R.O. P92/SAV/193, 250.   [92] G.L.R.O. P92/SAV/219, 281.

[93] This is also evidence that the 1603 returns were compiled accurately in this area; for doubts as
   to the accuracy of the 1603 returns see, Cornwall 1970: 32.

[94] P. S. Seaver, *The Puritan Lectureships, the Politics of Religious Dissent 1560–1662*, California, 1970,
   p. 199.

[95] T. Sutton, *Jethroe's Counsell to Moses, or A Direction for Magistrates*, London, 1631.

[96] S. Mayor, *The Lord's Supper in Early English Dissent*, London 1972, p. 49; Tolmie 1977: 30; Finlay
   1981: 22.

[97] Cockburn 1982: 263, 276, 277, 284, 286, 298.

[98] Clark and Slack 1976: 72.

[99] Notes on the 1618 book labelled John and James Craven and Walter Trotter as anabaptists,
   G.L.R.O. P92/SAV/207. See also Burrage 1912: 2, 305–8.

'persecuted beyond measure by the clergy and Bishops' Courts'.[100] It is also questionable to what extent the members of the sect operated outside the framework of the Anglican Church since all three so-called Anabaptists baptised children in the parish church and accepted and paid for communion tokens. The whole sect was arrested by the parish authorities in 1641.[101] The three Brownists identified in the Boroughside between 1618 and 1624 were operating outside the Anglican Church, possibly as part of the conventicle captured at Newington in 1632.[102] One of these individuals moved to St George's where he died excommunicated in 1619.[103] Another, Richard Ewer, a poor householder in Goat Yard consistently failed to accept communion tokens. There were no Brownist centres in Southwark in 1641, according to a list compiled in a polemical pamphlet of that year.[104] The churchwardens' presentments for the 1630s confirm that few householders were presented for failure to receive annual communion and also indicate that separatism was rare.[105]

The Anglican framework, represented here by the services of baptism, churching and Holy Communion, does not appear to have significantly deteriorated before 1640. After that date attacks were made on the Laudian railed altar, as they were elsewhere in London.[106] Many of the 1641 attacks could have represented popular anti-Catholicism rather than radical religious dissent and may have displayed a concern over the ritualised format of religious ceremony, a point which has been emphasised by Spufford.[107] Furthermore, as noted in Chapter 2, it was only after 1640 that under-registration of baptisms became a significant problem in Southwark, as in the rest of London. There is also some evidence that in Southwark the ceremony of churching was neglected after this date.[108]

The collapse of religious consensus in the 1640s was mirrored by a parallel growth in reluctance to return or accept communion tokens. In 1641, between Easter and Whitsuntide, 3580 tokens were returned compared to

---

[100] Tolmie 1977: 71; Burrage 1912: 2, 305–6.
[101] Manning 1978: 71; Malden 1967: 2, 38.   [102] Burrage 1912: 1, 204.
[103] Thomas Aspley of Horsehead Alley had 'gone' according to the 1619 token book. He moved to neighbouring St George's. The burial register of that church contains the following entry: '9 May 1623 Thomas Aspley A Browning or Anabaptist being excommunicated was by some of his own sect buried in St George's field'.
[104] Burrage 1912: 1, 205–7.
[105] See G.L.R.O. P92/SAV/522–573.   [106] Manning 1978: 44–57.
[107] Margaret Spufford, *Contrasting Communities. English Villagers in the Sixteenth and Seventeenth Centuries*, Cambridge, 1974.
[108] See above Chapter 2. See also Finlay 1981: 23. An undated petition recorded complaints that Southwark inhabitants 'will not kneel at receiving the Holy Communion, but some will stand, some sit' and that some 'women refuse to give God thanks for delivery in childbed as is appointed'. The British Library suggests 1630 as a possible date for this petition although its content and overall context suggests that 1640 is more likely, see, *Humble Petition of the inhabitants of the Borough of Southwark and other parts near adjacent being all true Protestants*, London, 1640?

4120 in the same period in 1637 (see Table 10.3). In 1643 only 2339 tokens were delivered to the *entire* parish, 44% of the number delivered out in 1636, and explicit cases of refusal to accept tokens were recorded. Hence Mrs Irons in Montague Close 'sayeth that she will not have no tokens nor would not come to the church'.[109] This decline in acceptance of communion tokens reflects the collapse of both ecclesiastical authority and also the important voluntary element on which the token book system operated. That such a system could not function in the face of mass opposition may in itself be a sign of the religious consensus within the parish before 1640: a series of ceremonies and associated popular beliefs that may have provided a 'common belief system', albeit on the lowest common denominator, for the neighbourhood, uniting individuals of different occupations, wealth and social and economic standing.

The church may also have played a significant part in the reinforcing of neighbourhood bonds within streets and alleys. Frequent attendance at church by the whole population of the parish every Sunday could not be enforced in St Saviour's and no administrative system was developed, as it was in at least one London parish, to ensure a good regular attendance.[110] In 1633 and 1634 in reply to the fifth article of the Bishop of Winchester's visitation concerning non-attendance the churchwardens replied that 'the parish being very great we know not who doth therein offend and there is no money taken of any'.[111] Presentments for such dereliction were, therefore, rare and normally confined to papists or separatists. Full attendance, despite the legal penalties imposed on absentees, was not a realistic proposition since, despite its size, the body of the church could not have held anything like the total population of the parish at any one time.[112] Nor can it be assumed that low attendance at church reflects peculiarly metropolitan irreligion since, as far as it is possible to judge, similar levels occurred in the countryside.[113]

Despite the impossibility of enforcing universal and frequent church attendance a fragment of a church seating plan suggests that the church-wardens of St Saviour's were at least attempting to ensure a modest level of attendance from male household heads.[114] In London and elsewhere at this time householders were the chief objects of attendance drives and other

---

[109] G.L.R.O. P92/SAV/235.
[110] See, Dingle 1974: 62–3, 228; Williams 1955: 8–9.
[111] G.L.R.O. P92/SAV/529, 533.
[112] Collinson 1982: 210. See also, Thomas 1978: 189.
[113] For non-attendance at church in London and high levels of excommunication see, Dingle 1974: 61–3. For rural areas see, R. Marchant, *The Church Under the Law*, Cambridge, 1969, p. 227; Thomas 1978: 189–90; Wrightson 1982: 220.
[114] G.L.R.O. P92/SAV/408. The existence of 'pew books' in the early seventeenth century is recorded regularly in the vestry minute book of St Saviour's at the accounting sessions held in March of each year, G.L.R.O. P92/SAV/450, passim.

London parishes are known to have drawn up similar seating plans.[115] Since the document is only fragmentary it cannot tell us anything about actual levels of attendance at church but it can be used to deduce the criteria by which pew seats were allocated. The names of the householders on the document, dated between 1616 and 1617, can be linked to the 1618 token book and the 1617 assessment for the wages of the provost marshall.[116] As has been pointed out above, one of the most important criteria in placing householders was social standing. The seating plan, which covers only pews in Mayhew's gallery, confirms the influence of wealth. The richer householders were styled as 'Mr Aldridge (or) Mr Austen' and sat together in their own pews. The 'Low seats' in Mayhew's gallery contained seven pews of which all but number seven held ten householders. Seat number three was 'all for the bankside'. If the remaining fifty householders, who were all Boroughside inhabitants, are broken down according to wealth it emerges that the first two pews were occupied primarily by subsidy payers In fact the primary determinant of the order of seating in these 'low seats' was residential location. The first two pews were allocated to the wealthier householders resident in the Boarshead Alley – Swan Alley district and to those on the east side of the High Street. The remaining three pews were all allocated to small areas in the New Rents. The overall effect of this, therefore, was that close neighbours shared the same pew in church. Each pew represented a very small locality within the parish and, to a limited extent, reflected its relative wealth. This meant that a subsidy man living in a generally poor area could find himself seated in the same pew as his less fortunate neighbours. The criteria on which pew seats were allocated, therefore, could have played some part in promoting social contacts between neighbouring households and underlining the existence of common religious behaviour.

The ubiquitous victualling houses and taverns, probably more so than the local parish church, provided local meeting places wherein many of the social relationships discussed in the previous Chapter might be formed, maintained or indeed broken. The localised nature of much of the social activity within the Boroughside took place in the presence of more formal institutions. Participation in and contact with the organs of the local administration was extensive. This was particularly so for the wealthier social groups but elements of some institutions of government, notably those associated with poor relief and the collection of communion dues, regularly touched poorer households. In the early seventeenth century the local social system in this part of Southwark was underpinned by comprehensive and (given what we now know of population increase and

[115] See, Thomas 1978: 190; Dingle 1974: 63; Kennedy 1924: 3, 344–6; Nicholson 1843: 169; Heales 1872: 148–9.   [116] G.L.R.O. P92/SAV/1340, 207.

residential mobility within that area) surprisingly effective local government. There is evidence too that, through a combination of effective administrative devices, and perhaps an element of popular demand, most eligible inhabitants participated in the sacraments of the Anglican Church, baptism and Holy Communion, and in the churching of wives following childbirth. This could well represent the existence of a 'common belief system' in the neighbourhood or, since individual perceptions and interpretations of their participation must have differed according to social, educational and cultural background, at least common public participation in standard church ceremonies, a 'lowest common denominator' or consensus of what were the basic constituents of lay church life in the neighbourbood.

11

Conclusion: neighbourhood and society in seventeenth-century London

Demographically Southwark and its component parts were very much part of the metropolitan whole. Like London, Southwark's population increased most rapidly in the second half of the sixteenth century and grew progressively more slowly as the seventeenth century wore on. The district, however, always increased at a slower rate than the capital, although faster than its central areas. In the early seventeenth century about one in ten of London's population lived in one of the four Southwark parishes. St Saviour's, Southwark, containing more than a third of Southwark's total population, displayed a pattern of population growth similar to that of the rest of London. The parish, to a striking degree, also shared in the demographic experience of the capital, experiencing similar mortality crises and seasonal patterns of births and deaths. Epidemic disease seems to have been largely an autonomous influence over the lives of the inhabitants of St Saviour's. The latter did not suffer unduly in periods of hardship caused by cold weather, depressions in the cloth industry or high bread and fuel prices. Members of this society gained more protection against these latter types of hardship than the inhabitants of some rural communities.

Such resilience seems to have derived in part from the protection conferred by local government institutions, poor relief administration and the provision of subsidised fuel. Evidence from the Boroughside district of St Saviour's, the subject of an intensive area study, also suggested that the local economy possessed more in-built flexibility than has been supposed hitherto. Amongst the most vulnerable sections of the population, such as manual labourers and unskilled workers, multi-occupation was common and other sources of income, taking in lodgers or keeping livestock, were commonly available. Further flexibility derived from the short-term credit obtained by pawning personal possessions to wealthier neighbours. The Boroughside district too, it was suggested, in possessing a varied and heterogeneous occupational structure with few trades and crafts dominating

289

may have been markedly less vulnerable to the periodic depressions in the cloth industry.

Wealth was distributed unequally among the inhabitants of the Borough-side. This was important because wealth determined (or was associated with) not merely local social status, and local power and influence, but also familial experience, that is household size and structure. Aging and marital status were further factors likely to influence social standing in this society. The elderly were more likely to fall into abject dependence on parish institutions losing even elementary householder status; widowed females were particularly likely to fall into this parlous social position. The wealthiest members of this society tended to be large-scale manufacturers, wealthy retailers or professionals. However, occupational groups were not socially homogeneous. Behind the bland labels of many trades and crafts lay a wide range of wealth and status.

The unequal distribution of wealth did not involve a physical segregation of particular social groups. The housing stock was sufficiently heterogeneous to allow a certain amount of residential intermingling of householders of different social and economic standing. Moreover, where people chose to live was determined not only by the dictates of wealth or occupation but was also influenced by patterns of property ownership, kinship and life-cycle stage. Short residential moves to meet new family or financial circumstances were common. Such moves were not hampered by great tenurial security since very few householders owned the freehold of their dwelling house. Local landlord–tenant relations may have been an important social force in this society, particularly among those who dwelt in back alleys which were often held as a single property by a local landlord.

Where comparison is possible many aspects of Boroughside society resemble social forms found elsewhere in pre-industrial England. Wealth was distributed unequally in most seventeenth-century English communities. Wealthy yeomen monopolised the important village offices as their manu-facturing and trading counterparts did in the Boroughside.[1] Household size and structure was another variation of a form found all over early modern England. The relatively poor social and economic position of women was common to both rural and urban environments. In many respects the realities of social life in the Boroughside would not have struck the rural immigrant as particularly unusual.

In other respects the social patterns revealed in the Boroughside differed from those found in the country. Kin were probably less frequently found in the Boroughside than in Terling, Essex, but in other ways the pattern

---

[1] For the wealth of village officials in Terling see, Wrightson and Levine 1979: 104–6. See also Wrightson 1982: 35–6.

of kinship was similar. Kinship networks were rarely extensive and few possessed any generational depth. The density and type of kinship network could well be related to population growth rates and mobility *per se* rather than to any inherently generic quality possessed by the rural or urban environment. Moreover to the newcomer the value of what kin contact there was available might have been greater in the metropolis. In the Boroughside, as in some nineteenth-century cities, kinship certainly influenced choice of residential location. Whether this was a familial reaction to the metropolitan environment or a more universal social phenomenon is a question that cannot be answered without knowing more about how the residential geography and settlement patterns of Tudor and Stuart villages affected social relations. Residential propinquity to kin was also found in rural villages in the nineteenth century.[2]

As in English rural society, many Boroughside householders may have possessed geographically restricted social horizons, living out much of their lives within a local social system. Such a society contained many networks of relationships between landlord and tenant, employer and employee, borrower and lender, kin and neighbours. Marriage partners, too, were sought within a limited geographical area. Such local ties were the biggest single source of financial, emotional and social support for Boroughside householders. The informal social institutions of neighbourhood life were bolstered and underpinned by a surprisingly pervasive parochial administration in which many inhabitants participated and all were involved with at one or more levels. Neighbourhood ties were also reinforced by widespread participation in the basic church ceremonies of baptism, churching and Holy Communion. Conscious or unconscious recognition of the bonds of neighbourhood and, possibly, the lack of known alternatives, may have lain behind the widespread but short-range residential mobility in the Boroughside. Householders moved from house to house and from street to street in response to social and economic forces but kept within the same familiar area. Overall population turnover within the Boroughside district was not markedly less than in parts of rural England.

There is some fragmentary evidence, too, that within the neighbourhood emphasis was placed on neighbourly values such as keeping the peace. Neighbours could and did inform on each other to enforce particular codes of behaviour. The Boroughside searcher for inmates relied on neighbours to inform against unwanted newcomers.[3] In 1594 it was reported that,

[2] See, D. R. Mills, 'The residential propinquity of kin in a Cambridgeshire village, 1841', *Journal of Historical Geography* 4, 3 (1978), 265–76.

[3] See the case of one Agnes Cooper, a vagrant ejected by the searcher for inmates in 1619. The searcher received information about Cooper from witnesses in the yard where she lodged. G.L.R.O. P92/SAV/1419, 1420, 1421. For neighbourliness in rural England, see, Wrightson 1982: 51–61.

William Lynch, hath William Honor his wife and a child and one Thomas Cooke and his wife. This Cooke and Honor cannot agree, the neighbours complain, and say Cooke sweareth he will kill Honor.[4]

Cases of scolding and 'backbiting' were similarly presented to the church courts although most of these latter records are not extant.[5] One of the most revealing cases to have survived was that of,

Chester Harrison and Jane his wife for common drunkards grievous blasphemours and taking God's name in vain by cursing and swearing and for continual abusing of their neighbours as the common fame goeth.[6]

Similar examples of neighbourly values can be identified in other parts of the capital.[7]

As in rural England the localised nature of much social activity should not be taken to suggest that the Boroughside was a *self enclosed* neighbourhood, an inward looking urban community. The local social system of the Boroughside, like the original sociological definition, was only partial.[8] The limited social area of the villagers of Terling did not preclude contacts with outsiders in other eastern counties of England; one villager had a contact with someone in the New World![9] Similarly in the Boroughside membership of city companies, family or property ties to rural areas and participation in national and international trading networks must have made 'extra local' claims on many inhabitants. The evidence suggests, however, that neighbourly contacts were of paramount importance in day-to-day life. It might well be the case, too, that the pattern of social activity and width of social horizons was particularly broad at the top of the social scale but narrowed progressively further down. The social world of the wealthy and literate lawyer, city merchant or gentleman, in contact by letter or in person with distant kin, outlying property and trading networks was likely to be far wider and more cosmopolitan than that of humble tradesmen and artisans who lacked the financial resources, time and perhaps literacy to maintain more distant connections.[10] Nor should the concept of the local social system be taken to mean that neighbourly relations were invariably supportive and friendly. Clearly poor relations between neighbours and kin must have occurred in the Boroughside, as they did in rural villages. The activities of local officials, as we have seen, sometimes led to resentment

---

[4] G.L.R.O. P92/SAV/1315.
[5] For the case of a scold presented to the diocesan court, see, G.L.R.O. P92/SAV/572.
[6] G.L.R.O. P92/SAV/550.
[7] See, Pearl 1979: 24; Forbes 1971: 36, 39.
[8] Stacey 1969: 140.　　　　[9] Wrightson and Levine 1979: 76.
[10] Wrightson 1982: 40–4; Houlbrooke 1984: 39–58. For similar sentiments about the social worlds of the inhabitants of nineteenth-century cities see, A. Sutcliffe, 'In search of the urban variable: Britain in the later nineteenth century', in D. Fraser and A. Sutcliffe (eds.), *The Pursuit of Urban History*, London, 1983, p. 246.

and abuse.[11] It is rather the fact of such contact, rather than its content, which is important; the local basis of much social and economic activity is not really compatible with the sociological concept of anomie sometimes thought to be applicable to the metropolitan environment.[12]

The unsurprising notion that individuals should be most conscious of their immediate surroundings forms the basis of the urban local social system. It has been pointed out that the mental map of the urban environment which each individual possesses may be of some importance in determining his or her social area. Many people in practice 'know and live in but a limited area' of towns and cities.[13] Modern day Cairo, for example,

is not one community but rather many separate social communities...a member of one community may pass daily through the physical site of communities other than his own, neither 'seeing' nor admitting their relevance to his own life. But within his own community, there is little if any anonymity.[14]

Restricted social perceptions of this sort may explain the vague general terminology used by the Boroughside searcher for inmates to describe other neighbourhoods. He used the term 'Bankside' to describe that part of the Clink liberty in much the same way as he used the term 'Cheapside' or 'Westminster' to describe more distant parts of the metropolis.

London society may be conceived of more fruitfully as a mosaic of neighbourhoods rather than as one single amorphous community. The point at which the capital ceased to be seen as one entity to those inhabiting it will probably never be determined. If population size is related to the phenomenon we might perhaps date the crucial period to the late sixteenth century when the capital's population passed the 100,000 mark, the threshold beyond which urban societies are thought by some to develop distinctive social and anthropological characteristics.[15] Given that antiquarian descriptions of towns and cities are visions of how their authors perceived the world they lived in, it may be significant that one of the first antiquarian *parish* histories, of St Andrew Holborn, was produced in London in the 1580s.[16] By the mid-seventeenth century there is more concrete

[11] See, Wrightson and Levine 1979: 110–11, 122–41; Wrightson 1982: 54.

[12] For such opinions see, Laslett 1971: 168; Burke 1975: 19; Carr 1974: 170–1.

[13] See, R. J. Johnston and D. T. Herbert, 'Introduction: social areas in cities', in R. J. Johnston and D. T. Herbert (eds.), *Social Areas in Cities*, Chichester, 1978, p. 26; Bell and Newby 1971: 60–2.

[14] See, C. Bell and H. Newby, 'The sociology of the inner city; introduction', in C. Bell and H. Newby (eds.), *The Sociology of Community*, London, 1974, p. 147.

[15] See, Burke 1975: 19; Burke 1983: 81; Finlay 1981: 155.

[16] P. Clark, 'Visions of the urban community: antiquarians and the English city before 1800', in D. Fraser and A. Sutcliffe (eds.), *The Pursuit of Urban History*, London, 1983, pp. 105–24. For the author of the parish history of St Andrew Holborn see, Caroline Barron, *The Parish of St Andrew Holborn*, London, 1979, p. 31.

evidence of neighbourhood activity in the metropolis. The fortification of London in the 1640s was organised partly by neighbourhood and Mahony has put forward the idea of the 'religious social area' to explain the geographical concentration of Baillie's Presbyterian organisation in the Commonwealth period in London.[17] By the later seventeenth and early eighteenth century it became commonplace for contemporaries to remark on the heterogeneous mosaic of neighbourhoods of which the capital was made up.[18] Such social areas may have become more sharply defined as population growth rates slowed down, as an increasing proportion of Londoners came to be born and bred in the capital and as social polarisation and environmental segregation occurred in London after the Restoration.[19] Size, however, was probably the biggest single factor in the fragmentation of the metropolitan community. Until the early nineteenth century London was the only city in England with more than 100,000 inhabitants. Thereafter as cities like Manchester, Liverpool and Birmingham exceeded that threshold, reaching more than 200,000 or 300,000 by the middle of that century so they, in turn, suffered a similar fate. As such cities grew 'their residents arguably found it harder to comprehend their totality and were increasingly absorbed into the local cultures generated by the emergence of distinct functional and social areas'.[20]

This book, therefore, suggests that a particularly fruitful method of studying metropolitan society would be to reconstruct other parts of the capital. Differences in local government, wealth and occupational composition might well have produced distinctive neighbourhoods. Even within Southwark there were marked occupational and social differences between the Boroughside, the Clink and Paris Garden liberties, and eastern Southwark. For example, the heavy concentration of watermen could have given the two out-liberties of St Saviour's the distinctive identity of riverside districts observed in other early modern cities, and the large numbers of alien immigrants in eastern Southwark may have led quite different lives in self-contained ghettos.[21]

The present study has examined the nature of urban life in one part of the metropolis at one period of time. Many more questions remain to be answered. How far was the Boroughside typical of other parts of the metropolis? And how did metropolitan society change over the seventeenth century? More specifically, how did neighbourhoods adjust to ideological

[17] Manning 1978: 217; Mahony 1979: 106.
[18] George 1966: 77; Corfield 1982: 77.
[19] See, Wareing 1980: 244; Power 1978b: 167–85; Corfield 1982: 77–81. For the associated architectural changes see, in particular, J. Summerson, *Georgian London*, Harmondsworth, revised edn 1978, pp. 17–83.
[20] Sutcliffe 1983: 244.   [21] Prior 1977: 6–9; Ellis 1984: 208–14.

fragmentation, to the rise of open religious dissent, and to the growing withdrawal of significant numbers of persons from even the most basic Anglican services?[22] By studying other parts of the metropolis in similar detail we may be able to understand more fully not only what it was like to live and work in London in the seventeenth century, but also how far life in the capital was distinctively different from the experience of the rest of English society.

[22] For the cultural alienation of religious dissenters and the divisive effect of religious dissent in rural communities, see, Wrightson 1982: 184, 217–18. For the possible effects of the emergence of religious dissent in Restoration London, see, T. J. G. Harris, 'Politics of the London crowd in the reign of Charles II', Cambridge (1984), pp. 84–93.

Bibliography

MANUSCRIPT SOURCES

Greater London Record Office

Records of the Corporation of Wardens of St Saviour's, Southwark

P92/SAV/61 Bill for the interment of Richard Bird

P92/SAV/81–83 Bills of Henry Cawdery, plumber 1613

P92/SAV/174–5 Bills for communion wine

P92/SAV/176 Certificate of population of Boroughside 1631

P92/SAV/177 List of communion tokens brought in and counted

P92/SAV/186–235 Sacramental token books for Boroughside 1584–1643

P92/SAV/250–257 Sacramental token books for Clink and Paris Garden liberties 1601–9

P92/SAV/267–289 Sacramental token books for Clink liberty 1618–41

P92/SAV/296–319 Sacramental token books for Paris Garden Liberty 1618–41

P92/SAV/406 Parish clerk's notebook 1619–25

P92/SAV/408 Fragment of seating plan for church c. 1617

P92/SAV/409 Letter on seating arrangements in church 1634

P92/SAV/450 Vestry Minute book of St Saviour's, Southwark 1580–1628

P92/SAV/490 Arrears of tithes in Rochester House

P92/SAV/499 Deposition of Thomas Oliver 1622

P92/SAV/517 Churchwardens' replies to Visitation Articles 1635

P92/SAV/520 Letter on pew dispute 1639

P92/SAV/521 Presentment of usury case 1596

P92/SAV/522–573 Churchwardens' presentments to bi-annual visitations of Bishop of Winchester 1632–40

P92/SAV/664 Tithes owing in Close since 1595–1605

P92/SAV/673 Passes issued to vagrants 1627

P92/SAV/675 Passes issued to vagrants 1627

P92/SAV/682 Bill of Richard Cliff, carpenter 1621

P92/SAV/685 Itemised bill sent in by vestry clerk

P92/SAV/692 Tradesman's bill

P92/SAV/749–786 Undated petitions from the poor to Vestry of St Saviour's

P92/SAV/787–798 Objections and proceedings to bill against the 30 vestrymen 1606

P92/SAV/802 Draft petition from wardens to Bishop of Winchester

P92/SAV/815 Inventory of goods of Mary Kirton, almswoman

P92/SAV/816 Inventory of goods of Widow Poulson

P92/SAV/817 Inventory of goods of John Coleman 1631

P92/SAV/1310 Assessment for repair of highways 1583

P92/SAV/1314 A view of inmates and divided houses 1593

P92/SAV/1315 A view of inmates and divided houses 1594–5

P92/SAV/1320 List of victuallers licensed in the Boroughside by Lord Mayor 1633

P92/SAV/1330 Draft certificate of poor and divided tenements c. 1637

P92/SAV/1331 Return of poor and divided tenements 1637

P92/SAV/1332 List of tenements chargeable 'since Pentecost last' 1637

P92/SAV/1333 Schedule of poor and divided tenements 1637

P92/SAV/1335 View of inmates and divided houses 1637

P92/SAV/1336 Return of new buildings 1635

P92/SAV/1340 Assessment for wages of Provost Marshall 1617

P92/SAV/1352–1354 Boroughside Ship Money assessments 1635–7

P92/SAV/1357 Petition to Lord Mayor from Boroughside inhabitants 1637?

P92/SAV/1397 Accounts of the collectors of the poor

P92/SAV/1398 Money gathered from vestrymen for relief of poor 1608

P92/SAV/1400 Accounts of the Overseers of the Poor for the Boroughside 1621–2

P92/SAV/1401 Accounts of the warden of the general poor 1627

P92/SAV/1419–1421 Depositions of witnesses against Agnes Cooper 1619

P92/SAV/1422 Report of searcher for inmates 1619

P92/SAV/1423 Report of searcher for inmates 1622

P92/SAV/1465 Survey of the poor in the Boroughside 1618

P92/SAV/1466–68 Certificates of numbers of poor 1631–4

P92/SAV/1471 Vestry petition to Lord Mayor

P92/SAV/1524 Letters Patent confirming ordinances of College of the Poor

P92/SAV/1529 Ordinances and statutes of College of the Poor 1584

P92/SAV/1577–1583 Accounts of College of the Poor 1605–41

P92/SAV/1585 Bricklayer's bill 1641

P92/SAV/1589 Glaziers' bill 1627

P92/SAV/1595 Bill of John Inman 1627

P92/SAV/1596 Accounts of College of the Poor 1627–8

P92/SAV/1601 Petition of William Shaw 1630

P92/SAV/1760–1764 Accounts of the charity of Henry Smith 1632–4

P92/SAV/1766 Account of gift of coals from Sir John Fenner, Paris Garden

P92/SAV/1767 Account of the charity of Henry Smith 1635

P92/SAV/1769 Account of gift of coals from Sir John Fenner, Paris Garden 1635

P92/SAV/1770–1781 Accounts of the charity of Henry Smith 1636–40

P92/SAV/1960 Inventory of goods of John Boston 1625

HI/ST/A1/5 Minute book of Governors of St Thomas's Hospital 1619–77

HI/ST/E26 Fine book of St Thomas's Hospital 1573–1751
HI/ST/E105 Surveys of property belonging to St Thomas's Hospital
SKCS 19–40 Court minutes and orders of the Surrey and Kent Commission of
  Sewers 12 May 1608 – 25 Oct. 1642

Parish registers
P92/SAV/356a, 3001–3004 Marriages, baptisms and burials, St Saviour's, South-
  wark, 1538–1680
P92/CTC/55/1 Baptisms and burials, Christchurch, Southwark, 1670–80
P71/OLA/9–11 Marriages, baptisms and burials, St Olave's, Southwark,
  1583–1628, 1639–80
P71/TMS/1358A, 1358B, 1359 Marriages, baptisms and burials, St Thomas's,
  Southwark, 1614–80

Archdeaconry of Surrey Will Registers
DW/PA/7/7 Herringman Register
DW/PA/7/8 Berry Register
DW/PA/7/9 Stoughton Register
DW/PA/7/10 Peter Register
DW/PA/7/11 Yeast Register
DW/PA/7/12 Farmer Register
DW/PA/7/13 Harding Register

Corporation of London Record Office

Repertories 25–59 (Proceedings of the Court of Aldermen) 1599–1642
Southwark Box 2 Presentments of jurors of Guildable Manor 1620–39; Present-
  ments of jurors of King's Manor 1620–4
Southwark Box 4 Presentments of jurors of Great Liberty Manor 1622–40
Southwark Box 9.7 Survey of chief landlords in Southwark 1617
Ms 39c Courts of the Manors of Southwark 1539–64

Guildhall Library

Quest book of the Whitebakers' Company Ms No. 5181
Tylers' and Bricklayers' Company Apprenticeship bindings 1612–1894 Ms No.
  3045
Parish Clerk's memoranda books of the parish of St. Botolph Aldgate 1584–1601
  Ms No. 9234/2–7

British Library

Harleian Ms 595.250 1603 Communicant returns
Lansdowne Ms 351.18–23
Additional Ms 34112 Proceedings of Commissions of Sewers for the River Thames
  1612–17

St Olave's Grammar School, Orpington

Minutes of the governors of the Free Grammar School of St Saviour's

Parish church of St George the Martyr, Southwark

Parish register; marriages, baptisms and burials 1602–80

Public Record Office, Chancery Lane

E179/186/377 1601 subsidy assessment, St Saviour's, Southwark
E179/186/407 1622 subsidy assessment, St Saviour's, Southwark
E179/257/22 1643 Land tax assessment, St Saviour's, Southwark
E179/184/154, 173, 145 1660s Hearth tax assessments, Boroughside
E179/188/481 1660s Hearth tax assessments, Boroughside
E179/258/7 1660s Hearth tax assessments, Boroughside
E163/18/18 Fees taken by Southwark Bailiff 1630
E178/4600 Special Commission 1605
E180/140 Butchers' and victuallers' recognisances 1620
STAC8/125/7 Star Chamber case, James Davies 1624
STAC8/228/8 Star Chamber case, Richard Wright *v.* Widow Payne 1613
REQ2/304/22 Court of Requests, Michael Nichollson 1621
REQ2/388/9 Court of Requests, Daniel Tiberkin 1624
SP14/23 Notes of taxations of subsidy in London 1606
SP14/120/79 Certificate of butchers that kill flesh without licence 1620
SP14/137/10 Stranger dyers 1622
SP/16/92/5 Petition of watermen 1629
SP16/135/130 Muster of seamen 1629
SP16/135/4 Muster of watermen 1629
SP16/158/21 Examination of Richard Wright 1628
SP16/216/114 Property owned by St Thomas's Hospital 1632
SP16/359/23 Returns of poor and divided tenements 1637
SP16/408/65 Returns of new buildings 1638
SP16/453/117 Opposition to collection of coat and conduct money 1640
PROB4/5184 Inventory of goods of Roger Askew, victualler
PROB4/1414 Inventory of goods of Philip Butcher, distiller

Prerogative Court of Canterbury, Will Registers.

	Register		Folio numbers
PROB11/117	Wood	1611	1–58
PROB11/136	Soame	1620	65–120
PROB11/138	Dale	1621	64–109
PROB11/141–2	Swann	1623	1–130
PROB11/143–4	Byrde	1624	1–118
PROB11/145–7	Clarke	1625	1–147

PROB11/148–50	Hele	1626	1–154
PROB11/151	Skynner	1627	1–59
PROB11/156	Ridley	1629	60–113
PROB11/158	Scroope	1630	64–117
PROB11/159–60	St John	1631	1–138
PROB11/162	Audley	1632	1–126
PROB11/163–4	Russell	1633	1–117
PROB11/169–8	Sadler	1635	45–132
PROB11/170	Pile	1636	1–42
PROB11/173	Goare	1637	1–58
PROB11/176–8	Lee	1638	1–183
PROB11/179	Harvey	1639	1–65
PROB11/182–4	Coventry	1640	1–173
PROB11/189	Cambell	1642	43–85
PROB11/192	Rivers	1644–5	1–56
PROB11/195–6, 198	Twisse	1646	1–101, 149–95
PROB11/202	Fines	1647	202–60
PROB11/206	Essex	1648	150–91
PROB11/209	Fairfax	1649	117–53
PROB11/212	Pembroke	1650	55–109
PROB11/222	Bowyer	1652	107–53
PROB11/231	Brent	1653	319–67
PROB11/234	Alchin	1654	51–100
PROB11/254, 258	Berkeley	1656	105–54, 313–62
PROB11/295	Pell	1659	457–510
PROB11/299	Nabbs	1660	106–60

PRINTED SOURCES

Acts of the Privy Council of England 1615–1616. London, 1925.
Acts of the Privy Council of England 1616–1617. London, 1927.
Acts of the Privy Council of England, 1617–1619. London, 1929.
Acts of the Privy Council of England 1629–1630. London, 1960.
Acts of the Privy Council of England 1630 June–June 1631. London, 1964.
Bannerman, W. B. (ed.). 1899. *The Visitations of the County of Surrey Made and Taken in the Years 1530;...1572...and 1623....* Harleian Society Publications 43.
British Parliamentary Papers: 1851 Census of Great Britain, Population 6. Shannon, Ireland. 1970.
Calendar of State Papers, Domestic Series, James I, 1603–1610. London, 1857.
Calendar of State Papers, Domestic Series, James I, 1611–1618. London, 1858.
Calendar of State Papers, Domestic Series, James I, 1619–1623. London, 1858.
Calendar of State Papers, Domestic Series, James I, 1623–1625. London, 1859.
Calendar of State Papers, Domestic Series, Charles I, 1625–1626. London, 1858.
Calendar of State Papers, Domestic Series, Charles I, 1627–1628. London, 1858.
Calendar of State Papers, Domestic Series, Charles I, 1629–31. London, 1860.
Calender of State Papers, Domestic Series, Charles I, 1636–37. London, 1867.

City of London: Schedule C: Population of the City of London in A.D. 1631. 1881. Report of the City Day Census.

Cockburn, J. S. (ed.). 1982. *Calendar of Assize Records Surrey Indictments James I.* London.

Craib, T. (ed.). 1912. 'Surrey chantries', *Surrey Archaeological Collections* 25, 3–32.

Crawford, R. P. (ed.). 1917. *The Parish Register of East Grinstead, Sussex, 1558–1661.* Sussex Record Society 24.

Freshfield, E. (ed.). 1890. *The Vestry Minute Book of the Parish of St Bartholomew by the Exchange in the City of London 1567–1676.* London.

Freshfield E. (ed.). 1887. *The Vestry Minute Book of the Parish of St Margaret Lothbury in the City of London 1571–1677.* London.

Giuseppe, M. S. (ed.). 1899. 'The Parliamentary surveys relating to Southwark', *Surrey Archaeological Collections* 14, 42–71.

Kirk, R. E. G. and E. F. (eds.). 1900–7. *Returns of Aliens in the City and Suburbs of London from Henry VIII to James I.* Huguenot Society Publications 10. 4 vols.

Longstaffe, W. (ed.). 1857. *The Acts of the High Commission Court Within the Diocese of Durham.* Surtees Society 2. Durham.

Norman, P. (ed.). 1901. 'The accounts of the Overseers of the Poor of Paris Garden, Southwark, 17 May 1608–30 September 1671', *Surrey Archaeological Collections* 16, 54–123.

Overall, W. H. and H. C. (eds). 1878. *Analytical Index to the Series of Records Known as the Remembrancia Preserved Among the Archives of the City of London. A.D. 1579–1664.* London.

Parliamentary Accounts and Papers 16 Charities, Session 8 February 1898–12 August 1898. LXVII, 1898.

Steele, R. R. (ed.). *Bibliotheca Lindesiana: A Bibliography of Tudor and Stuart Proclamations 1485–1714.* 2 vols. Oxford.

PUBLISHED WORKS

Allison, K. J. 1962. 'An Elizabethan village "census"', *Bulletin of the Institute of Historical Research* 35, 93–103.

Anderson, M. 1971. *Family Structure in Nineteenth-Century Lancashire.* Cambridge.

Appleby, A. 1975. 'Nutrition and disease: the case of London, 1550–1750', *Journal of Interdisciplinary History* 6, 1–22.

Appleby, A. B. 1978. *Famine in Tudor and Stuart England.* Liverpool.

Armstrong, W. A. 1971. 'The use of information about occupation', in E. A. Wrigley (ed.), *Nineteenth-Century Society*, Cambridge, pp. 191–310.

Ashton, R. 1979. *The City and the Court.* Cambridge.

Ashton, R. 1983. 'Popular entertainment and social control in Later Elizabethan and Early Stuart London', *London Journal* 9, 3–19.

Avery, D. 1969. 'Male occupations in a rural Middlesex parish', *Local Population Studies* 2, 29–35.

Baily, J. 1898. 'Book of Easter offerings, small tithes and "outen" tithes of the parish of Ryton', *Archaeologia Aeliana*, n.s., 19, 39–46.

Barnes, T. G. 1970. 'The prerogative and environmental control of London building in the early seventeenth century: the lost opportunity', *California Law Review* 58, 1332–63.

Barron, Caroline. 1979. *The Parish of St Andrew Holborn*. London.

Barton, N. J. 1962. *The Lost Rivers of London*. London.

Beier, A. L. 1981. 'The social problems of an Elizabethan country town: Warwick, 1580–90', in P. Clark (ed.), *Country Towns in Pre-Industrial England*, Leicester, pp. 46–85.

Beier, A. L. 1978. 'Social problems in Elizabethan London', *Journal of Interdisciplinary History* 9, 203–21.

Bell, C. and Newby, H. 1978. 'Community, communion, class and community action', in D. T. Herbert and R. J. Johnston (eds.), *Social Areas in Cities*, Chichester, pp. 283–301.

Bell, C. and Newby, H. 1971. *Community Studies*. London.

Bell, C. and Newby, H. 1974. 'The sociology of the inner city', in C. Bell and H. Newby (eds.), *The Sociology of Community*, London, pp. 145–8.

Bell, W. G. 1917. 'Wardmote inquest registers of St Dunstans-in-the-West', *Transactions of the London and Middlesex Archaeological Society*, n.s., 3, 56–70.

Berry, B. M. and Schofield, R. S. 1971. 'Age at baptism in pre-industrial England', *Population Studies* 25, 453–63.

Bittle, W. G. and Lane, R. T. 1976. 'Inflation and philanthropy in England: a re-assessment of W. K. Jordan's data', *Economic History Review*, 2nd ser., 29, 203–10.

Bittle, W. G. and Lane, R. T. 1978. 'A re-assessment reiterated', *Economic History Review*, 2nd ser., 31, 124–8.

Bonomi, Patricia U. and Eisenstadt, P. R. 1982. 'Church adherence in the eighteenth-century British American colonies', *William and Mary Quarterly* 39, 245–86.

Boulton, J. 1984. 'The limits of formal religion: the administration of Holy Communion in late Elizabethan and early Stuart London', *London Journal* 10, forthcoming.

Boulton, J. 1986. 'Residential mobility in seventeenth-century Southwark', *Urban History Yearbook*, forthcoming.

Bourchet, J. 1981. 'Urban neighbourhood and community: informal group life, 1850–1970', *Journal of Interdisciplinary History* 11, 607–31.

Bowden, P. 1967. 'Agricultural prices, farm profits, and rents', in J. Thirsk (ed.), *The Agrarian History of England and Wales*, IV, Cambridge, pp. 593–695.

Boynton, L. 1962. 'The Tudor Provost Marshall, *English Historical Review* 77, 437–55.

Brett-James, N. G. 1935. *The Growth of Stuart London*. London.

Brown, R. L. 1981. 'The rise and fall of the Fleet marriages', in R. B. Outhwaite (ed.), *Marriage and Society. Studies in the Social History of Marriage*, London, pp. 117–36.

Burch T. K. 1972. 'Some demographic determinants of average household size: an analytic approach', in P. Laslett (ed.), *Household and Family in Past Time*, Cambridge, pp. 91–102.

Burke, P. 1975. 'Some reflections on the pre-industrial city', *Urban History Yearbook*, 13–21.

Burke, P. 1981. 'The early modern town – its history and historians: a review article', *Urban History Yearbook*, 55–7.

Burke, P. 1977. 'Popular culture in seventeenth-century London', *London Journal* 3, 143–62.

Burke, P. 1983. 'Urban history and urban anthropology of early modern Europe', in D. Fraser and A. Sutcliffe (eds.), *The Pursuit of Urban History*, London, pp. 69–82.

Burn, R. 1824. *The Ecclesiastical Law*. 8th edn. 4 vols. London.

Burrage, C. 1912. *Early English Dissenters*. 2 vols. Cambridge.

Caldin, W. and Raine, H. 1971. 'The plague of 1625 and the story of John Boston, parish clerk of St Saviour's, Southwark', *Transactions of the London and Middlesex Archaeological Society* 23, 90–9.

Carrington, R. C. 1971. *Two Schools, a History of the St Olave's and St Saviour's Grammar School Foundation*. London.

Carter, H. 1979. 'The map in urban history', *Urban History Yearbook*, 11–31.

Chartres, J. A. 1977a. 'The capital's provincial eyes: London's inns in the early eighteenth century', *London Journal* 3, 14–39.

Chartres, J. A. 1977b. 'Road carrying in England in the seventeenth century: myth and reality', *Economic History Review*, 2nd ser., 30, 73–94.

Chaytor, Miranda. 1980. 'Household and kinship: Ryton in the late 16th and early 17th centuries', *History Workshop Journal* 10, 25–60.

Cheney, C. R. (ed.). 1945. *Handbook of Dates for Students of English History*. London.

Clark, Alice. 1982. *Working Life of Women in the Seventeenth Century*. London.

Clark, P. 1972. 'The migrant in Kentish towns 1580–1640' in P. Clark and P. Slack (eds.), *Crisis and Order in English Towns 1500–1700*, London, pp. 117–63.

Clark, P. 1978. 'The alehouse and the alternative society', in D. H. Pennington and K. Thomas (eds.), *Puritans and Revolutionaries: Essays in Seventeenth-Century History presented to Christopher Hill*, Oxford, pp. 47–72.

Clark, P. 1979. 'Migration in England during the late seventeenth and early eighteenth centuries', *Past and Present* 83, 57–90.

Clark, P. 1983a. *The English Alehouse, a Social History 1200–1830*. London.

Clark, P. and Clark, Jennifer. 1983b. 'The social economy of the Canterbury suburbs: the evidence of the census of 1563', in A. Detsicas and N. Yates (eds.), *Studies in Modern Kentish History*, Maidstone, pp. 65–86.

Clark, P. 1983c. 'Visions of the urban community: antiquarians and the English city before 1800', in D. Fraser and A. Sutcliffe (eds.), *The Pursuit of Urban History*, London, pp. 105–24.

Clark, P. and Slack P. 1976. *English Towns in Transition 1500–1700*. Oxford.

Clark, P. and Slack, P. 1972. 'Introduction', in P. Clark and P. Slack (eds.), *Crisis and Order in English Towns 1500–1700: Essays in Urban History*, London, pp. 1–55.

Clarkson, L. A. 1960a. 'The leather crafts in Tudor and Stuart England', *Agricultural History Review* 14, 25–39.

Clarkson, L. A. 1960b. 'The organisation of the English leather industry in the late sixteenth and seventeenth centuries', *Economic History Review*, 2nd ser., 13, 245–53.

Coleman, D. 1956. 'Labour in the English economy of the seventeenth century', *Economic History Review*, 2nd ser., 8, 280–95.

Coleman, D. C. 1977. *The Economy of England 1450–1750*. Oxford.

Coleman, D. C. 1978. 'Philanthropy deflated: a comment', *Economic History Review*, 2nd ser., 31, 118–20.

Collinson, P. 1980. 'Cranbrooke and the Fletchers: popular and unpopular religion in the Kentish Weald', in P. N. Brooke (ed.), *Reformation Principle and Practice: Essays in Honour of A. G. Dickens*, London, pp. 173–202.

Collinson, P. 1982. *The Religion of Protestants*. Oxford.

Connell, J. 1973. 'Social networks in urban society', in B. D. Clark and M. B. Gleave (eds.), *Social Patterns in Cities*, London, pp. 41–52.

Cook, Ann. J. 1981. *The Privileged Playgoers of Shakespeare's London 1576–1642*. London.

Corfield, Penelope 1976. 'A provincial capital in the late seventeenth century: the case of Norwich', in P. Clark (ed.) *The Early Modern Town*, London, pp. 233–72.

Corfield, Penelope J. 1982. *The Impact of English Towns 1700–1800*. Oxford.

Cornwall, J. 1970. 'English population in the early sixteenth century' *Economic History Review*, 2nd ser., 23, 32–44.

Cox, J. C. 1910. *The Parish Registers of England*. London.

Cressy, D. 1976. 'Describing the social order of Elizabethan and Stuart England', *Literature and History* 3, 29–44.

Cressy, D. 1980. *Literacy and the Social Order: Reading and Writing in Tudor and Stuart England*. Cambridge.

Cressy, D. 1970. 'Occupations, migration and literacy in East London 1580–1640', *Local Population Studies* 5, 53–60.

Currie, R., Gilbert, A. and Horsley, L. 1977. *Churches and Churchgoers: Patterns of Church Growth in the British Isles since 1700*. Oxford.

Dale, T. C. (ed.). 1931. *The Inhabitants of London in 1638*. London.

Darlington, I. 1955b. 'The Reformation in Southwark', *Proceedings of the Huguenot Society of London* 19, 65–81.

Darlington, I. 1954a. 'The manorial and parish records of Southwark', *The Genealogist's Magazine* 2, 435–40.

Darlington, I. 1954b. 'The manorial and parish records of Southwark, cont.', *The Genealogists' Magazine* 2, 470–7.

Darlington, I. (ed.). 1955a. *St George's Fields: the Parishes of St George the Martyr Southwark, and St Mary Newington*. Survey of London 25.

Darlington, I. (ed.). 1950. *Bankside – the Parishes of St Saviour and Christchurch, Southwark*. Survey of London 22.

Darlington, I. and Howgego, J. 1964. *Printed Maps of London c. 1553 and 1850*. London.

Daunton, M. J. 1979. 'Towns and economic growth in eighteenth-century England', in P. Abrams and E. A. Wrigley (eds.), *Towns in Societies: Essays in Economic History and Historical Sociology*, Cambridge, pp. 245–78.

Davies, E. J. 1924. 'The transformation of London', in R. W. Seton-Watson (ed.), *Wealth and Power in Sixteenth-Century England: Tudor Studies presented to A. F. Pollard*, London, pp. 287–314.

Dennes, R. and Daniels, S. 1981. '"Community" and the social geography of Victorian cities', *Urban History Yearbook*, 7–23.

De Vries, J. 1984. *European Urbanization 1500–1800*. London.

Dobson, M. 1980. '"Marsh Fever" – the geography of malaria in England', *Journal of Historical Geography* 6, 357–89.

Drake, M. and Hammerton, P. 1974. *Exercises in Historical Sociology*. Milton Keynes.

Dyer, A. 1973. *The City of Worcester in the Sixteenth Century*. Leicester.

East London History Group. 1968. 'The population of Stepney in the early seventeenth century', *Local Population Studies* 3, 39–52.

Elliott, V. B. 1981. 'Single women in the London marriage market: age, status and mobility, 1598–1619', in R. B. Outhwaite (ed.), *Marriage and Society. Studies in the Social History of Marriage*, London, pp. 81–100.

Ellis, Joyce. 1984. 'A dynamic society: social relations in Newcastle 1660–1760', in P. Clark (ed.), *The Transformation of English Provincial Towns*, London, pp. 190–227.

Everitt, A. 1967. 'The marketing of agricultural produce', in J. Thirsk (ed.), *The Agrarian History of England and Wales*, IV, Cambridge, pp. 466–592.

Everitt, A. 1973. 'The English urban inn 1560–1760', in A. Everitt (ed.), *Perspectives in English Urban History*, London, pp. 91–137.

Eversley, D. E. C. 1966. 'Exploitation of Anglican parish registers by aggregative analysis', in E. A. Wrigley (ed.), *An Introduction to English Historical Demography*, London, pp. 44–95.

Ewart, W. 1897. 'On the decrease of ague and aguish affections in London', *Journal of Balneology and Climatology* 1, 24–48.

Ferguson, W. C. 1976. 'The Stationers' Company Poor Book, 1608–1700', *The Library* 31, 37–51.

Finlay, R. 1980. 'Natural decrease in early modern cities', *Past and Present* 92, 169–74.

Finlay, R. 1981. *Population and Metropolis: The Demography of London 1580–1650*. Cambridge.

Fisher, F. J. 1948. 'The development of London as a centre of conspicuous consumption in the sixteenth and seventeenth centuries', *Transactions of the Royal Historical Society*, 4th ser., 30, 37–50.

Fisher, F. J. 1950. 'London's export trade in the early seventeenth century', *Economic History Review*, 2nd ser., 3, 151–61.

Fisher, F. J. 1954. 'The development of the London food market, 1540–1640', in E. M. Carus-Wilson (ed.), *Essays in Economic History*, vol. 1, London, pp. 134–51.

Fisher, F. J. 1976. 'London as an engine of economic growth', in P. Clark (ed.), *The Early Modern Town*, London, pp. 205–15.

Flinn, M. 1981. *The European Demographic System 1500–1820*. Brighton.

Foakes, R. A. and Rickert, R. T. (eds.), 1961. *Henslowe's Diary*. Cambridge.

Foakes, R. A. (ed.). 1977. *The Henslowe Papers*. 2 vols. London.

Forbes, T. R. 1980. 'Weaver and cordwainer: occupations in the parish of St Giles-without-Cripplegate, London, in 1654–1693 and 1729–1743', *Guildhall Studies in London History*, 4, 119–32.

Forbes, T. R. 1979. 'The changing face of death in London', in C. Webster (ed.), *Health, Medicine and Mortality in the Sixteenth Century*, Cambridge, pp. 117–39.

Forbes, T. R. 1971. *Chronicle from Aldgate: Life and Death in Shakespeare's London*. London.

Foster, F. F. 1977. *The Politics of Stability: a Portrait of the Rulers in Elizabethan London*. London.

George, M. D. 1966. *London Life in the Eighteenth Century*. Peregrine edn. London.

Gibson, J. S. W. 1974. *Wills and Where to Find Them*. Chichester.

Glanville, P. 1980. 'The topography of seventeenth-century London', *Urban History Yearbook*, 79–83.

Glass, D. V. 1972. 'Notes on the demography of London at the end of the seventeenth century', in D. V. Glass and R. Revelle (eds.), *Population and Social Change*, London, pp. 275–85.

Glass, D. V. 1976. 'Socio-economic status and occupations in the City of London at the end of the seventeenth century', in P. Clark (ed.), *The Early Modern Town*, London, pp. 216–32.

Glass, D. V. (ed.). 1966. *London Inhabitants Within the Walls 1695*. London Record Society 2.

Glass, D. V. 1974. 'Two papers on Gregory King', in D. V. Glass and D. E. C. Eversley (eds.), *Population in History*, London, pp. 159–220.

Goose, N. 1980. 'Household size and structure in early Stuart Cambridge', *Social History* 5, 347–85.

Goose, N. 1982. 'The "Dutch" in Colchester: the economic influence of an immigrant community in the sixteenth and seventeenth centuries', *Immigrants and Minorities* 1, 261–80.

Gough, R. 1981. *The History of Myddle*. Harmondsworth.

Gould, J. D. 1954. 'The trade depression of the early 1620s', *Economic History Review*, 2nd ser., 7, 81–90.

Gould, J. D. 1978. 'Bittle and Lane on charity', *Economic History Review*, 2nd ser., 31, 121–3.

Grantham, W. 1931. *List of the Wardens of the Grocers' Company from 1345 to 1904*. 2nd edn. London.

Grassby, R. 1970. 'The personal wealth of the business community in seventeenth-century England', *Economic History Review*, 2nd ser., 23, 220–34.

Grassby, R. 1978. 'Social mobility and business enterprise in seventeenth-century England', in D. H. Pennington and K. Thomas (eds.), *Puritans and Revolutionaries: Essays in Seventeenth-Century History presented to Christopher Hill*, Oxford, pp. 355–81.

Graunt, J. 1973. *Natural and Political Observations...Made Upon the Bills of Mortality*, London 1662, reprinted in P. Laslett (ed.), *The Earliest Classics: John Graunt and Gregory King*. Farnborough.

Greaves, R. L. 1981. *Society and Religion in Elizabethan England*. Minneapolis.

Gwynn, R. D. 1976. 'The distribution of Huguenot refugees in England, II; London and its environs', *Proceedings of the Huguenot Society of London* 22, 509–68.

Habbakuk, H. J. 1950. 'Marriage settlements in the eighteenth century', *Transactions of the Royal Historical Society*, 4th ser., 32, 15–30.

Hadwin, J. F. 1978. 'Deflating philanthropy', *Economic History Review*, 2nd ser., 105–17.

Hareven, T. K. (ed.). 1977. *Family and Kin in Urban Communities, 1700–1930*. London.

Hart, W. H. 1865. 'Further remarks on some of the ancient inns of Southwark', *Surrey Archaeological Collections* 3, 193–204.

Harte, N. B. 1976. 'State control of dress and social change in pre-industrial England', in D. Coleman and A. H. John (eds.), *Trade, Government and Economy*, London, pp. 132–65.

Heal, Felicity. 1984. 'The idea of hospitality in early modern England', *Past and Present* 102, 66–93.

Heales, A. 1872. *The History and Law of Church Seats or Pews*. London.

Herlan, R. W. 1976. 'Social articulation and the configuration of parochial poverty in London on the eve of the Restoration', *Guildhall Studies in London History* 2, 43–53.

Herlan, R. W. 1977a. 'Poor relief in the London parish of Dunstan in the West during the English revolution', *Guildhall Studies in London History* 3, 13–36.

Herlan, R. W. 1977b. 'Poor relief in the London parish of Antholin's Budge Row, 1638–1664', *Guildhall Studies in London History* 2, 179–99.

Hey, D. 1974. *An English Rural Community. Myddle Under the Tudors and Stuarts*. Leicester.

Higham, F. 1955. *Southwark Story*. London.

Hill, C. 1971. *Economic Problems of the Church*. London.

Hill, C. 1964. *Society and Puritanism in Pre-Revolutionary England*. London.

Hill, C. 1975. *The World Turned Upside Down*. Harmondsworth.

Holderness, B. A. 1975. 'Credit in a rural community 1660–1800', *Midland History* 3, 94–115.

Hollingsworth, M. F. and T. H. 1971. 'Plague mortality rates by age and sex in the parish of St Botolph's-without-Bishopsgate, London, 1603', *Population Studies* 25, 131–46.

Hooper, W. 1915. 'The Tudor sumptuary laws', *English Historical Review* 30, 433–49.

Hoskins, W. G. 1957. *Exeter in the Seventeenth Century: Tax and Rate Assessments 1602–1699*, Devon and Cornwall Record Society. n.s., 2.

Hoskins, W. G. 1976a. 'English provincial towns in the early sixteenth century', in P. Clark (ed.), *The Early Modern Town*, London, pp. 91–105.

Hoskins, W. G. 1976b. 'The Elizabethan merchants of Exeter', in P. Clark (ed.), *The Early Modern Town*, London, pp. 148–67.

Houlbrooke, R. 1979. *Church courts and the people during the English Reformation 1520–1570*. Oxford.

Houlbrooke, R. 1984. *The English Family 1450–1700*. Harlow.

Houston, R. and Smith, R. 1982. 'A new approach to family history?' *History Workshop Journal* 14, 120–31.

Howes, E. 1631. *Annals, or a General Chronicle of England…Continued Unto the End of 1631*. London.

Humble petition of the inhabitants of the Borough of Southwark and other parts near adjacent. 1640? London.

Humpherus, H. 1981. *History of the Origins and Progress of the Company of Watermen and Lightermen of the River Thames 1517–1859*. 2nd end. 3 vols. London.

Hutchins, B. L. 1899. 'Notes towards the history of London wages', *Economic Journal* 9, 599–605.

Ingram, W. 1978. *A London Life in the Brazen Age: Francis Langley 1548–1602*. Harvard.

Innes, Joanna. 1983. 'The King's Bench prison in the later eighteenth century', in J. Brewer and J. Styles (eds.), *An Ungovernable People*, London, paperback edn, pp. 250–98.

Jack, Sybil, M. 1977. *Trade and Industry in Tudor and Stuart England*. London.

James, T. B. and Price, N. A. 1976. 'Measurement of the change in populations through time: capture – recapture analysis of population for St Lawrence parish, Southhampton, 1454 to 1610', *Journal of European Economic History* 5, 719–36.

Johnson, D. 1969. *Southwark and the City*. London.

Johnston, R. J. and Herbert, D. T. 1978. 'Introduction: social areas in cities', in R. J. Johnston and D. T. Herbert (eds.), *Social Areas in Cities*, 2nd edn, Chichester, pp. 1–34.

Jones, D. W. 1972. 'The "Hallage" receipts of the London cloth markets, 1562–1720', *Economic History Review*, 2nd ser., 25, 567–87.

Jones, E. 1980. 'London in the early seventeenth century: an ecological approach', *London Journal* 6, 123–33.

Jones, P. E. 1976. *The Butchers of London: a History of the Worshipful Company of Butchers of the City of London*. London.

Jones, P. E. and Judges, A. V. 1935. 'London population in the late seventeenth century', *Economic History Review* 6, 45–63.

Jordan, W. K. 1959. *Philanthropy in England 1480–1660*. London.

Jordan, W. K. 1960. *The Charities of London 1480–1660*. London.

Keene, D. 1984. 'A new study of London before the Great Fire', *Urban History Yearbook*, 11–21.

Kellett, J. R. 1958. 'The breakdown of gild and corporation control over the handicraft and retail trade in London', *Economic History Review*, 2nd ser., 10, 381–94.

Kennedy, W. P. M. 1924. *Elizabethan Episcopal Administration, vol. 3, 1583–1603*. Alcuin Club Collections 27.

Kerridge, E. 1953. 'The movement of rent 1540–1640', *Economic History Review*, 2nd ser., 6, 16–34.

King, G. 1973. 'L.C.C. Burns Journal', reprinted in P. Laslett (ed.) *The Earliest Classics: John Graunt and Gregory King*. Farnborough.

Kirby, D. A. 1970. 'The radicals of St Stephen's, Coleman Street, London, 1624–1642', *Guildhall Miscellany* 3, 98–119.

Kitching, C. (ed.). 1980. *London and Middlesex Chantry Certificate 1548*. London Record Society 16.

Laithwaite, M. 1973. 'The buildings of Burford: a Cotswold town in the fourteenth to nineteenth centuries', in A. Everitt (ed.), *Perspectives in English Urban History*, London, pp. 60–90.

Laithwaite, M. 1984. 'Totnes houses 1500–1800', in P. Clark (ed.), *The Transformation of English Provincial Towns*, London, pp. 62–98.

Lang, R. G. 1971. 'London's aldermen in business: 1600–1625'. *Guildhall Miscellany* 3, 242–64.

Lang, R. G. 1974. 'Social origins and social aspirations of Jacobean London merchants', *Economic History Review*, 2nd ser., 27, 28–47.

Langton, J. 1977. 'Late medieval Gloucester: some data from a rental of 1455', *Transactions of the Institute of British Geographers* n.s., 2, 259–77.

Langton, J. 1975. 'Residential patterns in pre-industrial cities: some case studies from seventeenth-century Britain', *Transactions of the Institute of British Geographers* 65, 1–27.

Langton, J. 1978. 'Industry and towns' in R. A. Dodgshon and R. A. Butlin (eds.), *An Historical Geography of England and Wales*, London, pp. 173–98.

Laslett, P. 1971. *The World We Have Lost*. 2nd edn. London.

Laslett, P. 1972a. 'The history of the family', in P. Laslett (ed.), *Household and Family in Past Time*, Cambridge, pp. 1–90.

Laslett, P. 1972b. 'Mean household size in England since the sixteenth century', in P. Laslett (ed.), *Household and Family in Past Time*, Cambridge, pp. 125–58.

Laslett, P. 1977a. 'Clayworth and Cogenhoe', in P. Laslett, *Family Life and Illicit Love in Earlier Generations*, Cambridge, pp. 50–101.

Laslett, P. 1976. 'Societal development and aging', in R. H. Binstock and E. Shanas (eds.), *Handbook of Aging and the Social Sciences*, New York, pp. 87–116.

Laslett, P. 1977b. 'Characteristics of the western family considered over time', *Journal of Family History* 2, 89–115.

Latham, R. and Mathews, W. (eds.), 1970–83. *The Diary of Samuel Pepys*. 10 vols. London.

Lawton, R. 1979. 'Mobility in nineteenth-century British cities', *Geographical Journal* 145, 206–24.

Lee, T R. 1978. 'Cities in the mind', in D. T. Herbert and R. J. Johnston (eds.), *Social Areas in Cities*, 2nd edn, Chichester, pp. 253–81.

Leonard, E. M. 1900. *The Early History of English Poor Relief*. Cambridge.

Lindley, K. 1983. 'Riot prevention and control in early Stuart London', *Transactions of the Royal Historical Society*, 5th ser., 33, 109–26.

Llewellyn-Smith, H. 1939. *The History of East London*. London.

Lupton, D. 1632. *London and the Country Carbonadoed*. London.

MacCaffrey, W. T. 1975. *Exeter 1540–1640*. London.

MacCampbell, Alice. E. 1976. 'The London parish and the London precinct 1640–1660', *Guildhall Studies in London History* 2, 107–24.

Macfarlane, A. 1977. *Reconstructing Historical Communities*. Cambridge.

Macfarlane, A. 1978. *The Origins of English Individualism*. Oxford.

Macfarlane, A. 1970. *The Family Life of Ralph Josselin, a Seventeenth-century Clergyman: an Essay in Historical Anthropology*. Cambridge.

McInnes, Eileen. 1963. *St Thomas's Hospital*. London.

McIntosh, Marjorie. 1984. 'Servants and the household unit in an Elizabethan English community', *Journal of Family History* 9, 3–23.

Mcintyre, Sylvia. 1981. 'Bath: the rise of a resort town, 1660–1800', in P. Clark (ed.), *Country Towns in Pre-Industrial England*, Leicester. pp. 198–249.

McLaren, D. 1974. 'The Marriage Act of 1653: its influence on the parish registers', *Population Studies* 28, 319–27.

Maclean, D. 1929–33. 'London in 1689–90 by the Revd R. Kirk', *Transactions of the London and Middlesex Archaeological Society*, n.s., 6, 322–42, 487–97, 652–61.

McLeod, H. 1978. 'Religion in the city', *Urban History Yearbook*, 7–22.

McMaster, J. 1916. *A short history of the royal parish of St Martin-in-the-Fields London WC*. London.

Mahony, M. 1979. 'Presbyterianism in the city of London, 1645–1647, *Historical Journal* 22, 93–114.

Malden, H. E. (ed.). 1967. *The Victoria History of the Counties of England, Surrey*. 2nd edn. 4 vols. London.

Maltby, B. 1969. 'Easingwold marriage horizons', *Local Population Studies* 2, 36–9.

Manning, B. 1978. *The English People and the English Revolution*. Harmondsworth.

Marchant, R. A. 1969. *The Church Under the Law*. Cambridge.

Mayor, S. 1972. *The Lord's Supper in Early English Dissent*. London.

Mills, D. R. 1978 'The residential propinquity of kin in a Cambridgeshire village, 1841', *Journal of Historical Geography* 4, 265–76.

Mitchell, B. and Deane, Phyllis. 1962. *Abstract of British Historical Statistics*. Cambridge.

Mitchell, J. C. (ed.). 1969. *Social Networks in Urban Situations*. Manchester.

Morgan, W. 1682. *London Etc. Actually Surveyed – Including a Prospect of London and Westminster – Taken at Several Stations to the Southward thereof*. London.

Nef, J. U. 1954. 'The progress of technology and the growth of large-scale industry in Great Britain, 1540–1640', in E. M. Carus-Wilson (ed.), *Essays in Economic History*, 1, London, pp. 88–107.

Newman Brown, W. 1985. 'The receipt of poor relief and family situation', in R. M. Smith (ed.), *Land, Kinship and Life-Cycle*, Cambridge, pp. 405–22.

Nicholson, W. 1843. (ed). *The Remains of Edmund Grindal*. Cambridge.

Ormsby, H. 1924. *London on the Thames*. London.

Palli, H. 1975. 'The seasonality of marriage in Estonia', *Local Population Studies* 14, 50–1.

Palliser, D. M. 1979. *Tudor York*. Oxford.

Palliser, D. 1982. 'Civic mentality and the environment in Tudor York', *Northern History* 18, 78–115.

Palliser, D. 1983. *The Age of Elizabeth. England Under the Later Tudors 1547–1603*. Harlow.

Patten, J. 1973. 'Rural-urban migration in pre-industrial England', *University of Oxford, School of Geography Research Paper* 6, 1–61.

Patten, J. 1978. *English Towns 1500–1700*. Hamden, Conn.

Patten, J. 1977. 'Urban occupations in pre-industrial England', *Transactions of the Institute of British Geographers*, n.s., 2, 296–313.

Pearl, Valerie. 1961. *London and the Outbreak of the Puritan Revolution*. London.

Pearl, Valerie. 1979. 'Change and stability in seventeenth-century London', *London Journal* 5, 3–34.

Pearl, Valerie. 1978. 'Puritans and poor relief. The London workhouse, 1649–1660', in D. H. Pennington and K. Thomas (eds.), *Puritans and Revolutionaries. Essays in Seventeenth-Century History presented to Christopher Hill*, Oxford, pp. 206–32.

Pearl, Valerie, 1981. 'Social policy in early modern London', in V. Pearl, H. Lloyd-Jones and B. Worden (eds.), *History and Imagination: Essays in Honour of H. R. Trevor-Roper*, London, pp. 115–31.

Pearl, Valerie. 1982. 'The capital per caput', *The Times Literary Supplement*, 22 January, 72.

Peel, R. F. 1942. 'Local intermarriage and the stability of rural population in the English Midlands', *Geography* 27, 22–30.

Pelling, Margaret. Forthcoming. 'Appearance and reality: barbersurgeons, the body and disease in early modern London', in A. L. Beier and R. Finlay (eds.). *The Making of the Metropolis*.

Phelps Brown, H. and Hopkins, Sheila V. 1981. *A Perspective of Wages and Prices*. London.

Phythian-Adams, C. 1979. *Desolation of a City*. Cambridge.

Phythian-Adams, C. 1976. 'Ceremony and the citizen: the communal year at Coventry 1450–1550', in P. Clark (ed.), *The Early Modern Town*, London, pp. 106–28.

Phythian-Adams, C., Wilson, K. and Clark P. 1977. *The Fabric of the Traditional Community*. Milton Keynes.

Pooley, C. G. 1979. 'Residential mobility in the Victorian city', *Transactions of the Institute of British Geographers*, n.s., 4, 258–77.

Pound, J. F. 1976. 'The social and trade structure of Norwich 1525–1575', in P. Clark (ed.), *The Early Modern Town*, London. pp. 129–47.

Pound, J. F. (ed.). 1971b. *The Norwich Census of the Poor 1570*. Norfolk Record Society 40.

Pound, J. 1971a. *Poverty and Vagrancy in Tudor England*. London.

Pound, J. F. 1981. 'The validity of the freemen's lists: some Norwich evidence', *Economic History Review*, 2nd ser., 34, 48–59.

Power, M. J. 1987b. 'The east and west in early modern London', in E. Ives, R. J. Knecht and J. Scarisbrick (eds.), *Wealth and Power in Tudor England: Essays Presented to S. T. Bindoff*, London, pp. 167–85.

Power, M. J. 1978a. 'Shadwell: the development of a London suburban community in the seventeenth century', *London Journal* 4, 29–46.

Power, M. 1972. 'East London housing in the seventeenth century', in P. Clark and P. Slack (eds.), *Crisis and Order in English Towns 1500–1700: Essays in Urban History*, London, pp. 237–62.

Prest, W. R. 1976. 'Stability and change in Old and New England: Clayworth and Dedham', *Journal of Interdisciplinary History* 6, 359–74.

Raine, Helen. 1969. 'Christopher Fawcett against the inmates', *Surrey Archaeological Collections* 6, 79–85.

Ramsay, G. D. 1975. 'Industrial discontent in early Elizabethan London: clothworkers and merchant adventurers in conflict', *London Journal* 1, 227–39.

Ramsay, G. D. 1978. 'The recruitment and fortunes of some London freemen in the mid sixteenth century', *Economic History Review*, 2nd ser., 31, 526–40.

Ramsay, G. 1982. *The English Woollen Industry 1500–1750*. London.

Rappaport, S. 1983. 'Social structure and mobility in sixteenth century London, Part 1', *London Journal* 9, 107–35.

Ratcliffe, T. 1620. *A Short Summe of the Whole Catechisme for the Greater Ease of the Common People of Saint Saveries Southwark*. London.

Reddaway, T. F. 1963. 'Elizabethan London – Goldsmith's Row in Cheapside, 1558–1645', *Guildhall Miscellany* 2, 181–206.

Reddaway, T. F. 1966. 'The livery companies of Tudor London', *History* 51, 287–99.

Reed, M. 1981. 'Economic structure and change in seventeenth-century Ipswich', in P. Clark (ed.), *Country Towns in Pre-Industrial England*, Leicester, pp. 88–141.

Reeder, D. A. 1977. 'Keeping up with London's past', *Urban History Yearbook*, 48–54.

Rendle, W. 1878. *Old Southwark and Its People*. London.

Rendle, W. and Norman, P. 1888. *The Inns of Old Southwark*. London.

Roque, J. 1981. *A Plan of the City of London and Westminster and the Borough of Southwark*, London, 1746, reprinted in R. Hyde (ed.), *The A to Z of Georgian London*. Lympne Castle.

Roy, I. and Porter, S. 1980. 'The social and economic structure of an early modern suburb: the tything at Worcester', *Bulletin of the Institute of Historical Research* 53, 203–17.

Rudé, G. 1971. *Hanoverian London: 1714–1808*. London.

Schofield, R. S. 1970. 'Age-specific mobility in an eighteenth century rural English parish', *Annales de Démographie Historique*, 261–74.

Schofield, R. S. 1979. 'Microdemography and epidemic mortality: two case studies', in J. Sundin and E. Soderlund (eds.), *Time, Space and Man: Essays in Microdemography*, Stockholm, pp. 53–68.

Schofield, R. S. 1983. 'The impact of scarcity and plenty on population change in England 1541–1871', *Journal of Interdisciplinary History* 14, 265–91.

Schofield, R. S. and Wrigley, E. A. 1979. 'Infant and child mortality in England in the late Tudor and early Stuart period', in C. Webster (ed.), *Health, Medicine and Mortality in the Sixteenth Century*, Cambridge, pp. 61–96.

Schwarz, L. D. 1982. 'Social class and social geography: the middle classes in London at the end of the eighteenth century', *Social History* 7, 167–85.

Schwarz, L. D. 1979. 'Income distribution and social structure in London in the late Eighteenth Century', *Economic History Review* 32, 250–9.

Schwarz, L. D. 1985. 'The standard of living in the long run: London, 1700–1860', *Economic History Review*, 2nd ser., 38, 24–41.

Scott, W. R. 1910–12. *The Constitution and Finance of English, Scottish and Irish Joint-Stock Companies to 1720*. 3 vols. Cambridge.

Scouloudi, I. 1938. 'Alien immigration into and alien communities in London, 1558–1640', *Proceedings of the Hugenot Society of London* 16, 27–49.

Seaver, P. S. 1970. *The Puritan Lectureships. The politics of Religious Dissent 1560–1662*. California.

Sharlin, A. 1978. 'Natural decrease in early modern cities: a reconsideration', *Past and Present* 79, 126–38.

Sharlin, A. 1980. 'Natural decrease in early modern cities: a rejoinder', *Past and Present* 92, 175–80.

Sharpe, J. 1980. 'Enforcing the law in the seventeenth century English village', in V. A. C. Gatrell, B. Lenman and G. Parker (eds.), *Crime and the Law: the Social History of Crime in Western Europe Since 1500*, London, pp. 97–119.

Simpson, A. 1958. 'Thomas Cullum, Draper, 1587–1664', *Economic History Review*, 2nd ser., 11, 19–33.

Slack, P. 1977. 'The local incidence of epidemic disease: the case of Bristol 1540–1650', in P. Slack (ed.), *The Plague Reconsidered*, Local Population Studies Supplement, pp. 49–62.

Slack, P. 1972. 'Poverty and politics in Salisbury 1597–1666', in P. Clark and P. Slack (eds.), *Crisis and Order in English Towns 1500–1700*, London, pp. 164–203.

Slack, P. 1979. 'Mortality crises and epidemic disease in England', in C. Webster (ed.), *Health, Medicine and Mortality in the Sixteenth Century*, Cambridge, pp. 9–59.

Slack, P., Phythian-Adams, C., Corfield, P., O'Day, R. 1977. *The Traditional Community Under Stress*. Milton Keynes.

Smith, R. M. 1978. 'Population and its geography in England 1500–1730', in R. A. Dodgshon and R. A. Butlin (eds.), *An Historical Geography of England and Wales*, London, pp. 199–237.

Smith, R. M. 1981b. 'Fertility, economy, and household formation in England over three centuries', *Population and Development Review* 7, 595–622.

Smith, S. R. 1973a. 'The social and geographical origins of the London apprentices, 1630–1660', *Guildhall Miscellany* 4, 195–206.

Smith, S. R. 1973b. 'The London apprentices as seventeenth-century adolescents', *Past and Present* 61, 149–61.

Smith, S. R. 1981a. 'The ideal and the reality: apprentice–master relationships in seventeenth-century London', *History of Education Quarterly* 21, 449–60.

Souden, D. 1984. 'Migrants and the population structure of later seventeenth-century provincial cities and market towns', in P. Clark (ed.), *The Transformation of English Provincial Towns*, London, pp. 133–68.

Sperber, J. 1982. 'Roman Catholic religious identity in Rhineland-Westphalia, 1800–70: quantitative examples and some political implications', *Social History* 7, 305–18.

Spufford, Margaret. 1974. *Contrasting Communities, English Villagers in the Sixteenth and Seventeenth Centuries*. Cambridge.

Spufford, M. 1981. *Small Books and Pleasant Histories*, London.

Stacey, M. 1979. 'The myth of community studies' *British Journal of Sociology* 20, 134–47.

Stern, W. M. 1956. 'The trade, art or mystery of silk throwers of the City of London in the seventeenth century', *Guildhall Miscellany* 1, 25–30.

Stone, L. 1966. 'Social mobility in England, 1500–1700' *Past and Present* 33, 16–55.

Stow, J. 1971. *A Survey of London*. London, 1601. Kingsford, C. L. (ed.). 2nd edn. 2 vols. Oxford.

Strype, J. 1720. *A Survey of London*. 2 vols. London.

Styles, P. 1963. 'The evolution of the law of settlement', *University of Birmingham Historical Journal* 9, 33–63.

Summerson, J. 1978. *Georgian London*. Revised edn. Harmondsworth.

Supple, B. 1959. *Commercial Crisis and Change in England 1600–42*. Cambridge.

Sutcliffe, A. 1983. 'In search of the urban variable: Britain in the later nineteenth century', in D. Fraser and A. Sutcliffe (eds.), *The Pursuit of Urban History*, London, pp. 234–63.

Sutherland, I. 1972. 'When was the Great Plague? Mortality in London, 1563 to 1665', in D. V. Glass and R. Revelle (eds.), *Population and Social Change*, London, pp. 287–320.

Sutton, T. 1631. *Jethroe's Counsell to Moses or, A Direction for Magistrates*. London.

Tate, W. E. 1969. *The Parish Chest*. 3rd edn. Cambridge.

Taylor, J. 1973. *The True Cause of the Watermen's Suit*, in, *All the works of John Taylor, the Water Poet*. London, 1630, facsimile edn. Menston.

Taylor, J. 1637. *The Carrier's Cosmographie*. London.

Taylor, W. 1833. *Annals of St Mary Overy; an Historical and Descriptive Account of St Saviour's Church and Parish*. London.

Tebbut, Melanie. 1983. *Making Ends Meet: Pawnbroking and Working-Class Credit*. New York.

Te Brake, W. 1975. 'Air pollution and fuel crises in pre-industrial London, 1250–1650', *Technology and Culture* 16, 337–59.

Thale, M (ed.). *The Autobiography of Francis Place, 1771–1854*. Cambridge.

Thirsk, Joan. 1983. 'The horticultural revolution: a cautionary note on prices', *Journal of Interdisciplinary History* 14, 299–302.

Thomas, K. 1976. 'Age and authority in early modern England', *Proceedings of the British Academy* 62, 3–46.

Thomas, K. 1978. *Religion and the Decline of Magic*. Harmondsworth.

Tolmie, M. 1977. *The Triumph of the Saints. The Separate Churches of London 1616–1649*. Cambridge.

Underwood, E. and Farrant, J. H. 1977. 'Marriage mobility in Brighton's rural hinterland', *Sussex Family Historian* 3, 32–7.

Unwin, G. 1957. *Industrial Organisation in the Sixteenth and Seventeenth Centuries*. 2nd edn. Oxford.

Unwin, G. 1938. *The Gilds and Companies of London*. 3rd edn. London.

Vann, R. T. 1979. 'Wills and the family in an English town: Banbury, 1550–1800', *Journal of Family History* 4, 346–67.

Wales, T. C. 1985. 'Poverty, poor relief and the life-cycle', in R. M. Smith, (ed.), *Land, Kinship and Life-Cycle*, Cambridge, pp. 351–404.

Walker, R. B. 1973. 'Advertising in London newspapers, 1650–1750', *Business History* 15, 112–30.

Walker, R. B. 1966. 'Religious changes in Cheshire 1750–1850', *Journal of Ecclesiastical History* 17, 77–94.

Wall, R. 1978. 'The age at leaving home', *Journal of Family History* 3, 181–202.

Wall, R. 1979. 'Regional and temporal variations in English household structure from 1650' in J. Hobcraft and P. Rees (eds.), *Regional Aspects of British Population Growth*, London, pp. 89–113.

Wall, R. 1982. 'The household: demographic and economic change in England 1650–1970', in R. Wall (ed.), *Family Forms in Historic Europe*, Cambridge, pp. 493–512.

Wallington, N. 1869. *Historical Notices of Events Occurring Chiefly in the Reign of Charles I.* Webb, R. (ed.). 2 vols. London.

Ward, D. 1980. 'Environs and neighbours in the "Two Nations"; residential differentiation in mid nineteenth-century Leeds', *Journal of Historical Geography* 6, 133–62.

Wareing, J. 1980. 'Changes in the geographical distribution of the recruitment of apprentices to the London Companies, 1486–1750', *Journal of Historical Geography* 6, 241–9.

Watson, R. 1975. 'A study of surname distribution in a group of Cambridge parishes, 1538–1840', *Local Population Studies* 15, 23–32.

Webb, S. and B. 1908. *English Local Government from the Revolution to the Municipal Corporation Act: The Manor and the Borough.* 2 vols. London.

Webb, S. and B. 1963. *The History of Liquor Licensing.* London.

Whiteman, E. A. O. 1973. 'The census that never was: a problem in authorship and dating', in E. Whiteman (ed.), *Statesmen, Scholars and Merchants: Essays in Eighteenth-Century History presented to Dame Lucy Sutherland,* Oxford, pp. 1–16.

Williams, D. A. 1960b. 'London Puritanism: the parish of St Botolph-without-Aldgate', *Guildhall Miscellany* 2, 24–38.

Williams, D. A. 1955. 'Puritanism in the city government 1610–1640', *Guildhall Miscellany* 1, 3–14.

Williams, N. (ed.). 1960a. *Tradesmen in Early Stuart Wiltshire.* Devizes.

Wilson, F. P. 1927. *The Plague in Shakespeare's London.* Oxford.

Wilson, H. S. (ed.). 1923. *Constitutions and Canons Ecclesiastical 1604.* Oxford.

Wilson, T. 1925. *Discourse upon Usury.* Tawney, R. H. (ed.). London.

Winchester, I. 1970. 'The linkage of historical records by man and computer: techniques and problems', *Journal of Interdisciplinary History* 1, 107–24.

Woodward, D. 1975. 'The impact of the Commonwealth Act on Yorkshire parish registers', *Local Population Studies* 14, 15–31.

Woodward, D. 1981. 'Wage rates and living standards in pre-industrial England', *Past and Present* 91, 28–46.

Wrightson, K. 1982. *English Society 1580–1680.* London.

Wrightson, K. and Levine, D. 1979. *Poverty and Piety in an English Village, Terling 1525–1700.* London.

Wrightson, K. 1981a. 'Household and kinship in sixteenth-century England', *History Workshop Journal* 12, 151–8.

Wrightson, K. 1981b. 'Alehouses, order and reformation in rural England 1590–1660', in Eileen and S. Yeo (eds.), *Popular Culture and Class Conflict,* Hassocks, pp. 1–27.

Wrightson, K. 1983. 'Two concepts of order', in J. Brewer and J. Styles (eds.), *An Ungovernable People,* London, paperback edn, pp. 21–46.

Wrigley, E. A. 1967. 'A simple model of London's importance in changing English society and economy 1650–1750', *Past and Present* 37, 44–70.

Wrigley, E. A. 1966. 'Family reconstitution', in E. A. Wrigley (ed.), *An Introduction to English Historical Demography,* London, pp. 96–159.

Wrigley, E. A. 1973. 'Clandestine marriage in Tetbury in the late seventeenth century', *Local Population Studies* 10, 15–21.

Wrigley, E. A. 1977a. 'Births and baptisms: the use of Anglican baptism registers as a source of information about the numbers of births in England before the beginning of civil registration', *Population Studies* 31, 281–312.

Wrigley, E. A. 1977b. 'The changing occupational structure of Colyton over two centuries', *Local Population Studies* 18, 9–21.

Wrigley, E. A. 1985. 'Urban growth and agricultural change: England and the Continent in the Early Modern Period', *Journal of Interdisciplinary History* 15, 683–728.

Wrigley, E. A. and Schofield, R. S. 1981. *The Population History of England 1541–1871*. London.

Wrigley, E. A. and Schofield, R. 1983. 'English population history from family reconstitution: summary results 1600–1799', *Population Studies* 37, 157–84.

Yates, N. 1979. 'Urban church attendance and the use of statistical evidence, 1850–1900', in D. Baker (ed.), *The Church in Town and Countryside*, Studies in Church History 16, pp. 389–400.

Young, W. 1889. *A History of Dulwich College*. 2 vols. London.

Young, M. and Willmott, P. 1957. *Family and Kinship in East London*. London.

UNPUBLISHED WORKS

Archer, J. L. 1934. 'The industrial history of London 1603–1640 with special reference to the suburbs and those areas claiming exemption from the authority of the Lord Mayor', London University M. A. thesis.

Boulton, J. P. 1983. 'The social and economic structure of early seventeenth-century Southwark', Cambridge University Ph.D. thesis.

Carlin, Martha. 1983. 'The urban development of Southwark c. 1200–1550', Toronto University Ph.D. thesis.

Carr, G. 1974. 'Residence and social status', Harvard University Ph.D. thesis.

Dingle, A. M. 1974. 'The role of the householder in Early Stuart London c. 1603–1630', London University M. Phil thesis.

Elliott, V. B. 1978. 'Mobility and marriage in pre-industrial England', Cambridge University Ph.D. thesis.

Finlay, R. A. P. 1977. 'The population of London 1580–1650', Cambridge University Ph.D. thesis.

Harris, T. J. G. 1984. 'Politics of the London crowd in the reign of Charles II', Cambridge University Ph.D. thesis.

Hibberd, D. J. 1981. 'Urban inequalities. Social geography and demography in seventeenth-century York', Liverpool University Ph.D. thesis.

Kerby, G. A. 1983. 'Inequality in a pre-industrial society: a study of wealth, status, office and taxation in Tudor and Stuart England with particular reference to Cheshire', Cambridge University Ph.D. thesis.

McGrath, P. V. 1948. 'The marketing of food, fodder and livestock in the London area in the seventeenth century with some reference to the sources of supply', London University M.A. thesis.

Marshall, J. D. 1977. 'Social structure and wealth in pre-industrial England', The 139th Annual Meeting of the British Association for the Advancement of Science 31 August to 7 September, 1–56.

Power, M. J. 1971. 'The urban development of East London 1550–1700', London University Ph.D. thesis.

Power, M. J. 1981. 'Hearth and homes in pre-Fire London', paper delivered at Conference on London Economic and Social History 1500–1700, London, 27 June.

Prior, M. L. 1977. 'Fisher Row. The Oxford Community of fishermen, bargemen and canal boatmen 1500–1800', Oxford University Ph.D. thesis.

Rappaport, S. 1981. 'Social structure and mobility in sixteenth-century London', paper presented at Conference on London Economic and Social History 1500–1700, London, 27 June.

Sheail, J. 1968. 'The regional distribution of wealth in England as indicated by the Lay Subsidy Returns of 1524/5', London University Ph.D. thesis.

Shearer, B. 1981. 'Expanding suburbs', paper presented at Conference on London Economic and Social History 1500–1700, London 27 June.

Souden, D. 1981. 'Pre-industrial English local migration fields', Cambridge University Ph.D. thesis.

Thomson, D. W. 1980. 'Provision for the elderly in England, 1830 to 1908', Cambridge University Ph.D. thesis.

Wright, S. J. 1982. 'Family life and society in sixteenth- and early seventeenth-century Salisbury', Leicester University Ph.D. thesis.

Index

In the index, places, districts and institutions within the metropolis are entered under London. Southwark and its districts are treated separately.